Apple Pro Training Series

Advanced Editing and Finishing Techniques in Final Cut Pro 4

DigitalFilm Tree

Apple
Certified

Apple Pro Training Series: Advanced Editing and Finishing Techniques in Final Cut Pro 4

DigitalFilm Tree
Copyright © 2004 by DigitalFilm Tree

Published by Peachpit Press. For information on Peachpit Press books, contact:

Peachpit Press
1249 Eighth Street
Berkeley, CA 94710
(510) 524-2178
Fax: (510) 524-2221
www.peachpit.com
To report errors, please send a note to errata@peachpit.com.
Peachpit Press is a division of Pearson Education.

Contributing Writers: Andrew Balis, Daniel Fort, Steve Martin, Mary Plummer, Yan Shvalb, Martin Sitter, Michael Wohl
Editor: Serena Herr
Production Editor: Connie Jeung-Mills
DigitalFilm Tree Project Director: Ramy Katrib
DigitalFilm Tree Project Managers: Donna Madrigal, Joshua Reis, Zed Saeed
DigitalFilm Tree Design and Illustration: Sazeer Kader
DigitalFilm Tree Technical Editors: Tom Maroney, John Taylor, Larry Jordan, Joshua Reis, Zoe Mougin
Technical Editors: Matthew Geller, Stephen Kanter
Technical Reviewers: Dean Chamberlain, Ralph Fairweather, Adam Green, Stephen Kanter
Copy Editor: Darren Meiss
Compositor: Happenstance Type-O-Rama
Indexer: Karin Arrigoni
Cover and Interior Design: Frances Baca
Cover Illustration and Production: Aren Howell

ISBN 0-321-19726-7
9 8 7 6 5 4 3 2 1
Printed and bound in the United States of America

To the memory of Maurice Katrib—
his spoken and edited word lives on

and

In memoriam: Ralph Fairweather,
a valued colleague, cherished friend, and
respected member of the Final Cut Pro community.

Acknowledgements When DigitalFilm Tree was asked to take on the advanced Final Cut Pro 4 book, we dove right in, in keeping with our history. To those who have been waiting on this book, we hope the effort, with all its colors and shades, serves you well. We thank and congratulate the incredibly talented concert of writers who made this book possible. May it bring love and peace to you and yours, or at least shed some light on the many faces of Final Cut Pro. And of course, we would like to thank the Final Cut Pro team for unleashing a revolutionary technology on the masses.

Thanks and gratitude to all:

Joshua Reis and **Donna Madrigal**, for your singular and unwavering persistence, focus, and excellence,

The DigitalFilm Tree team, for helping out, while dodging bullets and fireballs,

Zed Saeed, for the experience, guidance, and laughter,

Walter Murch, for your contribution to the book and Final Cut Pro history,

Serena Herr, for making a book like this possible, and your extraordinary support and guidance,

Patty Montesion, for providing us the opportunity, and your tireless work on this and all the Apple Pro Training Series books,

The Footage providers, who contributed a rich array of imagery: Anthony Assini, Howard and Michelle Hall, Stephen Purvis, Joshua Reis, and Brett Shapiro.

Contents at a Glance

Table of Contents

Working with Film and 24p

Foreword

Film editing celebrates its hundredth birthday in 2003. It is strange to think that something so essential was not born in 1889 along with cinema itself, but that the movies discovered editing—like most of us discover sex— when they were fourteen years old.

And like sex, the ability to mingle and juxtapose moving images is simultaneously wonderful, improbable, life-enhancing—and the movies would probably not have survived long without it. Louis Lumière, cinema's father on the French side of the family, despaired that his child was "an invention without a future." But he was thinking of the short, static, single-shot Lumière documentaries such as *Workers Leaving the Factory* (1895), or *Arrival of a Train at the Station* (1896).

On the other hand, Edwin Porter's *Life of an American Fireman* and *The Great Train Robbery* (both released in 1903) told dramatic stories with thrilling conclusions (Fire! Theft!) and gave the illusion of continuous reality through a series of discontinuous images, a paradox that remains at the heart of film editing to this day. Despite—or probably because of— that paradox, Porter's films were sensationally successful, single-handedly reviving the flagging fortunes of the young film industry. In the hundred years since, movies have acquired a voice and burst into color, they have become much longer and the density of images in them much greater, but the paradoxical path Porter set for us is the one we are still exploring.

In fact, the edited moving image has now become so ubiquitous in our culture—in theaters, on television, in home movies, on DVDs, in lectures, in video games, on the Internet—that it has surged over the banks of the theatrical film industry and now poses a problem with a broader social and technical context: how best to channel and choreograph the flow of all these images, the lingua franca of the twenty-first century, across the widest possible landscape? A system is needed that is technically sophisticated, easy to use, reliable, infinitely adaptable, and easily affordable. Until recently, there was no such system.

As different as they are, the machines that film editors used through the twentieth century shared one trait in common: their development costs and technical specifications were extremely high compared to the narrow market at which they were aimed. There are just not that many film editors in the world, compared to, say, doctors. As an inevitable result, editing machines were expensive, usually priced as much or more than a luxury automobile. I remember how shocked I was as a film student in 1965 to discover that even a roll of splicing tape—scotch tape with sprockets— would set me back twelve dollars, at a time when a loaf of bread could be had for 25 cents.

The difficulty is this: the images may be increasingly ubiquitous, but the control and organization of those images, even on a computer, has been a complicated, cumbersome, and expensive proposition, subject to periods of technical inertia and bottlenecks. This is a difficult but surmountable problem for commercials or large-budget feature films, but it is just plain difficult for almost everyone else. How to bend this iron triangle of high specifications, high cost, and narrow market?

There is no question of lowering the technical specifications—films are extraordinarily demanding in this regard—but the other two sides of the triangle have started to yield in the last few years, compressed by different aspects of the same force: the inexorable increase in processing speed of computers. This has both expanded the markets in which motion pictures can function (think of how rapidly DVDs have become commonplace) and has enabled computers equipped with the right software to process high-quality images and sounds without the need for expensive and proprietary additional hardware.

As it turns out, the ordinary laptop that I am using to write this has also been one of the machines I have been using to edit Anthony Minghella's $80 million film *Cold Mountain*. This would not have been feasible a few years ago. In fact, *Cold Mountain* is the first large-scale feature motion picture to be edited from start to finish on Final Cut Pro, Apple's software-only film editing program.

I had been curious about the development of Final Cut as a video editing tool from the time that Apple took over the program from Macromedia in 1999, but I became particularly interested a year or so later when Apple acquired the company FilmLogic and integrated their software with Final Cut, since FilmLogic (renamed Cinema Tools) gave Final Cut Pro the capability to handle 35mm film.

In the spring of 2002, my assistant Sean Cullen and I approached DigitalFilm Tree, a Post/Design house in LA specializing in Final Cut Pro instruction and implementation, and asked what they thought about our using Final Cut on the upcoming *Cold Mountain*. The people at DFT were enthusiastic—they had been hoping something like this would come along—and together we developed a workflow that integrated my usual editing methods within the structure of Final Cut.

Three months later, in July 2002, Sean and I were on location in Bucharest, Romania with four Final Cut Pro stations, including four Apple G4 processors, 1.2 terabytes of Rorke Data hard disk storage, Aurora Igniter capture cards, NTSC monitors, tape decks, sound mixers, video switchers, and other devices, all of which was assembled by DFT for less than the cost of one typical computer-based NLE workstation.

As it turned out, all the equipment performed flawlessly during the five months of shooting and the seven months (ongoing as I write this) of post-production. On previous films, with just two workstations, we frequently had to negotiate awkward priority conflicts, which was a bit like trying to cook a banquet on a two-burner stove. Our four FCP "burners" proved essential to keep everything running smoothly, since we were screening an average mile of film each day, for a total of just under 111 hours of workprint.

In addition, Sean and I were able to offload chunks of media onto our laptops, which were also equipped with Final Cut Pro software, and edit small sections of the film away from direct connection to the central hard drives. At one point, we had four of these satellites (one of them an older iMac) working in addition to the four "official" machines.

In this way, we were also able to give hands-on editing experience to our two film assistants, Walter and Dei; our two Romanian apprentices, Ilinca and Mihai; and our BBC intern, Susannah. When one of their sketches was complete, they would simply network the sequence icon back to home base, relink it to the media on the hard drives, and then integrate it into the flow of the film.

I can't stress enough how important this flexibility is, not only for the health and economy of the individual film, but also for the film industry at large. In one stroke, it solves the problem of how to get through logjams on days when there is a surge in the amount of film being shot. Just as important, it solves a dilemma that has been growing over the last 25 years, which is the increasing specialization of tasks (film assembly, data entry, etc.) in the editing room, something that has prevented assistants and apprentices from gaining experience in actual editing.

It is hard to imagine a better present for the hundredth birthday of film editing than Final Cut Pro 4, released in June of 2003. It is a profound rewriting and improvement of the Final Cut Pro 3 software that served us faithfully on location in Romania, and this advanced manual for FCP 4, which has evolved as a joint effort between Peachpit Press, Apple Computer, and DigitalFilm Tree, has been assembled and authored by a number of the same people who have been personally instrumental in helping us to climb our Cold Mountain.

—*Walter Murch*

Introduction

DigitalFilm Tree was started in 1998 by a group of mavericks with a dream: to change the world of post-production with Final Cut Pro and related technologies.

When Final Cut Pro 1.0 was released, we were some of the first people to think of the software as redefining the future of post, as opposed to just editing the latest family video. In early 2000, a small group consisting of an editor, a negative cutter, and a software designer gathered in a small apartment in Hollywood and conducted a groundbreaking test. The test was designed to see if it was possible to edit films at 24 frames per second using Final Cut Pro with FilmLogic (which later became Cinema Tools) and create frame accurate negative cut lists, resulting in a 100-percent reliable negative assembly. The test was a success, and the dream was on its way to becoming a reality.

Almost four years later, we have just finished shepherding the largest feature film ever to be created in Final Cut Pro: *Cold Mountain*. Edited by the Academy Award–winning Walter Murch, who also wrote the foreword to this book and has films such as *The English Patient, The Unbearable Lightness of Being,* and *Apocalypse Now* to his credit, this Miramax megabudget film features an all-star cast of Jude Law, Nicole Kidman, Donald Sutherland, Natalie Portman, and Renee Zellweger. *Cold Mountain* is being directed by Academy Award winner Anthony Minghella of *The English Patient* fame.

Along the way, from that small apartment to *Cold Mountain*, DigitalFilm Tree has pushed Final Cut Pro further and further into the professional realm. We have designed the workflows for many large-scale projects and helped edit numerous TV shows (such as NBC's *Scrubs*) and films on Final Cut Pro. Today, DigitalFilm Tree is firmly rooted as a post-production and design company specializing in Final Cut Pro implementation and education.

When Peachpit and Apple approached us to do an advanced book on Final Cut Pro, we knew how we wanted to do it. Instead of taking the run-of-the-mill approach of having one author write the entire book, we wanted the top Final Cut Pro experts to each write sections which best suited their backgrounds and expertise. You are holding the results in your hands.

This book features the stellar talents of some of the most respected names in the Final Cut Pro arena. Michael Wohl, a principal designer of Final Cut Pro, wrote the editing and media management chapters, and several of the effects chapters. Andrew Balis, who along with being an editor and cinematographer has also worked closely with Apple to create their official courseware, wrote the remaining effects chapters and the extensive color correction section. Mary Plummer, a respected editor for films and TV who is a fine musician as well, wrote the Soundtrack chapters. Martin Sitter, a noted music and DVD producer, was the logical choice for the chapters on audio finishing. Steve Martin, a titling wizard and longtime Apple-certified trainer, penned the LiveType sections. Yan Shvalb, one of the leading DVD and multimedia experts in the world, wrote the Compressor chapter. And when it came to editing film and High Definition video in Final Cut Pro, there was no other choice but Daniel Fort, one of the original pioneers of film editing on Final Cut Pro.

This book is the fruit of our collective efforts.

Getting Started

Welcome to the official advanced training course for Final Cut Pro 4, Apple's dynamic and powerful non linear editing package. This book is a detailed guide to advanced editing and finishing techniques using Final Cut Pro, as well as the three programs that come bundled with it: Soundtrack, LiveType, and Compressor. The premise of this book is to build upon your knowledge of Final Cut Pro, providing you with practical, professional techniques that you will use on a daily basis in your editorial projects.

The Methodology

The emphasis of this book is hands-on training. Each exercise was designed to help you start editing in Final Cut Pro at a professional level as quickly as possible. The book assumes a basic level of familiarity with the Final Cut Pro interface and with the fundamentals of post production. If you are new to Final Cut Pro, it would be helpful for you to start at the beginning and progress through each lesson in order. Since every section (and every lesson) is self-contained, if you are familiar with Final Cut Pro you can start with any section and focus on that topic.

Course Structure

This book was designed to help you master the most critical professional-level editing and post-production techniques in Final Cut Pro. Each lesson expands on the basic concepts of the program, giving you the tools to customize your project workflows and use the program for your own purposes. Finally, the book delves into features that are not frequently touched on, with a special section on editing film and HD video presented in PDF format on the DVD. The lessons fall into the following categories:

Lessons 1-2	Advanced editing and trimming
Lessons 3-9	Advanced effects
Lessons 10-14	Color correction

Lessons 15-18   Working with Soundtrack and audio

Lessons 19-20   Titling with LiveType

Lessons 21–23   Project management, encoding, and outputting

Lesson 24   Working with film and 24p

Appendix A   Film and 24p editing basics

Appendix B   Working with 16x9

Copying the Lesson Files

All the necessary files you will need to complete the lessons are found
on the two-sided *APTS_Advanced FCP* DVD-10 that comes with this
book. On each disk, the files are located inside a single folder named
Adv_FCP_Book_Files.

Installing the Lesson files

1   Insert the *APTS: Advanced FCP* Disk 1 DVD into your DVD drive.

2   For best results, drag the entire *Adv_FCP_Book_Files* folder from Disk
    1 to the top level of a single fast hard drive. Then eject the disk, flip it
    over, reinsert it, and drag the contents of the *Adv_FCP_Book_Files*
    folder from Disk 2 to the new *Adv_FCP_Book_Files* folder on your
    hard drive. There is a total of 8.3 GB of data.

    NOTE ▶ When you keep all the lesson files and media files from both
    disks together in one single *Adv_FCP_Book_Files* folder on your hard
    drive, just as you find them on the DVD, you will ensure that the
    tutorial project files for each lesson will open with their media files
    all correctly linked, and ready for you to begin the lesson.

3   To begin each lesson, launch the application for that lesson and then
    open the project file or files listed at the beginning of each lesson.

Reconnecting Broken Media Links

For any number of reasons, you may need to separate the lesson files from the media files when you install and use them. For instance, you may choose to keep the project files in a user home directory and the media files on a dedicated media drive. In this case, when you open a project file, a window will appear asking you to reconnect the project files to their source media files.

Reconnecting files is a simple process, whether you are using Final Cut Pro, Soundtrack, LiveType or Cinema Tools. For Final Cut Pro, just follow the steps below.

1 When you first open a lesson's project file, a Final Cut Pro dialog will appear listing one or more files that are offline. Click the Reconnect button.

A Final Cut Pro Reconnect Options window appears.

2 Leave the reconnect options set at their default choices: Offline should be the only box checked. (Do not check the Connect Files Manually choice unless you are already familiar with connecting and reconnecting files in Final Cut Pro.) On the Reconnect Options dialog box, Click OK.

A new and larger Mac OS X Reconnect dialog will appear.

3 Navigate to the location you have chosen for the Media folder from the DVD, and then to the specific numbered media subfolder for the lesson you are working on.

A single media source file should be highlighted in the right pane of the Reconnect dialog box. You may need to scroll to see it.

Pay close attention that the number of the media subfolder containing the highlighted media file matches the number of the lesson file you are reconnecting. Some media clips are used in more than one lesson, and therefore appear in more than one numbered media subfolder.

4 With the media file selected, click the highlighted Choose button in the Reconnect dialog.

5   Repeat steps 3 and 4 until all project files have been reconnected.

6   Be sure to Save the newly reconnected project file, or you will have to perform the reconnect operation every time you open it.

See *Lesson 22, Reconnecting Offline Files,* if you have any difficulties when connecting broken links between project files and media files.

System Requirements

Before beginning to use this book, you should have a working knowledge of your computer and its operating system. Make sure that you know how to use the mouse and standard menus and commands and also how to open, save, and close files. If you need to review these techniques, see the printed or online documentation included with your system.

Basic system requirements for Final Cut Pro include:

- Mac OS X 10.25 or higher
- 604/250 MHz or better
- 128 MB RAM or more
- DVD Drive
- Separate hard drive for media is recommended

Resources

This book is not intended as a comprehensive reference manual, nor does it replace the documentation that comes with the application. For comprehensive information about program features, refer to these resources:

- The Reference Guide. Accessed through the Final Cut Pro Help menu, the Reference Guide contains a complete description of all features.
- Apple's Web site: http://www.apple.com.
- Stay current: As Final Cut Pro is updated, check www.peachpit.com/apts.advfcp for revised lessons.

About the Apple Pro Training Series

Advanced Editing and Finishing Techniques in Final Cut Pro is part of the official training series for Apple Pro applications developed by experts in the field. The lessons are designed to let you learn at your own pace. Although each lesson provides step-by-step instructions for creating specific projects, there's room for exploration and experimentation. Each lesson concludes with a review section summarizing what you've covered.

Apple Pro Certification Program

The Apple Pro Training and Certification Programs are designed to keep you at the forefront of Apple's digital media technology while giving you a competitive edge in today's ever-changing job market. Whether you're an editor, graphic designer, sound designer, special effects artist, or teacher, these training tools are meant to help you expand your skills.

Upon completing the course material in this book, you can become an Apple Pro by taking the certification exam at an Apple Authorized Training Center. Certification is offered in Final Cut Pro 4, DVD Studio Pro 2, Shake 3, and Logic 6. Successful certification as an Apple Pro gives you official recognition of your knowledge of Apple's professional applications while allowing you to market yourself to employers and clients as a skilled, pro-level user of Apple products.

To find an Authorized Training Center near you, go to www.apple.com/software/pro/training.

For those who prefer to learn in an instructor-led setting, Apple also offers training courses at Apple Authorized Training Centers worldwide. These courses, which use the Apple Pro Training Series books as their curriculum, are taught by Apple Certified Trainers and balance concepts and lectures with hands-on labs and exercises. Apple Authorized Training Centers have been carefully selected and have met Apple's highest standards in all areas, including facilities, instructors, course delivery, and infrastructure. The goal of the program is to offer Apple customers, from beginners to the most seasoned professionals, the highest quality training experience.

Advanced Editing

Michael Wohl is best known as the principal designer of Final Cut Pro, a role he held for more than five years. He has also had success as a director and editor for more than 15 years. His 1993 film "Theatereality" won the coveted CINE Golden Eagle award and his latest feature film "WANT" is playing to acclaim on the international film festival circuit. He is currently in development on a new feature film and will be directing an original stageplay in early 2004 in Los Angeles.

1

Lesson Files	Lessons > Lesson_01 > 01_Project_Start.fcp
Media	Media > Lesson_01_Media
Time	This lesson takes approximately 120 minutes to complete.
Goals	Apply basic editing techniques to real-world projects
	Learn to select the best footage
	Fine-tune edit points using ripple and roll
	Use an insert or a cutaway to cover a bad edit
	Create split edits to smooth transitions
	Use Ripple Delete to clean up rough edits
	Use Replace edits with In and Out points
	Use Gang Sync mode to simplify repetitive edits

Lesson 1
Applied Editing

Welcome. This book starts off with applied editing techniques because they are the foundation of any advanced-level work you'll do in Final Cut Pro. Many of the other topics covered in the book— such as advanced effects, color correction, adding soundtracks, titling, and media management—assume a certain level of editing skill as a prerequisite.

Mastering the art of video editing in Final Cut Pro involves more than learning what buttons to press and how each tool works. A great deal of the craft of editing requires understanding editing techniques and knowing when to use the various powerful tools that Final Cut Pro provides.

This lesson focuses on applying standard editing tools such as Ripple, Roll, Replace, and others to real-world situations. Further, you will tackle common editing challenges such as screen direction errors, sync errors, overlapping dialogue tracks, and building inter- view sequences.

Basic Dialogue Editing

In the following exercises, you will create a simple dialogue sequence from scratch. You'll use different tools as the real-world situation requires.

1   Open Lessons > Lesson_01 > **01_Project_Start.fcp**.

2   Double-click the Scene 2 Clips bin.

This opens the bin in its own window. This bin contains all of the source footage for the scene.

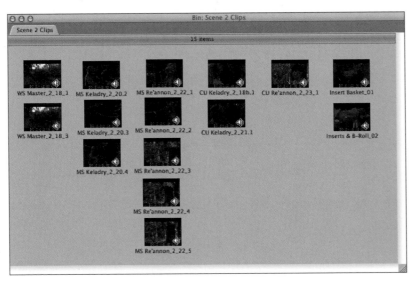

The shots have been arranged so that multiple takes of the same shot are stacked vertically. There are five primary shots, plus two shots stacked on the right that contain inserts and additional coverage.

3   Drag the bin (by its tab) back into the Browser window to conserve your Desktop real estate.

This scene was shot in a very traditional method, providing you with adequate coverage to choose from. The entire scene was covered in nearly every shot, giving you myriad editing choices for assembling the scene.

Familiarizing Yourself with the Footage

Before you begin to edit a scene, it's important to assess the footage you have to work with.

1   Double-click the clip **WS_Master_2_18_1** to open it into the Viewer.

This is a wide shot covering the entire scene.

2   Play the clip in the Viewer.

Keladry (with blond hair on the left) and Re'annon (with dark hair on the right) hang clothes from a basket while they cook up a plan to run away. Play the scene several times through, to familiarize yourself with the dialogue and action, playing close attention to the interaction with the basket.

Although this shot is useful to acquaint you with the dialogue in the scene, for the majority of the shot, the girls are facing away from the camera.

3   Double-click and play **MS Keladry_2_20_2**.

This shot shows the entire scene, but it focuses only on Keladry. There are three versions (or *takes*) of this shot. Each one has a different performance and may have different problems or benefits. The director's preference is listed in one of the Comment columns, so let's go find it.

4   In a gray area of the Browser window, Ctrl-click to access the contextual menu for the bin and choose View as List.

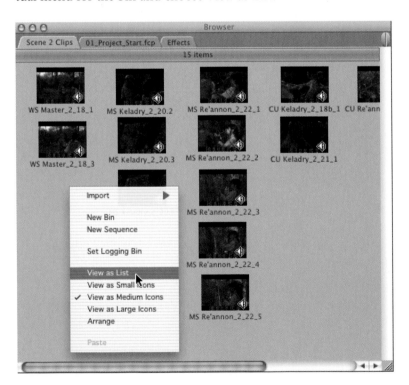

5   Scroll the window until the Master Comment 1 column is visible.

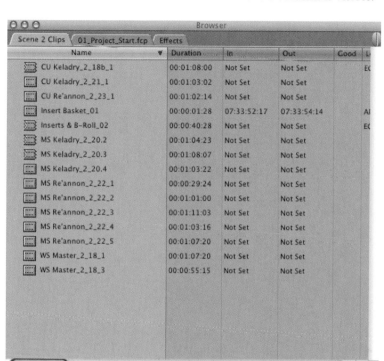

Here you can view the director's comments about the shots. These comments were entered from the camera log book when the footage was logged.

6   Ctrl-click again and choose View As Medium Icons.

7   Double-click the clip **MS Re'annon_2_22_1** and play it in the Viewer.

This shot is a reverse of the previous shot, so you will be able to cut back and forth between the two shots. Unfortunately, Re'annon is facing away from the camera for most of the shot, making it a bad take.

8   Review the next take, **MS Re'annon_02_22_2**.

This time the performance has improved, but the lighting has changed, and there is a shadow in front of Re'annon's face, making this shot unusable, too. Fortunately the crew noticed this and set up a large scrim to soften the sun for the remainder of the takes. It is up to you to review all of the clips to find the best take of each shot.

Assembling the Scene

The best way to begin assembling a scene like this one is to edit the master shot in first and then overwrite the close-up shots individually until the scene is assembled. You should focus on building the overall structure of the scene and then go back and fine-tune each of the edits.

1   Double-click **WS Master_2-18_1**.

2   Set an In point just before the two girls appear on the left side of the frame and set an Out point just after they exit at the end of the scene.

3   In the Timeline, you should see the **Empty Scene 2** sequence already open. If not, double-click the **Empty Scene 2** sequence from the Scene 2 Sequences bin to open the Canvas and Timeline.

4   Edit the clip into the sequence.

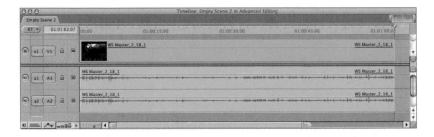

5 Play the sequence and set an In point just before Re'annon says, "I know, it's the same at my house," (approximately 11-12 seconds into the shot).

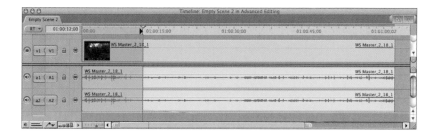

6 Open any one of the **MS Re'annon** shots (your choice, but you might want to open List view again and select the take the director tagged as Best in the Master Comment 1 column). Set an In point just before Re'annon says the same line. Set an Out point after she says, "…for stealing Jack's toys."

7   Overwrite this clip (the medium shot of Re'annon) into the sequence by dragging from the Viewer to the Canvas.

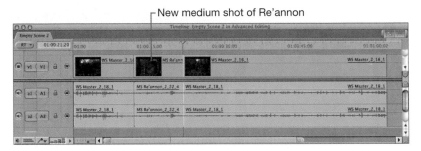

New medium shot of Re'annon

8   Play back the sequence.

If the actors' performances are consistent across the shots and takes, each time you add a shot, the edit from this medium over-the-shoulder shot back to the master shot should be smooth. If the medium shot was performed faster or more slowly than the master, you may need to fine-tune the edit later.

9   Open **MS Keladry_2_20.3** in the Viewer and find the end of Keladry's line, "It's not fair!" Set your In point there. Set an Out point after Keladry says, "That's it!"

Keladry

Re'annon

10 Overwrite the clip (**MS Keladry_20_30.3**) into the sequence directly after the second clip.

Now that you've reached the emotional height of the scene (when the girls get the idea that will drive the rest of the film), you will want to draw the viewer further into the scene. This would be an excellent time to move from the medium over-the-shoulder shots to close-ups.

11 Open **CU Re'annon_2_23_1** into the Viewer. Find the moment where Re'annon responds to Keladry's, "That's it!" with, "What, get rid of…?" Set your In point there and set the Out point after Re'annon says, "That's a magnificent idea."

12 Overwrite that clip (**CU Re'annon_2_23_1**) into the sequence right after your last edit, and play back the whole sequence.

13 Mark In and Out points around the section of the sequence when Keladry says, "No, what if we got rid of ourselves instead?"

14 Open **CU Keladry_2_21_1**. Set an In point just before she says "No, what if we…"

15 Overwrite that clip into the sequence.

Now the sequence progresses from Re'annon's close-up to Keladry's close-up and then back to Re'annon.

16 Play back the sequence.

Depending on how well you marked your clips, some of your edits may feel abrupt. The same audio may play twice, or there may be a delay before a reaction, creating an unnatural effect.

Choosing exactly when to make your edits and which shots to cut to is an art that you will master over time. In general, you should only cut when there is some new information that could not be revealed in the previous shot. In dialogue sequences, it is often more important to see someone's reaction than to see the speaker's moving lips. There are countless ways to edit the same sequence, and there is no "right" way.

Refining Your Edits

Once you have your sequence roughed together, you will probably need to go back and clean up the edit points, adjust the timing, and generally smooth out the look and feel of the scene.

Rather than using the Scene 2 sequence you edited, this exercise will use a different rough cut of the same scene.

1   Open **Rough Scene 2** from the Scene 2 Sequences bin.

2   Play back the sequence to familiarize yourself with this version of the edit.

   You will fix this scene edit by edit. The first problem is that there is an unnatural pause between the first two cuts, when Keladry says, "It's not fair," and Re'annon answers, "I know," (approximately 12 seconds into the scene).

3 Play the sequence and stop the playhead as soon as Keladry finishes saying, "It's not fair."

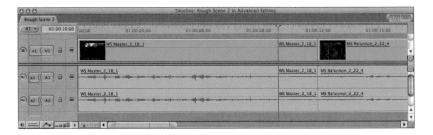

4 Select the Ripple tool from the Tool palette or type *RR*.

5 Click on the right edge of the outgoing clip and drag to the left, shortening the clip until you reach the playhead position. If snapping is enabled, the edit will snap to the playhead.

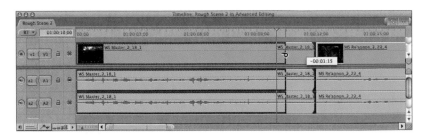

6 Play back the sequence.

Now the timing is right, but because of the business with the basket, Re'annon is in the wrong position, causing a jump cut. There are two ways to solve this: use an insert shot or split the shot.

Use an Insert Shot

1 In the Scene2 Clips bin, open the clip called **Insert Basket_01**.

There should already be In and Out points set.

2 Play the clip from In to Out by pressing Shift-backslash.

This clip can be used to cover the action of the girls standing up and beginning to hang the wash on the line.

3 Untarget the audio tracks in the Timeline by dragging the Source controls away from the Destination controls.

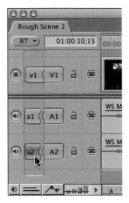

Now the next edit will not modify the audio tracks.

4 In the Timeline, position the playhead on the edit point between the first two clips.

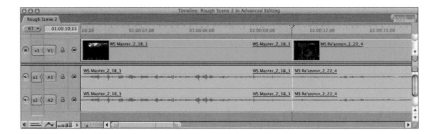

5 Overwrite the **Insert Basket_01** clip into the sequence by dragging it to the Canvas.

6 Play back the sequence.

Using this insert shot effectively covers the continuity error between the two shots. There is, however, another way to solve this problem.

Split the Edit

1 Press Cmd-Z to undo the last edit.

2 Select the Roll tool from the Tool palette or press R.

3 Press and hold the Option key to override Linked Selection and click the Video edit point.

4 Drag the edit point to the right until the left side of the Canvas displays a frame where Re'annon is fully standing. When you have lined up the edit on the desired frame, release the mouse.

NOTE ▶ If snapping is enabled, it may be difficult to line up on the correct frame. In that case, press the N key to turn off snapping.

5 Play back the sequence.

Because you are using a long shot and Re'annon is facing away from the camera, you can get away with playing the dialogue from the second clip over the first, even though she wasn't actually speaking.

Using Ripple Delete to Remove an Unwanted Sound

The next edit in the sequence contains the same action twice: the unwanted repetition of a sound. Keladry sighs in the outgoing clip and then sighs again in the incoming clip before saying her line. To solve this problem, you must eliminate the duplicate frames and offset the video and audio cuts.

1 Set an In point in the sequence right after Re'annon says "…stealing Jack's toys" and before Keladry begins her first sigh, (approximately 21 seconds into the scene).

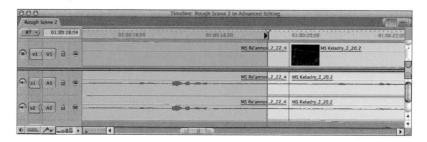

2 Set an Out point in the sequence just before Keladry sighs again in the third clip.

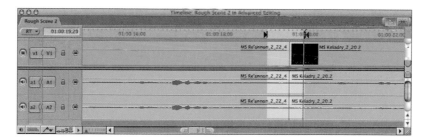

3 Choose Sequence > Ripple Delete or press Shift-Delete.

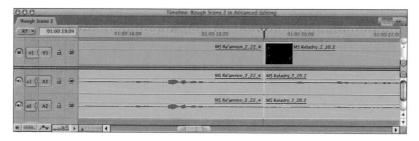

You have now successfully removed the double sigh, but the edit may still feel somewhat abrupt because the cut occurs precisely at the beginning of Keladry's next line, "I hate him." This is aggravated by the way the actress delivers the line: she swallows the beginning of it.

4 Turn off Linked Selection by clicking the button in the Timeline button bar.

5 Using the Selection tool, click on the edit point on track A1.

When you select an edit with the Selection tool, it is selected as a roll.

6 Cmd-click on the edit point on Track A2 so that both audio tracks are selected.

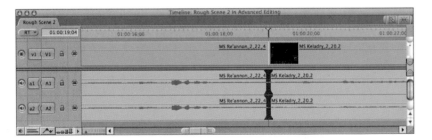

7 Type *+110* and press Return.

A window appears in the Timeline, indicating that you are performing a numeric roll.

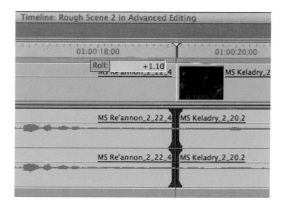

8   Press Return.

This should clean up the edit by rolling your audio edit forward past the sigh. Make sure the audio from the outgoing clip matches the video of Keladry's lips in the incoming clip.

9   Press the backslash key to play around the current edit.

Using Replace Edits

The next two edits play smoothly, but Keladry has an important line that is delivered entirely off-camera. To improve the sequence, you will cut to her for her line, and then cut back to Re'annon for her reaction.

1   Play back the sequence.

2   Mark In and Out points around the section where Keladry says, "Well, think about it," (approximately 40 seconds into the scene).

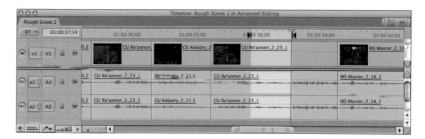

To edit a shot of Keladry into this section and maintain sync throughout the sequence, you could load the close-up of Keladry into the Viewer, find the exact spot where the line begins, and hope that it aligns precisely with the other shots in the sequence. But there's an easier way.

3 Park your playhead over the previous close-up of Keladry in the Timeline.

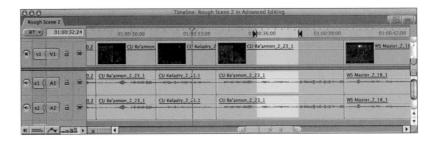

4 Choose View > Match Frame > Master Clip, or press the F key.

The master clip opens into the Viewer, cued to the same frame as the Canvas.

5   Retarget the audio tracks by dragging back together the Source controls and the Destination controls for tracks A1 and A2.

6   Drag the clip from the Viewer to the Canvas and drop it on the Replace edit section of the Edit Overlay.

7 Play back the section by pressing the backslash key.

Replace edits match the Viewer and Canvas/Timeline playheads to each other and use this matched frame as a starting point to edit in material, both forward and backward, until the boundaries of the edit points before and after the playhead are reached. However, if there are In and Out points set in the sequence (such as in our example), material lays in only between those set In and Out points.

Since we just used Match Frame to make sure the Viewer was displaying the same frame as the Canvas, and since the pace of Keladry's close-up was relatively similar to that of the sequence, the edit placed the line of dialogue we wanted from Keladry's close-up into the right place and maintained sync.

Ganging the Viewer and Canvas

Another way to take advantage of Replace edits is to use the Gang controls, which lock the Canvas and the Viewer into sync.

1 Go back and park your playhead over any part of Keladry's close-up.

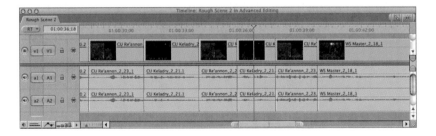

2 Perform a Match Frame by pressing F.

3   In the Viewer, set the Gang Sync mode to Gang.

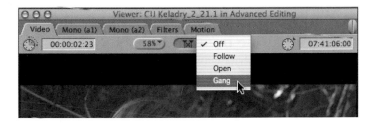

This ties the Canvas and Viewer playheads together. As you move the Canvas playhead, the Viewer playhead moves by the same amount, and vice versa.

4   Play the sequence and stop right after Re'annon says, "I know where my mom keeps our money," (approximately 46 seconds into the scene).

5   Choose Sequence > Add Edit or press Ctrl-V.

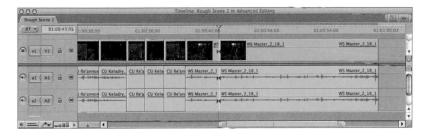

6   Play forward until Re'annon says, "…all the land." Add another edit at the end of her line.

7 Add a third edit after she says, "When shall we leave?"

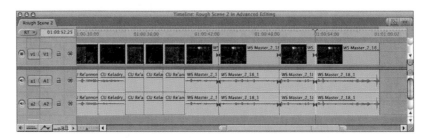

8 Place your Timeline playhead anywhere between the last close-up of Re'annon and the first edit you added.

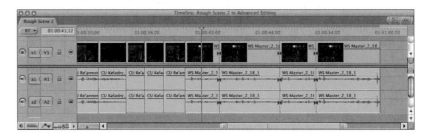

9 Drag the match framed clip in the Viewer (**CU Keladry_2_21_1**) to the Replace target in the Canvas.

Because the two windows were ganged after a match frame, the new edit will be in sync with the surrounding clips.

10 Park your playhead between the next two edit points that you created.

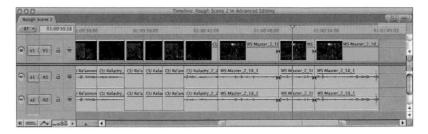

11 Perform another Replace edit.

12 Play back your sequence.

You have now edited two close-ups of Keladry into the sequence. All that remains is to edit one more close-up of Re'annon.

13 Park your playhead over one of the close-ups of Re'annon already in the sequence.

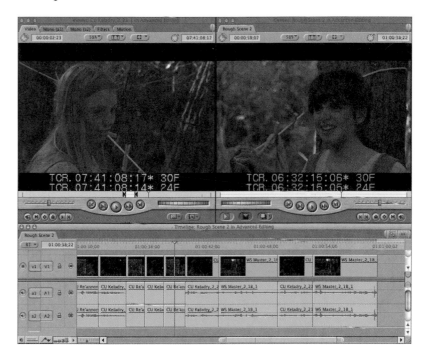

14 Press F to perform a Match Frame.

15 Set the Viewer to Gang mode.

16 Park your sequence playhead over the remaining segment of the master shot, between the two close-ups of Keladry.

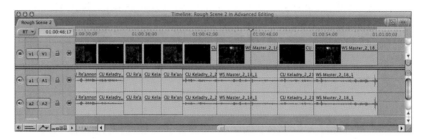

17 Perform a Replace edit to insert the close-up shot.

18 Play back your entire sequence. If you wish, you may spend some more time fine-tuning it with the Ripple tool and other tools we covered in the preceding exercises.

There Are No Right—or Wrong—Edits

As we said earlier, there are as many ways to edit a scene as there are editors. There is never just one way to composite shots or sync audio and video. But a good way to learn how to create really good scenes is to study the choices that others editors made.

1 Double-click **Fine Scene 2** from the Scene 2 Sequences bin.

2 Play back this version of the sequence.

This is the actual version that was cut for the film. You can learn from seeing the choices that the editor made. Notice that the opening cutaway to the basket is further enhanced with a shot of Keladry working on the laundry as Re'annon speaks.

Also notice that the editor chose to use the close-ups of the girls for the entire sequence. This may have been because the performances were best in these shots, but using the close-ups has the effect of flattening the arc of the scene.

3   Play the **Alternate Scene 2** sequence.

In this version, the editor cut out most of the dialogue in the second half of the scene. Often you can eliminate redundancy and sharpen a scene by cutting some lines of dialogue or by cutting out the beginning or end. This version uses only two audio clips for all the video, and also involves a lot of lip synching.

Experiment with the footage on your own time and create your own version of the sequence.

Cutting an Action Scene

Most of the same rules and techniques apply whether you are cutting a basic dialogue scene, an action scene, or any other type of scene. There are, however, certain issues that are likely to arise in particular situations. Action scenes, for example, rely very heavily on *continuity cutting* (following action across cuts), and you may encounter obstacles such as screen direction problems that are tricky to solve.

Continuity Cutting

In this exercise, you will make some continuity cuts to help the viewer follow the action more easily.

1   Open the **Water Scene** sequence and play it back.

This sequence is incomplete. You must add the remaining shots where the boy pours the bucket of water on the girls.

2 Open the **WS K&R get wet_1_11_1** clip from the Water Scene Clips bin.

In order to make a successful continuity cut, you must find an action that occurs in both shots and set the cut in the middle of that action.

3 Play back the clip in the Viewer and stop on the frame just as the boy is leaping off of the log. Set an In point.

4 Play back the sequence and find the frame in the last shot where the boy begins to leap to the left.

5 Overwrite the clip into the sequence at that point. Don't worry about where the Out point falls.

6 Play back your new edit.

You may need to fine-tune the edit with the Ripple and Roll tools to make the action look and sound fluid across the edit point, but your new edit should now follow the action with more continuity.

Solving Screen Direction Problems

However, there is a bigger problem. The screen direction changes across the two shots: In the first clip, the boy is moving right-to-left and in the second clip he is moving left-to-right. This occurred because the camera position changed between the two shots.

There are several different ways to solve this sort of screen direction problem, depending upon what footage you have to work with.

Using an On-Axis Shot

One of the easiest ways to fix incongruous screen direction is to replace the offending clip with a shot where the action is coming directly toward the camera, called an *on-axis* shot.

1   Undo the overwrite edit you just did in the previous exercise (**WS K&R get wet_1_11_1**).

2   Open **WS Start chase_1_16_6** from the Water Scene Clips bin and play it back.

This clip shows the same action from a wider, more neutral angle.

Notice that in this shot, the boy is not moving left-to-right or right-to-left, but rather he is moving directly toward the camera. Using an on-axis shot like this one is one way to get around a screen direction error. The clip is already marked with In and Out points.

3   Drag this clip to the Timeline and overwrite the very beginning of the **WS K&R** shot.

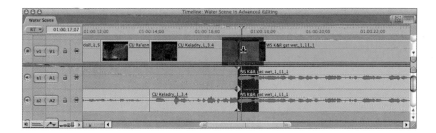

Although this is a fairly short shot, it should play smoothly as long as the action is continuous across the two cuts. The fast cutting also makes the action more dynamic, and heightens the drama of the scene.

Using the Flop filter

Another way to fix this type of screen direction error is to use the Flop filter.

1   Play the water sequence back and stop near the end, just after Keladry screams from having the water dumped on her.

2   Open **ECU Keladry_1_13b_2** from the Water Scene Clips bin. The In and Out points have already been set.

3   Perform an Overwrite edit by dragging the clip to the Canvas.

4   Open **CU Timmy_1_15_3** into the Viewer. Again, the In and Out points have already been set.

5   Overwrite this clip into the sequence right after Keladry's extreme close-up.

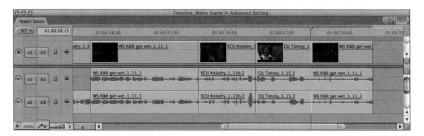

As long as you have not moved your sequence playhead, the clip will be overlaid immediately after the ECU of Keladry.

6   Play back your sequence.

Notice that Keladry and Timmy are both looking to the right in sub-sequent shots. If the two are supposed to be looking at each other, this breaks the basic rules of screen direction. The easiest way to solve this problem is to use the Flop filter.

7   Select the **ECU Keladry** clip in the Timeline.

8   Apply the Flop filter by choosing Effects > Video Filters > Perspective > Flop.

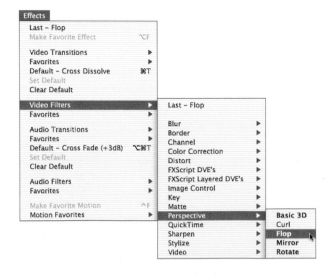

9 Play back the section of the sequence that you have changed.

Before

After

Now Timmy is facing right, Keladry is facing left, and they appear to be looking at one another.

The Flop filter only works in certain instances. If there had been any writing in the shot (such as a store awning or billboard in the background) it would appear reversed, creating a bigger problem than the incongruous eyelines. Also, if you needed to cut back to another shot showing a character on the left side of the frame, you would have simply traded one bad cut for another.

Fortunately in this sequence the flop works fine and can be reinforced by ending the sequence with another shot where Timmy is on the left and Keladry is on the right.

10 Open **WS Start chase_1_16_6** into the Viewer.

11 Even though In and Out points are already set, mark a new In point just as Timmy begins to run away and Keladry lifts her leg to step over the log.

12 Edit this clip into the sequence directly after the **CU Timmy** shot at the end of the sequence.

13 Play back the entire sequence.

You have all of the footage to create your own versions of these sequences. Take some time to experiment with different shots and discover new ways of constructing the scene. Remember, there is no right way to construct a scene.

Bonus Section: Cutting Interview Footage

Interviews and narration are another common type of footage you'll encounter while editing. Like dialogue or action footage, there are specific techniques that are ideal for working with interview footage. We've include a special bonus section on these techniques, in PDF format, in the Lessons > x_Bonus_Lesson folder on the DVD that comes with this book. Take some time now to master these techniques.

What You've Learned

- The Ripple and Roll tools can be used to fine-tune edits.
- A cutaway or insert shot can cover a difficult edit.
- You can split edits to smooth dialogue.
- Ripple Delete cleans up an edit point.
- Replace edits speed the editing and synching of clips.
- Gang Sync mode keeps clips aligned and simplifies the process of editing dialogue.
- Time continuity cuts to sync action shots.
- Overwrite shots and/or use the Flop filter to solve incongruous screen direction errors.

2

Lesson Files	Lessons > Lesson_02 > 02_Project_Start.fcp
Media	Media > Lesson_02_Media
Time	This lesson takes approximately 90 minutes to complete.
Goals	Learn when to use the Trim Edit window versus the Timeline
	Master the basic trimming controls
	Learn to trim on the fly using the JKL keys
	Use dynamic trimming to speed editing
	Perform complex trims across multiple tracks
	Create split edits with asymmetrical trimming in the Timeline
	Perform asymmetrical trims in the Trim Edit window
	Trim edits underneath transitions

Advanced Trimming

Editing, like most complex tasks, typically follows the 80/20 rule The last 20 percent of the work typically takes 80 percent of the time. You can usually knock out a rough assembly of your video fairly quickly, and even refine it into a rough cut soon after, but getting from that point to a polished final piece involves a great deal of work. You must finesse each edit point to its optimal location, split your edits so your audio and video don't begin and end at the same time, and trim away extraneous frames to make your program as tight and concise as possible.

In this lesson, you will explore some of the more advanced trimming techniques, such as basic multi-track trimming, asymmetrical trimming, dynamic trimming, and trimming an edit under a transition effect.

Fortunately, Final Cut Pro has a plethora of tools designed to make this work as fluid and painless as possible. The single most important tool to master, however, is the Trim Edit window.

The Trim Edit window is like a zoomed-in view of an individual edit point. You can see the frames of the outgoing and incoming clips in full detail and make adjustments to both. Although the functionality of the Trim Edit window is simple, it is also quite powerful.

The Trim Edit Window

For the most part, the work you do in the Trim Edit window can also be done in the Timeline. The advantages to the Trim Edit window are primarily precision and fluidity You can make decisions while playing the clip. Deciding when to use the Timeline rather than the Trim Edit window depends on the circumstances of the edit and your personal preference.

1   Open the Lessons > Lesson_02 > **02_Project_Start.fcp** project.

2   Play back the open sequence (**Night Woods Chase_01**).

You can probably see that even though the overall sequence is intact, several edit points need to be adjusted.

3 Double-click on the first edit point with the Selection tool to open the Trim Edit window. (Be sure to turn on Linked Selection first, so that both audio tracks and the video track are highlighted and loaded for trimming.)

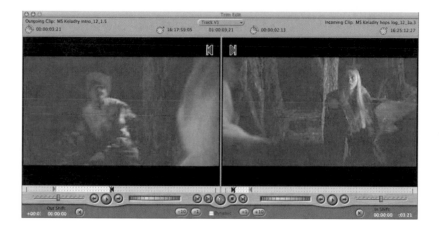

Although trimming in the Timeline can be efficient for some edit points, the Trim Edit window can be especially useful when you need to add frames to your edit.

In the first cut, the ogre is barely visible before the edit cuts away to the girl's reaction. Here you need to add frames to the outgoing clip without changing the incoming clip.

4 Click on the left side of the window (the outgoing clip).

This sets the trim type to a Ripple Outgoing. The Trim Edit window changes so that only the clip on the left (the outgoing clip) has a green bar over it. Also, the Timeline changes to indicate a Ripple Outgoing trim.

5 Position the cursor over the left clip.

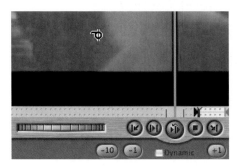

The position of the cursor determines which clip your JKL keys will affect. Positioning the cursor over the left side of the window controls the outgoing clip. Positioning the cursor over the right side of the window controls the incoming clip. No clicking is necessary. The active clip's Play button appears light blue.

Most editors find that making decisions while playing is the best way to make subtle, effective changes. The edit you are adjusting could be corrected in the Timeline—you could grab the Ripple tool, drag the left side of the edit point to the right, and watch the two-up display in the Canvas until you felt that the ogre was onscreen long enough— but watching the edit frame by frame makes it difficult to determine how long is "long enough." The Trim Edit window, in contrast, allows you to make that decision while playing.

NOTE ▶ Make sure you do not have the dynamic check box selected for the following steps.

6 Press the J key to back up the clip slightly, and then press the L key to play forward. Let the playback run beyond the Out point until the ogre is visible for "long enough." At exactly that moment, press the K key to stop playback.

There is no exact frame that makes the edit "correct." The preceding figure illustrates one possible end frame.

7 Experiment a little. Back up and play the clip a few times until you consistently stop on the same frame.

8 When you have settled on the new frame, click the Mark Out button or press the O key.

This performs a Ripple trim, adding the additional frames to the end of the outgoing clip.

9   Press the spacebar to watch your new edit.

Playback will automatically loop around the edit point. (You can set the amount of pre- and post-roll in your User Preferences.)

If you are happy with the new edit—the ogre is onscreen long enough to see him clearly, but not too long as to slow down the action—you are finished.

10   If you are not satisfied, use the JKL keys to find a different Out point for the first clip. (Be sure your cursor is still over the outgoing clip.)

11   When you stop on the new Out point, press the O key to execute the ripple.

Creating Complex Trims

This same technique can be used to quickly correct more complicated editorial problems.

1   In the Timeline, double-click the fourth video edit (between **WS_Ogres_12_5.2** and **MS Keladry hops log_12_3a.3**). Again, be sure Linked Selection is turned on.

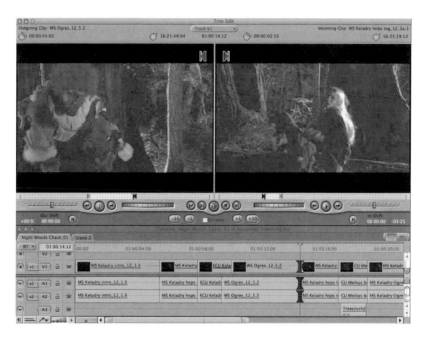

The Trim Edit window updates to display the new edit point. The problem with this edit is that the action overlaps in the two clips The girl jumps over the log in the first shot, then jumps it again in the second clip. Let's eliminate the redundant action.

2   Press the U key to toggle the trim type to Ripple Incoming, or click the right side of the window, so the green highlight is only over the incoming clip on the right.

3   Position the cursor over the right clip to activate it for JKL playback.

4   Use the JKL keys to position the playhead in the middle of Keladry's twirl, just after she turns her face away from the camera.

You can use the frame in this figure as a guide for where to position the playhead.

5   Click the In button (or press the I key) to set a new In point.

6   Press the U key again to switch to a Ripple Outgoing and work on the outgoing clip.

7   Position your cursor over the left side of the window. (Note that the play button on the left window highlights blue.)

8 Use the JKL keys to position the playhead in the middle of Keladry's twirl on the outgoing clip.

You can use the frame in this figure as a guide. In addition to the JKL keys, you can also use your left and right arrow keys to move one frame at a time.

9 Click the Out button or press the O key.

10 Use the spacebar to watch your edit.

The movement across the edit point should look continuous. The only problem is that the action of the ogre jumping onto the log is missing.

Because you have established continuity across the edit point, you can now Roll the edit to any frame, and the action should feel continuous.

11 Press the U key until the edit point is selected as a Roll. Alternately, click on the bar between the two frames in the Trim Edit window. The green bar should light up above both clips.

12 Position your cursor over the left (outgoing) clip. Don't click, or you'll change the trim to a Ripple.

13 Use the JKL keys to find the frame where the ogre first lands on the log.

You can use the frame in this picture as a guide.

14 Press the O key to set the new Out point.

15 Use the spacebar to play around your new edit.

The girl's movement should still look natural and continuous across the edit point.

Speeding Work with Dynamic Trimming

Once you get the hang of trimming while playing, you'll probably grow to love it. You can very quickly make all of your timing decisions while playing, which is far more efficient and more intuitive than dragging and counting frames. You can even navigate from edit to edit from within the Trim Edit window.

1 With the Trim Edit window still open and active, press the down arrow key three times to move to the third-to-last edit (between **MS Keladry Ogres close in_12_7.1** and **CU Ogres close in_12_8.3**).

In this edit, the ogres are not moving at the start of the close-up shot. By now you should have a sense of how to fix this, but this time you will use dynamic trimming to speed the work.

When dynamic trimming is enabled, one step is eliminated from the process you used in the last two examples Pressing the K key automatically stamps the In or Out key to perform the trim.

2   Click on the incoming clip in the Trim Edit window (or press U on the keyboard until the edit point is selected as an Incoming Ripple).

3   Check the Dynamic box at the bottom of the Trim Edit window to enable dynamic trimming.

4   Position your cursor over the incoming clip on the right and press the L key to advance the clip forward.

5   After the director calls, "Action," and the ogres start moving, press the K key.

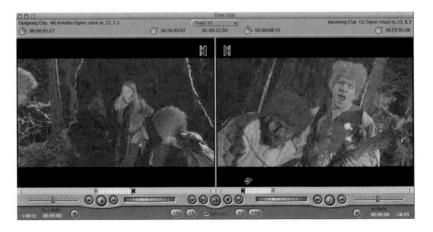

The In point is changed, and the edit is automatically updated.

NOTE ▶ You can also use the spacebar or Esc key to stop playback and not apply the edit.

6   Use the spacebar to play around your new edit.

If you aren't satisfied with the edit, continue to make adjustments using the JKL keys to change the frame where the edit falls.

Multi-Track Trimming

Often, the adjustments you make to an edit point require changing both the picture and the soundtrack, and often you will encounter edits where many different tracks must all be trimmed in order to keep your sequence in sync.

1   Close the Trim Edit window.

2   Find the clip in the sequence called **CU Meikus bangs Log_12_6a.1** and zoom in on it (in the middle of the sequence, at approximately 14–15 seconds).

3   Play across the clip to watch it.

This clip starts too early. The ogre should already be midswing at the beginning of the shot. To fix this, you'll need to make an Incoming Ripple, which you'll do this time in the Timeline.

4   Select the Ripple tool from the Tool palette (or press RR) and click on the incoming edge of the edit point to select both the audio and video for trimming. (Be sure Linked Selection is turned on.)

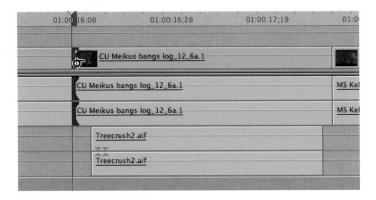

5   Drag the edit to the right until the ogre lifts the club over his head, and then release the mouse to make the trim.

6 Play back the new edit.

You will immediately notice that the sound of the club hitting the log is no longer in sync with the picture.

To correctly trim this edit, you must edit all four audio tracks in addition to the video track.

7 Choose Edit > Undo to undo the last edit you made; you may have to repeat the undo command a few times, depending on how you got to this point. Your Timeline should now look like the figure shown in step 3, except the edit point will be selected.

8 If the edit point is not selected, use the Ripple tool to select the edit point as a Ripple Incoming.

9   Cmd-click on the right side of the edit point on Track 3 and Track 4 to select both edit points.

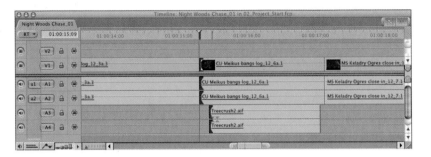

Now when you perform your edit, all of the tracks will be trimmed simultaneously.

10   Drag the edit points to the right until the ogre's club is raised over his head, and then release the mouse.

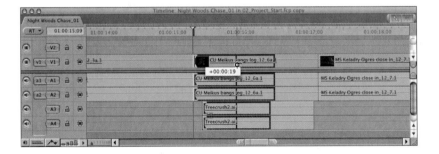

11   Play back the sequence.

This time, the sound effect is moved along with the corresponding picture, and everything is in sync.

Asymmetrical Trimming in the Timeline

In addition to being able to trim multiple clips on multiple tracks, you can select different sides of each edit point to execute different types of trims.

You can even go so far as to trim two clips in opposite directions. This is called *asymmetrical trimming*.

1   Double-click the **Scene 2** sequence.

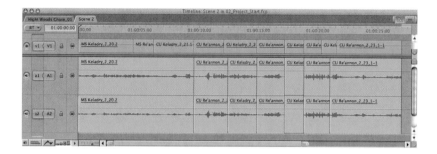

2   Play back the sequence to get familiar with it.

Dialogue sequences often benefit from extensive use of *split edits* to tie the audio and visual elements together. Asymmetrical trimming is a way to create a split edit in one step. The audio and video edits are moved in opposite directions, offsetting the edit points.

The third edit (between **CU Keladry_2_21.1-1** and **CU_Re'annon_2_23_1-1**) is a perfect example of where a split edit will improve the sequence. In this edit, Keladry says, "Re'annon, that's it!" and then, after the edit, Re'annon responds. The sequence would be better if it cut to Re'annon when Keladry says her name.

Using asymmetrical trimming, you can do this in one step.

3   Select the Ripple tool (RR) from the Tool palette.

4   Click the outgoing (left) side of the video edit point.

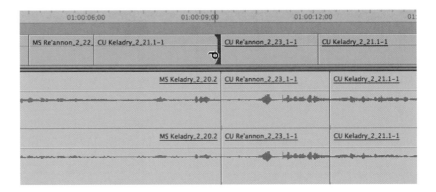

5   Cmd-click to also select the incoming (right) side of both audio edits.

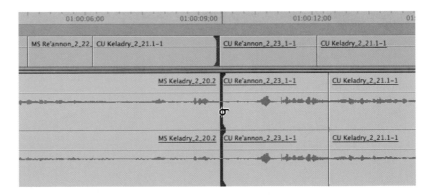

You can use the audio waveforms in the Timeline to guide your trim.

6   Drag the mouse to the left approximately one second, so the new edit point is after the word "Re'annon" and before "That's it!"

As you trim the Out point of the outgoing video on the left, reducing its duration, you are also trimming the In point of the incoming audio on the right, which reduces its duration as well. Further, you are now left with a split edit point, where the video and audio cut at different times. Because you cut to the incoming video clip first, you get to see Re'annon's face after Keladry calls her name and then watch Re'annon's reaction to Keladry's statement. This allows you to cut on the height of the action, one of the fundamental goals of good editing.

7   Play around your edit point (use the backslash key) to see how your new edit looks. You may want to undo and redo the trim a few times to really see what is happening.

Asymmetrical Trimming in the Trim Edit Window

You can also make asymmetrical trims in the Trim Edit window, which offers the benefit of being able to set the edit on the fly.

1   Skip ahead two edit points (between **CU Keladry_2_21_1-1** and **CU Re'annon_2_23_1-1**).

Select this edit point in the same asymmetrical pattern as the last.

2 With Linked Selection on, use the Ripple tool to Option-click the outgoing video clip so that only the video edit is selected.

Option-Cmd-click to add the audio edits one at a time as a Ripple Incoming.

3 Double-click on a selected edit point to open the Trim Edit window.

The edit should remain selected in an asymmetrical manner. The Trim Edit window will display a green bar above the outgoing clip, indicating the state of the V1 track.

4 Uncheck the Dynamic box so that you can work more slowly and see how the edit changes.

5 Position your cursor over the left (outgoing) clip, but do not click to activate JKL playback for the outgoing clip.

6 Using the JKL keys, back the clip up and play forward. Stop with the K key after Keladry says "ourselves" and just before she says "instead."

7 Press the O key to set the new Out point and perform the trim.

The same phenomenon happens here as it did in our previous trim. Both the audio and video are trimmed shorter from opposite directions, which results in a split edit point. Most importantly, the trim drives the excitement of the scene because the viewer is privy to Re'annon's reaction as it forms before Keladry finishes her sentence. This also tightens the dialogue.

You can also undo and redo the trim while watching the Timeline update to better understand the change.

8 Use the spacebar to play around your new edit. If you don't like the timing, use your JKL keys to change it until it looks and sounds fluid and natural.

Trimming Under Transitions

All of the same trimming controls are available to you, regardless of whether the edit point you are modifying is a straight cut, a split edit, or contains a transition effect, such as a dissolve or wipe. Often, you will need to trim the edit beneath a transition effect to improve its effect.

1 Open the **Transition Effect** sequence.

2 Play the sequence back to familiarize yourself with the edit.

Depending on your RT settings and the capability of your machine, you may need to render the sequence in order to see it play back properly.

In this example, the wipe effect is intended to follow the girls' movement as they exit in the outgoing shot. Simultaneously, their entrance in the incoming shot should follow the wipe.

With a wipe, it is easier to make this trim if the transition is set on Start On Edit or End On Edit, rather than the default Center On Edit. However, working this way will require one non-intuitive step.

3 Ctrl-click on the transition and choose Transition Alignment > Start On Edit from the shortcut menu that appears.

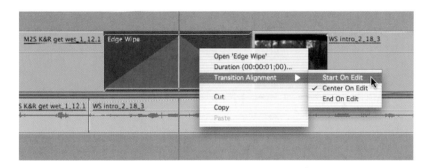

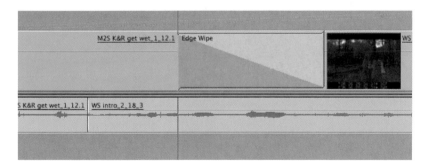

4 With the Selection tool active, double-click the video edit point (not the transition effect) to open the Trim Edit window with both the audio and video edits selected.

You may need to zoom in on the edit in order to select the edit point instead of the transition effect. Alternately, use the Edit Select tool (G) and drag a lasso around the edit.

5 Click on the right side of the Trim Edit window to perform a Ripple Incoming trim. Then position the cursor over the right side of the window and use the J key or drag left to find the first frame in which Keladry (the blond girl) is fully visible in the shot.

6   Stamp the trim by pressing the I key.

7   Change the transition from Start On Edit to End On Edit.

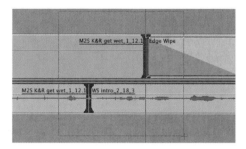

The Trim Edit window closes automatically.

8   Reopen the Trim Edit window by double-clicking the edit point (now at the end of the transition icon).

9   Click on the left side to activate an Outgoing Ripple. Keep the cursor on the left side of the window and navigate to the last frame, before the last girl (Keladry) is gone completely.

10   Perform the trim by pressing the O key, but do not review your edit or move the playhead yet.

Now this is where you need to take an extra, non-intuitive step. To accommodate the offset created when the edit was switched from Start On Edit to End On Edit, you must reset the incoming clip's In point.

11 Click on the right side of the Trim Edit window to change the trim to a Ripple Incoming.

12 Without moving the playhead, press the I key or click the Mark In button to reset the In point.

13 Change the transition alignment back to Center On Edit.

14 Close the Trim Edit window and render the sequence.

15 Play back the final effect and confirm that the timing is to your liking.

The edge of the wipe should follow the girls out of the frame, and the movement of the girls' entrance should follow closely behind.

What You've Learned

- Double-click or drag with the Edit Select tool to open the Trim Edit window.
- Click in the Trim Edit window to control what sort of trim will be performed—Ripple Outgoing, Roll, or Ripple Incoming.
- Use the JKL keys to control playback of incoming and outgoing clips in the Trim Edit window.
- Enabling dynamic trimming eliminates the step of stamping the In or Out key to perform the trim.
- Cmd-click to perform multi-track trims in the Timeline or in the Trim Edit window.
- Asymmetrical trimming trims two clips in opposite directions.
- Dynamic trimming, asymmetrical trimming, and other trimming controls can all be applied underneath a transition effect.

Advanced Effects

Andrew Balis has worked in the film industry since 1990 as a cinematographer, editor, and post-production consultant. He regularly teaches classes in Final Cut Pro to industry professionals, and has lectured at Apple, UCLA, Moviola, AFI, and IFP. He is the co-author of the original Apple-certified training curriculum for Final Cut Pro in introductory, advanced, and effects classes, developed at Moviola Education.

Michael Wohl is best known as the principal designer of Final Cut Pro, a role he held for more than five years. He has also had success as a director and editor for more than 15 years. His 1993 film "Theatereality" won the coveted CINE Golden Eagle award and his latest feature film "WANT" is playing to acclaim on the international film festival circuit. He is currently in development on a new feature film and will be directing an original stageplay in early 2004 in Los Angeles.

3

Lesson Files	Lessons > Lesson_03 > 03_Project_Start.fcp
	Lessons > Lesson_03 > 03_Project_Finished.fcp
Media	Media > Lesson_03_Media
Time	This lesson takes approximately 120 minutes to complete.
Goals	Become familiar with motion properties and the ways in which they can be altered
	Create motion effects with keyframe animation
	Create and modify motion paths
	Use Bézier handles to customize effects
	Copy effects to additional images
	Remove artifacts and otherwise finesse the final sequence
	Create a template to reuse a composition and replace the images

Lesson 3
Motion Effects

Motion effects are an integral element of television programming. They are used to create anything from a simple split screen to a pan-and-scan on a still photograph, or for more eye-catching animations such as images flying across the screen for the intro to a show. By mastering motion effects, you can create exciting visuals as well as solve simple, everyday editing problems.

In this lesson, you will first learn the fundamentals of motion properties and then create a finished composition—an opening sequence for a TV travel magazine show. Along the way, you will learn how to animate effects settings; reshape, distort, reposition, and crop images; save time by building on previous work, and refine your effects for professional results.

Working with Motion Properties

Using motion properties to animate sequences is rather like creating a collage from pictures in a magazine. However, instead of using just still photographs, you also use titles, onscreen graphics, and multiple images. And instead of using scissors and glue to cobble together static images, you animate digital images by modifying their motion properties with such tools as Rotation and Scale.

Let's start by examining some basic approaches to altering motion properties and learning some keyboard shortcuts that give you additional flexibility and control.

1   Open Lessons > Lesson _03 > **03_Project_Start.fcp**.

2   From the Clips bin in the Browser, locate **kelp forest intro** and add it to the beginning of the sequence, called **Sequence**, which should already be open.

3   Position the Timeline playhead so that it's over the clip, and make sure the clip is visible in the Canvas.

4   In the Timeline, double-click to open the clip into the Viewer, and then click the Motion tab.

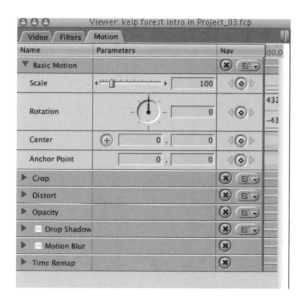

The parameters listed in the Motion tab are the default settings. Almost all of these parameters can be manipulated in the Viewer or directly in the Canvas.

5   In the Canvas, click the View button and choose Image+Wireframe from the pop-up menu.

With the clip selected in the Timeline, an X should appear over the clip in the Canvas.

The Wireframe view allows you to make changes to an image's properties in a graphic way, as you will see in the following exercises.

NOTE ▶ If an X does not appear in the Canvas, it means the clip in the Timeline is not selected. Click the clip to activate its wireframe in the Canvas.

Setting Up the Wireframe

When working with a wireframe image, you will be clicking very near the edge of the windows. It's a good idea to resize the Canvas and Viewer windows in order to move the wireframe away from the edge of the window. To do this, you'll use the window resizing feature.

1   Position the cursor between the Viewer and Canvas, near the bottom of the windows, as shown in the following figure.

When positioned directly over the connecting boundaries of the two windows, the cursor changes into a resize icon.

2   Click and drag left slightly to widen the Canvas a bit. Notice that the wireframe is now separated from the edge of the window by a small gray border.

With the Canvas slightly wider than the image, there is now a clear separation between the wireframe and the window edge, which will make it easier to choose to work with either one without accidentally affecting the other.

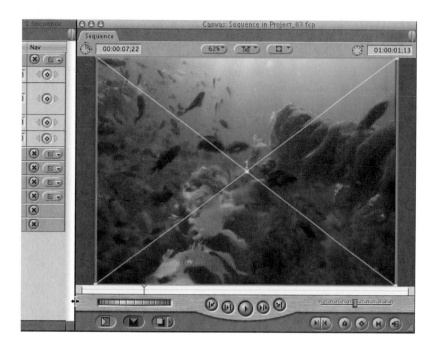

Scaling and Rotating Images

Several of the properties that can be altered graphically in Wireframe mode are grouped together in the Viewer under the heading Basic Motion. These settings are Scale, Rotation, Center, and Anchor Point.

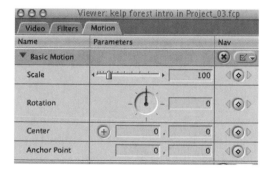

1   In the Canvas, position the cursor over one of the four white-colored corner points of the wireframe. The cursor becomes a crosshair.

2   Click one of these corner points and drag inward toward the center.

The image scales down accordingly. Notice that this adjustment is also reflected in the Scale setting in the Viewer.

Scaled image in Canvas

Scaling is used to fit multiple images on the screen together.

TIP In most cases, avoid scaling an image larger than 100%, because that in effect zooms in past the image's native resolution, which may result in the image appearing softer and more pixilated.

3 Click anywhere inside the wireframe and drag it to one side of the frame. This change will be reflected in the Motion tab of the Viewer, in the Center coordinates settings boxes.

4   Click the green image-boundary line at one of the four sides of the image and drag to rotate the image.

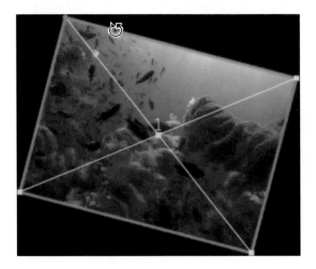

5   Cmd-drag on a corner point to simultaneously scale and rotate the image.

6   In the Viewer motion tab, click the red X reset button for Basic Motion to reset all parameters back to 100% and recenter the image on the screen.

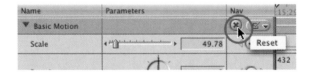

Cropping Images

Cropping is used to hide extraneous information along the edges of an image. This focuses attention on the remaining portion of the image and highlights the area of interest. Cropping is also frequently used to fit two or more images on a split screen.

1   In the Motion tab of the Viewer, click the disclosure triangle next to Crop to display the crop parameters. These settings can be manipulated right here, but as you are about to see, some of them can be modified in a more visually dynamic way in the Canvas.

2 Select the Crop tool from the Tool palette or press C.

3 Position the cursor over one of the four sides of the green image-boundary line in the Canvas. The cursor turns into the crop icon.

4 Click and drag inward to crop one of the four sides.

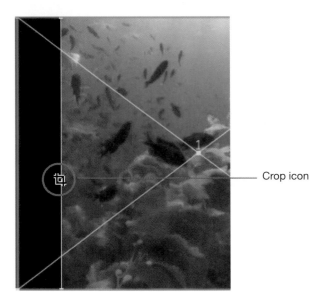

Crop icon

5 Uncrop by dragging back out (or undo with Cmd-Z).

6   Position the cursor at a corner point and click and drag inward. This crops the height and width of the image at the same time.

Crop Points in the Canvas

Once you have cropped the image, new points appear in the wireframe. These new crop points indicate where you can click to recrop an image that has already been cropped. Instead of clicking and dragging a corner of the wireframe, you now click and drag one of the new white boundaries or corner points to modify the clip's cropping.

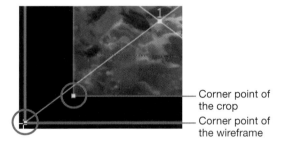

Corner point of the crop
Corner point of the wireframe

1   Position your cursor over the corner point of the wireframe. The cursor becomes a crosshair icon. If you click and drag on this point, even with the Crop tool selected, you will scale—not crop—the image.

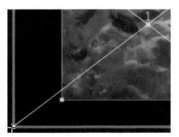

2 Position the cursor over a crop corner point. The cursor becomes the crop icon again. You would click here if you wanted to modify the crop settings of the clip.

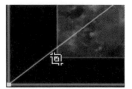

Cropping and the Keyboard

Depending on where you click and what key combination you use, you can modify cropping behavior to crop one, two, or all four sides together, proportionally or not. As different situations call for different approaches, the following options will afford you the most flexibility.

1 To trim two sides proportionally, press and hold Shift as you click along the corner point with the Crop tool.

This is helpful when an image is positioned in a corner of the frame, and only the outside edges need to be adjusted.

2   To crop two parallel sides evenly, press and hold Cmd while you click
     and drag one side.

3   To crop all four sides, Cmd-click-drag on a corner point.

4   To crop all four sides by the same amount, press Shift-Cmd while you
     click and drag on a crop corner point.

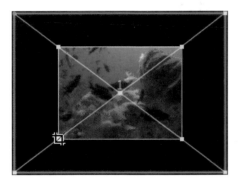

Using Shift-Cmd while you drag is a fast way to set all four sides to
the same crop setting dynamically and efficiently. In the Motion tab of
the Viewer, notice that settings for all four sides have been updated to
reflect your changes. You will use some of these key combinations
during the next exercise to modify several settings at once.

▼ Crop			⊗ ☑
Left	◀——⬜—┴—┴—┴—▶	20.97	◁ ◈
Right	◀——⬜—┴—┴—┴—▶	20.97	◁ ◈
Top	◀——⬜—┴—┴—┴—▶	20.97	◁ ◈
Bottom	◀——⬜—┴—┴—┴—▶	20.97	◁ ◈
Edge Feather	◀⬜—┴—┴—┴—┴—▶	0	◁ ◈

5   Click the red X button to reset Crop settings to their default values.
     Also reset Basic Motion if you have adjusted any of these settings.

Distorting Images

The Distort motion property is useful for mixing 4x3 and 16x9 material, for creating a sense of perspective, and for making an image look distressed, squeezed, or stretched. Like Scale and Crop, Distort can also be used to create split screens, but it squeezes the two images rather than resizing or cropping them.

1   In the Motion tab of the Viewer, click the disclosure triangle to hide the Crop parameters and then click the triangle to display the Distort parameters.

2   Click and drag the Aspect Ratio slider left and right. The image in the Canvas alternately squeezes in both directions. The Aspect Ratio parameter is a quick way to distort an image proportionally, either horizontally or vertically.

3   To try this out in the Canvas, select the Selection tool from the Tool palette and then Shift-click and drag on a corner point in the Canvas. This modifies Aspect Ratio and Scale together in one adjustment.

Resetting Attributes

In the previous exercises, you altered settings from three different sections of the Motion tab. Although settings can be manually reset, the Remove Attributes command is an efficient way to globally or selectively restore default settings and return a clip back to its original state without having to use the reset buttons in each section of the Motion tab.

1   Ctrl-click **kelp forest intro** in the Timeline and choose Remove Attributes from the contextual menu.

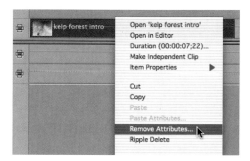

2   In the Remove Attributes dialog box that appears, check the settings you want to restore and then click OK. Those settings will be returned to their default state.

TIP ▶ Remove Attributes can be used to remove different attributes from multiple clips at once. For instance, one clip may have a filter and another clip an altered motion setting. Simply select all clips with effects before Ctrl-clicking and choosing Remove Attributes. Then select any and all boxes in the dialog box for those effects to be removed.

Creating Dynamic Motion Effects

Now you know how to alter motion properties to create some basic *static* effects. Static effects remain unchanged for the duration of a clip—for example, if the image is scaled to 40%, it stays at 40% for the entire time that it plays. Effects are more dynamic if they change over time. This is accomplished using *keyframe animation*.

Keyframes are considered the basic building blocks of motion effects, as they are a way of stamping a particular setting on a clip at any given time. Between any two keyframes, in-between values are automatically determined. Keyframes can be used to animate all of the motion settings that you have explored so far in this lesson, as well as many others. If the Scale parameter is keyframed, for example, an image can be made to change size over a predetermined period of time.

In the following exercises, you will use keyframe animation to create dynamic motion effects. You will use the clip from the previous exercises as well as other clips to create an opening sequence for an imaginary TV travel show. You'll start by using keyframe animation to introduce one image, have it cross the screen, and then exit the frame.

Configuring the Workspace

To set and modify keyframes easily, let's rearrange the interface windows so that they're more amenable to effects work.

1   Reposition the Viewer, Browser, and Timeline so that the Viewer can be stretched out fairly wide. Use the following illustration as a guide when setting up a computer display for working with effects.

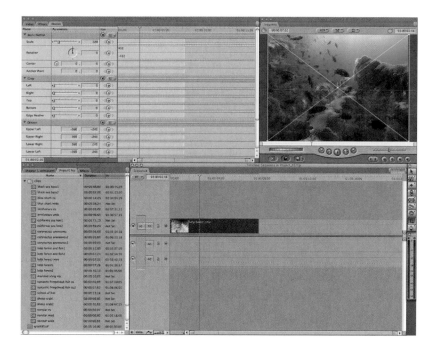

2 Choose Window > Arrange > Save Layout. A Save dialog box appears, with an option for naming the layout to be saved.

3 Choose an intuitive name for this layout, such as *Animating Effects*, and then click Save.

Now this screen arrangement will be available for you to use any time you are working with effects.

TIP Be sure to save window layouts to the default location in the Window Layouts folder.

Creating a Keyframe Animation

Now you will create the first motion effect by using the Scale and Rotation motion properties so that the first clip in the sequence starts out full frame, then scales down and rotates offscreen.

1 To see the final effect, as well as the rest of the composition that you will be working on, double-click **Finished Sequence** in the Browser to open it.

2   Play back the clips in the Timeline (render if needed).

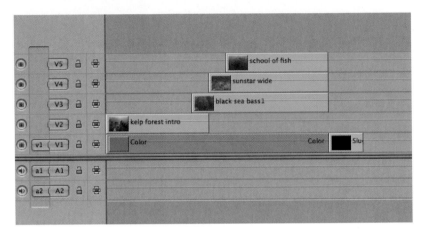

3   Switch back to the **Sequence** Timeline by clicking on its Timeline tab.

4   In the Timeline, open the clip **kelp forest intro** into the Viewer again and click the Motion tab, if not currently active.

The area to the right of the Motion settings is called the *keyframe graph*. This is where keyframes will be placed. Let's take a quick look at it.

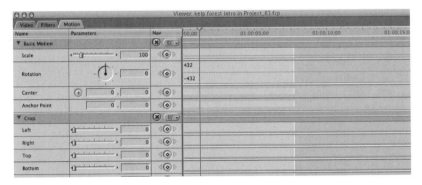

The ruler at the top of this tab is like looking at a slice out of the Timeline, and both the Timeline and this area reflect one another. If you scrub the playhead, you will see both Viewer and Timeline playheads moving together.

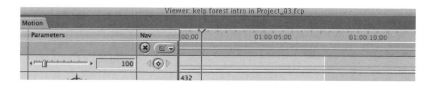

The lighter area represents the clip in the Viewer. When setting keyframes for the clip, they will be contained to this area.

The darker areas to the left and/or right of the light areas represent the Timeline sections adjacent to this clip.

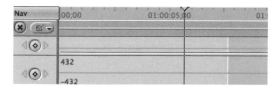

Now let's set some keyframes.

5   Move to the tail (end) of the clip in the keyframe graph in the Viewer.

> **TIP** ▶ Press Shift-I to move to the head of a clip in the Viewer and Shift-O to move to the Out point of the clip. This is preferable over the use of the Up and Down arrows keys, which may open up other clips from the Timeline into the Viewer.

6   While the Viewer is active, press Shift-left arrow twice to move the playhead back two seconds from the end of the clip.

7   At this playhead position, add a Scale keyframe by clicking on its keyframe button. This first keyframe will act as an anchor for the effect.

The keyframe is added on the graph at this position, and it is represented by the green dot at the playhead location.

8   Move to the end of the clip by pressing Shift-O.

9   Set a keyframe here for Scale. Now there are two keyframes for Scale, but they have the same values so there is no effect.

10   Click and drag down on the keyframe at the end of the clip until it touches the bottom of the graph. As you drag, a tooltip will display the value. When it reaches the bottom of the scale, 0, release the mouse.

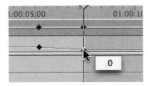

11   Play back this motion effect. Render if needed.

12 If your computer is capable of real-time playback, this would be a good opportunity to take advantage of the options of RT Extreme. In the RT menu in the Timeline, choose Unlimited RT.

If your playback isn't real-time at High quality, you can choose Medium or Low. Even at Low quality, you can still judge certain aspects of your effects. With a motion effect such as Scale, you can still observe the timing or pacing of the effect. Once that is tweaked and locked into place, you may switch to a higher quality to fine-tune the look of the images.

TIP Unless you are using a capture card, you can increase native RT playback by turning off external video in the View menu.

13 Move the Viewer playhead until it is roughly midway between the two Scale keyframes. Exact positioning is not necessary.

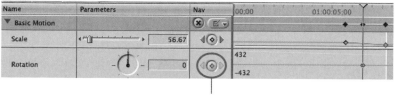

Rotation keyframe button

14 Set a Rotation keyframe here.

15 Move the playhead to the last frame of the clip (Shift-O).

16 In the Rotation dial control, click and drag clockwise and set the angle to approximately 270 degrees.

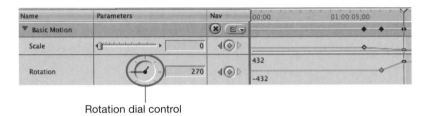

Rotation dial control

This automatically adds a keyframe at the playhead position. In this case, using the dial control is easier than dragging on the wireframe in the Canvas, because the image has been resized down to 0% at this position.

TIP ▶ To set an angle to any even increment of 45 degrees, press and hold the Shift key as you drag around the dial.

17 Play back the motion effect.

It's not quite finished. You have rotated the image out of frame, but the effect is still rough and somewhat jerky.

Adjusting the Pacing

There are two basic approaches to smoothing out the pacing of a motion effect. One is to change the distance between two keyframes—the further apart the keyframes, the slower the effect.

But in this case, making the animation longer would devote too much screen time to one image, so instead you'll use the other method for smoothing the pacing of motion effects: altering the keyframe type. Currently, the effect uses *corner point* keyframes, which means that there is a constant velocity (speed) between them. By changing the keyframe type, you can accelerate or decelerate the in or out motion of an effect.

Before you make this change, let's get a better view of the keyframe graphs for Scale and Rotation.

1 Position the cursor on the separator line between Scale and Rotation in the keyframe graph area. When you are directly over the line, the cursor will change into a resize icon.

2 Click and drag downward on this line to open up the working area for the Scale graph.

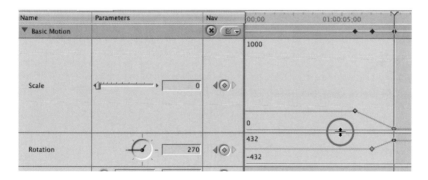

TIP You can resize the keyframe graph for many types of effects. The result is larger spacing between the values for the effect, allowing you to make smaller, subtler changes.

3 Do the same for the Rotation graph area: give it more space by dragging downward on the separator line below Rotation.

4   In the Viewer, Ctrl-click on the start keyframe for Scale. Choose Smooth from the contextual menu that appears.

A Bézier handle now stretches away from the keyframe, smoothing out the top angle on the graph.

5   Ctrl-click on the start keyframe for Rotation and choose Smooth from the contextual menu.

6   Play back the motion effect.

Notice that the animation starts off more slowly and then accelerates as it progresses, making the animation appear smoother than it did before. There is no need to change the end keyframes in this particular example, as the image disappears gracefully with corner point keyframes.

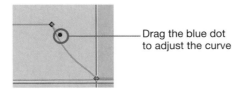

Drag the blue dot to adjust the curve

TIP ▶ The default curves created with the addition of the Bézier handles in this animation are adequate to create a nice smooth effect. When your aim is different, you may click and drag on the end of the Bézier handle (the dark blue dot) to alter the angle of the curve stretching toward the next keyframe.

Generating Motion Paths

Continuing with our imaginary TV opening sequence, let's animate an image flying into frame and coming to rest on the opposite side of the frame.

To do so, you will set keyframes to create a motion path that the image will follow across the screen. You'll use the Viewer to navigate through the clip and set keyframes on the Motion tab, but you will do most of the animating work in the Canvas, which offers a very dynamic way to create motion paths.

1   From the Browser, locate the clip **black sea bass1** and drag it to the Timeline, beginning right after **kelp forest intro** ends, and dropping it on the blank space above V1. This will automatically create a new video track, V2.

Don't worry about setting an In or Out for the clip. Simply use the whole clip.

2   Select the **black sea bass1** clip on V2.

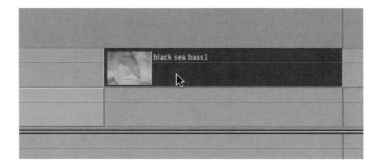

3   Type *–15* and press Return.

The clip moves to the left, overlapping the clip on V1 by 15 frames. This clip will begin an animation into the frame just before the first image disappears from the frame.

4   Open the clip **black sea bass1** from V2 into the Viewer and click the Motion tab.

5   Move the playhead to the first frame of the clip (Shift-1).

6   Set Scale to about 40%. Do not set any keyframes for Scale.

7   Click **black sea bass1** in the Canvas and move it to the upper-left part of the Canvas until it is mostly out of frame. In the next few steps, you will move it fully offscreen. (Be sure you are still in Image+Wireframe mode in the Canvas.)

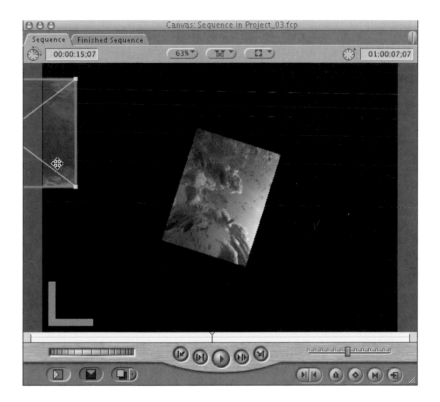

8   Click the Zoom button at the top of the Canvas and choose Fit All from the pop-up menu. This action resizes the Canvas, and you will now be able to see the offscreen area where you placed the image.

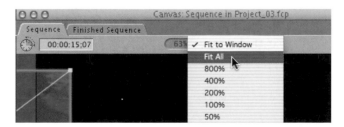

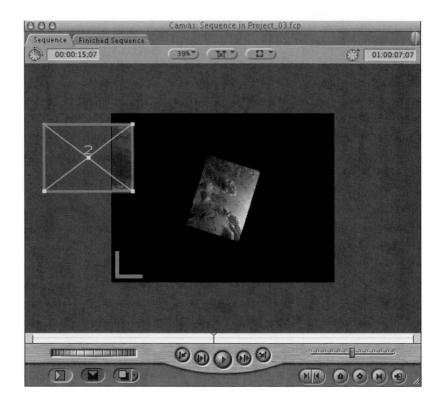

9   Now that you can see the area outside the frame, click and drag to the
    left on the image until the wireframe is fully outside the Canvas frame.

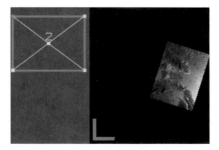

10 With your playhead still on the first frame of the clip, set a keyframe for Center in the Motion tab of the Viewer by clicking its keyframe button. This locks in the offscreen position at the beginning of the clip.

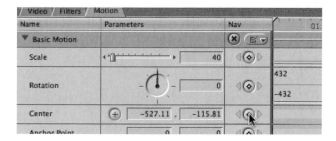

11 Move the playhead forward one second (Shift-right arrow).

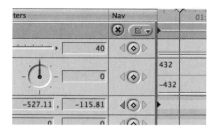

12 In the Canvas, click and drag the image to its final position at the right center of the image, as shown. (Don't worry about positioning it exactly.)

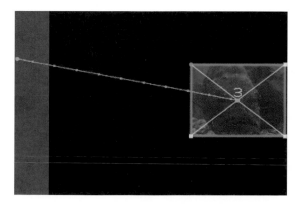

As you drag, Final Cut Pro displays a purple line from the image's original location to its new position. This line, called the *motion path*, indicates animation from one spot to another. The green dots on either end of the path indicate keyframes.

NOTE ▶ If you do not see the purple line in the Canvas, you have not created an animation. Be sure to set an initial keyframe, advance the playhead, and then move the image.

In addition, a Center keyframe is automatically created in the Viewer.

Notice that the two Center keyframes in the Viewer do not look the same as keyframes for scale or rotation, which can be modified in the keyframe graph area. With Center keyframes, it is much easier to make changes directly in the Canvas, as you will do in the next exercise.

13 Play back the motion path.

TIP ▶ To examine the pacing of a motion path, it's not necessary to view the image, so in the Canvas, choose View > Wireframe to play back a wireframe outline but no image. In Wireframe mode, you can play back the motion effect in real time, independent of real-time capabilities. Switch back to the Image+Wireframe mode when you need to see content and access images that are placed outside of the frame.

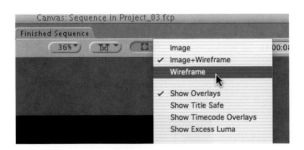

Modifying Motion Paths with Bézier Handles

You may recall that the example for this exercise shows the image moving in a smooth curve across the screen, decelerating as it goes and coming to rest at a slightly rotated angle. Currently, the motion is straight and evenly paced. To make the motion more graceful, you'll manipulate the Bézier handles to control the arc and velocity of the image's movement.

1 Move the Viewer playhead to a point midway between the two Center keyframes to temporarily move the wireframe out of the workspace.

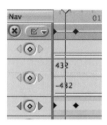

2 Ctrl-click the green dot in the Canvas that represents the end keyframe and choose Ease In/Ease Out from the contextual menu to change the keyframe type.

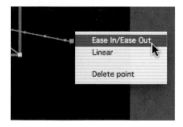

NOTE ▶ This contextual menu is not available from the Viewer. Be sure to Ctrl-click on the green point representing the keyframe on the right in the Canvas.

We've added a Bézier handle to the keyframe, but it is hidden along the animation path.

3   Make the Canvas window active by clicking the title bar. Don't click inside the workspace.

4   Press Cmd-+ twice to zoom in and use the scroll arrows to center in on the end keyframe.

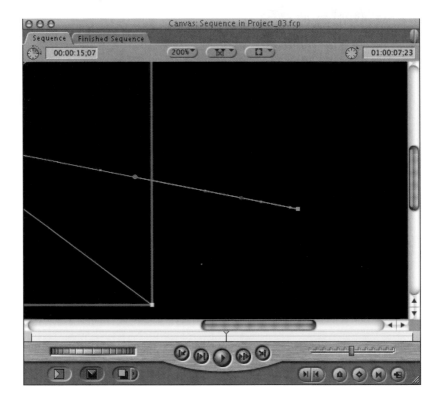

NOTE ▶ Zooming does not magnify the actual image. It simply lets you see your work area up close.

5   Locate the larger purple dot along the motion path (not the smaller purple dots on the line). This is the end of the Bézier handle.

6 Click and drag the dot up and to the right to move it away from the motion path. Notice that this action curves the path leading toward this keyframe. By dragging the keyframe around, you can alter the path as desired. Set the position of the handle as shown.

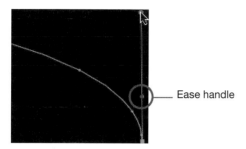

Ease handle

Notice that there is a single, smaller purple dot along the Bézier handle. This is the *Ease* handle for the keyframe. An Ease handle is used to slow down or to speed up the clip as it approaches the keyframe.

NOTE ▶ Clicking on the animation path instead of the Bézier handle will create a new keyframe. To avoid this, notice that the cursor changes into a pen icon when positioned over the path instead of the Bézier handle. If you accidentally set a new keyframe, press Cmd-Z to undo the action and try again.

7 Click and drag up and down on the Ease handle. Notice that this action changes the spacing of the small purple ticks running along the motion path.

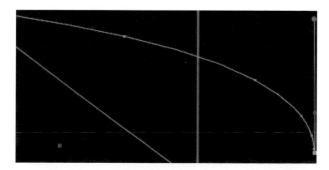

These ticks represent the relative velocity of the image's movement at different spots along the path. In other words, they show the speed of the motion along the path. When they are further apart, the motion is relatively quick. When they are close together, the motion is slowed down.

8   Click and drag the Ease handle toward the keyframe so that the purple ticks bunch up at the keyframe point.

This will cause the image to slow down as much as possible before reaching a stop point (without adjusting the animation duration).

The default ease setting, set by choosing Ease In/Ease Out for the keyframe type, is often just fine for starting or ending an effect. Here, you added more easing because the effect was relatively quick.

9   In the Canvas, zoom back to Fit to Window (Shift-Z).

10   Play back this effect (render if necessary).

Adding Rotation to Movement

As this image on V2 is settling on the screen, you will add another short animation so that the image rotates slightly as it is coming to a stop.

1 In the Viewer, move the playhead to a spot in the curve of the animation just before it lands at its final position. Watch the Canvas as a guide.

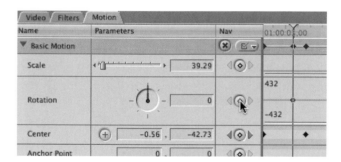

2 In the Viewer, set a keyframe for Rotation. This value for this keyframe will remain at 0, and the beginning of the animation will have no rotation.

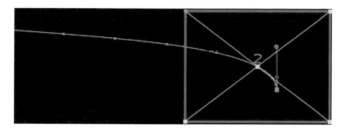

3   Move the playhead to the same frame as the last keyframe for Center.

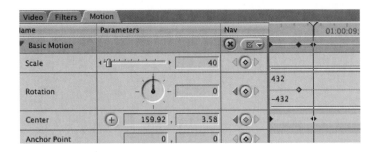

> **TIP** ▶ Align the playhead to a keyframe from another setting (in this case, Center) by clicking on that setting's previous or next keyframe arrows. To move to the next or previous keyframe for any setting, press Shift-K (next) or Option-K (previous).

4   In the Canvas, click the green boundary line of the wireframe and rotate the image clockwise about 15 degrees. Don't worry about a specific angle—you can approximate.

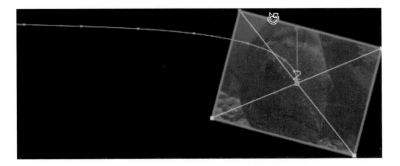

In the Viewer, there should now be a new keyframe for Rotation.

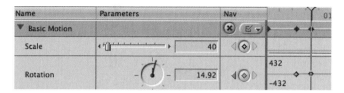

5   Ctrl-click on the end keyframe for Rotation and choose Smooth from the contextual menu to add a default slow-down for this effect.

6   Play back the clip.

    If you followed these steps closely, the image will move left to right, into and across the frame, rotating a bit as it settles into place.

Adding Another Motion Path

Now let's add another image into the fray and modify its Bézier handles to add variety to the new path.

1   From the Browser, locate the clip **sunstar wide** and edit it directly above the clip on V2, which will automatically create V3. Do not worry about setting an In or Out for the clip, simply use the whole clip.

2   With **sunstar wide** selected in the Timeline, type *+15* and press Return. The clip will move to the right so that it will animate into the screen just as the previous image is settling on the screen.

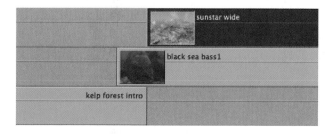

3 Open this clip into the Viewer and click the Motion tab.

4 Position the Viewer playhead at the first frame of the clip.

5 Set Scale for this clip at 40%.

6 In the Canvas, drag the wireframe for the V3 clip out of the frame (bottom-left corner). Remember to use Fit All to see the offscreen area.

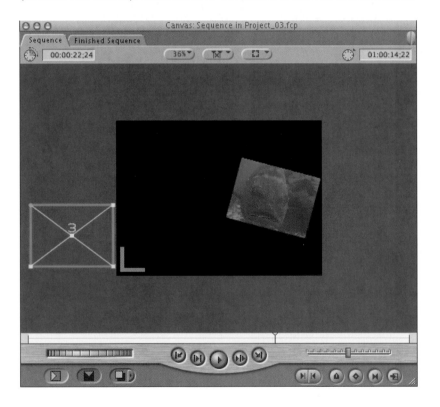

7 Set a start keyframe for Center at the first frame of this clip in the Viewer.

8 Move the playhead forward one second (Shift-right arrow).

9 Drag the wireframe into the frame, releasing the mouse when the image is in the upper-left part of the frame. Again, an approximate location is fine.

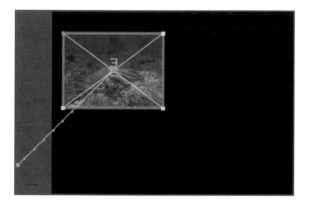

A motion path will be drawn from offscreen to this spot.

10 Ctrl-click on the start keyframe for this clip (the keyframe offscreen) and choose Linear from the contextual menu.

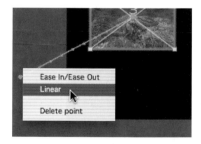

NOTE ▶ With Linear keyframes, the ease handle is placed in a neutral location so that it does not change the clip velocity. With Ease In/Ease Out, the ease handle is located closer to the keyframe. Either keyframe type can be customized with the ease handle.

TIP When changing the keyframe type, it is helpful if the wireframe for the image is not directly over the keyframe. In this case, leave the wireframe at the end keyframe's location while you work on the first keyframe.

11 Click the Bézier handle and stretch it to the right, as shown in the following figure. This will cause the image to move to the right and then curve upward. It's not a perfect path yet, so you will smooth it out in the next step.

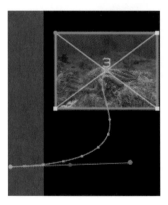

12 Move the playhead back to the beginning of the clip so that the wireframe moves away from the end keyframe, giving you a clearer view of this keyframe.

13 Ctrl-click the end keyframe and choose Ease In/Ease Out from the contextual menu.

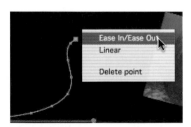

NOTE ▸ It may seem intuitive to click and drag the wireframe to move it out of the way, but doing so will add a new keyframe. Use the playhead to move the image.

The Bézier handle will jut slightly to the left. Let's alter this handle to finesse the curve of the motion path.

14 Click the ease handle for the end keyframe and drag toward the keyframe to bunch up the purple ticks along the motion path. This will slow the clip's speed as it reaches the keyframe position.

15 Click the end of the Bézier handle and drag to the right until the handle is aligned with the motion path. This will straighten out the motion path as it approaches the keyframe, resulting in a smoother path.

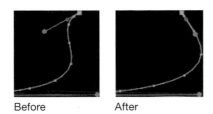

Before   After

16 Place the Viewer playhead just before the end keyframe and set a Rotation keyframe (leave the setting at 0).

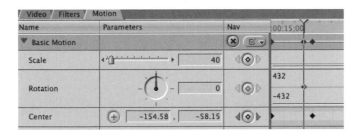

17 Move the Viewer playhead to the last Center keyframe.

18 In the Canvas, rotate the image slightly counterclockwise. This will add a new keyframe for Rotation at this position. As with the first clip that moves into frame, this one will also rotate slightly as it settles.

19 Ctrl-click on the end keyframe for Rotation and choose Smooth from the contextual menu to add a default slow-down for this effect.

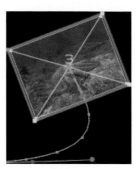

Creating a Multipoint Motion Path

To finish the sequence, let's move one final image into the frame. This image will hold position for a second, and then animate to fill the entire frame.

1 From the Browser, locate **school of fish** and open it into the Viewer.

2 Set an In point roughly midway through this clip, just before the school of fish starts to separate.

3 Drag this clip to the Timeline directly over **sunstar wide** on V3, starting at the same point. This automatically creates a new video track.

4 Select **school of fish** in the Timeline and type *+15* to move it to the right, overlapping **sunstar wide**.

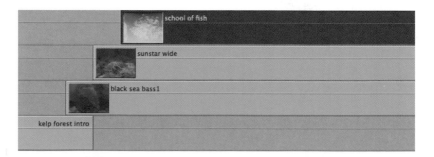

5 Open **school of fish** into the Viewer from the Timeline and click the Motion tab.

6 Set Scale to about 40%.

7 At the first frame of the clip, add a Center point keyframe and move the image offscreen above the frame.

8 Move the playhead forward by one second, and then move the wireframe into position near the bottom of the frame, overlapping the other images on the screen. A new keyframe is automatically created for this new position.

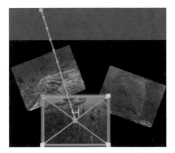

9 Move the playhead back to just before the end keyframe and insert a Rotation keyframe (leave the setting at 0).

10 Move the playhead to the last keyframe for the Center parameter and set another Rotation keyframe by rotating the image slightly counter-clockwise in the Canvas.

11 Ctrl-click on the end keyframe for Rotation and choose Smooth from the contextual menu to add a default slow-down for this effect.

Setting a Hold Position

To make the image stay in one position for a moment before animating it to another position, you need to add an extra set of keyframes.

1 Move the Viewer playhead forward one second after the last Center keyframe.

2 Add keyframes at this point for Scale, Rotation, and Center, but do not change parameter values. This ensures that the image will stay in its current size and position up to this point in time. Adding and changing keyframe values after this point (later in time) will cause the image to animate again.

3 Move the playhead forward two seconds.

4 Set keyframes again here for Scale, Rotation, and Center. Make the Scale 100%, set Rotation to 0 degrees, and set Center to 0,0.

Video	Filters	Motion				
Name		Parameters		Nav	01:00:04:00	01:00:06:00
▼ Basic Motion				⊗ ☑⌄		
Scale		◄—⎴—►	100	◄◎▷		
Rotation		◉	0	◄◎▷	432 / -432	
Center		⊕ 0 , 0		◄◎▷		

5 Play back the end of the composition, including the last clip. Switch to Wireframe mode to avoid rendering.

The last clip will enter the frame, rotating a bit as it settles. The clip will hold its position for one second, and then take two seconds to scale up and fill the frame, ending the composition.

Smoothing Out the Animation

The motion path may still feel stilted at this point, so let's add some Ease In/Ease Out keyframes. It is helpful to set keyframes first and then go back and add smoothing as needed. This will ensure that the Bézier handles are, by default, in line with the direction of the motion path.

1 Move the Viewer playhead back to the beginning of the clip. This moves the wireframe out of the way, so you can get a closer look at the path of the Center keyframes.

2 Ctrl-click over the second Center keyframe in the Canvas and choose Ease In/Ease Out from the contextual menu. This will cause the image to slow down before it stops moving.

3 Ctrl-click over the third Center keyframe in the Canvas and choose Ease In/Ease Out from the contextual menu. The image will start off slowly, and it will gain speed as it starts to fill the frame.

NOTE ▶ All other keyframes for this clip may be left as corner point keyframes. Adding a Bézier handle isn't always required for smooth motion. If you want the image to continue at a steady velocity, leave the keyframes as corner point keyframes.

Fine-Tuning the Composition

With the animated elements in place, it's time to fine-tune the composition by adding a background, changing its color, and making other minor adjustments as needed.

Unifying the Out Points

In your composition, the clips are all trimmed to different Out points, and the first thing you need to do is unify them. To do that, you perform an *extend edit* to roll all selected Out points to one common point. The clips' Out points can all be rolled together, regardless of whether they are to the left or right of the playhead, as long as they are all selected and contain enough handle length to complete the trim.

1   Move the Timeline playhead to a point just after the school of fish fills the frame.

2   Choose the standard Selection tool if it is not currently selected.

3   Cmd-click the end of the clips on V2, V3, and V4 to select them all.

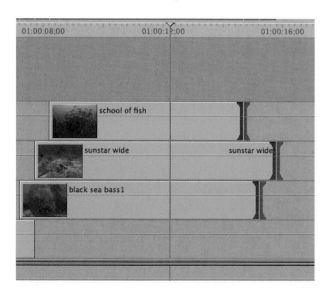

4 Press E to perform an extend edit. If all clips have enough media handle available, they will be trimmed (shortened or lengthened) to the position of the playhead.

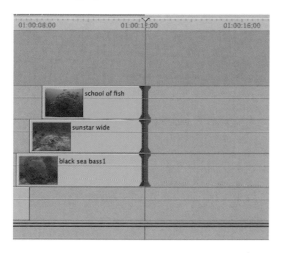

Adding a Background

You will start making room in the Timeline for a new background by moving the entire composition up one track.

1 In the sequence **Sequence** you have been working on, select all clips in the Timeline (Cmd-A).

2 Press Option-up arrow. This will move the clips up one track.

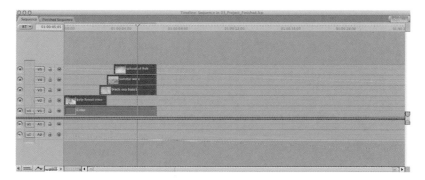

3   From the Generator pop-up menu on the Video tab in the Viewer, choose
     Matte > Color. This will load a new a color matte into the Viewer.

4   Edit the color matte onto track V1, directly beneath the composition,
     starting at the beginning of the first clip and extending to the end of
     the last clip.

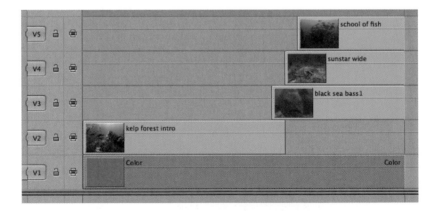

5   Double-click the color matte in the Timeline to open it back into the
     Viewer.

6   Click the Controls tab.

7 Click in the color box to open the Color Picker.

8 Choose a color for this background.

If your Color Picker isn't currently set to the color wheel (if it displays crayons, for example), then click the color wheel icon in the upper-left corner of the window. Choose a color that it is midway on any radius of the color wheel and set the brightness slider about a third of the way from the top of the scale. Click OK to accept the new color.

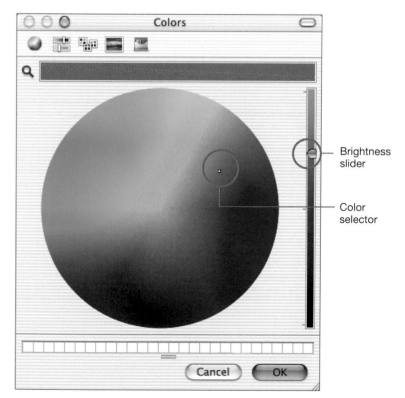

Animating with Color

Now you will animate the background color so that it gets richer and deeper as the final video image fills the frame.

1   Option-click the V1 visibility button. This will leave V1 visible and turn off visibility on all other tracks.

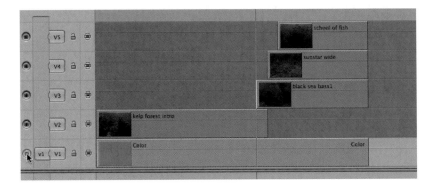

This is a quick way to isolate the color matte. You will animate the color matte alone and activate the other tracks again later. Fewer visible items require less processing time and can improve real-time playback if your machine is real-time capable.

NOTE ▶ If there are rendered items in the Timeline, turning off track visibility will discard the render files for those tracks. This is not a problem, because you will be adding a new element to the composition, so the final composition will need to be re-rendered anyway.

2   On the Controls tab in the Viewer, press Cmd-+ to zoom in on the keyframe graph area for the color matte.

3   Press Shift-O to move to the end frame of the matte.

4   Move the playhead back two seconds by pressing Shift-left arrow twice.

5   Set a keyframe here for Color by clicking the keyframe button next to
    the color box. This sets the current color in the color box at this point
    in the clip.

6   Move to the end of the clip (Shift-O).

7   Click the color box to open the Color Picker. Choosing a new color
    now will automatically create a second keyframe for color at this point
    in time.

    Use the Color Picker controls to pick a darker color, one that is closer
    to the edge of the color wheel. Click OK when you have chosen the
    color. You will now notice the new keyframe for color in the keyframe
    graph.

8   Play back this color matte to see the how the color changes.

9   Option-click the V1 visibility button to turn all video tracks back on.

    NOTE ▶ When animating color across hues, such as from magenta to
    blue, be sure to use the color direction button when setting the color
    in the first keyframe. Look at the relationship of the colors in the wheel
    and choose clockwise or counterclockwise to create the shortest ani-
    mation path between the two hues.

Cleaning Up the Edges

Now that you have added a background, you can clearly see the edges of each of the images onscreen. Whenever an image is scaled down, as you have done, the edges, normally not seen on television, are well within the frame. Left untreated, this may draw the viewer's attention to possible unwanted artifacts or image distortions along the edges. Such "defects" are normal but are usually outside of the viewing area. Additionally, any hard diagonal edges may result in harsh, jagged edges when viewed on interlaced televisions such as NTSC.

1 Position the Timeline playhead at a point when the images in V3, V4, and V5 are all visible onscreen in the Canvas.

In this composition, black edges are visible on the right side of each of the scaled images. You'll remove these offending artifacts by cropping and feathering the edges. If you have an external monitor set up, this would be a good time to turn it on (if it's not already on). An NTSC monitor (or standard TV) will more clearly show the interlace artifacts you must contend with.

2   Double-click to open the clip on V5 into the Viewer, and then click the Motion tab.

3   Click the disclosure triangle next to Crop to open up its settings.

4   Set cropping to 2 on all four sides, and add an Edge Feather of 5, as shown here.

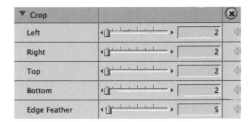

This will remove any fringe elements and soften the edges.

NOTE ▶ Although cropping is usually necessary for scaled down images, using Edge Feather to soften image borders is optional. Edge feathering can be helpful in disguising the inherent limitations of the digital video format, including the unflattering jagged edges that result from the sharp, high-contrast, diagonal lines that border the edges of the images.

Adding Drop Shadows

The addition of a subtle drop shadow around an image is a great way to add depth and separation between overlapping images.

1   In the Motion tab of the Viewer, check the Drop Shadow box. A drop shadow is added at its default settings.

2   Click the disclosure triangle for Drop Shadow to modify the shadow.

3   Set the Offset to 3 to position the shadow closer to the image.

4   Set Softness to about 30 to blur the edges of the shadow, making it
    less pronounced.

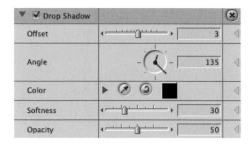

Pasting Attributes to Other Clips

At this point, you have finessed the edges and added a custom drop shadow
to one of the images in the composition. Instead of doing the same work
on all the other clips, you can use a shortcut. Most effects that need to be
applied to multiple clips can be applied first on one clip, and then transferred as customized settings to other clips.

1   Select **school of fish** on V5 in the Timeline.

2   Ctrl-click **school of fish** and choose Copy from the contextual menu
    (or press Cmd-C). This copies the clip and all its individual settings
    (attributes), including motion settings.

3   Deselect the clip in the Timeline.

4   Cmd-click to select the clips in V2, V3, and V4 together.

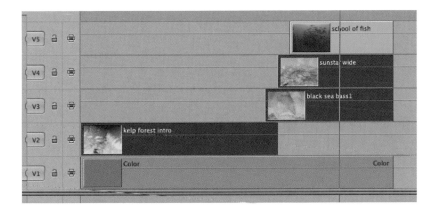

5   Ctrl-click on any of the selected clips and choose Paste Attributes from the contextual menu.

A dialog box will open, offering you a choice of attributes that can be pasted.

6   Check the Crop and Drop Shadow boxes and click OK.

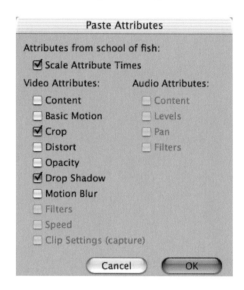

Now all the clips are cropped and have a drop shadow.

7   Do a final render and play back the composition at full quality.

> **NOTE** ▶ The very beginning and end of the composition reveal the edges of the color matte in the Canvas, because we cropped the full-frame video that begins and ends the sequence. This is not a concern when outputting to NTSC, because these edges are beyond the action safe area. But if your output is intended for the Web, animate crop settings to uncrop when an image is full frame. Open the **Project_03_Finished** sequence, then open **kelp forest intro** to view an example of this technique.

Creating Templates

Since your composition is the intro for a weekly newsmagazine show, you want to do one more thing: use it over and over with images from the current week's show.

Pasting Content to Replace a Clip

Fortunately, your imaginary TV production crew can use the sequence you've created each week by employing Paste Attributes, a very handy feature that lets you easily swap new images into a composition.

1   In the Browser, locate **blue shark cu** and click it to select it.

2 Press Cmd-C to copy the clip, or Ctrl-click and choose Copy from the contextual menu.

3 In the Timeline, Ctrl-click **kelp forest intro** on V2 and choose Paste Attributes (or press Option-V).

4 Check the Content box in the Paste Attributes dialog box and then click OK.

The Browser clip will replace the clip in the Timeline. Any effects from the original Timeline clip will now be transferred to the new clip, with timing preserved. Notice that the name of the clip in the Timeline is updated to reflect the new clip.

NOTE ▶ If the clip you copy is too short to replace the clip in the Timeline, you will get an error message warning that there is insufficient content for the edit. In and Out points on the copied clip are ignored and do not affect this error, but sufficient media must be available.

Slipping Content

Once the new clip is in the Timeline, the content may need to be customized. This can be done with a slip edit on the new clip, but some care needs to be taken so that the keyframes continue to line up in the Timeline after the slip is complete.

1   Click the Clip Keyframes button in the Timeline to turn on the Filters/ Motion bars for each track.

A bar opens up under each track. The blue bar indicates that a motion effect has been applied to the clip. The notches on the bar represent keyframe positions.

2   Select the Slip tool from the Tool palette (or press S).

3   Click **blue shark cu** in the Timeline with the Slip tool and drag left to slip the content. Drag until you see the shark in both of the two-up displays in the Canvas. This indicates that once the clip is slipped, you will see the shark for the whole duration of this clip.

When you release the mouse, notice that the keyframes in the blue bar have moved in the direction of the slip edit.

This changes the timing of the effect, throwing the clip out of sync with the other clips in the composition.

4   Undo this slip edit, and the keyframes return to their original positioning. You will slip the clip again, but first *protect* the keyframes already on the clip.

5   Choose the Selection tool and select the clip on V2 (**blue shark cu**).

6   Press Cmd-C to copy it.

7   Double-click the clip to open it in the Viewer.

8   Position the cursor over the In or Out point in the Viewer. The cursor changes to a resize icon.

9   With the Slip tool still selected, Shift-drag left or right on the In or Out point.

    You should see the In and Out points move together. This is a standard slip edit, the same as if you had used the Slip tool in the Timeline. As you drag, watch the Viewer for a new In point and watch the Canvas for a new Out point (choose any new In and Out as you desire). Using the slip edit in the Viewer affords a larger two-up display, which makes it easier to look for new In and Out points.

10 In the Timeline, notice that the keyframe locations have changed again. That's OK. You will fix this in the next step.

11 Ctrl-click on the same clip in the Timeline and choose Paste Attributes (or press Option-V with the clip selected).

12 In the Paste Attributes dialog box, check all of the custom settings that you originally set: Basic Motion, Crop, and Drop Shadow. Click OK.

    Congratulations. You copied the settings before slipping the clip (to preserve the settings), and then after the slip edit, you pasted the original settings back on to the same clip, replacing the ones that were slipped. Your TV sequence is ready for prime time.

NOTE ▶ Although there were no keyframes set for Center or Drop Shadow, it is best to select all customized settings so that you don't accidentally forget settings you may need.

What You've Learned

- Scale, Rotation, Crop, and other basic motion properties can be adjusted in the Motion tab of the Viewer.

- The Remove Attributes command restores default settings from various areas of the Motion tab.

- Keyframe animation allows you to modify an effect over time, for example scaling up or scaling down.

- Bézier handles allow you to adjust the pacing of Scale and Rotation paths.

- Ease handles control the velocity of a motion path.

- Use Cropping and Edge Feather to remove artifacts from the edges of scaled images.

- Pasting attributes to additional images saves you from manually applying them to every image.

4

Lesson Files	Lessons > Lesson_04 > 04_Project_Start.fcp
Media	Media > Lesson_04_Media
Time	This lesson takes approximately 120 minutes to complete.
Goals	Create Favorite motions, filters, and filter packs
	Save and apply Favorites for static and animated effects
	Move an entire motion path
	Alter the timing of effects
	Create templates for generators
	Modify motion paths with Bézier handles
	Move multiple keyframes together

Customizing Motion and Filter Effects

In this lesson, you look at how to customize motion effects. This includes creating more complex compositions, adjusting the timing of effects, positioning elements more precisely onscreen, customizing motion paths, and coordinating effects from one clip to another. In addition, you will examine typical scenarios for altering the appearance of an image using filter effects and delve into how to best manage those effects.

You will create and use Favorite motions and filters, create generator templates, and examine other options so that you have a well-rounded understanding of the effects tools in Final Cut Pro.

Streamlining Effects Using Favorites

In the last lesson, you manipulated several motion properties in combination to create a final effect. As you probably noticed, building on a combination of adjustments and getting it all "just right" can require quite an investment of time.

So, what if you may want to use an effect again, in a slightly different scenario? Perhaps, for example, you've created an effect that is a good starting point for a more elaborate effect, or perhaps you've created an effect that you know you're going to use repeatedly for different projects. One way to streamline these tasks is to save *Favorite* motions and effects so they can be reused.

Creating Favorite Motions

In this exercise, you will create a composition in which multiple images pass through the frame in a seemingly random fashion. But instead of creating each motion from scratch, you will save one as a Favorite and use it as a starting point to create varied effects on the subsequent clips.

1   Open Lessons > Lesson_04 > **04_Project_Start.fcp**.

2   Open the **Opener 2 Finished** sequence into the Timeline, if it's not already open.

3   Render (if necessary) and play back the composition to see what you will be working on.

4   Open the empty **Opener 2 Sequence** into the Timeline, if it is not already open.

5   Switch to the custom window layout you created and saved in the Creating Dynamic Motion Effects exercise in Lesson 3. Or, arrange your Viewer now to be as wide as possible, to make working in the keyframe graph easier.

6 Locate **kelp forest and fish** in the Clips bin of the Browser and edit it into the **Opener 2 Sequence** Timeline.

7 Ctrl-click **kelp forest and fish** in the Timeline and choose Duration from the contextual menu. The Duration dialog box opens.

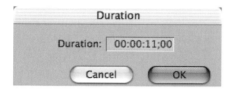

8 Type *400* in the Duration field and click OK. The clip will shorten to four seconds.

9 Choose Image+Wireframe from the View pop-up menu in the Canvas.

10 With the Selection tool, click on the image in the Canvas to select the wireframe and drag one of the four wireframe corner points to scale the clip down to approximately 25%.

11 Click and hold on the image in the wireframe and drag upward to move the image out of the frame. (Zoom the Canvas view to 50% if necessary.)

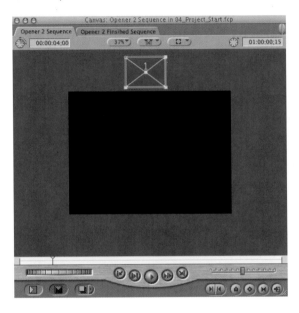

12 Open the clip from the Timeline into the Viewer and click the Motion tab.

13 Click the disclosure triangle next to Crop and set Left, Right, Top, and Bottom to 2. This ensures that you do not see any artifacts on the edges of the image.

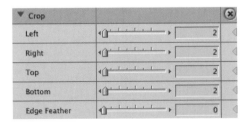

NOTE ▶ Be sure to click anywhere outside of the Crop input fields, or press Return, to force the 2 percent crop to take effect.

14 Move to the first frame of the clip in the Viewer (Shift-I).

> **NOTE ▶** Remember, use Shift-I and Shift-O instead of the up and down arrow keys in the Viewer so that you don't accidentally jump to the end of a clip and open the next clip in the Timeline into the Viewer.

15 Set a keyframe for Center by clicking the Insert/Delete keyframe button next to teh Center keyframe graph.

16 Move to the last frame of the clip (Shift-O).

17 In the Canvas, Shift-drag the image from the top of the frame down and out of the bottom of the frame. Pressing Shift ensures that the clip moves in a straight horizontal or vertical line.

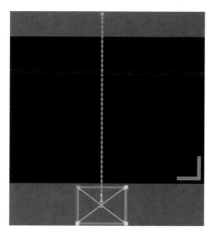

18 Play back the clip. It is a simple animation moving from top to bottom.

This effect will be used as a starting point for the remaining clips of the composition. Now you're ready to save the settings from this clip so that they may be applied to other clips.

19 Highlight the clip in the Timeline by clicking on it.

20 Choose Effects > Make Favorite Motion (or press Ctrl-F).

21 Click the Effects tab in the Browser. Choose Window > Effects if it is not visible.

22 Toggle open the disclosure triangle next to the Favorites bin. The effect you just created is listed here, named **kelp forest and fish (Motion)**.

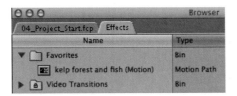

23 Give the effect a more descriptive name so that when you want to reuse it, you'll know what it does. Click the name field and change the name to *roll down frame*.

Static and animated (keyframed) Favorite effects include the following:

- Basic motion (Scale, Rotation, Center, and Anchor Point)
- Crop (all four sides and Edge Feather)
- Distort (all four corners and Aspect Ratio)
- Opacity

Because a Favorite motion saves all settings on the Motion tab, whether or not they have been adjusted, be aware that any previously set effects on the Motion tab will be replaced when a Favorite motion is applied.

Applying a Favorite Effect

In the finished example, you can see that all of the images move through the frame from top to bottom, but at varying times and horizontal positions. So let's apply the saved Favorite motion effect to another clip in your composition so that you don't have to re-create the same vertical motion path.

1 In the Browser, locate the clip **marbled sting ray** and edit the entire clip it into the Timeline on V1, after **kelp forest and fish**.

2   Drag your Favorite effect Roll Down Frame from the Favorites bin of the Effects tab of the Browser and drop it onto **marbled sting ray** in the Timeline.

3   Play back the clip.

Notice that **marbled sting ray** moves down the frame much more slowly than **kelp forest and fish**. This is because **marbled sting ray** is longer in duration than **kelp forest and fish**. As a result, the effect takes longer to move across the screen. If the second clip were shorter than the first, the effect would play faster.

You want all the vertical motion for all of the clips in your final composition to move at the same speed, so you have to do a little more tweaking.

4   Delete **marbled sting ray** from the Timeline.

Achieving Consistent Timing

Since all Favorite motion effects that are based on keyframed animation by necessity have a specific duration, let's first update the name of your Favorite to reflect that. Then you can apply it to other clips that are the same duration and be confident that the timing will be consistent.

1   In the Favorites bin, type *400* at the end of *roll down frame* to reflect the four-second duration of the Timeline clip where you created the effect.

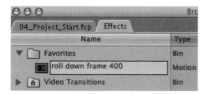

NOTE ▶ Favorites that are based on static effects with no animated keyframes can be applied to clips of any duration. Care is necessary only when applying Favorites with keyframed animation to clips with varying durations.

2   From the Browser, select **marbled sting ray** again and open it into the Viewer.

3   Place the Timeline playhead anywhere over the **kelp forest and fish** clip in the **Opener 2 Sequence** Timeline from the previous exercise. Be sure the **kelp forest and fish** clip is still set to a duration of four seconds.

4   Drop **marbled sting ray** in the Canvas using the overlay for Superimpose edit. It is edited to a new track above **kelp forest and fish**, at the same four-second duration.

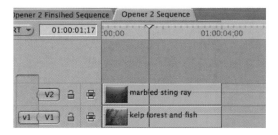

5   From the Browser, open the clip **sunstar med** into the Viewer.

Before you add **sunstar med** to the Timeline above **marbled sting ray** and **kelp forest and fish**, the Timeline targeting needs to be changed. When a new clip is superimposed, it will be placed above the highest targeted track, instead of inserting a new track and pushing up other clips in the Timeline.

6   Click the V2 destination control in the Timeline. This causes the source control to line up with V2.

7   Drag the **sunstar med** clip from the Viewer to the Canvas and again choose Superimpose.

8   Repeat steps 5 through 7 to add two more clips—**sheep crab2** and **corynactus anemones3**—into the Timeline. Before adding each clip, be sure to update targeting to the top-most track.

9   Select all the clips in the Timeline from V2 through V5.

10 Drag your Favorite motion roll down frame 400 from the Favorites bin of the Effects tab in the Browser and drop it onto the selected clips in the Timeline.

All clips now have the vertical motion path, at the same velocity, and you're ready to customize each one to make them all unique.

Moving an Entire Motion Path

Moving a motion path is an easy task that uses a simple keyboard-mouse combination to move the screen positioning of all Center keyframes together, keeping their positions relative.

1 Deselect the clips in the Timeline by clicking in a blank space, or press Shift-Cmd-A with the Timeline active.

2 Double-click the clip on V1 to open it into the Viewer, and click the Motion tab.

3 Move the Viewer playhead to the first Center keyframe.

Parking your playhead on an existing keyframe ensures that as you adjust the motion path, you don't create any unnecessary new keyframes. (You can do this in the Timeline, but in the Viewer keyframe graph you can more easily see that you are directly over an existing keyframe.)

4 In the Canvas, move your cursor over the active wireframe. Notice that the wireframe has a number 1 over its center, indicating it's the wireframe for the clip on V1.

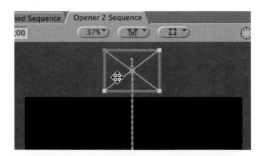

5   Press and hold Shift-Cmd. The cursor changes to a hand icon over the
    wireframe.

6   While still holding Shift and Cmd, click the wireframe and drag to the
    left. The entire motion path moves left with the first keyframe.

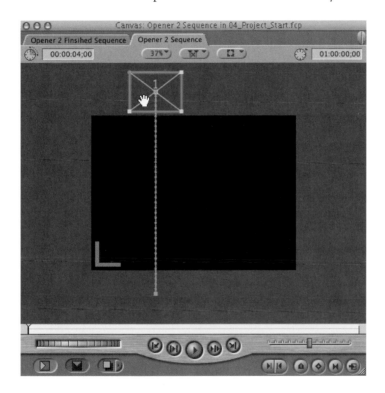

Fine-Tuning Clip Positions

Next you will spread the clips' motion paths out a bit around the Canvas,
and then adjust the timing of each clip's movement through the frame to
make each clip's appearance in the scene seem somewhat random.

1   Stagger the clips out to the right in the Timeline, so that each clip
    begins one second after the clip on the track below it. One quick way

to move a clip forward 1 second in the Timeline is to select the clip, type *1* (one-period), and press Enter.

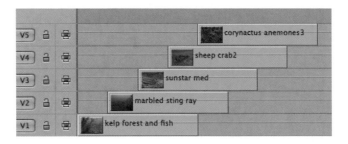

2   Move the playhead to the first frame of **marbled sting ray** (which is also the clip's first Center keyframe position).

3   Select **marbled sting ray** in the Timeline. Notice that the active wireframe in the Canvas is now labeled 2, corresponding to this clip's video track, and the center point is green, indicating the playhead is parked on a keyframe.

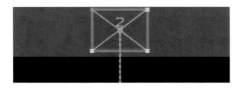

4   Shift-Cmd-click to select the active wireframe in the Canvas, and when the hand icon appears, move it right to space it out from the other motion paths.

5   Repeat steps 2 through 4 for **sunstar med**, **sheep crab2**, and **corynactus anemones3** to space out all of their paths, in no particular pattern or order.

6   In the Canvas, play back this series of clips and determine whether or not you want to make any further adjustments.

TIP ▶ This would be a good time to switch from Image+Wireframe to Wireframe only, to play back outlines of these tracks in real time independently of your RT playback capabilities. Switch back to Image+ Wireframe if you need to adjust the placement of the motion path, because wireframes cannot be selected when moved offscreen in Wireframe mode.

Using Favorites Versus Paste Attributes

Now that you've gotten the hang of Favorites, you may be wondering when to use Favorites versus Paste Attributes, which you learned about in Lesson 3.

One advantage to Paste Attributes is that you get the choice to apply your keyframed animation attributes to new clips *without automatically scaling the timing* of your animation to fit the varying duration of the new clip. On the other hand, when using a Favorite effect, the timing of the keyframed attributes is automatically scaled over time, so that the animation will appear to slow down or speed up in the second clip if the second clip is not the same duration as the original.

To apply animated effects without changing their timing, uncheck Scale Attribute Times in the Paste Attributes dialog box.

Favorites are often more convenient than Paste Attributes when you want to reuse effects across different projects (and/or when the original clip is unavailable) because Favorites are available in the Effects menu at any time; you don't have to have a specific clip with the desired effect open, as is the case with Paste Attributes.

Conversely, Paste Attributes is better when you want to reuse *only* selective effects from a clip. For example, you can opt to paste Basic motion settings independently from Crop and Opacity, whereas Favorites saves all of the Motion tab settings and applies them in an all-or-nothing manner.

Choreographing Effects Across Multiple Clips

When keyframing multiple images onscreen, it's often necessary to coordinate the timing of the effects of different clips as they appear and interplay in the full composited scene. Let's work on a new composition in which you'll learn a handy method for choreographing a series of multiple images onscreen so that they appear and disappear in unison.

Creating the Sequence

1 Open **Opener 3 Finished Sequence** from the Sequences bin into the Timeline.

2 Play back this series of clips to get an idea of what you will be working on next, and then close it.

3 Open **Opener 3 Sequence** from the Browser into the Timeline. It should be an empty sequence at this point.

4 Locate the clip **calm lake** from the Browser and edit it to V1 in the Timeline. Make it four seconds long.

5 Locate the clip **rocky coast** from the Browser and edit it directly above **calm lake** on V1, creating a new track, V2. Make it four seconds long. (A Superimpose edit would work well here.)

6 Locate the clip **sunset on beach** from the Browser and edit it directly above **rocky coast**, creating a new track, V3. Make it four seconds long.

7 Open the clip **sunset on beach** from the Timeline into the Viewer and click the Motion tab.

8 Under Distort, set the Aspect Ratio to *200*. This will squeeze the clip horizontally so that you can fit three images onscreen together.

9 Under Crop, set Left and Right to *2*.

You are cropping these edges so that you don't see any artifacts on the edges of the image as well as to add wider spacing between the three clips. These two Left and Right crop settings will not be keyframed.

10 Move the Viewer playhead to the first frame of the clip.

11 Set a keyframe for Bottom (in Crop) and set its value to *100*.

12 Move the playhead forward one second into the clip.

13 Set a keyframe here for Bottom and set it to *0*.

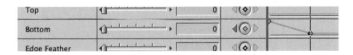

14 Play back the animation. The crop keyframes serve to reveal the image.

15 Select the **sunset on beach** clip in the Timeline and copy it (so you can paste its attributes to the other clips), then deselect it.

16 Select the other two clips in the Timeline: **rocky coast** and **calm lake**.

17 Ctrl-click **rocky coast** or **calm lake** and choose Paste Attributes from the contextual menu.

18 In the Paste Attributes dialog box, check the Crop and Distort boxes and then click OK. The custom Aspect Ratio and Crop keyframes are applied to all three clips.

Because the clips were all modified to the same Basic Motion parameters, they are now all stacked on top of each other in the Canvas.

19 Open the clip **sunset on beach** from the Timeline into the Viewer (if it is not still in the Viewer).

20 On the Motion tab, under Center in the Basic Motion section, set the coordinates to *240, 0*. This will position the clip on the right side of the frame. This setting will not be keyframed, so you don't need to have the playhead parked on an existing keyframe.

21 Open the clip **calm lake** from the Timeline into the Viewer.

22 Under Center, set the coordinates to *–240, 0*.

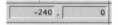

This will position the clip on the left side of the frame. Now, all three clips can be seen side by side.

23 Play back this composite. Right now, all three clips uncrop at the same time. In the finished example, these clips were revealed one after the other. Let's do that next.

Moving Multiple Keyframes

Now you will stagger the start of the crop animation on each clip so that the images make their grand entrance into the scene one after another, in a smooth rhythmic manner. To view or to change groups of keyframes, such as crop, you will use the motion bar in the Timeline.

1 Click the Clip Keyframes button in the Timeline to turn it on.

A blue bar appears under each of the three tracks, indicating that a motion effect has been applied to each clip. Two dots along the filter and motion bar for each clip represent the Crop keyframes you applied. If a filter were applied to a clip, there would also be a green line.

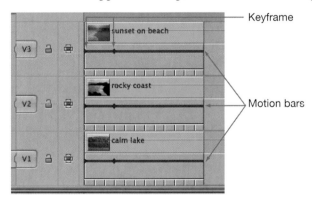

NOTE ▶ The keyframe at the head of each clip may be somewhat hard to see because it is at the same spot where the clip begins. Zoom your Timeline view in to get a better view.

2 Position the cursor over the blue bar for **rocky coast** but not directly over a keyframe. The cursor changes to the resize icon.

3 Click the blue bar and drag right. All of the keyframes on the clip move to the right. Drag until the first keyframe is midway between the two keyframes on the track below. This delays the start of the uncrop animation on the **rocky coast** clip.

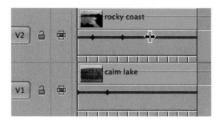

4 Repeat steps 2 and 3 for **sunset on beach**, moving its keyframes right until the first one is midway between the two keyframes of **rocky coast** and the first keyframe for each clip is staggered.

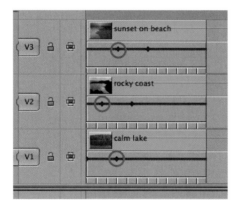

Stagger the first keyframe of each clip

5 Play back the composition. The clips will be revealed one after the other.

Selectively Keyframing Multiple Tracks

Now that you have carefully timed the entrance into the scene for each clip, you want to make the clips fade out of the scene in unison. Because you want them to all begin and end the final fade at the same time, but still maintain their staggered keyframes at the beginning, you will use the Add Keyframe button in the Canavas, rather than using Paste Attributes or a Favorite motion.

1   If they aren't displayed already, turn on Show Overlays in the Image pop-up menu in the Canvas.

2   Move to the last frame of the **Opener 3 Sequence** composition using Shift-O. You should see a greenish corner-shaped overlay in the bottom-right corner of the Canvas, which confirms you are parked at the last frame.

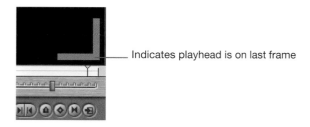

——— Indicates playhead is on last frame

3   Select **calm lake, rocky coast**, and **sunset on beach** in the Timeline.

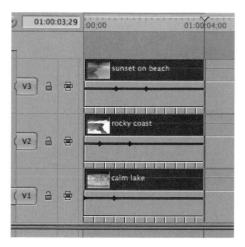

4 Ctrl-click the Add Motion Keyframe button in the Canvas.

 Add Motion Keyframe button

5 Choose Crop from the contextual menu that appears.

All four sides of the three clips have a keyframe set for cropping at this playhead position.

6 Move the Timeline playhead back one second by pressing Shift-left arrow.

7 Ctrl-click the Canvas keyframe button again and choose Crop from the contextual menu to add another set of keyframes for the clips. Be sure all three clips are still selected.

Now all you need to do is modify the keyframes for each clip, and you'll use a shortcut to do so.

8 Move the playhead back to the end keyframe position. Be sure the green corner bracket confirms you are on the last frame.

9   Open **sunset on beach** from the Timeline into the Viewer and click the Motion tab.

10   Toggle open the Crop parameters if they are not already open.

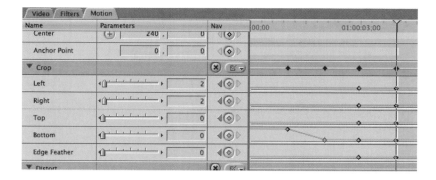

Notice that at this position (on the end keyframe), all four sides are cropped down to either 0 or 2. However, you want to crop all four sides of the image on these keyframes so that the entire image disappears.

11   From the View pop-up menu in the Canvas, activate Image+Wireframe.

12   Select the Crop tool by pressing C.

13   Click any empty spot in the Timeline to deselect the three clips.

14   Click the right-hand image in the Canvas (**sunset on beach** on V3) to make only its wireframe active.

15   While the playhead is still positioned on the end keyframe, press and hold Shift-Cmd as you click and drag on the corner of the wireframe in the Canvas. As you drag, the image will crop equally on all four sides.

Continue to drag inward until the image disappears. In the Viewer, the Crop number for all four sides is now 50 (meaning you have cropped opposing sides 50 percent).

Video	Filters	Motion				
Name	Parameters			Nav	00;00	01:00:03;00
Center	(+)	240 ,	0	◄⟨◇⟩▷		
Anchor Point		0 ,	0	◄⟨◇⟩▷		
▼ Crop				⊗ ☑ ▾		
Left	◄——☖——▸		50	◄⟨◇⟩▷		
Right	◄——☖——▸		50	◄⟨◇⟩▷		
Top	◄——☖——▸		50	◄⟨◇⟩▷		
Bottom	◄——☖——▸		50	◄⟨◇⟩▷		
Edge Feather	☖———▸		0	◄⟨◇⟩▷		

NOTE ▶ Pressing Shift while dragging preserves the aspect ratio of the clip. Pressing Cmd while dragging selects all four corners simultaneously.

16 Without moving the playhead, repeat steps 14 and 15 for **rocky coast** and **calm lake**.

17 Play back the composition. All three clips should now take their bow and disappear in unison.

Using Markers to Coordinate Keyframes

Would you like the clips to disappear a little sooner? To modify the timing of the crop-out on the three clips, you need to first line up the keyframes to a specific point in time.

1 Deselect the clips in the Timeline.

2 Set a Timeline marker approximately midway between the last frame of the composition and the next-to-last keyframes, as shown. Press M to set a Timeline marker at the playhead location.

NOTE ▶ If a clip is selected, the clip will receive the marker instead of the Timeline, so deselect all clips before pressing the M key.

3 Open any one of the clips from the Timeline into the Viewer and click the Motion tab.

Notice that the ruler above the keyframe graph has the marker from the Timeline.

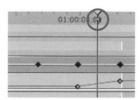

Any markers set in the Viewer or in the Timeline will be available in both locations. This is useful when you need a Timeline reference while keyframing in the Viewer.

4   Make sure that snapping is on. Grab any crop keyframe just to the right of the playhead and drag it to the playhead. Release when the keyframe snaps to the playhead.

5   Repeat step 4 for the other three end crop keyframes, so you've adjusted Top, Bottom, Left, and Right.

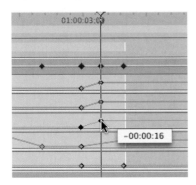

6   Repeat steps 4 and 5 for the other two clips, moving all the end keyframes to the marker position.

Now the crop-out has been shortened on all three clips using a Timeline marker as a reference.

Markers can also be used as a starting point when first setting up the timing for an animated scene. Simply set a marker to note where each desired change will happen. Then, as you set keyframes, you simply use the markers as a reference. Markers work particularly well when choreographing an animation to music or sound effects.

Positioning Clips Precisely

For any situation when accurate positioning of images onscreen is critical—such as a TV show closing credit sequence that uses split screens—it's helpful to use a grid as a guide, instead of trying to eyeball it. Final Cut Pro doesn't have a built-in background grid, but it's easy to import a custom grid created in Adobe Photoshop and use it to line up your images in the Canvas.

1   Double-click to open **Screen Positioning Sequence** from the Browser.

2   Scrub the playhead through this sequence.

    You should see four clips stacked in the Timeline. In the Canvas, you can also see that the four clips are roughed into a multi-image split screen. There are uneven spaces between the clips, making it look unprofessional. So let's finesse the positioning of the images in the split screen using an imported grid.

3   Locate the still image clip **grid480.tif** from the Browser and edit it to the Timeline on V5, above the clips already there. Make it the same length as the other clips.

4   Click the padlock icon next to V5 to lock the grid in place (or press F4 followed by the 5 key).

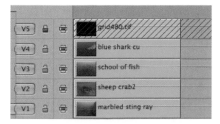

Once the track is locked, you cannot accidentally select its wireframe in the Canvas. And although it is on a higher video track, it was created semitransparent in Photoshop, so it blends into the background.

5   Using the Image+Wireframe view, align the images precisely in each screen quadrant, using the grid to position the wireframes. Set your Canvas view to 100% or 200% for precise control.

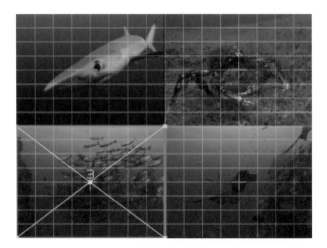

6   Experiment with different split screen configurations using Crop, Scale, or Distort as you wish. Use all four images or just two or three. Turn off track visibility on images that you want to hide.

7   When the images are placed exactly as you want them, either remove the grid from the Timeline or unlock track V5 and turn off the grid clip's visibility (Ctrl-click on the clip and deselect Clip Enable) before rendering for final output.

NOTE ▶ The grid used in this sequence is for digital video projects with a 720x480 frame size. A second grid on this book's DVD, **486grid.tif**, is for projects that use a 720x486 frame size. And you can, of course, create a different grid to your own specifications for projects with other requirements, using these grids as a starting point.

Modifying Motion Paths Using Bézier Handles

In addition to the various keyframing techniques we've covered in this lesson, you can also edit motion paths using Bézier handles. Single- and double-sided Bézier handles that extend from a keyframe provide extra control when altering an image's motion path.

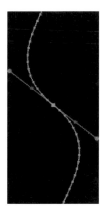

1   Switch to the **Opener 2 Sequence** you worked on in the first exercises in this lesson by clicking on its Timeline tab, or open it from the Browser. If your version doesn't look like the figure below, duplicate the **Opener 2 Finished Sequence** in the Browser for this exercise.

2   Choose the Selection tool if it is not active (press A).

3   Highlight any one of the Timeline clips and place the playhead over its first frame.

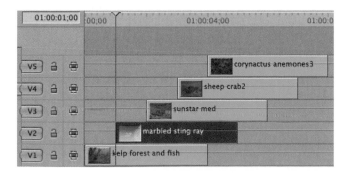

In the Canvas in Image+Wireframe mode, notice that the wireframe path goes from the top to the bottom of the frame.

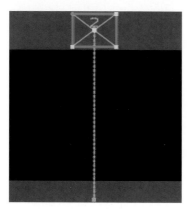

4   Position the cursor approximately in the middle of the motion path in the Canvas (on the purple line). The cursor turns into a Pen tool. Click to create a new keyframe, midway through the path.

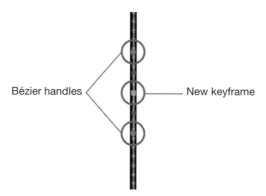

Bézier handles   New keyframe

5   Press Cmd-+ to zoom in slightly in the Canvas and get a better view of the Bézier handles now present on both sides of the new keyframe.

6   Click the upper Bézier handle and drag it to the left, as shown. This modifies the angle of the motion path coming into and moving away from this keyframe.

Release the mouse.

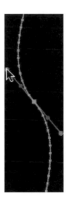

7   Shift-drag on one of the Bézier handles, pulling it away from
the keyframe. Shift-drag alters the length of only one side of the
two Bézier handles, but alters the angled position of both. Release
the mouse.

> **NOTE** ▶ The length of the handle controls the degree of curvature.
> The angle of the handle controls the direction of the curve. The dots
> around the midpoint of the handle control the velocity of the clip
> through the keyframe.

8 Cmd-drag one of the Bézier handles to the left or right. This alters the angle on only one side at a time but alters the length on both. Release the mouse.

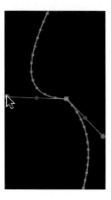

9 Shift-Cmd-click on one Bézier handle. This alters both handle length and angle. This key combination ensures that you alter only one side of the Bézier handle and do not affect the other side at all. Release the mouse.

10 Zoom back out to Fit to Window in the Canvas (Shift-Z).

11 Play back this motion path with different angles on the middle keyframe to see the effect of these Bézier handle adjustments on the clip's motion down the frame.

Working with Effects Filters

In this exercise, you'll begin to work with effects filters in ways that will seem familiar, since you already know how to work with motion paths. For example, you can save effects filters as Favorites and use Paste Attributes to copy filters across clips.

Creating Favorite Filters

Let's start by applying a filter and then saving it as a Favorite for reuse.

1 Open **Filter Sequence** from the Browser into the Timeline.

2 Move the playhead to the first clip in the Timeline, **sunset on beach**, and select it.

3 Choose Effects > Video Filters > Sharpen > Unsharp Mask to apply an unsharp mask.

4 Open the clip into the Viewer and click the Filters tab.

5 Toggle open Video Filters and Unsharp Mask. Set the Amount to *500*, and leave the other settings at their defaults. At these settings, the filter dramatically alters the texture of the image.

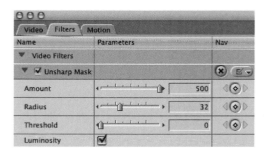

NOTE ▶ When applying a filter to a clip in the Timeline, be sure to select the clip first. If nothing is selected, all clips at the playhead position on every track with Autoselect enabled will have the filter added.

6 With the Viewer active, choose Effects > Make Favorite Effect (or press Option-F). The effect is saved into the Favorites bin with your custom settings.

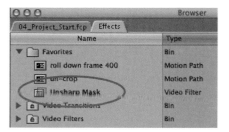

Creating Filter Packs

Sometimes an image can look too good, too clean. To create a surreal or dreamy quality, or make an image look aged, washed out, or discolored, you might want to apply a combination of filters to achieve a unique appearance.

In this exercise, you'll apply certain filters to your image to make it look distressed, and then you'll save the filters together as a group—or pack—so that they can be reused, in the same order, on other clips.

1 Add a strobe filter to **sunset on beach** by selecting it and choosing Effects > Video Filters > Video > Strobe. This filter adds a slight stuttering effect during playback.

2 Set the Strobe Duration to *2*.

3 Add a Desaturate filter by choosing Effects > Video Filters > Image Control > Desaturate. This filter removes all color from the image.

4 Set the Desaturate Amount to *50*.

A setting of 100 removes all color; a setting of 0 removes no color. A setting of 50 results in a muted look.

5 Add a Sepia filter by choosing Effects > Video Filters > Image Control > Sepia.

6 Set the Amount to *35* and Highlight to *30*.

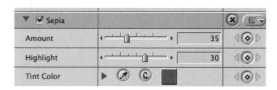

This adds a warm hue to the colors that were muted with the Desaturate filter.

Now you're ready to save these four filters as a Favorite.

7 Select **sunset on beach** in the Timeline and choose Effects > Make Favorite Effect (or press Option-F).

Notice that there is a new Favorites bin named Filter Sequence (Filters) in the Effects tab.

8 Toggle open the Filter Sequence (Filters) bin. Inside, you will see the four filters, in the order in which they were applied.

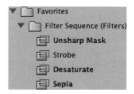

NOTE ▶ Do not double-click to open the filter bin because this may change the order in which the filters are listed, which will change the order in which they are applied.

9   Rename the Filter Sequence (Filters) bin to *distressed look*, or some other descriptive name.

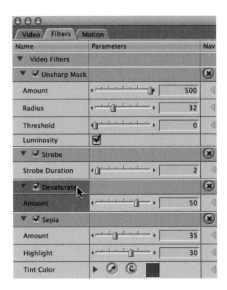

TIP ▶ If you want to save only one of the filters on the clip, highlight that filter by clicking on its name in the Filters tab in the Viewer and then choose Effects > Make Favorite Effect. Similarly, to remove an individual filter from a clip, highlight it and press Delete.

Applying a Filter Pack

It's easy to apply the combination of effects you just created to the other clips in this scene.

1   Select **bike angle1** and **bike angle2** in the Timeline.

2   Select the filter pack from the Effects tab of the Browser and drag it to **bike angle1** or **bike angle2** in the Timeline.

The effects are applied in the same order as on the original clip. Because a filter pack saves filters in a specific order, applying the whole bin to a clip adds all of the filters to the clip in the identical order.

NOTE ► Filter packs are easiest to apply by dragging from the Effects tab of the Browser. When using the Effects menu at the top of the screen, you can only select one Favorite filter at a time from the filter pack, so you need to click into the menu several times to apply multiple filters.

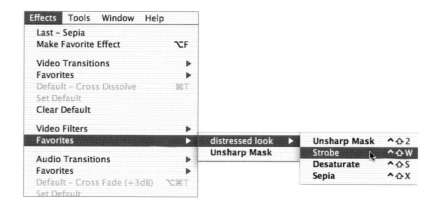

3   Spot-check and render a couple different portions of the Timeline to see how the effect works on all of the clips. Unless you want to, there is no need to render the entire sequence for this exercise.

Organizing Your Favorites Bin

Filter packs are an efficient way to sort effects in the Browser. When you rely on a lot of custom Favorites, you may want to spend some time organizing the contents of your Favorites bin so that you can locate what you need. In this exercise, you'll create some new Favorites bins and explore some ways to organize them.

1   Option-double-click the Favorites bin icon in the Effects tab of the Browser to open the bin as another tab in the Browser.

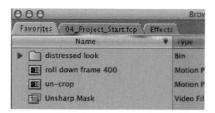

2 Ctrl-click a blank space inside the Favorites bin and choose New Bin from the contextual menu.

3 Rename your new bin as desired.

Once you have an assortment of bins and Favorites, you can put a Favorite in any bin. For instance, you might have a bin called Old Looks, in which you store filter packs, individual filters, or motion effects that are used whenever you need to build a *new* old look.

NOTE ▶ Although you may store Favorite filters, transitions, and motion effects in the same bin, you cannot apply them together. Only filter packs containing all the same type of effect can be applied as one to a clip. When the effects in a given bin are different types (filter, transition, or motion), they must be applied individually.

Moving and Preserving Favorites

As you build up your collection of Favorites, you will need to take special steps to preserve them, in case of a system problem on your workstation or to move them to a new workstation. Why? When a filter, motion, or transition is saved to the Favorites bin, that information is stored by Final Cut Pro in its preferences file. If you re-install your system, move to a new system, or delete the preferences file as a part of regular system maintenance or troubleshooting, you will lose all your Favorites!

In this exercise, you will use a special method to carry over your Favorites into a new preferences file, in case you need to delete your preferences file for any reason. This method can also be used as a way to back up your Favorites beyond the preferences file, and to move them to any new workstation.

1 Create a Timeline with several clips, using slugs for the clips. Create one slug clip for every effect or group of effects you want to save. (When you use slugs instead of actual video clips, you won't be presented with an "offline media" warning when moving this project to a computer without the same media.)

2   Drag all effects to be saved to the different slugs in the Timeline. To
save any Favorite transitions, just apply them to any edit point between
the slug clips in the Timeline.

3   Customize the name of each slug clip by selecting it and pressing
Cmd-9 to call up the Item Properties dialog box. Each slug can have
its own name. Any custom transition names will be carried over automatically.

4   Save this project and name it *Favorites*, then quit Final Cut Pro.

5   At this point, you can move the project file to a different computer,
or safely trash the preferences files, or archive the project just in case
you need it in the future.

6   To restore the effects, first open your Favorites project. If you've
moved computers or trashed your preferences, you will notice the
Favorites bin is empty. Then, one by one, restore your Favorite effects
by simply selecting a slug in the Timeline, and choose Make Favorite
Motion or Make Favorite Effect. For any filter packs, go back to the
Favorites bin and name the newly created bin of effects by the customized name of the slug in the Timeline. For any Favorite transitions, just re-create the Favorite by dragging each transition from the
Timeline to the Favorites bin.

Filtering Only Part of a Clip

For creative reasons or to reduce rendering time, you may sometimes want
to limit an effect to only one part of a clip. Here's how to use video filters
on selective portions of a clip.

1   Click the Filter Sequence tab in the Timeline to select it, or open it
from the Browser.

2 Move the Timeline playhead forward to the clip **201_7**.

3 Choose the Range Selection tool (GGG). The cursor changes into a crosshair.

4 In the Timeline, position the cursor roughly in the center of the clip **201_7**.

5 Click and drag to the right across the clip and release before the end of the clip. As you drag, the selected portion of the clip in the Timeline is darkened.

6 Click in a blank spot of the Timeline to deselect the clip.

7 Make the selection again, watching the Canvas as you drag. The Canvas shows a two-up display of the currently selected start and end frames.

8 With only a range of the clip selected, choose Effects > Video Filters > Channel > Invert to invert the channel.

In the Timeline, notice that the render status line above the clip indicates that only part of the clip is filtered.

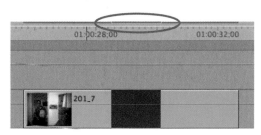

NOTE ▶ The color of the render line depends on your computer setup, RT choices, external video, and other factors.

9 Click the Clip Keyframes button to turn on the filter and motion bars in the Timeline.

The filter bar is only green for the section that's filtered, which also indicates that only part of the clip is filtered.

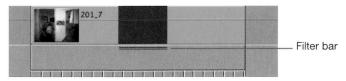

10 Play back the clip and notice how the effect instantaneously appears and then disappears.

This on/off technique can be used with one effect, or you may stack multiple filters on the clip, each new effect beginning when another effect pops off, creating a sort of strobe effect with the different looks. The next section shows how to adjust the exact start and end points for a filter.

11 Click the Clip Keyframes button to turn off the filter and motion bars.

Filter Slipping

Although Range Selection is a quick and easy way to apply an effect to part of a clip, you may want to go back and customize the start and end points more precisely. This is an easy task in the Viewer.

1 Activate the Selection tool (A), open the clip **201_7** into the Viewer, and go to the Filters tab. Be sure the Viewer is wide enough to see the keyframe graph area easily.

Notice the two vertical black lines above the keyframe area. They are located along the same strip as the name of the filter.

These lines represent the filter's boundaries, and the light gray section between the lines is the section of the clip that is affected.

2 Position the cursor inside the filtered section. It becomes a Slip icon.

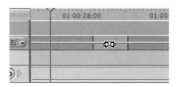

3 Click and drag left or right to slip the filtered section in either direction.

Adjusting Start and End Points

Whether or not you use Range Selection to apply the effect, you can customize the start and end points of a the filter's range at any time.

1 Position your cursor over one of the two black lines at the outside edges of the keyframe area. The cursor becomes a resize icon.

2   Click and drag left or right to change the filter start or end point.

Working with Text

So far, all of your sequences involve only images. Quite often, however, your program will require text. For subtitles and other text effects, Final Cut Pro includes built-in text generators, such as Outline Text. Although outlined text cannot be saved as a Favorite, it can be accessed at any time as a Browser clip.

Creating a Subtitle

To simplify your example, you're going create an English subtitle; imagine it's for hearing-impaired viewers.

1   Click the Filter Sequence tab in the Timeline to select it, or open it from the Browser.

2   Move the Timeline playhead to the clip **301_1**.

3   Play back the clip and listen to the dialogue.

A man says, "Hey," and a woman replies, "Hey, honey, hurry up. The movie is about to start."

4   Click the View button in the Canvas and choose Show Title Safe from the pop-up menu to turn on the title overlay.

5   Choose Text > Outline Text from the Generator pop-up menu at the bottom of the Video tab in the Viewer.

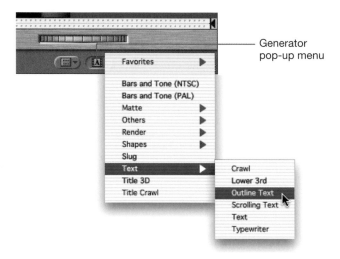

Generator pop-up menu

6   Place the Timeline playhead over the middle of **301_1**.

7   Edit the text into the sequence by dropping it on the Canvas overlay for Superimpose.

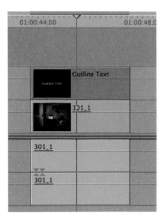

8   Double-click the Outline Text clip in the Timeline to open it back into the Viewer.

9 Click the Controls tab. In the text field, type the following:

- Hey.

- Hey. Hurry up, the movie is about to start.

10 Make the type easier to read by changing to a sans serif typeface such as Geneva. Make the point size 26 so that it's not too small, and change the line width to 15 to create a thin, dark outline between the background video and the color of the title. Finally, change the text color to light yellow to reduce the contrast between the title and the background video.

11 Click the text clip in the Timeline to highlight the wireframe in the Canvas. Turn on Image + Wireframe mode in the Canavas if necessary.

12 Adjust the position of the title in the frame by Shift-dragging the title downward in the Canvas until it's positioned just above the inside of the title safe line.

Fine-Tuning the Position of Text

Lines of text often look good in the Canvas, but their appearance in NTSC format might be radically different. That's because computer screens are progressive scan monitors, which makes text appear nice and sharp, whereas interlaced scanning television screens may be blurry or display artifacts.

Before signing off on any final text or subtitles, evaluate it on an external video monitor. In fact, if you have an external monitor set up, use it to see the difference in the subtitle you just created and to complete this exercise. (If not, don't worry. Complete the exercise anyway.)

1   Click the Motion tab in the Viewer for the text clip.

2   Click the Center crosshair to activate it (but do not click the Canvas).

3   Press Option-down arrow a couple of times to nudge the clip in the Canvas downward.

    Notice on the external monitor that the text repositions each time it moves, lining up somewhat differently with the scan lines on the monitor.

4   With the Center crosshair in the Motion tab active, continue to press Option–down arrow until the text snaps into sharpness. You should find that it cycles between soft and sharp on every nudge.

    TIP ▶ To nudge in finer increments, press Cmd-Option-down arrow. This is helpful when moving narrow horizontal objects, such as lines. You may need to press this key combination several times before you can see any perceptible change onscreen.

Saving a Title as a Template

You started this exercise intending to create a title template, so let's do that now.

1   Drag the text clip from the Timeline or Viewer to the Project tab in the Browser. This creates a copy of the text as a new Browser clip and sets its status as a master clip.

2   Click the name of the outline text, and change it to *Subtitle*.

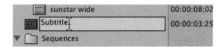

Now anytime you need that particular configuration of the outline generator, simply edit the Subtitle Browser clip to the Timeline, open it into the Viewer, and change the lines of text as desired.

TIP ▶ You can copy text from a word processing program and paste it directly into the text field of any text generator. Use the Dock to switch between Final Cut Pro and the word processor.

Additional Exercises

A sequence named **More Finished Examples** is in the Sequences bin in the Browser. For more practice, play back these examples in the Timeline and try to re-create them. To see how the examples were animated, open the clips from each composition into the Viewer and note the Motion tab settings.

What You've Learned

- Favorites are available in the Effect menu for reuse at any time.
- Filter effects can also be saved as Favorites.
- Keyframes can be adjusted in the Viewer, Canvas, Timeline, keyframe editor, and/or filter and motion bars.
- Organize Favorite effects and filters in bins.
- Use the Range Selection tool to apply a filter to only part of a clip.
- The Outline Text generator can be used to create subtitles.

5

Time   This lesson takes approximately 90 minutes to complete.

Goals   Apply basic speed manipulations to clips

Learn to read the speed indicators in the Timeline

Use the Time Remap tool to add and manipulate keyframes

Manipulate Time keyframes in the motion bar

Customize the Clip Keyframes control for different uses

Create freeze frames using variable speed controls

Make part of a clip play backward

Smooth speed keyframes to create gradual changes

Save a speed setting as a Favorite

Variable Speed

Speed effects are one of the most common and versatile effect types available in Final Cut Pro. Basic speed changes, such as slow motion, can be employed for dramatic effect, and increasing playback speed can simulate time lapse. The real fun happens when you employ variable speed effects (often called *time ramping*) to vary a clip's speed throughout playback. For example, a shot can begin playing in slow motion, speed up, and then return to another playback speed at the end of the shot. A speed-varied shot can slow to a freeze frame, or play back in reverse. Final Cut Pro displays time remapping data in several different ways. Learning how to read time controls is essential to mastering the variable speed tools.

Basic Slow Motion

Before delving into variable speed effects, it's important to review how Final Cut Pro handles constant speed changes such as slow motion.

1   Open Lesson_05 > **05_Project_Start.fcp**. The sequence **Golfer 1** should be open in the Timeline. Play the sequence.

2   Select clip **6E_1** (the third clip) and choose Modify > Speed.

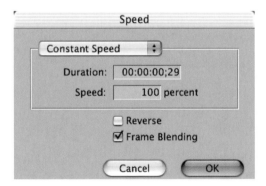

3   Check the Frame Blending box if it's not on already. Frame Blending generates new frames by blending the surrounding frames. This creates a smoother slow motion effect.

4   Set the Speed to 50 percent and click OK.

In the Timeline, you can see that slowing down the clip rippled it to the right and made it longer.

5 Click the button in the lower-left corner of the Timeline to turn on Clip Keyframes.

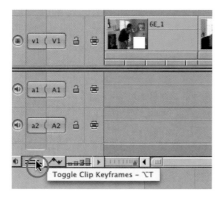

The Clip Keyframes button turns on the speed indicators beneath clips in the Timeline. Notice that the tick marks beneath **6E_1** are farther apart than they are in the surrounding clips. The distance between the ticks indicates the speed of the clip. The farther apart the ticks, the slower the clip will play back.

6 Render and play your sequence.

NOTE ▶ If you play the sequence using Unlimited RT instead of rendering, you can preview the effect, but Frame Blending will not be applied until you render.

You may notice that even with Frame Blending enabled, **6E_1** still appears to have a strobe or stuttering quality. The fourth clip (**6F_3**) was photographed in slow motion. You can compare the difference between the two clips. Creating slow motion in-camera will always produce a smoother result than applying an effect in post-production.

If you must slow a clip in post-production, adding Motion Blur can often improve the effect.

7 Double-click **6E_1**, the third clip in the **Golfer 1** sequence, to open it into the Viewer.

8   Click the Motion tab.

9   Turn on Motion Blur and click the triangle to reveal its settings.

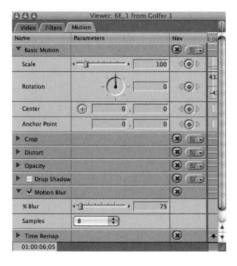

10   Set % Blur to 75 and Samples to 8.

11   Render and play your sequence.

Motion Blur uses frames before and after the current frame and combines them to create an effect similar to the natural blur that occurs in-camera when shooting in slow motion. The Samples setting equals the number of frames both before and after the current frame that are used to create the effect. % Blur sets the amount of blur applied to these sampled frames. Because of this, Motion Blur is a render-intensive effect. Higher settings will take longer to render. Remember: A little bit goes a long way with motion blurring.

Variable Speed Effects

Slowing only a portion of a clip is accomplished by using a Variable Speed effect.

1   Double-click the **Golfer 2** sequence to open it into the Timeline.

This clip contains a single clip of the golfer swinging his club.

2 Select the clip, play the sequence, and set a marker just as the golfer begins the downward motion of his swing.

3 Select the Time Remap tool from the Tool palette.

4   Click once on the clip at the frame where you want to set a speed remapping keyframe.

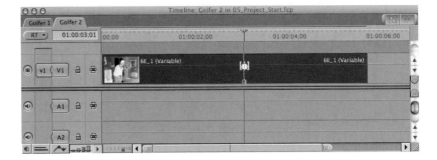

Setting this keyframe prepares the clip so that the speed changes you make will affect the clip from this point forward. The word "variable" appears next to the clip's name in the Timeline to indicate that speed keyframes have been applied.

5   Click and hold the Time Remap tool near the right edge of the clip. Turn off Snapping (N key) if necessary. You might see the tool turn into an arrow near the right edge, but if you click and hold, a tooltip will appear to inform you of the changes about to occur.

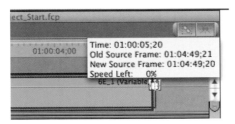

6   Drag the Time Remap tool to the left until the tooltip indicates that Speed Left equals approximately 50%.

The clip should play at normal speed until the golfer begins his swing, and then switch to slow motion for the duration of the swing.

7   Turn on Clip Keyframes in the Timeline.

Notice that the tick marks in the speed indicator spread out during the section of the clip that is in slow motion. Also, the blue motion bar indicates where keyframes have been set.

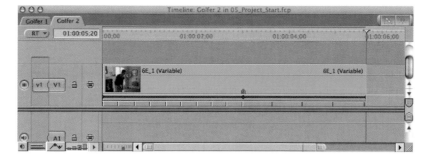

Creating a Freeze Frame

Variable speed effects can be used to make a clip play at normal speed, and then stop and hold on a particular frame. This is sometimes used in title sequences and trailers to introduce characters.

1   Double-click the **Character Intro** sequence to open it into the Timeline.

2 Play the sequence and stop when the girl is visible full frame, from head to toe (approximate timecode 01:00:11:10).

3 Select the Time Remap tool and click at the playhead position to add a single speed keyframe.

4 Type +3. (three-period) to move your playhead forward three seconds.

5 Add a new keyframe by clicking with the Time Remap tool.

6 Turn on Clip Keyframes.

The Clip Keyframes control aids in performing keyframing operations in the Timeline. In addition to displaying speed indicators and a motion bar, a keyframe editor also appears and can display speed keyframes for manipulation directly in the Timeline.

Although the Clip Keyframes button itself simply turns the visibility of controls in the Timeline on and off, you can make it more useful by customizing the controls it displays and which keyframes are visible.

7 Ctrl-click the Clip Keyframes button and uncheck Video > Filters Bar
in the contextual menu. Leave the other three selections checked.

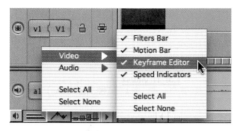

8 Ctrl-click the Clip Keyframes button again and check Audio >
Select None.

Now the settings that are helpful for variable speed effects will be the
only ones visible in the Timeline tracks.

9 Ctrl-click the blue motion bar under the clip and choose Hide All
from the contextual menu. By default, keyframes for all parameters
are visible. After choosing Hide All, no keyframes will be displayed
in the motion bar.

This menu allows you to choose which keyframes will be displayed in
the motion bar. You can have multiple parameters displayed simultaneously, but you will not be able to tell them apart by looking at the
motion bar. In this case, you want to view only speed keyframes.

10 Ctrl-click again on the blue motion bar and choose Time Remap > Time Graph from the contextual menu. Now only speed keyframes will be displayed in the motion bar.

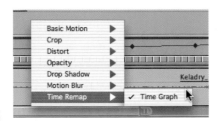

11 Ctrl-click in the area between the blue motion bar and the speed indicator, where the keyframe editor appears, and then choose Time Remap > Time Graph from the contextual menu.

This contextual menu allows you to choose which keyframe graph will be displayed in the Timeline's keyframe editor. You can only view one parameter graph at a time. Graphs for all parameters are always visible in the Motion tab of the Viewer.

When the keyframe editor is visible, a small new control appears at the right edge of the track headers: This thin bar controls the height of the keyframe graph.

12 Click the thin, vertical black bar and drag it upward to increase height of the graph. This will give you more room to manipulate the Time Remap keyframes.

Now you will set the second speed keyframe to the same frame as the first to create a freeze frame effect.

13 Position your playhead at the first keyframe. (Turn Snapping back on, with the N key, if necessary.)

14 Choose View > Match Frame > Master Clip or press F.

This loads the source clip into the Viewer, parked on the identical frame.

15 Make sure Snapping is turned on. Using the Time Remap tool, click and hold on the position of the second keyframe in the Timeline. Do not click in the keyframe graph, click the clip itself.

The speed tooltip appears.

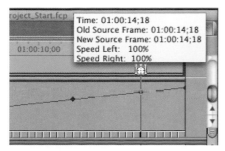

The Canvas displays the frame currently assigned to the place in time where you clicked. As you drag the Time Remap tool, the Canvas updates to display the new frame you are assigning to that time position.

16 Drag the tool to the left until the frame in the Canvas matches the exact frame displayed in the Viewer. As you drag, match the number on the Source Timecode Overlay in the Canvas to the Current Timecode position in the Viewer.

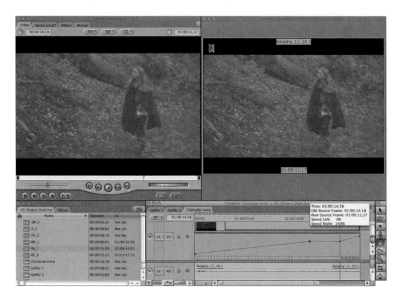

The keyframe graph and speed indicator can also assist you in identifying when you have achieved the freeze frame. The keyframe graph will display a horizontal line, and the speed indicators will not contain any tick marks for the duration of the freeze.

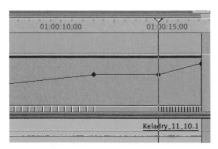

To finalize the effect, you must set the remaining portion of the clip back to regular speed.

17 Click the Time Remap tool on the last frame of the clip and drag it to the left until the tooltip reads Speed Left: 100%.

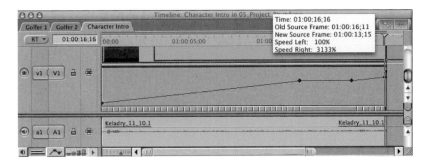

Ignore the Speed Right value because none of those frames will be played. If you have trouble setting the speed value to a precise number, you will use the keyboard modifiers Shift and Cmd next to restrict the movement of the Time Remap tool.

18 Click and hold the last frame with the Time Remap tool.

19 Press Shift to constrain movements to 10% increments or press Cmd to restrict movements to 1% increments.

This allows you to set precise values for speed effects.

20 Play your sequence and view the freeze frame effect.

21 Using the text generator, create a title, identifying the actor as "Kel."

22 Set the duration of the text generator to 3:00.

23 Edit the text clip onto V2 beginning at the first speed keyframe.

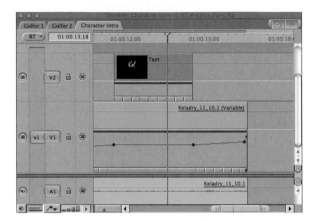

Modifying Existing Speed Keyframes

Once you've applied speed keyframes, you can modify their position in time to alter the variable speed effect. For example, speed can be altered to play in fast motion leading up to the freeze frame.

The Time Remap tool normally does what its name implies: it remaps, or moves, a particular clip frame to the current position in sequence time where the tool is clicked. It then speeds up or slows down intermediate frames in front of and behind that particular frame to execute this remap.

When you Option-click with the Time Remap tool, however, you move the current frame to a different position in time. Frames speed up and slow down on either side of this repositioned frame to compensate for the move.

To reflect this difference, a tooltip displays the Old Time and New Time, rather than the old and new Source Frame. In both cases, you are modifying the speed of the clip, so the Speed Left and Speed Right information is still visible.

1   Option-click and hold anywhere in the clip with the Time Remap tool at the location of the first keyframe. A tooltip appears.

NOTE ▶ Clicking or Option-clicking the clip with the Time Remap tool sets a new keyframe if there was not one there already. When adjusting settings for an existing keyframe, activate snapping to aid precision.

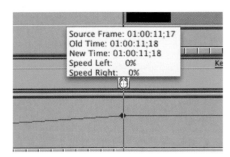

2   Drag the keyframe to the left until Speed Left reads approximately 250%.

NOTE ▶ You may have trouble getting the speed to line up to 250% exactly. When Option-dragging, you are moving the clip one frame at a time, so the speed may jump, from 226% to 278%, for example. If it is imperative that you set the speed exactly to 250%. Option-drag until it is as close as possible, then use the standard Time Remap tool (no Option key) to fine-tune the speed.

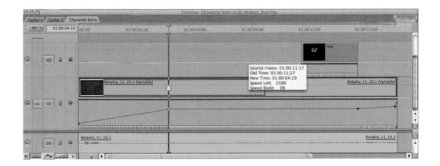

As you can see, using the Option key combined with the Time Remap tool allows you to extend this freeze frame for about six additional seconds. To accomplish this, the beginning frames that were playing normally are now squeezed together in time to play back at approximately 250%. This is reflected in the Timeline by the speed indicator, which shows the tick marks very close to each other. Now, however, the title no longer lines up with the effect, so let's fix that.

3 Change back to the Selection tool (press A) and drag the entire clip on V2 so it begins at the same time as the freeze frame.

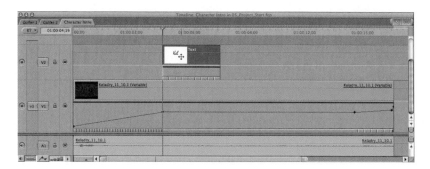

4 Option-drag the second speed keyframe with the Time Remap tool, or simply drag the keyframe point in the graph to line up with the end of the title.

Before the effect is complete, you must reset the speed between the last two keyframes so the clip will play back at 100% speed.

5 Option-click the last frame of the clip with the Time Remap tool and drag to the left until Speed Left equals 100%. Make sure you are adjusting the existing keyframe, not adding a new keyframe. Zoom in to Timeline and use snapping if necessary.

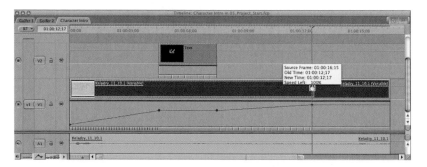

Due to the original duration of the sequence, a few extra frames remain at the end of the shot.

6   Using the Selection tool, drag the right edge of the clip until it lines up with the last keyframe.

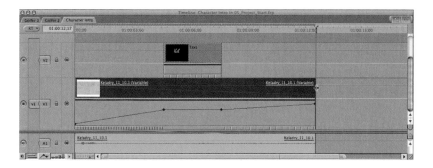

7   Play the sequence.

When creating freeze frames, it's important to check how the output looks on an interlaced, external monitor to be sure no field artifacts are visible in the frozen frame. If you select a frame that contains fast, horizontal movement, the freeze frame might look good on your computer screen but will flicker when displayed on a TV monitor.

If you see flicker in the freeze frame, choose a frame that doesn't contain such lateral movement. If you must choose a frame that contains movement, eliminate the flickering effect by applying the De-Interlace filter to the range of the clip that has the freeze frame (choose Effects > Video Filters > Video > De-Interlace). Be aware, however, that removing the interlacing from the clip can have a negative effect on slow motion speed effects, enhancing the strobe or stutter effect discussed earlier in the lesson.

Complex Speed Effects

Once you have mastered the basics of variable speed effects, you can make increasingly complex effects using many keyframes. You can even switch between forward and backward play.

1   Close all of your open sequences and then open the **Head Turn** sequence and watch it once.

In preparing for his golf swing, the actor makes an interesting, some-what comical head roll.

2 Identify the frame where the actor begins his head roll.

3 Set a keyframe at that point by clicking the clip with the Time Remap tool.

4 Ctrl-click the keyframe graph and choose Time Remap > Time Graph from the contextual menu.

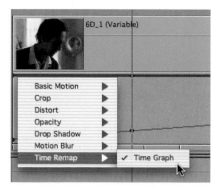

5   Find the frame where the head movement ends.

6   Option-click that frame and drag it to the left, compressing the time
between the two keyframes to approximately 200%.

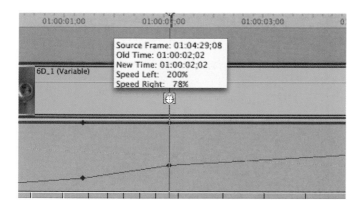

7   Move the playhead one second to the right of the last keyframe.
Click and drag to the left with the Time Remap tool (do not hold
down the Option key) to create a new keyframe with a Speed Left
value of approximately –155%.

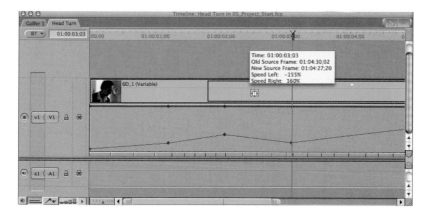

You have just set the clip to play backward between the second and
third keyframes. The speed indicator displays red tick marks for the
duration of reverse playback. Notice that the keyframe graph displays
a downward slope.

8   Move the playhead forward two seconds beyond the third keyframe and click-drag to the left with the Time Remap tool (no Option key). Watch the Canvas and stop when the last frame of the head movement appears.

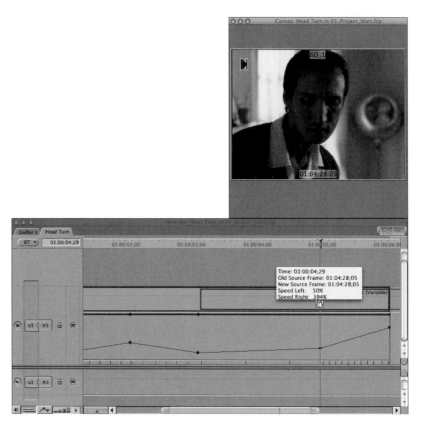

This adjusts the speed between keyframes three and four to about 50%.

9   Play your sequence.

You can continue adding additional keyframes to extend that short head turn for great comic effect.

Gradual Speed Changes

The speed effects you have created thus far transition abruptly from one speed to another—the clip plays at 100% until it reaches a new keyframe and then suddenly switches to 50% speed. This creates dramatic effects, but you can further improve your speed effects by controlling the ramping velocity of the speed changes.

1 Ctrl-click the second keyframe in the keyframe graph and choose Smooth from the contextual menu.

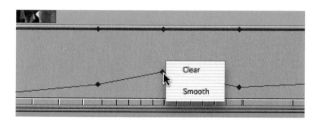

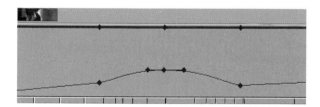

The transition from forward to reverse speed now occurs gradually, creating a subtle and natural-looking effect. The Bézier handles that appear when you choose Smooth allow further manipulation of the transition.

Be careful when manipulating these handles. Small movements can have dramatic effects and completely alter the subtlety of the speed settings you just established.

2   Zoom in to get a closer look at the keyframe you are about to manipulate. You can also enlarge the track height.

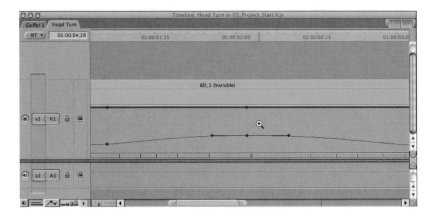

3   Drag the Bézier handle points towards the keyframe to reduce the duration of the transition. Be careful to keep the handles completely horizontal. By default, moving one handle automatically moves the other.

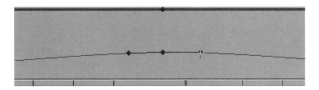

Lengthening the handles adds time to the transition between speed settings. Experiment with different settings to find the transition that feels most natural to you.

Once you smooth a keyframe, the Speed tooltip reports the Speed Left and Speed Right as Variable.

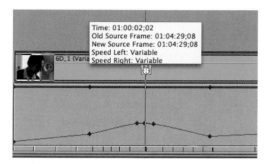

This makes it impossible to apply additional changes to the keyframe values. For good workflow, do not apply smoothing to your keyframes until speed value changes are final. Of course, you can always Ctrl-click the smoothed keyframe and set it back to a corner point, if necessary.

4 Apply the smoothing effect to all keyframes in the sequence. There is no need to adjust Bézier handles, because default settings provide adequate smoothing.

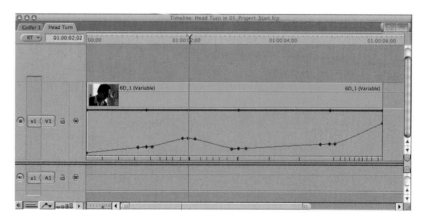

5 Play the finished sequence.

Using the Motion Viewer

The speed effects and controls used in the Timeline are also visible in the Time Remap section of the Motion tab in the Viewer.

1 Still in the **Head Turn** sequence, double-click with the Selection tool on **6D_1** to open it into the Viewer.

2 Click the Motion tab. Toggle open the Time Remap parameters.

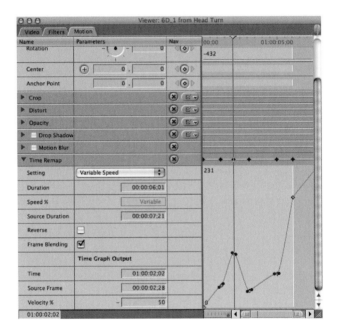

The graph displayed here is identical to the graph visible in the Timeline. Viewing this graph in the Motion tab allows you to compare it to keyframes applied in other motion parameters.

The primary disadvantage to making changes in the Motion tab is that, unlike using the Time Remap tool in the Timeline, you cannot view the frames interactively as they update in the Canvas, but only the result after you release the mouse.

The most useful control in the Motion tab is the Reset Button that removes all speed keyframes applied.

3   Click the Reset button for the Time Remap section of the Motion tab.

Copying and Saving Speed Effects

Speed effects are recorded in the Motion tab, so you can copy or save a clip's speed settings just as you can with any motion setting.

1   Open the **Copy Clip** sequence.

2   Play back the sequence.

Clip 1 has a variable speed effect applied to it, and Clip 2 plays at regular speed.

3   Select Clip 1 and choose Edit > Copy (or press Cmd-C).

4   Select Clip 2 and choose Edit > Paste Attributes (or press Option-V).

5   Check the Speed box and click OK.

If you are pasting attributes to a clip of a different length, checking the Scale Attribute Times box will scale your keyframes to fit the length of the new clip.

Let's save the speed settings so that they're available to use on other clips.

6   Select Clip 1 and choose Effects > Make Favorite Motion.

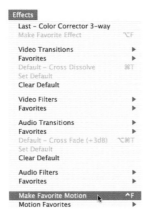

Make Favorite Motion stores all motion settings (Scale, Distortion, Drop Shadow, Speed, and so on) that are currently applied to the clip in the Motion tab.

7   In the Browser window, click the Effects tab and open the Favorites bin.

8 Rename **1M_3 (Motion)** to *My custom speed effect* and press Enter.

The custom effect also appears in the Effects > Motion Favorites submenu.

You can now apply this speed setting to any selected clip in any sequence.

What You've Learned

- Use Frame Blending when creating a slow motion, constant speed effect.

- Use the Time Remap tool to add and manipulate keyframes to create variable speed effects, such as freeze frames.

- Customize the controls displayed for clip keyframes in the Timeline by Ctrl-clicking to access its contextual menu.

- The keyframe graph displays speed effects.

- Play a clip backwards by giving a keyframe a negative Speed Left value.

- Choose the Smooth command in a keyframe's contextual menu to create gradual changes.

- Speed effects can be saved as Favorites and applied to other clips.

6

Lesson Files	Lessons > Lesson_06 > 06_Project_Start.fcp
	Lessons > Lesson_06 > 06_Project_Finished.fcp
Media	Media > Lesson_06_Media
Time	This lesson takes approximately 90 minutes to complete.
Goals	Edit one sequence into another to create a nested sequence
	Use the Nest Items command to convert clips into a nested sequence
	Apply effects to nested sequences
	Modify individual clips within a nested sequence
	Use nesting to work around Final Cut Pro's render order
	Mix sequence frame sizes to create scaling effects
	Use nesting to manage long-format shows

Lesson 6
Nesting Sequences

When working with complex sequences that involve multiple layers and many clips, you may want to treat a group of many continuous clips as a single object. For example, you may wish to apply a single filter to multiple items, or to scale or rotate several clips all at once. To efficiently accomplish such complex tasks, you can take advantage of Final Cut Pro's nesting features.

You can edit any full sequence into another sequence, in exactly the same way you edit any clip into the sequence. Whenever one sequence is thus embedded into another sequence, the embedded sequence is called a *nested* sequence, and the sequence it is embedded into is sometimes called the *parent* sequence. As well as editing a full sequence into another sequence to nest it, you can also select a group of clips already in a sequence and combine them into a nested sequence, in place, creating a new nest where the original clips were located within the original sequence.

Nested sequences are useful when organizing clips, but they also allow you to quickly add effects and perform tasks that would be otherwise time consuming. Learning to manage nested sequences will enable you to create powerful effects, as well as improve your overall workflow and flexibility within Final Cut Pro.

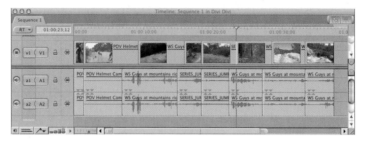

Unnested

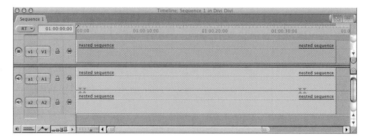

Nested

Basic Nesting

Nesting one sequence inside another is simple. Think of a nested sequence simply as a single clip that contains multiple items.

1   Open Lesson_06 > **06_Project_Start.fcp.**

The sequence called **Bike Jumps** should be open in the Timeline. If not, double-click it from the Browser to open it into the Timeline.

The sequence contains three clips on V1, and a title clip on Track 2.

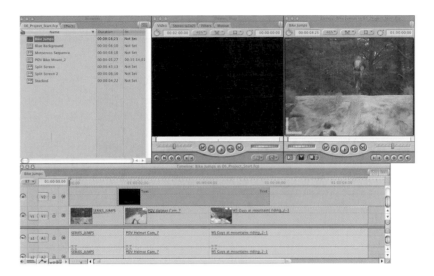

2   Double-click **Motocross Sequence** in the Browser. It opens as a second
    tab in the Timeline.

3   Activate snapping. Select the **Bike Jumps** sequence in the Browser. Edit
    it into the **Motocross Sequence** by dragging and dropping it into the
    Timeline as if it were a clip. Place it at the end of the first two clips.

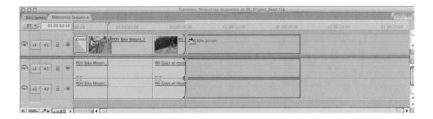

You have now nested one sequence inside of another sequence, with
a simple drag and drop edit The **Bike Jumps** sequence is the *nested
sequence*, often called simply the *nest*, and **Motocross Sequence** is the
main sequence, often called the *parent sequence*. You can see that the

new item is a slightly different color than ordinary clips in the Timeline. This helps you identify which items in your sequence are nested

When you play back **Motocross Sequence**, clips nested in the **Bike Jumps** sequence will play just as they were originally edited. Even the title from video track 2 of the **Bike Jumps** sequence will be visible.

Understanding Live Links

The link between a nested sequence and its parent sequence remains live: When you make changes inside a nested sequence, you will see those changes take effect when you play the parent sequence. All editing and effects changes made to any clips or other items inside a nested sequence will automatically be updated in the parent sequence which contains the nest.

1　Click the tab at the top of the Timeline to make **Bike Jumps** active.

2　Double-click the title clip on track V2 to load it into the Viewer.

3　In the Viewer, click the Controls tab. Type *Motocross Madness!* into the text box and click anywhere outside of the text box to force the text to update in the Canvas.

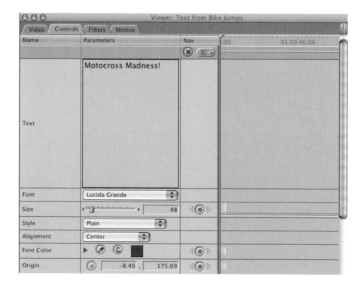

The Canvas should reflect the change. If your playhead isn't over the area of the title, drag it there to confirm that the text has been updated.

4   Click the tab at the top of the Timeline to make **Motocross Sequence**, the parent sequence, active.

5   Scrub the playhead through **Motocross Sequence** until you see the section where the title should appear. Notice that the text has been updated here as well.

If you make additional changes in the Controls tab of the Viewer for the title clip from the **Bike Jumps** nested sequence, the changes will continue to update live in **Motocross Sequence**, the parent sequence.

Applying Effects to Multiple Clips

You can use nesting to apply a single effect to multiple items at once. This saves time by eliminating the need to apply a filter to each clip individually. If you later decide to change the parameters of the filter, the changes will affect all the clips simultaneously.

In this example, you will tint all of the clips inside the nested sequence red.

1   Be sure that **Motocross Sequence** is open in your Timeline.

2   Select the **Bike Jumps** nested sequence in the Timeline.

3   Choose Effects > Video Filters > Image Control > Tint.

You see the tint effect on every clip in the **Bike Jumps** nested sequence.

The filter affects the image of each clip in the nest, but is actually applied to the Filters tab of the nest as a whole, and not the Filters tab of each clip inside the nest. To modify filter parameters on a nested sequence, you must open the nested sequence into the Viewer. Ordinarily, double-clicking a clip in the Timeline opens it up into the Viewer. Notice that when you double-click a nested sequence, it opens in the Timeline and Canvas as a new tab, just as a sequence does when you double-click it from the Browser.

4   Select the **Bike Jumps** nested sequence in the Timeline (if it's not already selected).

5   Press Enter on your keyboard, or choose View > Sequence, or Ctrl-click the nested sequence and choose Open in Viewer from the contextual menu.

The **Bike Jumps** sequence is now loaded in the Viewer as if it were an individual clip.

6   In the Viewer, click the Filters tab. The Tint filter controls should be visible.

7   Set the color of the tint to a pale red by clicking on the color selector and adjusting the color settings.

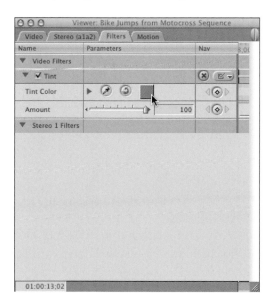

8   Play back **Motocross Sequence**. Notice that the new reddish tint affects the entire **Bike Jumps** segment.

You could accomplish the same results by applying the tint filter to each individual clip. If your client decided that he or she preferred a blue tint instead of red, however, you would then have to open the clips individually and then modify the filter settings. With nested sequences, you can modify filter settings and apply those changes to all items at once.

Applying Complex Geometric Settings

Some effects can be achieved only by using nested sequences. For example, by combining multiple clips into a single element in the Timeline, you can apply geometric attributes such as Scale, Rotation, and Motion to all of the clips as a single unit.

1   Double-click the **Split Screen** sequence in the Browser to open it into the Timeline.

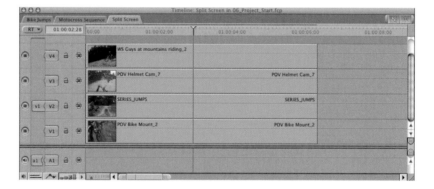

The **Split Screen** sequence contains four clips scaled down to 50% and arranged into quadrants in the Canvas so that all four images are visible onscreen at the same time. If your system is powerful enough, you may be able to play the sequence without rendering. If your Timeline displays a red line in the render bar area, you might not have Unlimited RT selected in the Real-Time Effects pop-up menu in the Timeline. Selecting Unlimited RT and low quality, instead of Safe RT, will allow you to play many effects in real time.

NOTE ▶ You must have a 500 MHz G4 (PowerBook G4 550) or a dual-processor G4 or faster to be able to choose Unlimited RT.

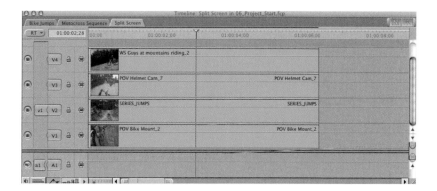

2   If necessary, render your sequence by pressing Option-R.

3   Play the sequence. The four video clips should play simultaneously.

In the following exercises, you will spin the four elements around a single anchor point, and then shrink the whole image to a single point, revealing a new image.

Nest Items in Place

Earlier in this lesson you created a nested sequence by dragging and dropping one sequence into another. In this exercise, you will create a new nested sequence directly inside an existing sequence, using the Nest Items command.

1   Drag a lasso around the four clips in the Timeline to select them.

2   Choose Sequence > Nest Item(s).

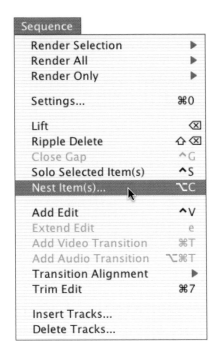

The Nest Items dialog box appears.

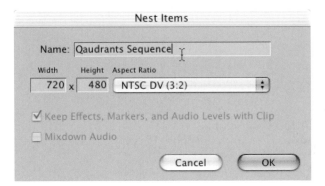

3 In the Name box, type *Quadrant Sequence.* Leave the other settings at their default values and click OK.

Now, instead of four clips on four tracks, the parent sequence contains one item: **Quadrant Sequence**. The image in the Canvas does not change. With rare exceptions, the Nest Items command will not change the visual output of your sequence. It affects only the grouping of the clips in the Timeline.

The Nest Items command automatically puts the new nested sequence on the lowest available track. If a clip already occupies the lowest track, the next available higher track will be used. In some cases, Final Cut Pro will generate a new track to make space for the item. The following screen shots show a case where V2 is the location of a nested sequence created from clips on V1 through V4.

Unnested

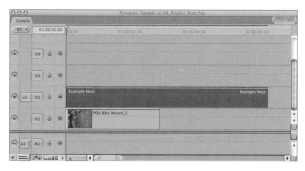

Nested

Nest Items also adds a new sequence icon to the Browser window, representing the nested sequence. This sequence can be used like any other sequence, but any changes you make to the nested **Quadrant Sequence** will modify the parent **Split Screen** sequence, because they contain live links.

Apply Motion Parameters

Because the four clips are now inside **Quadrant Sequence**, motion settings applied to it will affect all four of the clips. And because the four clips are geometrically connected, their relative positions will remain intact regardless of changes made to the sequence.

1   Open **Quadrant Sequence** into the Viewer by selecting it in the Timeline and pressing Enter, or by Ctrl-clicking on it and choosing Open Item in Viewer from the contextual menu.

2   In the Viewer, click the Motion tab.

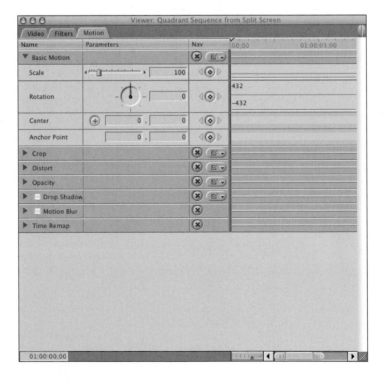

3   Press Home to bring your playhead to the beginning of the sequence in the Viewer.

4   Set a keyframe for the Rotation parameter.

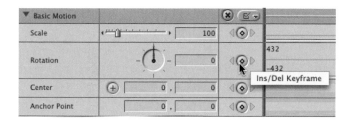

5   Move the playhead six seconds into the sequence in the Viewer by typing *+600*. (Or you can type *6* and then type a single period to enter double zeros.)

6   Set the Rotation value to *1440* degrees (four rotations) and press Enter. A second keyframe is automatically added. Because this rotation is render intensive, you will need to switch back to Safe RT mode and render this effect.

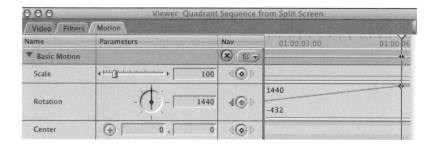

When you play this sequence, the four videos will spin in unison around a common center point. Setting similar rotation parameters for each clip individually would have resulted in each clip spinning around its own center point.

7   With your playhead on the last rotation keyframe, in the Motion tab of the Viewer, type –500 and press Enter to set your playhead to 01:00:01:00. This should move the playhead to five seconds before the second rotation keyframe.

8   Add a keyframe for the Scale parameter (leaving the value at 100).

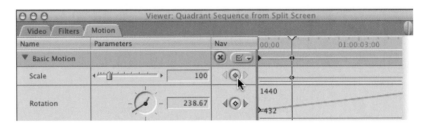

9   Move the playhead forward five seconds again so it lines up precisely with the Rotation keyframe.

10 Set the Scale parameter to 0 and press Enter. This will cause the four clips to shrink until they are invisible.

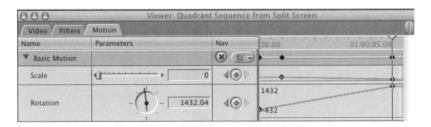

11 Make the Timeline or Canvas active and render the sequence if necessary (Option-R).

12 Play back the sequence.

The four clips spin around a single center point and then vanish into the distance.

Add a Background Element

At this point, the clips vanish into a black field. Let's use this effect as a transition, revealing another clip as the spinning clips disappear.

1   In the Timeline, Shift-drag **Quadrant Sequence** from track V1 onto track V2. Pressing Shift as you drag prevents the clip from moving left or right. Alternately, select the clip and press Option-up arrow.

2   Drag **Blue Background** from the Browser into the Timeline, dropping it on track V1 directly underneath **Quadrant Sequence**.

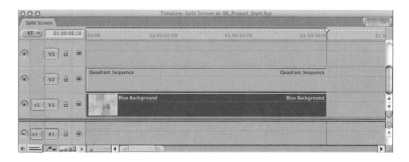

Now when the four clips scale down, **Blue Background** is revealed.

3 Render and play back the sequence.

Adjust the Anchor Point

In the **Blue Background** clip, the bike icon is slightly off center. To integrate the four quadrant clips with the background clip, let's alter the anchor point of the nested sequence so that the clips spin around and vanish into that bike icon.

1 In the Canvas, move the playhead near the end of the sequence and park on a frame where the bicycle graphic in the background is visible. Note the approximate position of the bicycle.

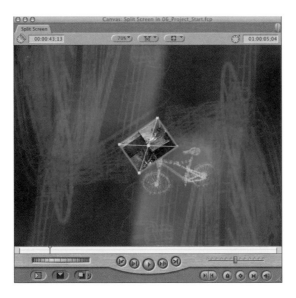

2 Select the Distort tool (D) and then press Home to bring the playhead to the beginning of the sequence.

3   Click the Canvas View button and choose Image+Wireframe from the pop-up menu. Place the cursor over the center point of the quadrant sequence in the Canvas and drag it to the approximate position of the bicycle.

This modifies the clip's anchor point, which is the point around which the object rotates and scales. What you see onscreen may be confusing. Final Cut Pro displays a representation of the change in the motion path, based on the rotation and scaling keyframes you set.

4   Render and play back the sequence.

The clips are now better integrated. To finesse this effect, you can apply a drop shadow or motion blur to the quadrant sequence, smooth out the scaling and rotational movement by applying Ease In/Ease Out settings, crop the black lines at the edges of the clips, or alter the timing of the four clips within so that they reach the apex of their jumps as they scale down and vanish.

Changing the Render Order

Effects are rendered in a specific order in Final Cut Pro. Filters are applied in the order they are listed, from top to bottom, in the Filter tab of the Viewer. Rearranging the render order can change the resulting effect. For example, if you apply a Mask Shape filter after applying a Blur, the edge of the matte will be sharp, but the image behind the matte will be blurred. If you apply the matte first and then add the Blur, the edge of the matte will blur along with the rest of the image.

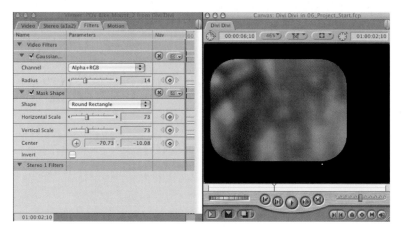

Blur before Mask Shape

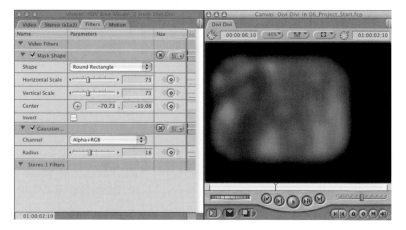

Mask Shape before Blur

Filters affect clips before motion parameters do. This is easy to remember, because the Filters tab appears to the left of the Motion tab in the Viewer—that is, first in reading order. So if you apply a distort filter, such as Wave or Ripple, and then reduce the size of the image, the filter will be applied before the scale operation. The distortion effect is limited to the clip's original size, so the effect may end abruptly at the edges of the clip.

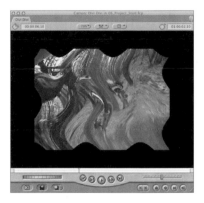 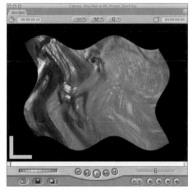

Wave filter first, scale second   Scale first, Wave filter second

If you scale the clip first and then apply the distortion to the reduced image, however, the edges of the clip will be properly processed, resulting in a clean edge.

Above you see the desired result, with no straight lines interrupting the wavy edges. To achieve it, you will use a nested sequence to work around Final Cut Pro's render chain.

1   Create a new sequence and call it *Render Order*. To make the effect more visible, set the Canvas background color to white using the Canvas View pop-up menu. Be sure your Selection tool is active.

2 Edit the clip **POV Bike Mount_2** into the new **Render Order** sequence.

3 With the Canvas in Image+Wireframe mode, drag one of the corner points with the Selection tool and scale the clip down to approximately 80 percent of its original size.

4 Double-click **POV Bike Mount_2** and select the Motion tab in the Viewer.

5 Check the Drop Shadow parameter box.

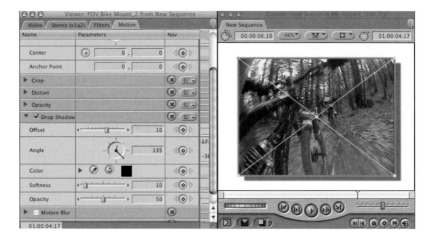

6 Select the clip in the Timeline and choose Sequence > Nest Items, or press Option-C.

7 Name the new sequence *POV Bike Mount Nested Sequence* and click OK.

8   Choose Effects > Video Filters > Distort > Ripple to apply a ripple
effect to the nested sequence.

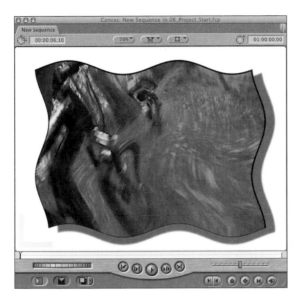

Applying the filter to the nested sequence allows the filtering effect
to be processed after the motion parameters are applied. In this case,
you can see how the drop shadow is distorted along with the image
itself.

Reordering Motion Effects

You can also use nesting to reorder effects within the Motion tab. In
an earlier exercise in this lesson, you changed an anchor point that
affected both scaling and rotation. Now let's change the anchor point
for the scaling, but leave rotation alone, by applying a second nesting
operation.

1   Open the **Split Screen 2** sequence.

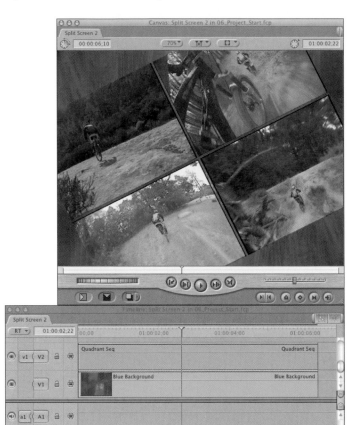

This sequence is just like the **Split Screen** sequence you modified earlier. The rotation has already been applied to the **Quadrant Sequence**, but the Scale and Anchor Point settings have not yet been modified.

2   Select **Quadrant Seq** and choose Sequence > Nest Items.

3   In the Nest Items dialog box, name the nested sequence *Rotating Quadrant Sequence* and set its frame size to 1140x760.

You made the nested sequence frame size larger to allow the clips plenty of room to rotate in virtual space without bumping into the edge of the frame.

4   Click OK.

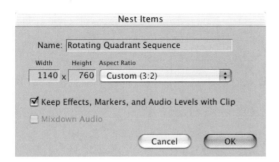

Although **Quadrant Sequence** is already a nested sequence, you can
nest it again. There is no limit to the number of times you can nest a
sequence.

5   Load **Rotating Quadrant Sequence** into the Viewer (using any of the
three methods you have learned earlier in this lesson) and click the
Motion tab.

6   Set a keyframe value of *100* in the Scale parameter at 01:00:01:00.

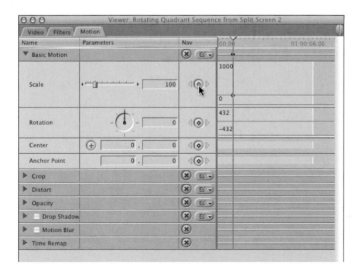

7   Set a second keyframe at 01:00:06:00 with a value of *0*.

8 Temporarily set the opacity for V2 to 20%, so you can see where to drag the anchor point.

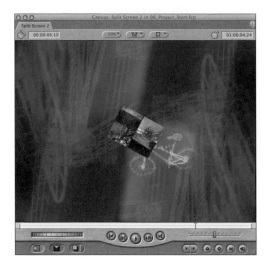

9 Press Home or drag the playhead to the beginning of the sequence.

10 Select the Distort tool and drag the center point of **Rotating Quadrant Sequence** to the approximate position of the bicycle.

11 Set Opacity back to 100% in the Motion tab of the Viewer. Render and play back your sequence.

The sequence will rotate around the center point of the four quadrants, but when it scales down, it will vanish into the center of the bike logo.

Mixing Sequence Sizes

The Nest Items dialog box allows you to modify the frame size for newly created nested sequences. Making use of variable frame size further expands the creative possibilities of nesting.

For example, if you want to build a background that comprises multiple video images and then pan across that background, you can construct a sequence with a large frame size, and then nest it into a standard NTSC-sized sequence. Let's do it.

1   Open the **Stacked** sequence from the Browser.

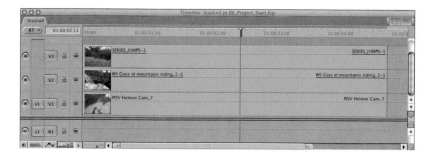

This sequence contains three clips that are stacked one on top of another. All are full-frame, standard DV resolution.

2   Select the three items and choose Sequence > Nest Items.

3   In the Nest Items dialog box, set the Aspect Ratio pop-up menu to Custom and define the new frame size as 2160x480. This is three times the width of a standard NTSC DV frame.

4   Name the new sequence *Wide Sequence* and click OK.

5   Double-click the new nest, **Wide Sequence**. A new Timeline tab appears.

The Canvas will display the wide sequence, reduced to fit into the viewable area, so that you can see your nonstandard frame size.

6   Set your Canvas background back to Black and then set the Canvas view to Image+Wireframe mode.

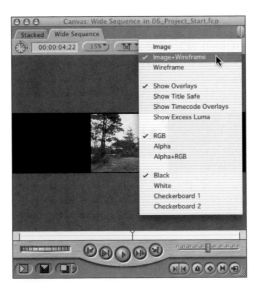

7   With the Selection tool, select the clip in track V3. Now, in the Canvas, drag the active (highlighted) clip to the left.

8 Now select the clip in track V2. Again, in the Canvas, drag this selected clip to the right of the frame.

All three clips should now appear side by side in the Canvas window.

9 Open a new text generator from the Generator pop-up menu in the Viewer.

10 Target track V3 and place the Timeline playhead in the center of the clips. Drag the Text clip from the Canvas to the Viewer and drop it on Superimpose. This places the text on a new track above the existing clips.

11 Double-click the text from track V4 in the Timeline to open it into the Viewer. It has now updated to the sequence size.

12 In the Controls tab in the Viewer, change the text to *Motocross*.

13 Set the text color to your liking. Set the font Size to 100.

The Canvas should update to reflect your changes.

14 In the Controls tab in the Viewer, use the Center control to adjust the text so that it is centered across the three images.

15 In the Canvas, click the **Stacked** tab to go back to the parent sequence. Currently, only the center portion of the nested **Wide Sequence** is visible in the parent sequence, because the parent sequence has a standard 720x480 DV NTSC frame size.

16 Set the Canvas Scale pop-up menu to Fit All so that you can see the entire wireframe boundary box of the nested sequence inside the **Stacked** parent sequence. It may help to think of this view as looking through the standard-sized window of the Stacked parent sequence into the wider nested sequence below.

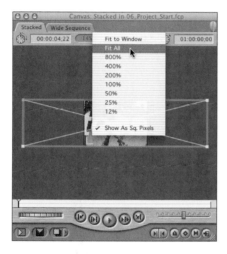

17 In the Canvas, drag the wireframe for the nested **Wide Sequence** to the right, until its left edge aligns with the visible area of your sequence.

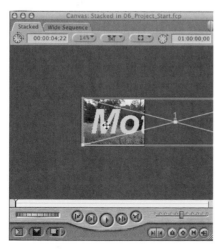

18 Press Home to move the playhead to the beginning of the sequence and then with the nest still selected, add a keyframe by clicking the Add Keyframe button in the Canvas, or by pressing Ctrl-K.

The wireframe for the nest turns green to indicate that a keyframe has been created.

19 Move the playhead to the last frame of the sequence.

20 In the Canvas, drag the nested sequence to the left until the right edge of the visible image aligns with the right edge of the boundary box. Use the white background to help guide your positioning.

A new keyframe is automatically added, and a motion path appears in the Canvas.

21 Render and play back your sequence. That's it!

Using Nesting as an Editing Tool

Although Final Cut Pro doesn't prevent you from building hours of program material in a single sequence, it's not the most efficient or practical way to work. When editing long format shows such as TV programming or feature films, most editors break the program into sections (often called scenes, reels, or segments) and treat each one as a separate sequence. When individual segments are complete, they are edited into a single main sequence for viewing and output.

To help you keep the terminology of nesting sequences straight, notice that when editors nest a scene or program segment into a longer main sequence, some will often call the main sequence a *master* sequence, instead of a *parent* sequence, and sometimes call the nested sequence a *subsequence* instead of a *nested* sequence. The differences in terminology are strictly a matter of preference. In Final Cut Pro, a master sequence is identical to a parent sequence, and a subsequence is identical to a nested sequence. Since the terms are often used interchangeably in everyday industry practice, we will use them interchangeably in this section, to help you get used to the terminology.

Nesting allows you to quickly rearrange entire segments so that you can experiment with scene order. You can manipulate the sequences as if they were a series of clips, trim nested sequences using the trimming tools, and add transition effects using In/Out points and Bézier handles. Nesting facilitates flexibility because you can modify individual scene sequences, and the master sequence will update to reflect the latest edits. Let's do some of these things now, starting with creating the master sequence.

1   Create a new sequence and name it **Master Sequence**.

2   Drag the **Stacked** sequence from the Browser directly into the Timeline.

The **Stacked** sequence is now nested in the master sequence, and is sometimes called a subsequence of the master sequence, in this situation. It looks small because the edit automatically reduces **Stacked** to 33.33%, due to the large format of **Wide Sequence**, which is nested inside of **Stacked**.

Mark a Sequence with In and Out Points

By setting an In or Out point in a sequence before you nest it, you define which portion of the sequence will be included in the master, or parent, sequence. Just like with editing a single clip, the portions of the sequence you want to nest that fall outside the In and Out points become handle frames, to accommodate transition effects, such as a cross dissolve, or close trimming of the edit points in the Timeline.

1   Double-click on the **Bike Jumps** sequence to open it in the Timeline.

2   Set an Out point at the end of the title on track V2.

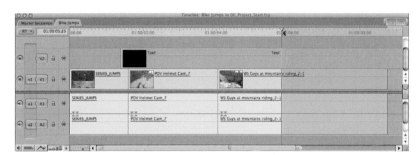

3   Click the **Master Sequence** tab in the Timeline to bring it to the foreground. Press the Down arrow or End key to make sure your playhead
is at the end of the sequence, one frame past the nested **Stacked** subsequence.

4   Edit **Bike Jumps** into **Master Sequence** by dragging it from the
Browser to the Canvas or Timeline.

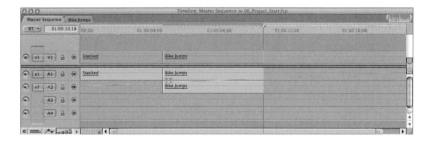

Now the master sequence contains two subsequences: **Stacked** and
Bike Jumps. Since nested subsequences follow all the standard rules of
three-point editing when edited into master sequences, the **Bike Jumps**
sequence ends in its master sequence at the Out point you designated
inside the **Bike Jumps** sequence, just like as if it were a clip and you
marked it with an Out point before editing it into the sequence.

Editing Within the Nested Sequence

Imagine these are the first two scenes of the finished program. You can continue to make editorial changes to clips inside the individual subsequences, and the master sequence will be updated automatically.

1 Place the playhead at the end of **Master Sequence**.

2 Press M to add a sequence marker.

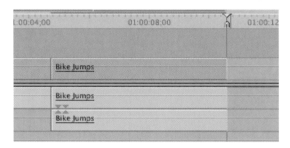

This marker will be used to illustrate how the editing changes in the nested sequences affect the parent sequence.

3 Double-click the **Stacked** sequence in the Browser to open it into its own Timeline tab.

4 Drag the clip **SERIES_JUMPS** from the Browser and drop it as an Insert edit at the end of the **Wide Sequence**.

5   Switch back to the **Master Sequence**.

When you added the clip to **Stacked** as an Insert edit, the master sequence was affected. In order to make room for the new clip, the sequence rippled to the right and the entire master sequence became longer, as you can see by the marker you added.

If you add, delete or trim the individual clips (or even another nested sequence) inside a nested subsequence—*that has no In or Out points marked in it*—the master sequence will ripple to the right or left, making the master sequence shorter or longer. Again, the editorial changes you make within the nested subsequences are automatically updated in the parent, as long as you have no In or Out point marked in the nested subsequence.

An Alternate Behavior

However, you should know that contrary to the trimming behavior of nested subsequences with no marked In or Out points, if you set an In or Out point in the nested subsequence *either before or after editing it into the master,* you will achieve somewhat different results.

1   Open the **Bike Jumps** sequence into the Timeline.

2   Drag the **SERIES_JUMPS** shot from the Browser into the Timeline to
add it to the end of this sequence.

Although this action makes this subsequence longer, the Out point set
earlier will still define the nested sequence's length within the parent,
master sequence.

3   Bring **Master Sequence** to the front.

Notice that nothing in **Master Sequence** has changed. Of course, you
can manually ripple the nested **Bike Jumps** subsequence in the master,
just like any clip, to reveal more of its content.

4   Using the Selection tool in the master sequence, drag the right edge of
the **Bike Jumps** subsequence to make it longer.

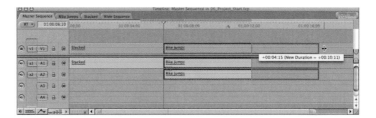

The additional content in the subsequence is now visible in **Master
Sequence**.

Editing the Content of a Subsequence

In all of the examples so far, you have been nesting several clips and treating
them as a whole to add effects or edits to a group of clips at one time.

Occasionally, you may need to perform a reverse technique to un-nest individual items within a nested sequence. This is necessary when making an Edit Decision List (EDL), which is a text list of all of the In and Out points for all of the clips in your sequence. If your master sequence contains a nested sequence comprising multiple clips, the EDL may mistakenly represent that nested sequence as a single clip. This will cause serious problems if you are using the EDL to re-create your sequence on another system.

1   Close all of your open sequences by closing the Canvas window.

2   Double-click on **complex sequence** in the Browser.

This sequence contains a series of clips, as well as a nested sequence. Nested sequences are a different shade than other clips in the Timeline.

The nested sequence **Complex Nest 1** is also located in the Browser. You will replace **Complex Nest 1** with the clips that comprise it, in its parent sequence.

3   Make sure snapping is enabled (N).

4   Select the **Complex Nest 1** sequence in the Browser and drag it over the Timeline. Position it directly over the exiting instance of the same nest, but do not release the mouse yet.

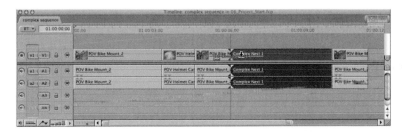

5 Press and hold the Cmd key.

The Timeline overlay identifies the individual clips within the sequence.

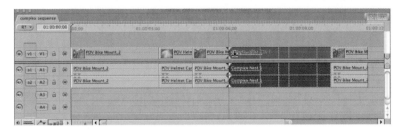

6 Make sure you are performing an Overwrite edit (not an Insert) by placing the cursor in the lower section of the Timeline track. Release the mouse to drop the five clips originally edited into **Complex Nest 1** as an Overwrite edit.

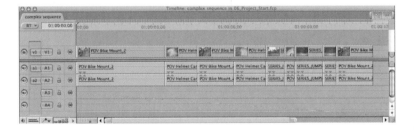

The nested sequence has been replaced by its original clip contents. You have "un-nested" the sequence, and your EDL will accurately reflect all of the individual clips used to build the master sequence.

NOTE ▸ After you complete this operation, there is no live link between the sequence and the individual clips. From this point forward, changes made to one clip will not affect the others.

Nesting is incredibly versatile. For audio-intensive projects, you can use nesting to combine groups of sounds to approximate the bussing features of audio-specific tools. For example, you might make a nest of different sound effects tracks, and then control the overall volume with a single slider. Or use nesting to output a sequence with Timecode Print filters applied to nests so that both sequence and source timecode are burned in on output to tape. As you become more adept at nesting, you will find countless ways to put it to use. Nesting is one of the fundamental tools for exploring the true depth and flexibility of Final Cut Pro.

What You've Learned

- Create nested sequences by dragging and dropping or use the Sequence > Nest Item command.

- Nested sequences contain live links to master, or parent, sequences, so changes made to one are also applied to the other.

- Final Cut Pro renders effects filters before motion parameters, unless you use nested layers to execute motion parameters before the effects filters.

- Nested sequences can contain other nested sequences.

- Nested sequences and their parent sequences are sometimes called subsequences and master sequences, in everyday industry practice.

- Perform an Overwrite edit with the Cmd key to "un-nest" a nested sequence from its parent, such as to create an accurate Edit Display List.

7

Lesson Files	Lessons > Lesson_07 > 07_Project_Start.fcp
	Lessons > Lesson_07 > 07_Project_Finished.fcp
Media	Media > Lesson_07_Media
Time	This lesson takes approximately 60 minutes to complete.
Goals	Learn how to apply various composite modes to clips
	Choose between the similar Add and Screen functions
	Create a "silk stocking" effect to soften and diffuse an image
	Project a video image onto a textured background element
	Modify opacity to lighten or darken a composite mode effect
	Combine composite modes with nesting effects

Lesson 7

Composite Modes

By now, you know how to add clips to multiple layers in the Final Cut Pro Timeline to create complex images and special effects. This lesson will introduce you to ways of combining, or *compositing*, images onscreen in order to create a wide variety of effects.

Understanding Composite Modes

In order to have more than one image occupy the same onscreen space and time, you must mix the two images together, or composite them. Final Cut Pro offers more than 10 composite modes. Each composite mode works by applying different mathematical equations to the pixels in the clips. You don't necessarily need to understand how the math works to use the different modes, but you do need to familiarize yourself with the look that each mode produces in order to know which one will best suit your needs.

1   Open the **07_Project_Start.fcp** file in the Lesson_07 folder.

2   Double-click on the **CompModes** clip in the Browser.

3   Play the clip in the Viewer.

   This clip contains examples of Final Cut Pro's various composite modes applied to the Sunset clip superimposed over a simple white-to-black vertical gradient.

   The gradient background is useful to help you understand how composite modes work. Some modes tend to make the overall image lighter; some tend to make it darker; others yield a combination of light and dark effects.

Applying a Composite Mode

To apply a composite mode, you must have two clips in your Timeline that overlap in space and time.

1   Double-click to open the **Basic** sequence in the Browser and play it back.

   You can view each clip by toggling the Track Visibility controls on and off.

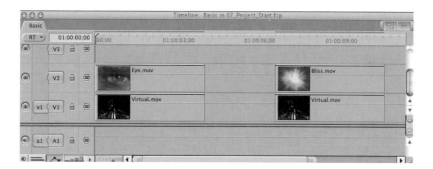

The **Basic** sequence contains two pairs of clips. You will apply a different composite mode to each one.

2   Select **Eye.mov** and choose Modify > Composite Mode > Add.

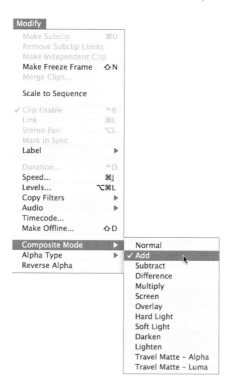

This mode adds the mathematical color value of each pixel to the clip beneath it. Areas that are black (0) remain unchanged (0 added to anything has no effect), whereas areas that are light in both images become brighter.

To view the playback of an effect, either render the sequence to see it in real-time or press Option-P to see it in "near-real-time."

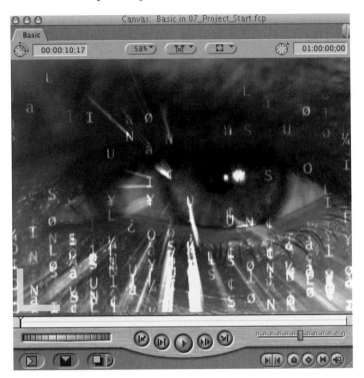

Add

Composite modes must be applied to the clip on the upper track. Applying a composite mode to a clip on track V1 will have no visible effect.

3   Position the playhead over the **Bliss.mov** clip.

4   Ctrl-click **Bliss.mov** to access the clip's contextual menu.

5   Choose Composite Mode > Subtract.

> **NOTE ▶** Changing a clip's composite mode from the contextual menu is the same as using the Modify menu.

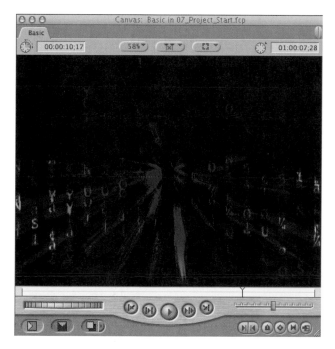

Subtract

Although the Subtract mode also performs a simple arithmetic operation on each pixel, the result may not be what you expect. Subtracting white from a color has the effect of inverting that color. Subtracting black always results in black.

Even if you can't follow the math that creates the various effects, you can learn by trial and error as you experiment with the various modes.

Experimenting with Modes that Lighten

Add, Screen, and Lighten are all similar modes that have an overall lightening effect when applied to a clip.

1   Open the **Lightening** sequence.

This sequence contains four sets of clips. The first three are identical, except that each has a different mode applied.

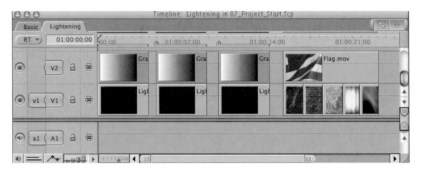

2   Render if necessary and play back the sequence to see the different effects.

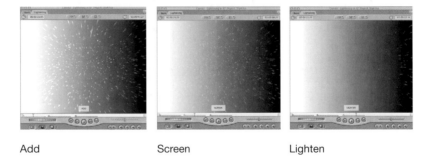

Add   Screen   Lighten

The Screen effect differs from the Add effect in that a ceiling is set at pure white, so no pixel will ever "bloom" and create the burning effect that the Add mode can create. The Lighten mode affects only pixels that are darker than 50% gray.

NOTE ▶ The Add mode can create clips that exceed broadcast-safe white levels. For more information on broadcast-safe levels, see Lesson 10.

3   Select **Flag.mov** and experiment with the Add, Screen, and Lighten modes to see the different results on each of the clips on V1.

You can easily see the difference in white levels between Add and Screen by viewing the sequence using the Waveform monitor in the Video Scopes and switching the composite mode for the V2 clip between Add and Screen.

Using Screen Mode to Create a Diffusion Effect

The Screen effect can be used to create a glowing diffusion effect to soften and brighten an image without losing any detail or sharpness. This is similar to what happens when you put a ProMist filter or a silk stocking on your camera lens.

1   Create a new sequence and name it *Silk Stocking*.

2   Edit **Lake** into the sequence on V1.

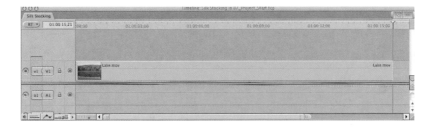

3   Duplicate **Lake** by Shift-Option-dragging the clip onto the V2 track, or use a Superimpose edit to edit another copy onto V2, above the V1 clip.

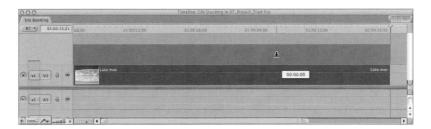

4   Select the clip on V1 and choose Effects > Video Filters > Blur > Gaussian Blur.

5   Double-click the clip to open it into the Viewer.

6   Click the Filters tab. The Blur controls should be visible.

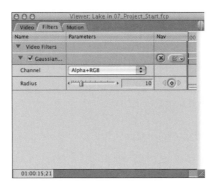

7   Set the Blur Amount to *10*.

The Canvas won't appear to change because the clip on V2 is completely obscuring the clip on V1 you are altering.

8   Select the clip on V2 and set the composite mode to Screen.

Before   After

You can expand this simple technique to create a wealth of unique and interesting effects. For example, instead of blurring the lower clip, try one of the Stylize filters at a low setting such as Diffuse or Find Edges. You can also experiment with different composite modes on the upper clip.

Using Screen Mode to Create a Lens Flare or Explosion Effect

Any time you want to add a bright light source such as a lens flare or an explosion to a clip without altering the overall look of the clip, Screen mode does the trick. It treats any black pixels as transparent, so even if your source clip has no predefined alpha channel (transparency), you can composite the clip successfully.

1   Using the sequence you just created, drag the **Ion Bubble** clip into the sequence on a track above the **Lake** shots.

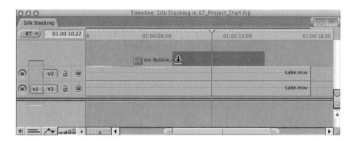

2   Set the composite mode for **Ion Bubble** to Screen.

3   Set the Canvas to Image+Wireframe.

4   Drag the **Ion Bubble** clip to the upper-left corner so that it looks like an explosion is occurring in the trees.

5   Render and play back the sequence.

Experimenting with Modes that Darken

Two of Final Cut Pro's composite modes typically darken the resulting composite: Multiply and Darken.

1   Open the **Darkening** sequence.

This sequence contains three sets of clips. The first two are set to Multiply and Darken, respectively.

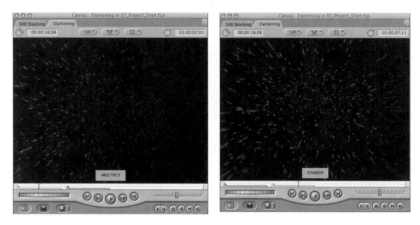

The difference between Multiply and Darken is similar to the difference between Screen and Lighten. Multiply treats white pixels as transparent and black pixels as opaque. The Darken mode affects only pixels brighter than 50% gray.

Multiply is one of the most commonly used composite modes. The pixel values in the two images are literally multiplied, but don't try to do the math yourself. The result merges the two images without adding brightness. This has the effect of combining the textures of the images into a single organic whole.

2   Select the **Flag.mov** clip on V2 and set the composite mode to Multiply.

3   Step through the clip to observe how the clip interacts with the different clips beneath it.

4   Set **Flag.mov** to Darken.

5   Observe the difference.

Using Multiply to Create a Textured Effect

The Multiply effect can be used to apply a texture from one clip to another.

1   Open the **Texture Text** sequence.

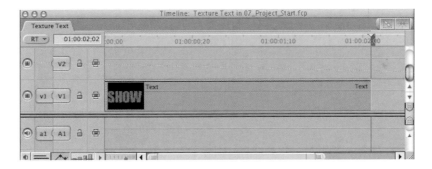

This sequence contains a text generator.

2   Drag **Stage** from the Clips bin in the Browser to the sequence and drop it on track V2 directly above the text clip.

3 Set the composite mode on **Stage** to Multiply.

The order of the clips affects how the composite mode is applied.

4 Reverse the order of the clips in the Timeline so **Text** is above **Stage**.

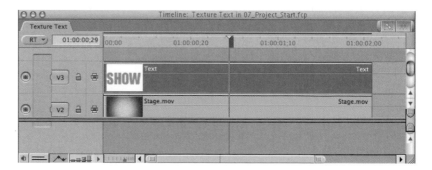

5   Set the composite mode for **Stage** to Normal.

6   Set the composite mode for **Text** to Multiply.

This gives the impression that the word *Show* is being projected onto a textured white background.

7 Delete the **Text** clip.

8 Drag the **Sunset** clip from the Browser into the sequence and place it on the track above the **Stage** clip.

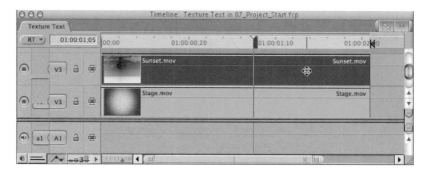

9 Set the composite mode for **Sunset** to Multiply.

The sunset clip looks like it is being projected onto the textured stage background. This trick is particularly effective when projected onto a static background image. Choose any texture file, such as a brick wall, canvas bag, or metal grate.

Using the Overlay Composite Mode

Overlay is a special composite mode that combines the effects of Screen and Multiply. Pixels darker than 50% gray are multiplied and clips lighter than 50% gray are screened. Overlay mode can be used when either a Multiply or Screen effect is too dramatic on its own.

1   Open the **Overlay** sequence.

2   Set the composite mode for the **Gradient** to Multiply.

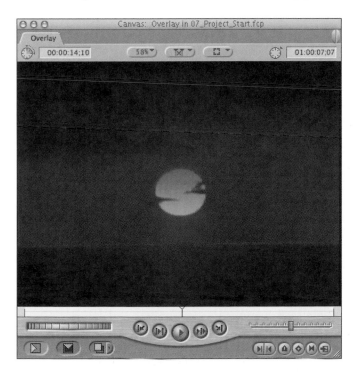

This composite effect is much too dark.

3   Set the composite mode for the **Gradient** to Screen.

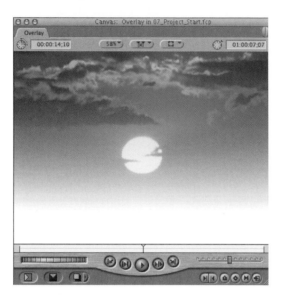

Now the whiter areas of **Gradient** wash out much of the sunset.

4   Set the composite mode to Overlay.

Now the dark areas successfully sharpen the sky, and the lighter areas sharpen the ocean.

5 Toggle the track visibility of the **Gradient** on V2 to see the difference.

Using Subtract and Difference Modes

The Subtract and Difference composite modes work similarly to the Invert filter (which we'll address next) in that they have the effect of changing pixel colors to values on the opposite side of the color wheel, depending on the clips that are being composited. There is no obvious application for Subtract and Difference modes when creating effects that suggest a real-world environment, but they can be used to create a variety of interesting specialized effects. Using black-and-white clips makes it easier to see how these modes work.

1 Open the **Subtract & Difference** sequence.

This sequence contains two pairs of clips. The first pair is monochromatic, and the second is full color.

2 Set the composite mode of **Binary Scan Vertical.mov** to Subtract.

This subtracts the pixel values of the two clips. Just like the opposite of adding, this tends to darken the image. If a pixel's combined value equals 0 or less it is represented as black.

3   Set the composite mode of **Binary Scan Vertical.mov** to Difference.

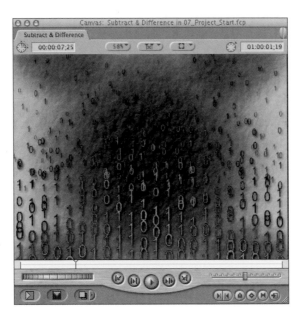

Difference creates a much more complex combination of the two images. Whereas Subtract stops at absolute zero (black) with its math, Difference will invert the image if the value goes below zero. In general, Difference results in a much more interesting and complex composite than Subtract.

Making Composite Effects More Versatile with the Invert Filter

You can use the Invert filter to modify one of the composited clips to reverse the effect of the composite mode. This trick can be employed with any composite mode setting, but it is most effective with the Subtract and Difference modes.

1   Select **Binary Scan Vertical.mov** and choose Effects > Video Filters > Channel > Invert.

2   Change the composite mode of **Binary Scan Vertical.mov** back to Subtract.

The Invert filter gives you two additional ways to use the effect.

Using Subtract and Difference with Color Clips

1   Select the **Pulse Rate.mov** clip and set the composite mode to Subtract.

Subtract   Difference

When subtracting one color from another, you may have unexpected results.

2   Select **Pulse Rate.mov** and set the composite mode to Difference.

3   Render and play back.

The Difference filter creates a rainbow on the pulse line as it moves across the variously colored pixels in the face and eye.

Modifying the Opacity of Composited Clips

You can further vary a composite mode's effect by altering a clip's opacity. Because changing the transparency of a clip can mute its colors or otherwise change its appearance, changing a clip's opacity can have dramatic effects on how the composite mode works.

1   Turn on Clip Overlays by clicking the button in the lower-left corner of the Timeline.

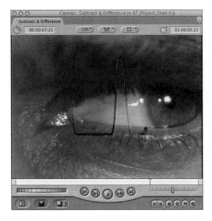 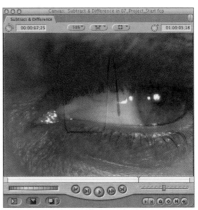

100% opacity   25% opacity

2 Adjust the opacity of **Pulse Rate.mov** to about 25%.

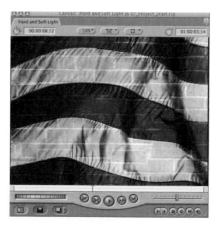

Reducing the opacity causes the colored highlights to disappear and the composited clip to become more integrated with the background clip. Whenever you experiment with composite modes, remember to adjust the clip's opacity to vary the effect.

Using Hard Light and Soft Light Modes

The Hard Light and Soft Light composite modes are designed to create the effect that the clip is being projected onto the background image either as a hard, high-contrast light source or as a soft, diffused light source that yields softer shadows.

1 Double-click on the **Hard and Soft Light** sequence to open it in the Browser.

2 Set the composite mode on **Flag.mov** to Hard Light.

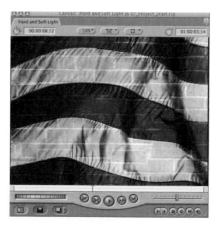

Hard light

3 Render and play back the sequence.

The four background clips illustrate how the effect looks when applied on various images. Notice how the shadows and folds of the flag are accentuated.

4 Set the composite mode of **Flag.mov** to Soft Light.

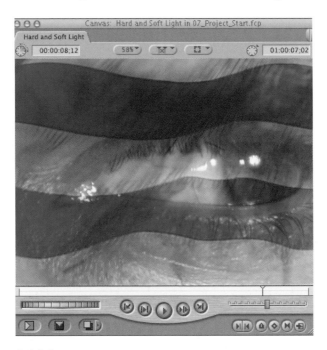

Soft light

In this mode, the white stripes become almost entirely transparent. The texture of the flag is softened, and the background becomes more prominent.

Complex Composite Mode Effects

Once you get the hang of the different composite modes, you'll find which ones you like best for different situations. In some cases, you can combine effects for even greater flexibility.

Combining Modes on Multiple layers

Every clip in a sequence has a composite mode that determines how it is mixed with the clips beneath it in the Timeline. In all of the previous examples, there have been only two clips in the Timeline. But sometimes you may want to composite three or more clips.

1   Open the **Complex** sequence.

This sequence contains the **Sunset Over Sea.mov** clip. In this exercise, you will make the clip look like it was shot on film, and that the film reel ran out during the filming.

2   Set an Out point at the end of the clip in the Timeline.

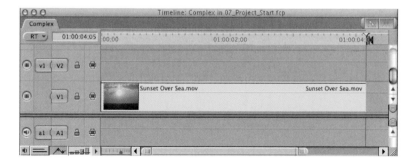

3   Edit the **Tail Burn 2** clip from the Clips bin in the Browser window onto track V2 in the Timeline. You may find that dropping the clip into the Canvas Superimpose overlay (with track V1 as the destination

track) works well when working with multiple layers of clips and composite modes.

The clip should appear on track V2 and end on the same frame as the Sunset clip.

4   Set the composite mode of **Tail Burn 2** to Screen.

5   Edit the **Film Scratch** clip from the Clips bin in the Browser to track V3 of the Timeline. It should line up with the beginning and end of the Sunset clip.

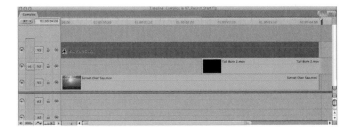

6   Set the composite mode of **Film Scratch.mov** to Subtract.

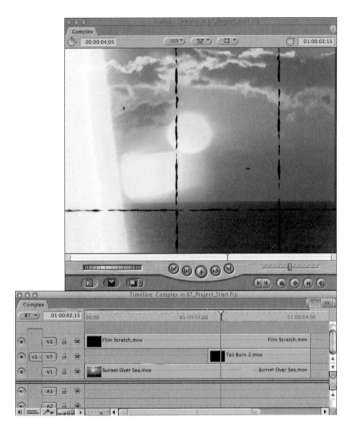

7   Render and play back your sequence.

Now the Sunset clip appears to have been taken from the very end of a scratched-up roll of film.

Use Nesting to Control and Combine Composite Modes

Sometimes, simply compositing one clip on top of another won't create your desired effect. You may want to control how one combined shot is composited with a third clip.

1   Create a new sequence by pressing Cmd-N. Name it *The Eye*.

2   In the Viewer window, access the Generators pop-up menu and load a
text generator.

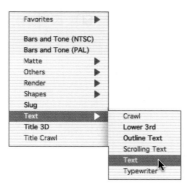

3   Click the Controls tab and type *EYE* into the text field. Use the default
font (Lucida Grande) and set the Size to 200. Make the Style bold and
the Font Color pink.

4   Edit the text clip into the sequence.

5   Return to the Generators pop-up and choose Render > Gradient to
load a gradient into the Viewer. Leave all the controls at their default
settings.

6 Edit **Gradient** to the track above the Text clip in the sequence.

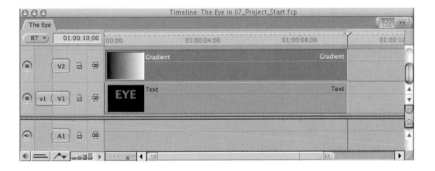

7 Set the composite mode of **Gradient** to Multiply.

This applies **Gradient** to the color of the text, leaving the remainder of the clip black.

8 Drag the two clips from tracks V1 and V2 onto V2 and V3.

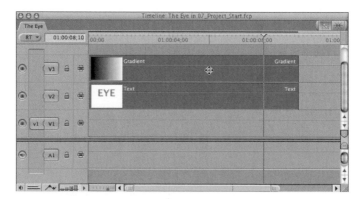

This makes room to use another clip as a background.

9 Drag **Eye** from the Clips bin in the Browser onto track V1 directly
beneath the two clips.

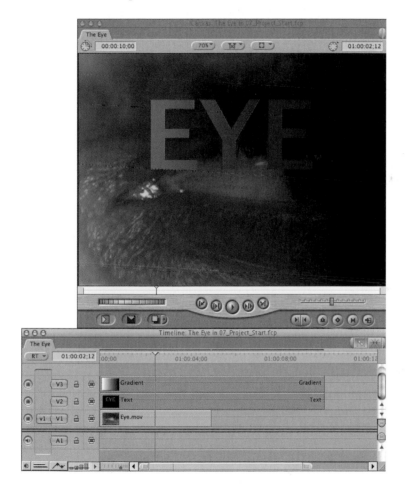

Because of the way composite modes work, the gradient on track V3
is darkening the right side of the **Eye** clip as well as the text on V2.
To eliminate this undesired effect, you must nest the clips on tracks
V2 and V3.

10 Select the **Text** and **Gradient** clips.

11 Choose Sequence > Nest Items.

The Nest Items dialog box appears.

12 Name the new sequence *Gradient Text* and click OK.

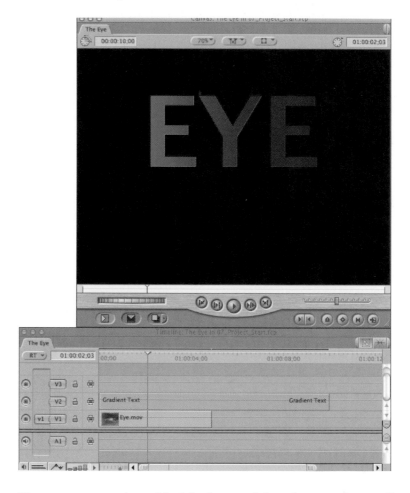

The new sequence has a black background that obscures the eye clip entirely.

13 Select **Gradient Text** and set the composite mode to Screen.

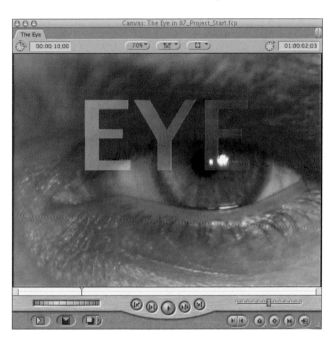

Now the gradated text is screened on top of the video clip. You could also try other modes such as Difference or Subtract to create alternate effects.

What You've Learned

- The effect of a composite mode varies depending on which clip is on top.
- Use the Screen composite mode to create a glowing diffusion or a lens flare effect.
- Apply an Invert filter to a composited clip to invert the effect.
- Modify a clip's opacity to lighten a composite mode.
- Nesting clips allows you to control how composite modes affect three or more clips.

8

Lesson Files   Lessons > Lesson_08 > 08_Project_Start.fcp

        Lessons > Lesson_08 > 08_Project_Finished.fcp

Media   Media > Lesson_08_Media

Time   This lesson takes approximately 60 minutes to complete.

Goals   Create travel matte composites

        Use travel mattes to create such effects as video-in-text

        Learn about the elements needed to achieve results with alpha and luma travel mattes

        Learn how to use gradients to improve the look of your travel matte effects

Travel Mattes

In this lesson, you will learn about travel mattes. Travel mattes offer another way to composite two images together, and are commonly used to create a video-in-text effect. That's where a video image is matted inside the shape of text. We'll use travel mattes to create a video-in-text effect, as well as explore some other scenarios where a travel matte is the perfect choice, including a gradient filter effect, dynamic lower-third backgrounds, and for revealing portions of video images.

What Are Travel Mattes?

First let's distinguish the differences between standard mattes (and masks) versus travel mattes. A standard matte is a filter used to cut out, or crop, an image by using defined points or shapes, leaving part of the frame transparent. Conventional matte treatments include 4- and 8-point garbage mattes to crop out miscellaneous parts of an image before blue- or green-screen keying. (Keying will be discussed in Lesson 9.)

Before   After

Travel mattes work a little differently in that they are more like compositing than matting. A travel matte is not a filter like a standard matte. A travel matte is a composite mode used to combine elements of two different images. Using a travel matte, one video image is matted by another.

Assume for a moment that you want to cut out an image in the shape of a word. This can be done by creating a travel matte that combines a video clip and a text clip. When the video is matted by the text, it appears as video-in-text.

There are two types of travel mattes: alpha and luma. Both are used to combine two images, yet they use different information to create the matte, as you will see during this lesson.

Alpha Travel Mattes

An alpha travel matte uses the transparency (alpha channel) from one clip to matte another clip.

Creating an Alpha Travel Matte

Let's give it a try.

1   Open Lesson_08 > **08_Project_start.fcp**.

2   If the **Travel Mattes1** sequence is not in front in the Timeline, click its Timeline tab to bring it to the front.

3   Move the Timeline playhead to the first clip in the Timeline, **circuit board**. This is one of the two clips you will use in this exercise.

4   Move the playhead to the next clip in the Timeline, a text generator.

    This clip will be used to matte the first clip, as you will see next.

5   Drag **circuit board** over the text clip, as shown, and drop it on V2.

6 Highlight the video clip on V2 and choose Modify > Composite Mode > Travel Matte - Alpha. Instantly, you should see a video-in-text effect.

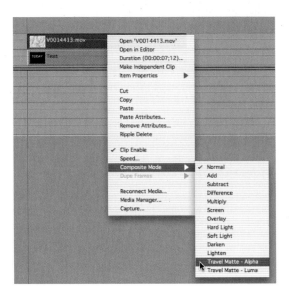

TIP ▶ You can also Ctrl-click a clip directly in the Timeline and choose Composite Mode > Travel Matte - Alpha from the contextual menu.

7 Render the composite and play it back.

This is one way to use a travel matte, to composite two clips. The top clip (also called the source clip) is a video image that is stamped into the shape of text. It is placed on a higher video track. The bottom clip (or the matte clip) is a text generator that contains an alpha channel. Any clip that has an alpha channel can be used to matte a source clip with an alpha travel matte. The matte clip is placed on a video track just below the source clip.

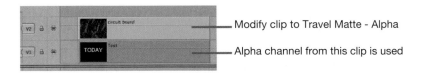

— Modify clip to Travel Matte - Alpha

— Alpha channel from this clip is used

To Blur or Not to Blur

When using travel mattes to create a video-in-text effect, you have the choice of whether or not you want to see the video clearly in the text. In other words, do you want to discern the content of the scene clearly, or is the video in the text simply a way to add texture to the text? In this exercise, you will blur the video clip to alter the result of the travel matte, creating a more subtle effect that shifts the emphasis from the video image to the text.

1 Double-click the **circuit board** clip in the Timeline to load it into the Viewer, and then click the Filters tab.

2 Choose Effects > Video Filters > Blur > Gaussian Blur to apply a Gaussian Blur filter.

3 Change the Radius of the blur to about *30*.

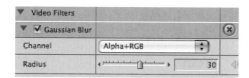

As you adjust the slider (increase the blur), watch the result in the Canvas.

The higher the blur, the less defined the image, eventually giving way to just a blur of light and color by the time the Radius is 30.

4 Render the composite and play it back.

The video in the text plays back as subtle shifts in light, color, and movement.

TIP ▶ When you want to create this type of textured text, choose a source clip with high-contrast areas, camera or subject movement, or varying color.

Adding a Background

When applying a travel matte, the source clip is matted into the shape of the matte clip, creating transparency in the resulting composite. At first, it may appear as though you have created video-in-text against a black background. If the composite is left as is, then this would be a black background, but there are many more possibilities.

1 Click the View menu in the Canvas to choose a checkerboard background.

Notice that the only portion of the image that is opaque (solid) is the shape of the text. The rest of the frame is transparent.

Because the travel matte has left a fairly large part of the frame transparent, any clip may be placed below the travel matte composite in the Timeline to create a background.

2 Switch the Canvas background back to Black.

3 Move the travel matte composite up one video track in the Timeline.

TIP To quickly move a clip or group of clips up in the Timeline, highlight both clips and press Option-up arrow.

4 Open the Clips bin in the Browser and locate the clip **sparkling water**. Edit it to V1 in the Timeline, under the composite. You now have added a background to the video-in-text effect.

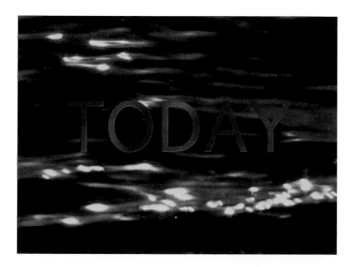

5   Optionally, add a sepia filter to the **circuit board** clip on V3 so that the text's hues are closer to the colors of the background. Choose Effects > Video Filters > Image Control > Sepia.

As you have now seen, the video used in the travel matte can be altered with filters, such as Gaussian Blur and Sepia, to create an entirely new look.

Fine-Tuning Travel Mattes

There are numerous ways to modify a travel matte composite, but the result will depend on which clip is altered. In the next exercise, you will make adjustments to the source clip, the matte clip, and the two clips together.

Adjust Source and Matte Clips Independently

Use the following steps to alter the results by making adjustments to each clip on its own.

1   Open the **Travel Mattes2** sequence by clicking on its tab in Timeline. (If it is not open, open it from the Browser.)

2   Move the playhead over the composite in the Timeline.

The clip **sunset on beach** is on V2. A text clip of the word "SUNSET" is on V1. The composite shows the video of the beach seen through the text. (A travel matte composite mode has been applied to the top clip.)

NOTE ▶ This text clip is created with a wide, heavy font so that you can see the matted image more clearly.

3   Switch to Image+Wireframe in the Canvas.

4   Select the video clip on V2 in the Timeline to activate its wireframe in the Canvas.

5   Shift-drag the active wireframe in the Canvas downward until you
can see the sun in the text. Pressing Shift while dragging constrains the
movement to only one direction, such as up and down or left and right.

Moving the source clip reveals different parts of the video seen in
the text.

6   Press Shift and grab a corner point of the Canvas wireframe, then
drag inward a bit to make the image smaller. Release before the
image is smaller than the text. Pressing Shift while you drag scales
the image out of proportion, making it possible to fit more of the
video frame inside the text.

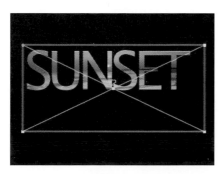

7   Select the text clip in the Timeline to activate its wireframe.

8   In the Canvas, click and drag on the text clip. Notice that the video remains still while the text moves, revealing different areas of the video image.

This would be undesirable if you wanted to move the text to a new location and still see the same area of the video in the text.

9   Press Cmd-Z to undo the text move in the Canvas.

10   Select *both* clips in the Timeline. In the Canvas, you should see both wireframes active.

11 In the Canvas, click and drag on either wireframe and move it around the screen.

The two clips reposition together. Depending on your goal, you can adjust the video seen in the text by moving the source clip's wireframe independently, or you can move the two wireframes together to reposition the text and video as one unit, keeping the video that is visible through the text the same.

Modify the Composite as a Whole

When you nest two clips together, you are able to treat them as one clip, and affect the entire composite as a single item when applying effects, animating a motion path, changing the scale, or other motion effect. When you create a motion path for the nest that contains the clips, as you will do next, all the clips move together in unison on the screen, because the animation is applied to the nest, instead of applied to one clip or the other.

Now you will animate the travel matte composite you have built so that it travels from one side of the screen to the other.

1 In the Timeline, highlight both clips of the travel matte composite.

2 Choose Modify > Nest Items (Option-C).

3 In the Nest Items dialog box, change the name to *Nested Composite* and then click OK.

4 Once the clips are nested, select the nest in the Timeline to activate its wireframe in the Canvas.

5 Click and drag the wireframe to the left until it is almost fully outside the frame.

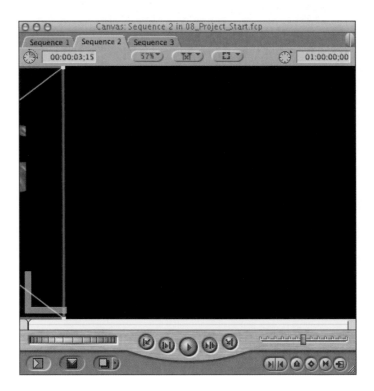

6 In the Canvas, choose Zoom > Fit All.

This resizes the Canvas view so that you can see the wireframe outside of the frame.

7   Continue to drag the clip to the left until it is fully out of the frame.

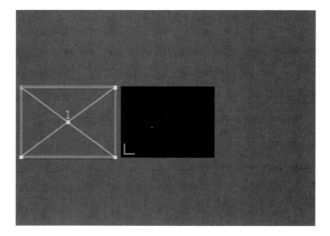

8   Press Home to move to the playhead to the head of the sequence (and the nest).

9   Set a keyframe at this point in the Canvas.

> **TIP** ▶ Ctrl-click the Add Keyframe button and choose Center to set a keyframe only for the Center point and not for all the motion settings.

10   Move the playhead near to the end of the nest in the Timeline.

11   In the Canvas, drag the wireframe to the right until it exits the frame.

You should now see a motion path from one side of the screen to the other.

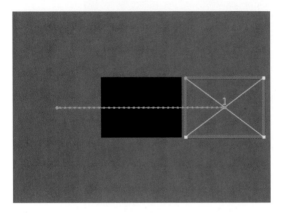

12 Render the animation and play it back.

In this exercise, you used nesting to treat the travel matte composite as one item, which made it easier to animate the two clips together.

Using a Gradient Source Clip

Any video or graphic can be used as the source clip in a travel matte, and using a gradient yields many interesting effects.

1 Open the **Travel Mattes2** sequence if it is not already open in the Timeline.

2 From the Generator pop-up menu in the Viewer, choose Render > Custom Gradient.

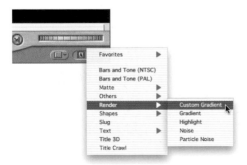

3   Edit this gradient into the Timeline on V2, into a blank space on the Timeline, to the right of the previous composition. Adjust it to a duration of four seconds.

4   Double-click the gradient from the Timeline to reopen it into the Viewer to modify it.

5   Click the Controls tab in the Viewer.

6   Set the Gradient Direction angle to 180 degrees, the Gradient Width to about 30, and set the Start coordinates to about 0, –100, to move the line of the gradient up the screen a bit. (There are two Start parameters; use the one nearer the top.)

Optionally, you can add a Gaussian Blur filter (set to 20) to soften the edge of the gradient clip a bit.

7   Create a new text clip. Use a somewhat wide font and large point size, such as 100-point Impact.

8   Edit this text clip to V1 in the Timeline, directly beneath the gradient.

9   Select the gradient clip in the Timeline and change its composite mode to Travel Matte-Alpha.

Depending on where the line of the gradient is, at this point you might see an image similar to this illustration, a full black frame, or text that is all white.

10   Select the gradient clip in the Timeline to activate its wireframe in the Canvas.

11   Click the gradient wireframe in the Canvas and slide it up or down in small increments to reveal the line of the gradient. Release when the line of the gradient is visible in the letters of the text.

There are many ways to use this effect by playing with the gradient and its position. You can make the text look as though it was fading away, with just the top of the text barely visible, for example. Or you can change the colors of the gradient to create other looks. If you animate the center point of the gradient clip itself, you can start with the text as one color, and transition over time into another hue.

TIP ▶ The Highlight Gradient can also be used to create the effect shown in the following figure.

Luma Travel Mattes

So far you've looked only at alpha travel mattes, but there is another type of travel matte available in Final Cut Pro: the luma travel matte. Luma travel mattes also produce an image matted by a clip placed below it, but they use luminance (brightness) levels of the clip image instead of an alpha channel to determine whether a pixel remains solid (opaque) or becomes transparent.

Here's how it works: Wherever there is pure black in the matte clip's luminance information, the matte is fully opaque and none of the source image on top (sometimes called the foreground image) shows through to the final composite you see in the Canvas. On the other hand, wherever there is pure white in the matte clip's luminance information, the matte clip is fully transparent, and all the pixels in the source image on top (foreground) show through the matte and are therefore preserved in the final composite. The really interesting stuff happens where there are shades of gray, which results in semi-transparency in the final composited image.

Let's dive into a few real-world scenarios where a luma travel matte is ideal for creating an effect.

Blending Two Images in a Luma Matte

In the last exercise, you used a gradient generator as a source clip. Now, you will use a gradient as a matte clip. As a default gradient ranges from black to white, it combines the two extremes used by a luma travel matte. Next, let's spend a moment seeing how grayscale information relates to matting an image.

1   Locate the clip **sunset on beach** from the Browser, and edit it to a blank area of the **Travel Mattes2** Timeline on V1.

2   Locate the clip **kelp forest and fish** in the Browser and edit it to the Timeline on V3, above the **sunset on beach**, leaving track V2 empty at this point.

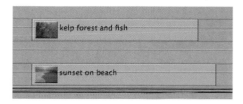

The images of these two clips will be blended together in the next steps.

3   Load a custom gradient into the Viewer, from the Generator > Render pop-up menu in the Viewer.

4   Edit the gradient onto V2, between the two clips already on V1 and V3.

5   Trim down all three clips to be the same length.

6   In the Timeline, Ctrl-click on the clip on V3 and choose Composite Mode > Travel Matte-Luma from the contextual menu.

In the Canvas, notice the result is a split screen of sorts. In the center of the screen, the two images blend together.

7   Compare the image in the Viewer and the Canvas to get a better idea of how the gradient on V2 is being used to blend together the clips on V1 and V3, based on the luminance (brightness) values of each pixel.

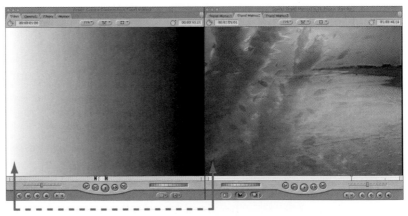

White in gradient   V3 image is preserved

Wherever the gradient is white, the image on V3 is preserved in the composite. Wherever there is black in the gradient, V3 is transparent and only V1 is visible. Wherever the gradient is gray, there is semi-transparency.

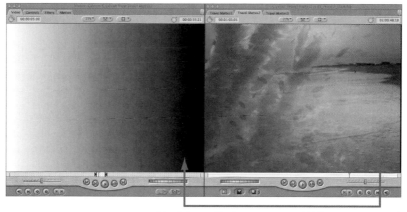

Black in gradient   V1 image preserved

8   In the Canvas, choose View > Image to turn off the wireframe.

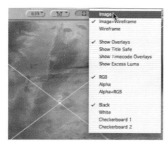

9   Double-click the gradient in the Timeline to open it back into the Viewer.

10   In the Viewer, click the Controls tab of the gradient.

11   To make the gradation line a bit smaller, change Gradient Width to *75*.

This adds a bit more contrast between the two images, as the left and right edges of the frame become less transparent. It also pushes the gradient line to the left too much, which you will correct next.

12 To reposition the gradient line, click the crosshair button next to Start. The button darkens when activated.

13 Move the cursor to the Canvas. The cursor appears as a crosshair.

14 Click and hold in the middle of the Canvas (do not release the mouse).

15 Drag left and right to see the line of the gradient change. It will continuously update as you move the cursor.

16 Release when the line is somewhat centered in the screen and you see an equal mix of the two images.

17 Set Gradient Direction to *135* to make a diagonal transition between the clips.

18 Because this last action also impacts the line of the gradient, use the Start crosshair to fine-tune the positioning of the gradient line to create a more equal mix of the two images.

19 Render and play back the composite.

This type of effect can also be used effectively in a narrative situation, as a way to show simultaneous action in two different scenes. It is also more film-like than a straight split screen.

Creating a Grad Filter Effect

Another handy use of a gradient as the matte clip is to emulate a grad lens filter. Grad is short for gradient. A grad lens filter graduates from clear to a color tint or a neutral density. Cinematographers often use grad filters to alter part of the frame without affecting the whole frame. Although a common use of these filters is to darken or intensify the color of a sky, grad filters can be used in a variety of situations.

In this exercise, you will use a gradient generator and a travel matte to intensify the color of the sky as if a grad filter had been used on the video camera.

1 Locate clip **L5-castlepeak-1** in the Browser and edit it into a blank spot in the **Travel Mattes2** Timeline on V1.

2 Duplicate this clip by Shift-Option-clicking on the clip, and then dragging upward. Place the copy on V3, leaving V2 empty. (Pressing

Option duplicates the clip; pressing Shift constrains the movement of the clip to one direction—up/down or left/right.)

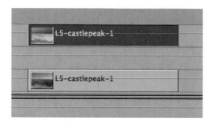

Now you'll blend parts of these two clip's images together to create the grad filter effect.

3   Select the clip on V3 and apply a brightness/contrast filter by choosing Effects > Video Filters > Image Control > Brightness/Contrast.

4   Open the V3 instance of **L5-castlepeak-1** into the Viewer and on the Filters tab, adjust the Brightness to approximately –25.

Now you'll add the gradient.

5   Edit a new custom gradient onto track V2, between the two video clips already in the Timeline, on V1 and V3. (Again, to access the custom gradients, click the Generator pop-up menu in the Viewer and choose Render > Custom Gradient.)

6   Open the gradient back into the Viewer and click on the Controls tab.

7   On the Controls tab in the Viewer, set the Gradient Direction angle to *180* to make it horizontal.

8   Set Gradient Width to about *50* to start. You will come back to these controls to fine-tune them later.

9   Ctrl-click the video clip on V3 and choose Composite Mode > Travel Matte-Luma from the contextual menu.

After the travel matte is applied to the clip on V3, then the gradient will serve to reveal the top of the clip on V3 (the darkened clip), and reveal the bottom part of the original, untouched clip from V1. In the Canvas, you should now see that the top of the image is dark, and the bottom of the image is normal.

10   Click the Video tab in the Viewer.

Notice the position of the gradient line and where that relates to the composite seen in the Canvas. The line separating the two images will still need to be fine-tuned because right now it falls in the greenery of the scene and should only be affecting the sky.

Clip on V3

Clip on V1

Next, you'll adjust the gradient so the lighter clip on V1 reveals the ground portion of the frame, and the darker clip on V3 reveals the sky portion of the frame. Additionally, setting the gradient line near the horizon line can help to disguise it and create a more realistic result.

11   Click back on the Controls tab of the Viewer to make adjustments to the gradient.

12 Click the crosshair for Start to activate it.

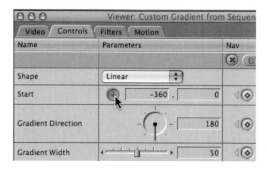

13 Move the cursor to the Canvas and click with the crosshair about two-thirds of the way up the screen.

This is a general starting point. You will need to fine tune this positioning a bit after the next step.

14 Change the Gradient Width to about *30*.

You should now see an image similar to the next example.

15 Continue to fine-tune the gradient Width, Start, or Direction as needed so that the line of the gradient is somewhat hidden along the horizon.

A Less-Than-Realistic Grad Filter Effect

Now you will continue to tweak the grad filter effect to produce a look that is bolder and somewhat surreal.

1 Add a Gaussian Blur filter to the gradient and set the Radius to *40*.

This will help to soften the line of the gradient as you intensify the look of the clip on V3 in the next steps.

2 On the Controls tab of the gradient, set the Gradient Direction angle to about *170* degrees.

3   Click the Start crosshair on the Controls tab in the Viewer and set it to the top-left corner of the Canvas, as shown in the following figure.

4   Adjust the Gradient Width as desired.

5   Open the clip on V3 into the Viewer and go to the Filters tab.

6   Set Brightness to about *−50* in the Brightness/Contrast filter.

7   Experiment with other variations by adding additional effects filters to the clip on V3 and/or modifying different elements of the gradient, this time without concern for hiding the line of the gradient.

Creating a Lower Third Gradient Background

In this exercise, you will create a luma travel matte (using a gradient as the matte clip) that produces a semi-transparent background that starts as a solid color on one end and becomes transparent on the other end. This techniques makes a lower third title stand out more distinctly than a plain solid background or no background at all.

1   Open the **Travel Mattes3** sequence.

This sequence contains a title over a video image. The title has no backdrop, and is fairly mundane. Let's spice it up with a new background.

2   Drag the text clip up to V4 to make room for a new text background.

TIP▶ Press Shift as you drag upward to constrain movement to one direction.

3   Open a color matte from the Generator pop-up menu in the Viewer. Keep the color somewhat dark and rich—no light pastels.

4   Edit this color matte to the Timeline on V3, just under the text clip. This clip will be the source clip when you create a travel matte.

5   Next, create a custom gradient. The default custom gradient is fine for now.

6   Edit this gradient clip to V2, just above the clip **rocky coast**.

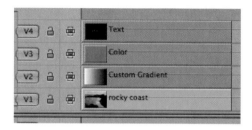

Your Timeline should look similar to the example shown here.

7   Select the color matte on V3 and apply a luma travel matte to this clip.

The color matte now graduates from your selected color to transparent, which is what you are aiming for. Currently, though, it fills the whole frame, which is not part of the final look.

8   Select the Crop tool and in Image+Wireframe mode in the Canvas, crop down the top and bottom of the color matte to see only a narrow horizontal band across the screen, surrounding the text.

The effect is nearly complete, but the line of the gradient could be enhanced a bit.

9 Open the gradient clip into the Viewer and adjust the Gradient Width to around *70*. This will make the gradient start to drop off a little closer to the center of the screen.

10 Optionally, you could move the Start of the gradient out more to the right (like the middle of the screen). This would make the left side of the color matte more dense and solid.

What You've Learned

- A travel matte composites two images together, resulting in the top (foreground) image being matted into the bottom (background) image, based on the luminance or alpha channel of a third matte clip, placed between them on the Timeline.

- An alpha travel matte uses the grayscale values of an alpha channel from the matte clip to composite one clip into another clip.

- A luma travel matte uses luminance values (brightness) of the pixels in the image of the matte clip itself, rather than an alpha channel, to composite one clip into another clip.

- Travel mattes are useful to create such effects as video-in-text, text that is fading away, a grad filter effect, and a lower third background.

9

Lesson Files	
Media	Media > Lesson_09_Media
Time	This lesson takes approximately 60 minutes to complete.
Goals	Identify good footage for keying
	Use the Chroma Keyer filter to create a transparent matte
	Modify the Chroma Keyer filter parameters over time
	Combine a foreground and background to make a composite
	Fine-tune a key through thinning, softening, and enhancing edges
	Apply color smoothing to DV footage before keying
	Apply spill suppression to eliminate unwanted remnants
	Eliminate unwanted edge elements with a garbage matte

Lesson 9

Keying

The Color Key is one of the most powerful and most commonly used tools in your compositing arsenal. It allows you to isolate (or matte) a foreground subject from its background and combine it with a different shot (often referred to as a plate). The key effect works by identifying all of the pixels of a certain color and making them transparent, so only the remaining pixels are visible. This is how Superman can appear to fly, or how a dinosaur can appear in the same shot as real actors.

The color used for keying is typically green or blue. This is because the most common subject is a human being, and human skin color falls on the opposite side of the color wheel from green and blue. But a key can be created from nearly any solid color. For example, if you were shooting a product shot of a green car, you might place it against a solid red background. Because there is nearly no overlap between green and red, Final Cut Pro would easily isolate all of the red pixels, leaving the green car to be composited onto a mountain top, inside a volcano or wherever you desire.

Identifying Good Source Footage

Keying is a very specialized craft. You can produce good results only when you start with shots that have been photographed against a solid background of a particular color expressly for the purpose of *pulling* a key. Although Final Cut Pro's keying tools are robust, it takes a properly shot source image to extract a clean matte and pull a successful key.

If the background color is inconsistent for some reason (such as improper lighting or a mix of paint types) or if it doesn't completely surround the subject, it may be impossible to pull a proper key. In these cases the only solution is to painstakingly paint the matte by hand, frame by frame, in a rotoscoping tool such as Shake or Commotion.

Well-shot footage for keying (sometimes referred to as green screen or blue screen footage) must also be shot and captured on a tape format with extremely high color fidelity. Unfortunately, standard DV does not qualify. One of the ways that DV compresses images is by throwing out a great deal of color information. This works great in most situations because our eyes are far more sensitive to gradations of light and dark than they are to nuances of hue. But when Final Cut Pro examines each pixel to identify whether it is green (and therefore part of the background) or not green (and so part of the subject), DV's true colors (or lack thereof) come out.

Formats that are adequate for creating a good key include the following:

- Uncompressed Standard Definition (SD) video
- High Data Rate M-JPEG compressed analog video
- DVCPRO-50
- HDCAM
- DVCPRO-HD

Formats that don't lend themselves to a good key include the following:

- MiniDV
- DVCAM
- DVCPRO-25

If you try to key footage shot in one of these formats, you will find that the edges of the key are prone to jagged edges and aliasing.

 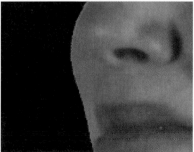

Basic Keying

When working with good source footage, performing a basic key in Final Cut Pro is very easy.

1 Open the project Lesson_09 > **09_Project_Start.fcp**.

2 The sequence **Cave Key** should open in the Timeline. If it's not, double-click it in the Browser to open it.

3 Select the clip **CU K Looks Back D_18_6B_8** and choose Effects > Video Filters > Key > Chroma Keyer to apply a Chroma Key filter.

Although nothing may appear to change, the filter has been applied.

Before you add the background effect, let's adjust the Chroma Keyer filter so you can see the results of removing the green color, by comparing the source footage to a simple black background.

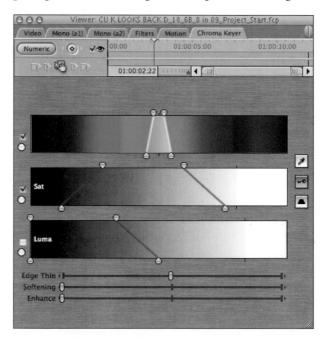

4   Open the clip into the Viewer, click the Chroma Keyer tab, and click the eyedropper at the right of the window.

5   Use the eyedropper to select a green spot in the Canvas. Click just one spot—don't drag.

Before   After

Immediately you should see that any area in the picture with the same color as the one you selected automatically becomes transparent and appears black. If there are still significant areas of green that need to be keyed, add to the selection as follows.

6   Select the eyedropper again.

7   Press Shift and choose another green spot in the Canvas.

When you press Shift, a tiny + appears next to the eyedropper cursor. You can Shift-click as many times as necessary until nearly all of the green has been selected.

Alternately, you can adjust the Color, Sat, and Luma bars in the Chroma Keyer filter. The diagonal lines across the bars indicate what areas will be keyed.

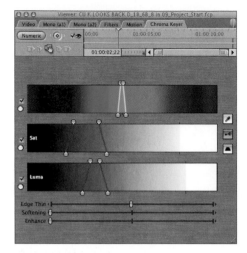

By dragging the button at the top of the line, you adjust the range of color, saturation, or luminance that will be keyed. By adjusting the bottom of the bars, you modify the softness, or *tolerance,* with which the effect is applied. Be careful not to include any areas of the subject in your selection.

After you have adjusted the color selector for maximum transparency, it can often help the look of a key to uncheck either the Sat or Luma sliders.

If the edges of your key are still green or jagged, don't worry. You'll continue to clean up and finalize the effect now.

Tools for Finessing the Key

Final Cut Pro has several tools that help you clean up your rough key. Two of them are the Key icon and the Invert button.

1   Click the Key icon on the right side of the Chroma Keyer window (below the eyedropper).

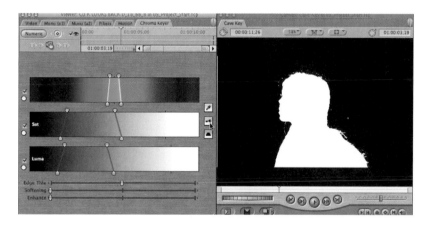

A black-and-white image appears in the Canvas. This image is the matte information. Black areas are transparent and white areas are opaque. The Key icon itself changes color to a black-and-white icon to let you know you are looking only at the matte.

2   Click the Key icon again.

The Key icon now turns blue. This indicates that the keying effect is temporarily disabled so you can view your original source image.

3   Click the Key icon a third time.

This returns you to the starting state, which shows your final output. The matted area is transparent, and the subject is opaque.

4   Click the Invert icon (directly below the Key icon).

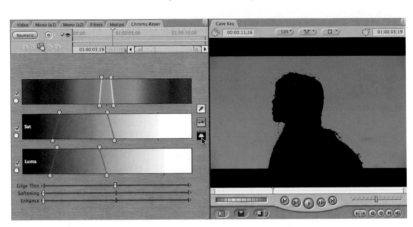

The Invert icon temporarily makes the transparent area opaque and the opaque area transparent. This can be helpful for viewing the matte edge when the subject is complex or blends with the background.

5   Click the Invert icon again to return to the normal state.

6   In the Canvas, choose View Options > Checkerboard 1.

Now, the Canvas background displays a checkerboard pattern, which will help you identify the matted area for clips where part of the subject is black. You can also set the background to white or an alternate checkerboard pattern.

Keyframing the Chroma Key Filter

Remember that all video images change over time. You may generate a perfect key on one frame, but five seconds into the shot, a shadow may appear that changes the background and requires different key settings. Fortunately, like all filters in Final Cut Pro, the Chroma Keyer filter can be keyframed.

1   Click the Numeric button in the Chroma Keyer tab.

This brings the Filter tab to the front.

2   Toggle open the filter parameters by clicking the disclosure triangle at the left of the filter name.

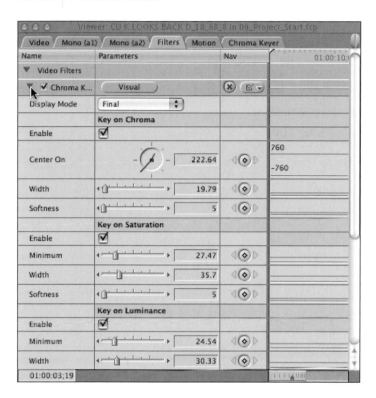

Each of the controls in the Chroma Keyer window is represented here numerically. To keyframe individual parameters, you must first decide which parameters will need to be changed in your video to improve the key.

3   To add keyframes for each individual parameter, click the Insert/ Delete Keyframe button to the right of each parameter name.

Or, if you are unsure which individual parameters need to be keyframed, you can keyframe all of the parameters simultaneously from the Chroma Keyer window.

4   Click the Visual button to return to the Chroma Keyer window.

In the upper-left corner of the window, there is a single Insert/Delete Keyframe button. This adds a keyframe to every filter parameter at the current playhead position.

Adding a Background

It's impossible to judge the quality of your key until you see how the foreground image works against the intended background. How convincingly the effect works will depend on many factors. Is the lighting the same in the two shots? Does the camera angle match? A successful key effect depends on the care and craft the production team uses when shooting the green screen shot and the corresponding plate.

Still, you can do your part by fine-tuning the key effect to best match the two shots together.

1   Drag **CU K LOOKS BACK D_18_6B_8** from track V1 in the Timeline up to V2.

2   Drag **background clip** from the Browser window and drop it onto track V1 directly beneath **CU K LOOKS BACK D_18_6B_8**.

You should immediately see the Canvas update, replacing the transparent areas with the **background clip**.

3   In the Canvas, click the View Options button and choose Image+Wireframe.

4   Choose 25% from the Canvas Zoom control menu.

5   Select the background layer on V1 in the Timeline.

6   In the Canvas, scale the background clip up by dragging one of the corners outward until the wireframe enclosing the cave image is larger than the screen. Dragging a corner without holding down any keys scales an image proportionately. (The approximate scale value is 85%.)

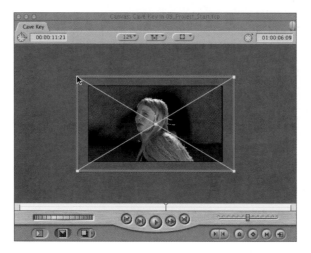

The wireframe in the Canvas has a number in the center to help iden-tify which layer is selected. In this case, the clip on V1 is selected, so the number is 1.

7   Move the background clip to the left so that the right edge of the clip aligns with the right edge of the wireframe.

8   Park the playhead at around 01:00:05:20 and then select the clip of the actor in the Timeline, on V2.

9   In the Canvas, move the clip to the right so her shoulder is near the right edge of the frame. Note also that the wireframe now shows the number 2 in the center, since a clip on V2 is selected.

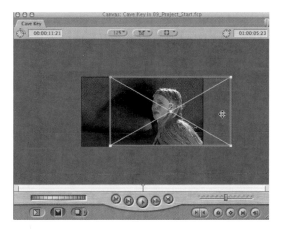

At this point the background and foreground are in approximately
the right positions. But the lighting conditions are different. The foreground has a much cooler feel than the background, due to the different color temperature of the lighting used in each scene.

10 Apply a tint filter to the **background clip** by selecting it and choosing
Effects > Video Filters > Image Control > Tint.

Although this makes the clip black and white, you can adjust the filter's settings to bring some color back into the image so that it better
matches the foreground.

11 Open the **background clip** from the Timeline into the Viewer window
and click the Filters tab.

12 Set the Color to a very dark blue and set the Amount slider to about 70.

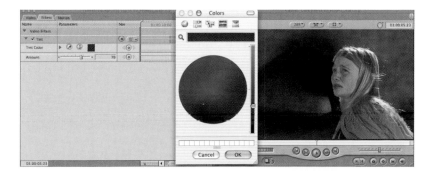

Finessing the Edges of the Matte

Now your key is almost complete. All that remains is fine-tuning the edges
of the matte. There are several controls that allow you to make fine adjustments to the edges of your keyed matte, including edge thinning, softening, and enhancement.

1   Double-click **CU K LOOKS BACK D_18_6B_8** in the Timeline to load it
into the Viewer.

2   Click the Chroma Keyer tab to bring it to the front.

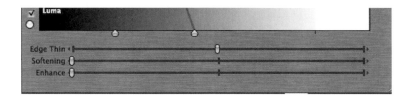

At the bottom of the Chroma Keyer window are three sliders. The first
is the Edge Thin slider. Edge thinning shrinks or enlarges the matte
slightly by working only on the gray pixels at the edge of the matte,
making them more or less transparent. As you experiment with these
three sliders, turn the Saturation and Luma Limit controls on and off
to get a feel for how these parameters all interact.

3   Drag the Edge Thin slider to the right.

If you drag too far, the edges of your subject will get too sharp.

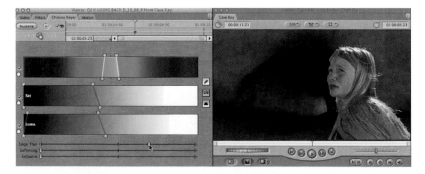

Once you get the edge of the matte as close to the subject as you can without edging into the subject itself, you may want to add a small amount of Softening to blur the edges of the matte. If Softening is too high, it can destroy the keying effect, but a tiny amount of blur may help the foreground blend into the background.

4 Click the tiny arrow on the right side of the Softening slider to add a subtle blur. Generally, only one or two clicks is sufficient.

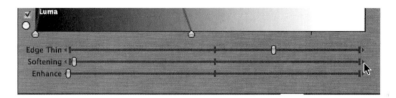

The third slider is Enhance. This effect controls the color of the semi-transparent pixels within your key. Typically, after the initial keying settings have eliminated nearly all of the key, a slight green halo remains around the subject. If you try to remove it with edge thinning, you may eat into the subject, and if you try to remove it through softening, the halo blurs but remains green. Specifically, Enhance turns any semi-transparent pixels in your matte the opposite color of the key color, to help cancel out the color of the key that may remain in any edges.

5 Drag the Enhance slider slightly to the right. Again, a little goes a long way.

Dragging it a small amount will have the effect of desaturating those areas of your matte.

Dragging too far will add the opposite color. This is usually undesirable.

Using Spill Suppression

Sometimes the color of the background from the green or blue screen may reflect (or *spill*) onto shiny surfaces in the subject. This will not be affected by the Enhance slider because the pixels are not semi-transparent. This spill color can be removed with the Spill Suppressor filter—choose Effects > Video Filters > Key > Spill Suppressor – Green.

Be sure to apply the Spill Suppressor filter *after* you apply the key filter, so the spill suppressor filter works on the end result of the keying process, not on the raw source image. In this lesson, the clip you have been manipulating does not have any visible spill, so this filter is not needed for this example.

Applying Color Smoothing

If you must attempt to pull a key with troublesome footage, such as DV footage or poorly lit non-DV footage, you can improve the results of your key by using the Color Smoothing 4:1:1 and Color Smoothing 4:2:2 filters.

These filters apply a slight horizontal blur to the color channels (leaving the luminance unmodified) to help smooth out difficult stepped edges in the color data, to make pulling a successful key easier.

Here is an example of how to use color smoothing to improve the keying of some DV footage.

1   Open the **Color smooth** sequence by double-clicking it in the Browser.

2   Select **Source.mov**. (This is a DV clip.)

3   Choose Effects > Video Filters > Key > Color Smoothing-4:1:1.

This filter has no parameters. (The 4:2:2 filter is for formats such as Motion JPEG, DVC-PRO 50, HDCAM or DVC-PRO HD.)

4   Next, apply the Chroma Keyer filter.

It is very important that you apply the Color Smoothing filter before the Chroma Keyer, so that the Chroma Keyer works on the smoothed color edges.

5   After applying the Color Smoothing and Chroma Keyer filters, you can then create the matte, following the steps in this lesson from the beginning through the "Finessing the Edges of the Matte" section.

Notice how color smoothing improves the stair-stepping artifact that normally occurs when keying DV footage.

Before color smoothing

After color smoothing

After you have pulled an acceptable key from this clip, let's add the Spill Suppression for good measure.

6   Choose Effects > Video Filters > Spill Suppressor – Green and adjust the amount until you remove the green cast from the subject's clothes, hair, and face.

Spill suppression sometimes adds an unwanted thick line along the perimeter of your key. You can tweak the Chroma Key settings to eliminate this.

Adding a Garbage Matte

Some footage requires the use of an additional matte to eliminate elements from the scene that are not part of the subject and cannot be removed through the Chroma Keyer filter alone.

Final Cut Pro's two garbage matte filters are designed to hide this "garbage" so that it will not be included in your final composite.

1   Open the **LS Key** sequence.

At the top of the frame, the edge of the green screen stage is visible. This was necessary in order to frame the medium shot of the subject.

2   Select **MS K STANDS_18_1B.4** in the Timeline.

3   Apply an eight-point garbage matte by choosing Effects > Video Filters > Matte > Eight Point Garbage Matte.

Numbered tags appear in the Canvas window, indicating the eight control points for the matte.

4   Open **MS K STANDS_18_1B.4** into the Viewer from the Timeline and click the Filters tab to bring it to the front.

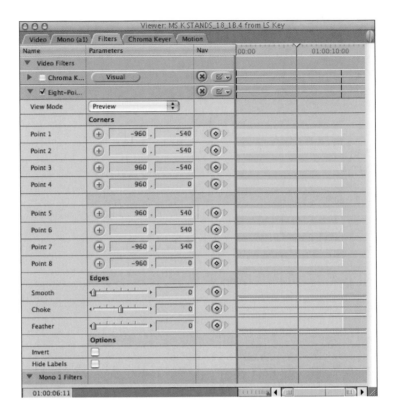

Each of the eight control points is represented in the Filters tab. You can use all eight points to create a shape that excludes the garbage elements you want to hide from view. Anything outside of the shape will be treated as transparent.

5   In the Filters tab, click Point 1.

6 In the Canvas, select a location in the green area near the upper-left corner.

The Canvas updates to show the change. The background clip is now visible in the upper-left corner.

7 In the Filters tab, click Point 2.

By default, Point 2 in the Canvas is midway across the top of the frame.

8 In the Canvas, click near the top center, in the green area, but safely above the girl's head.

If you click and hold, you can drag the new point around and see it update. Once you release the mouse, you will need to reselect the point control in the Filters tab to set a new point in the Canvas.

9 In the Filters tab, click Point 3.

By default, Point 3 in the Canvas is positioned at the upper-right corner of the frame.

10 In the Canvas, set the new position for the third control point near the upper-right corner, in the green area.

Your garbage matte is now complete.

11 The Chroma Keyer filter has already been applied to this clip. Activate the Chroma Keyer filter by checking its box in the Filters tab. (The necessary settings have already been applied.)

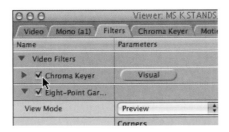

12 Hide the point controls in the Canvas by going to the Garbage Matte
controls in the Filters tab in the Viewer and setting the View Mode
to Final.

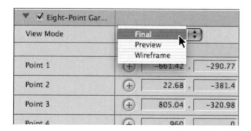

The key for this clip is now complete. In this example, the order of the
chroma key and garbage matte filters in the Filters tab do not affect the
final composite. However, as you use garbage mattes for other effects, such
as blurs, the order of the filters does matter. Experiment with the filter
order to see what works best for you.

The Garbage Matte filters offer additional controls in case the shape you need to matte out is more complex. Additionally, you can keyframe the Garbage Matte parameters in the event that the shape of the object that needs to be matted out changes over time.

Going Beyond the Basics

This lesson covered simple keying with only one forefround subject and one background plate. However, you can also easily combine many different elements, each photographed separately, into a single composited scene in Final Cut Pro. The software has several other keying and matting tools designed for specific compositing needs.

If there is any camera movement during the shot, keying gets a lot more complicated. If the camera movement can be recorded using a motion-control camera rig, the same movement can be applied to each shot, and you can key and composite the elements in Final Cut Pro just like you would with a static shot. Alternately, tracking marks can be applied onto the green screen, and then using a tool like Apple's Shake you can record the movement and apply it digitally to a new computer generated background element. Of course, the tracking marks also have to be manually removed from the green screen using a series of garbage mattes.

The power of keying is one of the most dazzling of all special effects. It is used commonly in major motion pictures to allow people to appear to frolic with dinosaurs or ghosts; training and educational films use keying to describe complex machinery; and television newscasts routinely show their weather forecasters standing in front of weather maps keyed with green screens.

As you master the various keying and matting tools in Final Cut Pro, you will undoubtedly come up with many new uses for this powerful effect.

What You've Learned

- Keying involves applying the Chroma Keyer filter to mask a foreground subject from the background.

- Keying is most successful when the source footage is filmed against a solid background, such as a green screen or blue screen.

- Add keyframes to the Chroma Keyer parameters in the Filters tab to accommodate changing lighting and shading conditions that occur across multiple frames.

- Use the Color Smoothing key filter to compensate for the stair-stepping artifact that occurs when keying DV footage.

- Fine tune the matte using the Edge Thin, Softening, and Enhance controls.

- Create a garbage matte to eliminate unwanted elements from a scene.

Color Correction

Andrew Balis has worked in the film industry since 1990 as a cinematographer, editor, and post-production consultant. He regularly teaches classes in Final Cut Pro to industry professionals, and has lectured at Apple, UCLA, Moviola, AFI, and IFP. He is the co-author of the original Apple-certified training curriculum for Final Cut Pro in introductory, advanced, and effects classes, developed at Moviola Education.

10

Evaluating Video Images

Color correction, the process of evaluating and enhancing the color and brightness of an image, is one of the final stages of post-production. A well-corrected sequence looks good, provides continuity shot-to-shot and scene-to-scene, supports the direction and mood of the sequence, and meets certain brightness and color requirements to be suitable for broadcast. Poorly corrected images not only look bad, they are unsuitable for broadcast and can even bleed into the audio signal of the program, creating distortion.

In this lesson, you will learn a critical piece of color correction: how to evaluate a video image. You'll look at three ways to evaluate an image: a quick method known as range checking, a detailed evaluation using Final Cut Pro's video scopes, and an old-fashioned reality check—viewing the image on an external monitor. We'll spend most of our time on the video scopes, since they're the most complicated and the most useful. In Lessons 11 through 14, we will use the various color correction tools available in Final Cut Pro, but we will always use them in conjunction with one or more video scopes.

Attributes of a Video Image

Let's start out by taking a look at the information we use to assess a video image. Final Cut Pro displays two types of information about a video image: luminance and chrominance.

Luminance

The *luminance* of a video image describes the brightness levels of the pixels that constitute the image. These levels range from the darkest black through various shades of gray to the brightest white.

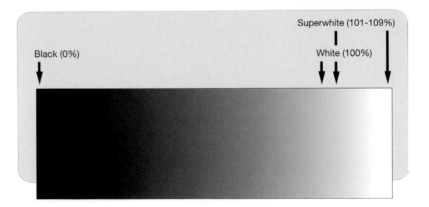

In Final Cut Pro, the range of possible luminance levels from black to white is represented along a scale as a percentage level, with pure black at 0 percent and pure white at 100 percent. Additionally, there is a small range of bright whites, known as Superwhite, from 100 percent up to 109 percent. When you read luminance levels in a video scope in Final Cut Pro, every pixel that makes up the image is represented as a percentage somewhere on this scale.

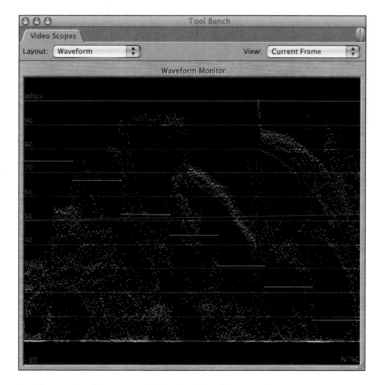

Luminance levels represented in the Waveform monitor

Chrominance

In Final Cut Pro, color information can be displayed graphically in multiple ways. These graphic representations of color are found in the color correction filters, the OS X color picker (used to assign color for various generators, including text), and the video scopes. One common element in all of these graphic interfaces is the use of a color wheel. A color wheel is simply a circular representation of possible colors.

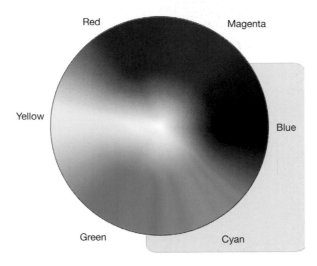

Red   Magenta

Yellow   Blue

Green   Cyan

A color wheel shows the range of possible colors.

The benefit of a color wheel is that it is an objective way to describe color. When referring to color, people tend to use fairly subjective words. For instance, you may say that something is a *warm red* or *navy blue*. These references may have different meanings to different people. The color wheel provides consistency when working with color.

Chrominance is the term used to describe the two color attributes that are represented in a color wheel: hue and saturation.

Hue

Hue is what we think of as an actual color, such as red or blue. It is represented on a color wheel as a location somewhere *around* the wheel. Any color hue can be represented as an angle on this wheel.

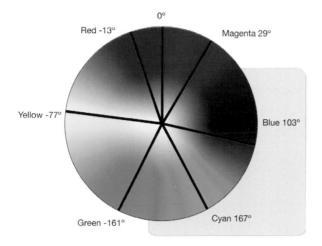

Saturation

Saturation describes the intensity of the color, such as bright or pale. It is represented on a color wheel as a point along a radius, from the center of the wheel to the outer rim.

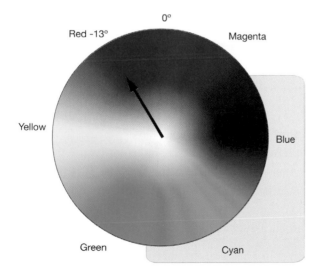

The closer to the outer rim of the wheel, the more intense, or saturated, the color. The closer to the center, the paler the color. For example, if the angle (hue) of a color is red, then different levels of saturation include everything from light pink to bright red. At the very center of the wheel is no color at all—no hue or saturation.

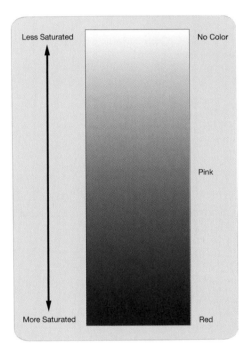

Keeping Color "Legal"

Video images need to meet certain brightness and color requirements to be suitable for broadcast—also referred to as being *broadcast legal*. If an image falls outside of these standards, it may be rejected by a network or broadcast facility. Even if you do not plan on broadcasting your program, you should still adhere to these broadcast standards, as it will affect display quality.

When you color correct in Final Cut Pro, keeping the luminance *legal* means setting the darkest black levels to 0 percent and the brightest white levels no higher than 100 percent. If pixels of white are in the

Superwhite range (above 100 percent), they are considered unsafe for broadcast. Additionally, in Final Cut Pro, 100 percent is often labeled simply as White and 0 percent as Black.

NOTE ▶ It's important to check with the intended broadcast facility for its specific standards.

In Final Cut Pro, this basic principle is appropriate for both digital and analog formats of video, as well as for different video systems like NTSC and PAL. For instance, the proper black level for both NTSC and PAL is 0 percent. Yet, in the analog world, when working with video formats like Beta SP or 3/4", NTSC has a black level standard of 7.5 IRE, and PAL has a black level standard of 0 IRE. Although the two systems have different analog standards for black, they are both represented by 0 percent in the digital realm.

> **NOTE** ▶ IRE is a measure of voltage in the video signal. This is a term used in the analog world to evaluate the luminance levels of the video. This term is not used in Final Cut Pro, as only luminance level percentages are used for digital readings.

In addition to luminance ranges, there are broadcast legal considerations for color saturation. As we explore the Vectorscope in this lesson, we will discuss the standards for legal color.

Range Checking

When all you need is a quick check of whether a video is broadcast legal, Final Cut Pro gives you a great option: Range Check. Available as an overlay in the Viewer or Canvas, these graphical notes tell you at a glance whether there are any problems with luminance levels or saturation.

When you need more detailed information about the image, that's where Final Cut Pro's video scopes come in. We will start out by examining the Range Check option, and then go into more detail about the image by looking into the video scopes.

Range-Checking Luminance

As you learned earlier, broadcast facilities set the maximum legal luminance at 100 percent. The Superwhite range of luminance between 100 percent and 109 percent might just as well be called *illegal white*, because white levels in this range are not broadcast safe.

In this exercise, you will spot-check your image for problem white areas, areas that are too bright for broadcast. You'll notice that the Range Check option flags these areas with green or red *zebra stripes* as an overlay in the Canvas or Viewer.

NOTE ▶ The Range Check option will display its zebra pattern at the current playhead position when the clip is paused or stopped. It is therefore a good idea to scrub your playhead to different areas within the clip to view how your white levels change.

1 Open Lesson_10 > **10_Project_Start.fcp**.

2 Ctrl-click in the Timeline.

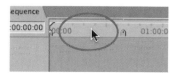

This brings up a contextual menu. At the bottom of the menu is a list of Timeline markers. Choosing a marker's name from this menu is a quick way to jump to that spot in the Timeline.

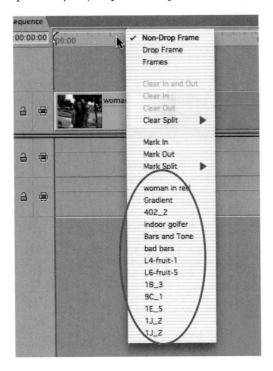

Timeline markers are listed in the contextual menu.

3   Choose **1E_5** from the contextual menu to navigate to this clip. This is a good clip to look at first, as its luminance levels are already broadcast legal.

4   Make sure the Canvas or Timeline window is active, then choose View > Range Check > Excess Luma. A new overlay appears in the Canvas, a green circle with a checkmark.

TIP ▶ Range Check for Excess Luma is also available as an option from the View pop-up menu in the Canvas.

The green checkmark in the Canvas indicates that there are no brightness levels above 90 percent in the image. It is broadcast legal, with room to spare.

5 Ctrl-click in the Timeline ruler and choose clip **1B_3** from the contextual menu.

Now you should see two new overlays. There is a green circle with a checkmark and a tiny arrow.

This indicates that the image is broadcast legal and all luminance levels are below 100 percent. Additionally, it indicates that the brightest areas of the frame are between 90 percent and 100 percent.

You should also see zebra stripes much like the diagonal stripes you find in many camera viewfinders that can be used to check exposure. In this case, the zebra stripes are green. This indicates that these areas of the video are between 90 percent and 100 percent.

6 Ctrl-click in the Timeline ruler and choose **woman in red** from the
contextual menu.

Two new overlays appear. One is a yellow triangle with an exclamation
point, and the other is red zebra stripes.

These overlays indicates that the video is not broadcast legal and that
some valucs are above 100 percent. The red zebra patterns are seen in
the areas where the levels exceed 100 percent. You will always see the
red zebra pattern and the yellow exclamation point together, an indication that there is a problem and that the video is not broadcast safe.

Range-Checking Saturation

In addition to range-checking luminance, you can range-check for saturation levels to see if any colors are too saturated for broadcast.

Going to View > Range Check offers three options:

- Excess Luma: This option was just explored previously. This checks
  for luminance levels that are above broadcast legal standards.

- Excess Chroma: This option checks for saturation levels that are above
  broadcast legal standards.

- Both: This options enables the checking of both luminance and
  chrominance levels that are above broadcast legal standards.

Excessive saturation is a particular problem in NTSC video, where red and yellow tend to bleed into surrounding colors as well as produce a color *ringing* or *buzzing* effect when viewed on an external video monitor.

The Excess Chroma overlay is similar to Excess Luma, as it also uses a yellow warning indicator and red zebra stripes—only this time, the indicators call out areas in the image that are above the broadcast legal limit for saturation.

1   At this point, the Timeline playhead should still be located over **woman in red** from the previous exercise. If not, Ctrl-click in the Timeline ruler and choose **woman in red** from the drop-down menu.

2   Choose View > Range Check > Excess Chroma.

Notice that the Range Check symbol changes to a green circle with a checkmark. This clip has unsafe *luminance* levels, but it does have legal *chroma* levels. When you are range-checking chroma, the green checkmark represents safe saturation levels.

3   Navigate to clip **L4-fruit-1** in the Timeline.

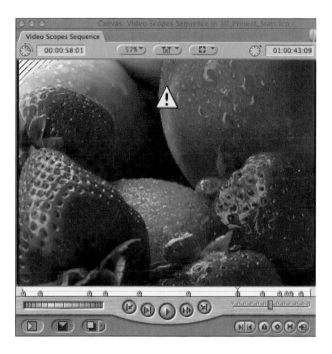

This clip has red zebra stripes and a yellow caution icon. This indicates that the clip has overly saturated areas and is not suitable for broadcast.

To summarize, a green circle with a checkmark means the image is legal. The yellow warning icon and red zebra strips mean the image contains illegal luma or chroma levels. If an image contains illegal levels of luma or chroma, it needs to be color corrected before it can be submitted for broadcast.

Accessing Video Scopes

There are four video scopes in Final Cut Pro. Each has a specific purpose, but in general they are used to obtain a more objective view of the video image than the human eye provides. Having this impartial viewpoint is essential for adjusting the image to meet broadcast specifications, and for creating consistency in the visual texture, or *feel,* of the video when you're comparing different images and matching scenes.

The four video scopes in Final Cut Pro are the Waveform monitor, the Vectorscope, the Parade scope, and the Histogram. Each scope displays different information about the video image—either its luminance, its chrominance, or a combination of the two.

Let's take a moment to open the Video Scopes window and look at the different scopes. One way to open the Video Scopes window is to choose from one of the window arrangement presets.

1   Move the Timeline playhead back to the clip **woman in red**. (Ctrl-click in the Timeline and choose **woman in red** from the menu.)

2   Choose Window > Arrange > Color Correction.

The Video Scopes window opens as a tab on the Tool Bench window. All four video scopes are displayed by default.

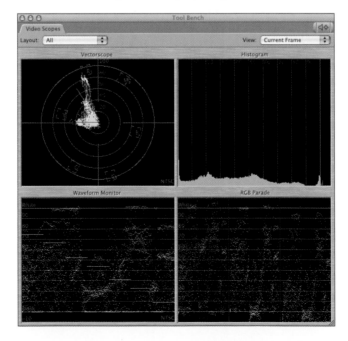

NOTE ► The Video Scopes display may also be opened by choosing
Tools > Video Scopes.

3 In the Video Scopes window, make sure that the View menu is set
to Current Frame. This ensures that the video scopes are reading the
current image in the Canvas.

Notice the overlay of the various colored dots in each of the graphs in
this window.

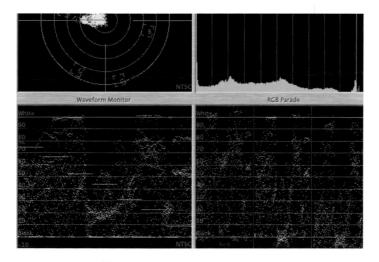

These dots represent the pixels that make up the image. They display
the luminance or chrominance of the video in the Canvas.

4   Move your cursor over the four displays. Notice that that in each one, a yellow line follows the cursor as it moves. Additionally, as you drag, a little window displays a percentage of luminance or chrominance that corresponds to the location of the cursor.

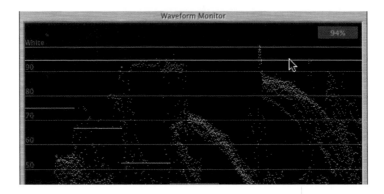

Once you learn how to read the windows, you will use this cursor to quickly spot specific luminance and chrominance values in areas of the image.

The Waveform Monitor

Two of Final Cut Pro's video scopes, the Waveform monitor and the Vectorscope, are used primarily to evaluate luminance and saturation to determine whether a video image is within broadcast standards. We'll look at the Waveform monitor first.

Checking Luminance Levels with the Waveform Monitor

In this exercise, you will learn how the Waveform monitor displays luminance levels and check an image to see if it falls within acceptable ranges.

1   In the Video Scopes window, choose Layout > Waveform to show just the Waveform monitor.

2 Ctrl-click the Waveform display and make sure that Saturation is *not* checked in the contextual menu.

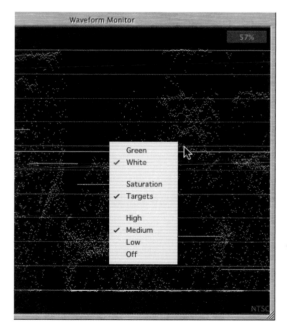

3 From the View pop-up menu in the Video Scopes window, choose None.

Now you have an unobstructed view of the scale along the left of the Waveform monitor. The effective range of the scale spans from –10 percent to 110 percent—in other words, below darkest black to super-white. Look along the left side of the Waveform monitor to view this scale. At 0 percent there is a line labeled *Black*, and at 100 percent there is a line labeled *White*.

NOTE ▶ There is a small range on the left side of the scale from 0 to –10 percent. For our purposes—checking luminance levels—0 percent is the bottom of the scale, and no blacks will fall below this line.

4   From the View pop-up menu in the Video Scopes window, choose Current Frame. The dots in the screen will reappear.

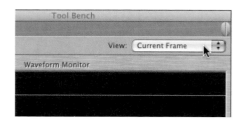

One of the goals of color correction is to make sure that blacks are at 0 percent and whites are no brighter than 100 percent. In this image, notice that some of the dots in the image do exceed 100 percent.

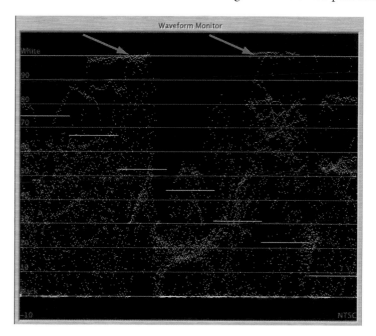

Next, look at how the Waveform monitor's display corresponds to a video image.

5   With the Timeline window active, press the down arrow to go to the next clip in the Timeline, **Gradient**.

In the Canvas, notice the clip's transition from white to black, from left to right.

In the Waveform display, note the line that stretches diagonally from white to black, from left to right.

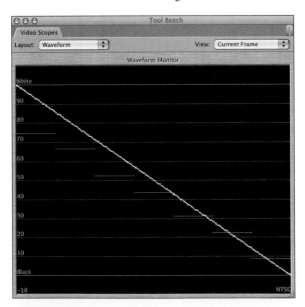

As you may already be able to see, the Waveform monitor represents the luminance of an image from left to right.

6   In the Timeline, press the up arrow to move back to the clip **woman in red**.

7   Turn off Range Check and observe the luminance level of the top left portion of the Canvas, the sky next to the woman's head.

Notice how close this section is to the left of the frame, then look at the Waveform monitor. The pixels near white, which represent the bright sky, are located near the left of the display, the same distance from the left of the frame as is the sky in the video.

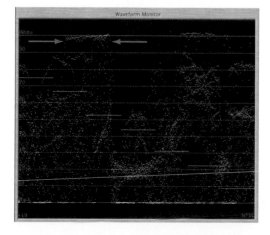

8   Move the cursor over the topmost dot in the Waveform monitor to check the luminance level of the sky.

A line follows the cursor up and down in the display. Look at the upper-right corner to see the corresponding percentage level.

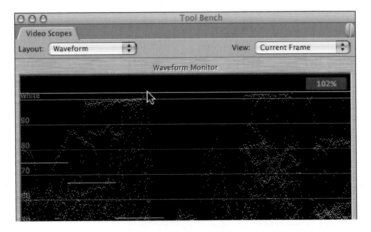

The brightest spot of this video falls just above 100 percent, outside of broadcast standards for NTSC.

9   Now check the luminance level of the darkest part of the woman's hair on her right side.

Notice that it is one of the darkest parts of this video frame, and nothing dips below 0 percent (black). When looking at only luminance in this scale, anything that should be black should be represented at this line. If the darkest part of the hair were higher than 0 percent, then what should be black would only look like a muddy gray.

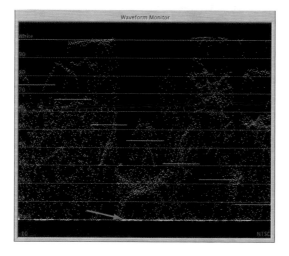

10 Ctrl-click in the Timeline ruler and choose **402_2** from the menu.

11 Move your cursor over to the upper-right corner of the Waveform monitor at the spot of the highest luminance values. These white values top out at around 102 percent, where the lamp would be represented, near the right side of the window. You can use the cursor to pinpoint any parts of the image in this way.

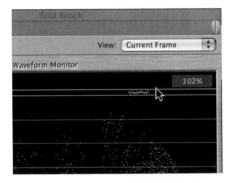

These values represent the glow from the lamp as you can see by comparing the image with the waveforms. This lamp is above 100 percent in the Waveform monitor and is also not proper for broadcast.

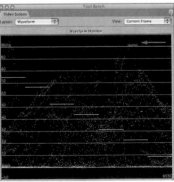

12 Ctrl-click in the Timeline ruler and choose **indoor golfer**.

13 Move your cursor over the Waveform monitor. Notice that this clip also has areas of the frame that exceed 100 percent, similar to the previous clips.

This clip also has another issue that would be problematic when displayed. The black levels of the image sit well above 0 percent. Visually, you will notice the "mushy" or grayish blacks instead of rich, deep blacks.

At first, it may not be apparent that the table legs or parts of the television aren't at ideal levels. In the Waveform monitor, most of these black areas are around 10 percent. For these objects to appear a rich, deep black, they should be 0 percent.

14 Press the up arrow to return to the previous clip in the Timeline.

This gives you a way of visually comparing the darkest part of the golfer clip with the clip of the couple watching TV. As you move between these two clips, notice that even without the Waveform monitor, you can see that the clip of the couple watching TV has richer dark parts of the frame, but in the clip of the golfer there is nothing that dark.

In order for the blacks in the golfer clip to look more natural, they should be color corrected (in this case, darkened). Later, you will use the Waveform monitor while color correcting to ensure that blacks are at 0 percent. This is a good guide to see whether the blacks are as black as they can be or if they need a little redirection.

Checking Relative Saturation with the Waveform Monitor

The Waveform monitor can also show us the relative saturation of different clips in a project. This information can be helpful when comparing the shots of an individual scene to see if the overall color intensity is remaining consistent. (You'll look at saturation with more precision using the Vectorscope, but the Waveform monitor gives you a quick way of checking relative saturation, and it's worth learning.)

In this exercise, you'll change a display option in the Waveform monitor to check relative saturation.

1 Ctrl-click over the Timeline ruler and choose **woman in red** from the drop-down menu.

2 Ctrl-click over the center of the Waveform monitor and choose Saturation from the drop-down menu.

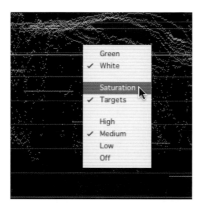

In the Waveform display, you will see that the dots have become thicker and fuller. These thicker areas represent the saturation of the image. Heavy saturation is shown by wider bars; lighter saturation by narrower bars. If there were no color in the image at all, you would see only dots, similar to when the saturation option is turned off.

Notice that the area represented by the dress is more saturated than other parts of the image.

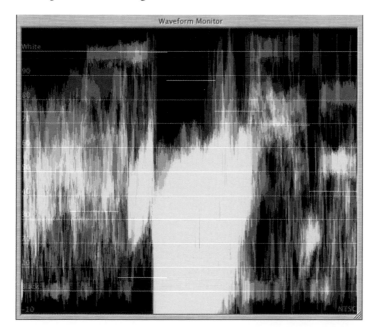

3 Ctrl-click again over the center of the Waveform monitor and turn off Saturation. In order to view luminance levels accurately, it's best if Saturation is left off in this display.

The Vectorscope

Final Cut Pro's Vectorscope is useful in a number of ways. One important function is monitoring the colors of the video primarily to determine whether saturation levels are broadcast legal. As mentioned earlier, colors that are too saturated (intense) can cause display problems like *blooming*, in which the edge of the color bleeds into adjacent areas of the image.

The Vectorscope is a graph that represents information about the chrominance in the video. Using the Vectorscope, you can read the hue and saturation of the various elements of the frame. This information is handy when you're trying to match colors in different scenes. It can also be used to evaluate flesh tones to determine whether people appear realistic and natural, which can be tricky with the eye alone.

Reading Hue and Saturation in the Vectorscope

The first step in using the Vectorscope is getting to know how it correlates to the video image.

In this exercise, we will look at a test image to see how it is represented in the Vectorscope. This will familiarize you with how a video image is displayed in the Vectorscope; the test image will also serve as a guide to understanding broadcast standards for saturation levels.

1 In the Video Scopes window, choose Layout > Vectorscope.

2 Ctrl-click over the Vectorscope display and make sure that Targets is checked.

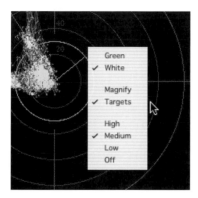

Before reading a video image, let's get familiar with this display. The circular shape is akin to the color wheel. You should also see six small, labeled pink boxes. These are *targets*, and they represent six hues in the wheel. The different mixes of these six colors represent the extent of the color palette with which you have to work.

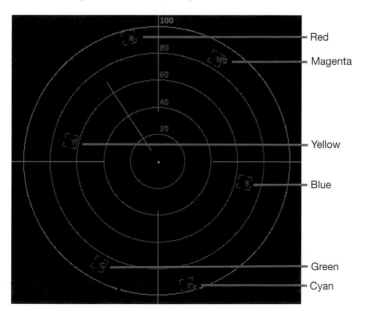

Colors in the video image are plotted on this circular graph. In a moment, you will study a test clip of color bars—but first, a little introduction on how to read color in this display. A color's location on the wheel depends on its hue and saturation. An orange color, for example, would be located in the Vectorscope somewhere between yellow and red, as orange is a mixture of those two.

3   Ctrl-click in the Timeline ruler and choose **Bars and Tone** from the drop-down menu to navigate to this clip in the Timeline.

The Vectorscope shows a number of crisscrossing lines. These lines, called *traces*, represent the colors in the sample image's color bars. Notice that they intersect in the six targets.

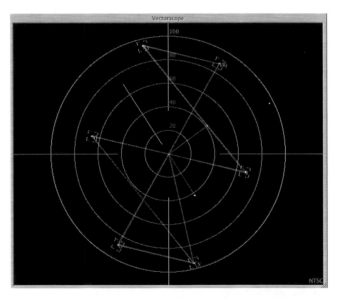

Also notice that these traces all point to the center of the target boxes. Each trace intersects in the middle of its respective target. This particular test image is accurate, as the colors in the bars have an accurate hue (a specific angle around the wheel) and are as saturated as can be within broadcast legal levels. If the traces were any farther outward (closer to the perimeter), the color would be too saturated for broadcast.

4   Look at the colors of these bars on your monitor, preferably an external NTSC monitor.

These are as intense as colors should get in the video image. As you should notice, even broadcast legal colors have issues when they are adjacent to other saturated colors The edges between colors seem to vibrate. Although colors can be this vibrant, it is a good idea to stay well under this color intensity, especially when vibrant colors are adjacent to one another, to avoid the harsh display that you see in this test image.

NOTE ▶ The previous step relates specifically to viewing on an external NTSC monitor (or TV). The computer monitor is not subject to the same limitations of NTSC video and therefore doesn't display the same problems. In other words, even if it looks terrific on the computer monitor, it may not look so great on the external NTSC monitor. If standard television is your intended medium, then you'll always want to look for video limitations on an external NTSC monitor.

5   Ctrl-click in the Timeline ruler and choose **bad bars** to navigate to that clip.

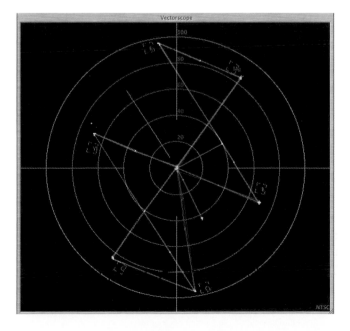

In the Vectorscope, notice that these traces do not intersect in the target boxes as they did for the previous color bars image. Instead, they miss their respective targets. This indicates that these hues are out of phase. They do not accurately display the colors that they are supposed to represent.

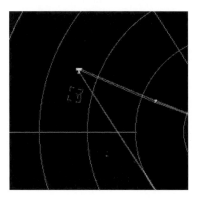

Checking Saturation Levels for Broadcast

The targets of the Vectorscope not only identify specific colors but also serve as a guide to ensure that saturation does not exceed broadcast standards. Just as you use the Waveform monitor to check for legal luminance values, you can use the Vectorscope to check for legal chrominance.

Remember, the closer a color is to the perimeter of the color wheel, the more saturated it is. As a rule of thumb, video is legal as long as no color's saturation extends beyond the center of any color target.

1   Ctrl-click in the Timeline ruler and choose **woman in red** from the drop-down menu.

    Notice no values extend beyond any of the color targets, although some traces are close to the red target. The traces that extend the farthest represent the woman's red dress.

2   Move the cursor over the Vectorscope to see an approximation of how close the saturation values of the red dress are to the closest color target, red. A circular line follows the cursor as you move it around the Vectorscope.

3 Move the cursor next to the dot that is the farthest away from the center. The dot will be close to the red target. This clip is safe for broadcast because the dots do not extend farther than the nearest color target—in this case, red.

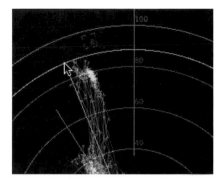

4 Ctrl-click in the Timeline ruler and choose **L4-fruit-1**.

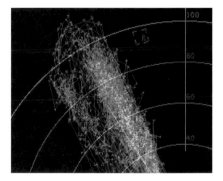

Notice that this clip has values that extend well beyond the red target. This clip is too saturated for broadcast and should be corrected to diminish the intensity of the fruit's color. Otherwise, the overly saturated colors could cause your program to be rejected by broadcasters.

Identifying Individual Colors

So far, you have seen that a color is represented by an angle in the Vectorscope, and that the intensity of the color (saturation) is displayed as a distance from the center of the color wheel. Now we're going to look at how individual colors in a frame are represented in the Vectorscope. The following technique, which uses cropping to isolate parts of the frame, shows how you can evaluate individual elements of the frame. This technique will be used throughout subsequent lessons on color correction to help identify and manipulate colors.

1 Ctrl-click in the Timeline ruler and choose **L6-fruit-5**.

The image is dominated by saturated red tones, and the Vectorscope shows the tallest spikes toward the direction of the red target.

As the clip has a lot of warm tones in the strawberries and the peaches, the predominance of saturated reds should be expected. But could you see each piece of fruit portrayed in the Vectorscope?

To get a sense of how the color of a piece of fruit is displayed, let's use cropping to exclude everything from the image except the fruit.

2 Choose View > Image+Wireframe in the Canvas.

3 Click the image in the Canvas to select it. The wireframe overlay should appear in the Canvas.

4 Select the Crop tool.

5 Crop the sides of the image until only the green apples are shown. To crop two sides at once, click and drag on a corner of the wireframe.

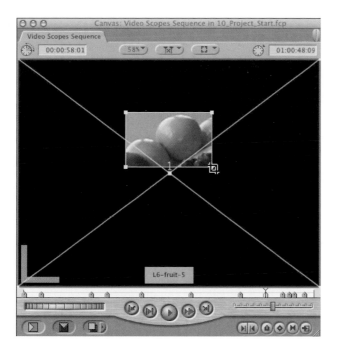

6   In the Vectorscope, notice that the spikes now represent only the green apples, and that the angle (hue) is between yellow and green, leaning closer to yellow.

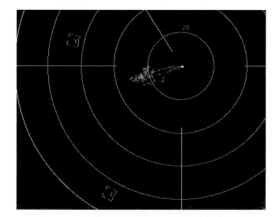

In other words, the green apples are actually closer to yellow than to green, even though they look green. The Vectorscope clarifies what isn't obvious to the human eye. Without cropping, you could see the whole picture. The traces for the apples were hidden in the overall display of the image. With cropping, you can get a fix on any part of the frame. As we continue, we will use this technique to help identify different elements of a frame and determine how an image should be color corrected. This will especially come in handy when evaluating skin tone (color) to determine whether it appears realistic and natural.

7 Ctrl-click over the clip in the Timeline and choose Remove Attributes to restore the image to full frame.

Understanding the Histogram

The other two video scopes in Final Cut Pro, the Histogram and the Parade scope, are most useful when making comparisons, either between two or more images or between the different areas of an individual shot. We'll start with the Histogram.

The Histogram displays the distribution of brightness, or levels of gray, in a video image. When two images are compared using the Histogram, you can identify major differences between them. This is helpful when you have to match different shots to one another.

When color varies too much between two shots that are supposed to have been taken at the same time under the same conditions, it can be distracting to the viewer. In other words, the clips shouldn't *feel* like they are substantially different from one another. There shouldn't be an unnatural change in the lighting as you cut from one image to another in a scene.

The Histogram is a handy way to detect and correct differences in contrast.

Evaluating the Brightness of an Image

In this exercise, you will get familiar with the Histogram and learn to interpret its displays.

1 In the Video Scopes window, choose Histogram from the drop-down menu.

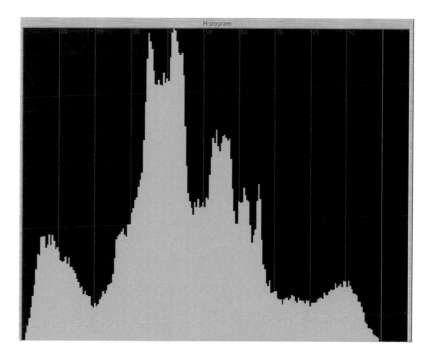

2 Ctrl-click over the Histogram display and make sure that Include Black is checked.

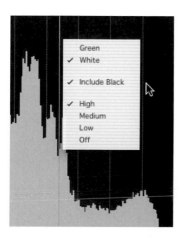

The Histogram is a bar graph representing luminance values of your clip from 0 percent to 110 percent. This luminance scale is similar to that of the Waveform monitor—but any similarities to the Waveform monitor end there.

3   Ctrl-click over the Timeline ruler and choose **1B_3** from the drop-down menu.

4   Move the cursor across the Histogram from left to right. Notice that a line follows the cursor, and an indicator appears showing you the brightness percentages wherever the cursor is positioned.

The height of the bar represents the number of pixels that have that particular luminance value. The horizontal position of the bar indicates the luminance value of those pixels.

5   In the Histogram display, take note of which bars spike, and how high. You should see a fairly high spikes from around 35 percent to 45 percent.

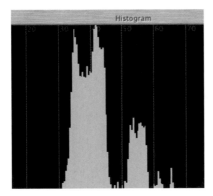

A spike indicates that there are a lot of pixels in that range. In this example, there are a lot of middle grays—in the shades of hair, skin color, shirt, and arms. This is an example of a low-contrast shot, which is the same as saying there is a lot of detail in the image.

Comparing the Contrast of Two Images

Next, we will compare this with a high-contrast image.

1   Press the down arrow to navigate to clip **9C_1**.

This clip of a house is high contrast. There are bright and dark portions of the frame, but very little in-between. In the Histogram, you should notice that the majority of pixels fall near black (left in scale) and white (right in scale).

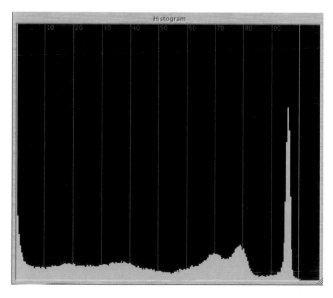

By evaluating clips in the Histogram, you can determine how the luminance levels of two images differ from one another. Next, you will navigate back and forth between the two clips of fruit in the Timeline, and observe any differences as they appear to the eye and in the Histogram.

2   Ctrl-click in the Timeline ruler and choose **L4-fruit-1**.

3   Play back this shot and continue on to the next one, the bowl of fruit. Notice that the transition from one clip to the next has a disturbing visual discontinuity. Somehow, it doesn't quite feel as though the two clips were shot together. Using the Histogram, you should be able to identify one specific difference between the two.

4   Go back to clip **L4-fruit-1**. Examine the spikes between 10 percent and 30 percent. The majority of values in this shot are mostly darker shades.

5   Press the down arrow to navigate to **L6-fruit-5**. Notice that the majority of values fall between 50 percent and 70 percent. The majority of values in this shot are mostly brighter shades. You could then determine that the luminance of the fruit is higher in this shot than in the previous one.

Evaluating Color Balance Using the Parade Scope

The Parade scope, also known as the RGB Parade, is a modified Waveform monitor. In a Waveform monitor, the brightness values of the entire image are shown on the same display. However, on the Parade scope, the red, green, and blue components of the image are broken down and shown on three separate Waveform displays.

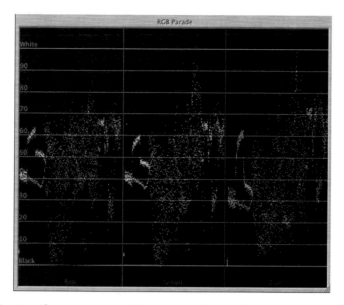

The Parade scope is used for monitoring and comparing the relative red, green, and blue levels between shots. In this exercise, you'll evaluate the color balance of individual images to determine whether there is a neutral color balance or any color tint in the scene.

1   Ctrl-click in the Timeline ruler and choose **1E_5**.

2   In the Video Scopes window, choose Layout > Parade.

The Parade scope displays red, green, and blue separately.

In this particular clip, the values from red, green, and blue are similar. There are about the same number of dots in the same locations in all three displays. This means that there is a fairly neutral color balance in the scene. The light in the scene is whitish.

3   Use the down arrow key to navigate to the next clip in the Timeline, 1J_2.

This clip has a noticeable color change. Exactly how it is different can be determined by a reading of the Parade.

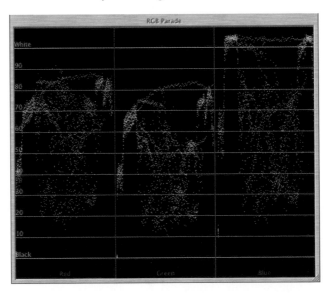

This clip has a higher range of blue values, which is seen as a bluish tint in the scene.

Often, one of the primary goals of color correction is creating a similar look in both clips so there is a more natural feel when cutting between them. Using the Parade scope, the task can be made easier, as you do not have to rely solely on your eye. The video scope can be used to quickly spot the mix of colors in each shot.

> **NOTE** ▶ In your exercises with the various video scopes, you have examined one frame from each clip. It is important to mention that looking at only one frame gives you simply a snapshot of that single moment. A scene can change quickly and dramatically. During your evaluation of images, you should examine many frames throughout each clip to look for changes in luminance and color shifts.

Using an External Monitor

If your intended output is NTSC—standard video displayed on a standard television or high-end monitor—then you should be evaluating the images in the next several lessons with the best external NTSC monitor you can afford.

The video scopes are analytic, but it's also important to see an approximation of how the video will look to your eventual audience. Because there are so many variables in the setup of consumers' televisions, and because it is hardly feasible to go to everyone's house to set up their televisions for them, you will just have to use some predetermined standards as well as a little intelligent guesswork.

> **NOTE** ▶ Lessons 11 through 14 assume you are viewing images on an external monitor rather than a computer monitor. All directions for the exercises are directed at a video image as it is viewed in NTSC, whether that is a high-end monitor or a television. If you do not have an external monitor, you can still follow the lessons. Use color correction to approximate the final look, and practice the techniques. It is more important that you have an external monitor when color correcting real projects that are meant for broadcast.

Monitor or TV?

Should you use a high-resolution monitor or a standard television? Preferably both. The monitor is a more qualified choice, and it has precise controls for helping to obtain a neutral setup. Additionally, the monitor may have more lines of resolution.

However, computer monitors do not represent how the video will look once displayed in NTSC, which has a more limited range of color and luminance latitude. And like it or not, most programs will probably ultimately be displayed on a standard television. Unfortunately, standard televisions don't have full options for setting up the color and luminance, and they may employ filtering that modifies incoming video.

So, if you have access to a high-resolution monitor, use it to perform color corrections. And having a standard NTSC TV available gives you added information when making decisions while color correcting.

Setting Up the External Monitor

To set up the external monitor or TV, we'll use a test image. This will make sure the TV accurately represents the color and luminance of the video. For example, if your external monitor's saturation is turned up too high, colors will appear more saturated than they actually are.

1   Navigate to the clip of **Bars and Tone** in the Timeline. This is the same video generator available by choosing Effects > Video Generators > Bars and Tone (NTSC).

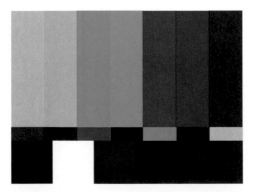

2   Choose View > External Video > All Frames to turn on external video to send an image to your output device. Hook up your external monitor to a FireWire device or capture card. (For these lessons, FireWire is appropriate, as the material is conformed to the DV format.) The **Bars and Tone** clip in the Timeline should now be visible on the external monitor.

3   In the monitor, dial Chroma (also called Color) all the way down. The bars should now be only shades of gray, with no color.

4   Increase the monitor's Brightness setting until you see three gray bars in the lower-right corner of the screen.

NOTE ▸ These three bars are visible only when viewing to the external monitor or TV. If you look in the Viewer or Canvas, you will see only one bar.

These three bars are called the PLUGE (picture line-up generating equipment) bars. The one on the left is blacker than video black, often referred to as Superblack. The middle one is video black. The one on the right is brighter than black. These are set up correctly when only one of the bars is visible.

5   Lessen the Brightness control on the monitor until the bar on the right is still just visible but the two bars on the left are not. This bar lines up directly underneath the red bar to the right.

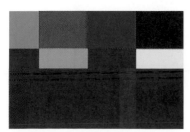

NOTE ▶ The red bar currently has no color. If you are unsure which bar is being referred to, then temporarily turn up the color to see. Once you have identified the red bar, turn the color back down.

The black and darker than black bars are now indistinguishable from one another, constituting just a single bar.

6   Dial up the Contrast control on the monitor (sometimes called Picture) to increase the intensity of the large white bar on the bottom left of the color bars. Brighten until the white starts to bloom, or bleed into the surrounding bars. Then dial down a little on the contrast until it isn't blooming.

7   If you are using a TV, skip to step 9.

8   If you use a monitor that has a blue-only setting, turn it on. The monitor now displays just shades of blue and black.

Set Chroma (color) until the bars on both the left and the right (light gray and blue) match the sub-bar beneath each of them. Then set Hue (tint) until the cyan and magenta bars (bars 3 and 5) match the brightness and color of the sub-bars beneath them. When you are finished, all blue bars match their sub-bars, and all that is seen is solid blue bars.

At this point, you can turn off the blue-only setting. The monitor is now calibrated.

9 If you do not have a blue-only switch on your monitor, you will have to set up the Chroma and Hue (color and tint) by eye. As a guide, the colors from left to right should be light gray (no color), yellow, cyan, green, magenta, red, and blue.

What You've Learned

- Final Cut Pro's video scopes can be used to view an image's luminance levels, color saturation, hue, and distribution of luminance and chrominance.

- For broadcast, the legal range for luminance is between 0 percent and 100 percent as read on the Waveform monitor.

- For broadcast, the saturation should not exceed the color target boxes in the Vectorscope.

- The Histogram can help to identify the contrast in an image as a bar graph.

- The Parade scope can be used to identify the color balance in an image.

- An external monitor can be used to evaluate the video image if it is set up in accordance with a test image of color bars.

11

Lesson Files	Lessons > Lesson_11 > 11_Project_Start.fcp
Media	Media > Lesson_10-14_Media
Time	This lesson takes approximately 60 minutes to complete.
Goals	Break down a video image into its components
	Incorporate video scopes in the grading process
	Use the Color Corrector 3-way filter
	Modify the contrast of an image
	Understand the terms *contrast*, *blacks*, *mids*, *whites*, *highlights*, *gamma*, and *grayscale*

Color-Correcting Contrast

Color correction is the process of enhancing a video image. It is sometimes called finishing, because it's the last step in finalizing the image. A color correction artist, or colorist, is charged with molding raw, photographed images into something fantastic. In some cases, color correction involves using broad strokes to dramatically change the look of a film. Other times, it's used for more subtle tasks, such as smoothing out variations in exposure and lighting from shot to shot, or fixing the occasional mistake. Color correction means different things depending on the project, but its success always depends on the skill of the colorist. In good color correction, the colorist's work may not even be noticeable in the final product.

This and the following lesson on color correction are meant as an introduction to the world of finishing. Professional colorists spend years honing their skills and their eye for color. If you want to know how to develop as a colorist, it's essential to learn to really *see* the video image—to grasp subtle color nuances and appreciate the subconscious effects of manipulating the color balance and contrast. This takes time, so be patient. That said, you can still have fun mastering the basics of color correcting, and even create effects that you may not have known were even possible.

Primary Color Correction

Color correction is an extension of the original cinematography. As a colorist, you are a collaborator in one step of the artistic process, and your ideas and contributions help to shape the final look and emotional impact of the film. You will most likely work closely with the cinematographer to gain a starting point for the direction of the color correction process, and the two of you may continue to work together to finesse the images into their final form. The producer and director may have a say about the look of the program, and this input can weave its way into the process, too. Color correction can also be used to experiment with ideas that may have been too difficult or costly to execute on the set.

Color correction, also called *grading*, can be broken down into two stages: primary and secondary. Primary color correction involves color-balancing images and enhancing contrast to achieve an overall look and feel for a film. For example, the film may warrant a cold, bluish tint, so primary color correction may include creating or enhancing that effect.

Conversely, if a film's bluish cast is an unintended error, color correction can rebalance the image to be more neutral.

Before

After, with bluish tint

Secondary color correction, which involves fine-tuning and finessing specific colors within the frame, rather than the overall frame, will be covered in Lesson 14. In this lesson, we will explore a single aspect of the primary color correction process: adjusting contrast.

Understanding Contrast

The term *contrast* is thrown around a lot and is perceived by different people to mean different things. Let's simplify and look at a basic definition: Contrast is the number of shades of gray, or gray steps, between black and white in an image.

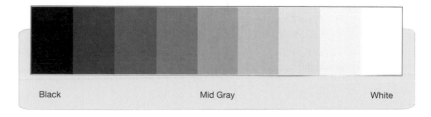

Black   Mid Gray   White

Let's do a simple exercise to see how an image can be broken down by its varying degrees of gray. This will be easier to do if the image you are studying has no color information to distract you.

1　Open the Lesson_11 > **11_Project_Start.fcp** project.

Let's use video scopes, since, as discussed in Lesson 10, they can be very informative when evaluating aspects of video images.

2　Choose Window > Arrange > Color Correction to open the Video Scopes tab.

3　On the Video Scopes tab, go to the Layout menu and choose Waveform to switch the view of the window. In the right of the window, make sure that the View pop-up menu is set to Current Frame.

4　Navigate to the first clip in the Timeline, **woman in red**, and select it in the Timeline.

5   Choose Effects > Video Filters > Image Control > Desaturate. The default setting of this filter will remove all color from the image.

6   Study the image: Notice that the woman's face is a light gray that would fall somewhere near the top of the grayscale. Her dress, meanwhile, is a darker gray, and the grass also has various shades of middle grays.

When an image has many varying degrees of gray—as in this example—it is called *low contrast*. Low contrast is often closest to representing how we see the world, which is with lots of gradations. It is fairly neutral and realistic.

When an image has a lot of white and black areas and fewer shades of gray, it is considered *high contrast*. The image on the following page is high contrast. Because high contrast images have substantially fewer gradations of grayscale, they are generally less natural and realistic and often lend a stylized approach to a scene.

Highlights Versus Shadows

Highlights describe the lightest elements in the frame, from light grays to full white.

When watching a video, a viewer's eyes follow the highlights like a cat chasing a string. Even when a viewer scans an entire image, his or her attention will keep shifting back to the lighter portions of the frame. Knowing this can help you focus your scene. (Of course, this doesn't take into account the content of the scene, which also has a strong influence on the viewer.)

Black, meanwhile, is the absence of light and color. Black is a great backdrop for other colors, which will stand out prominently against it. Having deep, rich black objects and shadows in a frame adds a crispness that can make an image appear sharper than it otherwise would.

In addition, objects in the shadows (near black) are harder to distinguish. A viewer's attention is not drawn to these objects, especially if there are lighter shades or movement in the frame.

High Versus Low Key

Terms such as high-key and low-key, originally used in lighting, have been carried over into color correction as ways to distinguish different types of images. High-key images comprise mostly light values. There may be black in the frame, but most light values are middle gray to white. High-key images are often used to convey a light mood, such as in a comedy.

A high-key image

Low-key images, conversely, have many dark values. There may be white in the frame, but the majority of values range from middle gray down to black. Low-key lighting is often used to indicate nighttime, or a serious, dramatic moment.

A low-key image

Now that you understand the terminology of contrast, let's learn how to control and manipulate it for specific end results.

Basic Contrast Grading

In this exercise, you will make simple adjustments to the contrast of a video clip. Next you will explore another way to enrich contrast, and then compare the two methods.

1 Move the playhead to the second clip in the Timeline, **3A_3**, and select it. Then, make sure that range checking is off. (Choose View > Range Check >Off.)

2   Choose Effects > Video Filters > Image Control > Brightness/Contrast
(Bezier) to add a Brightness/Contrast filter to the clip.

3   Open the clip into the Viewer and go to the Filters tab.

Here you should see two sliders, one for brightness and one for contrast.

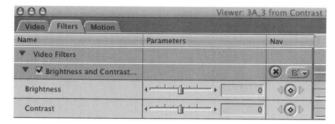

4   Drag the Contrast slider to the right all the way to 100, and then back
to 0.

As you drag the slider, note the change of contrast occurring in the
Canvas and the change in the distribution of dots in the Waveform
monitor.

When the slider is at 100 and contrast is increased dramatically, there
is less separation between different individual elements like the street,
the cars, and the sky.

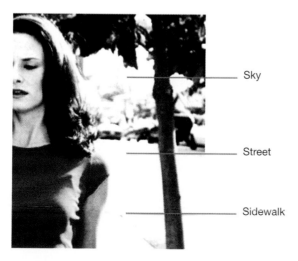

These areas now blend together more, resulting in less detail in the overall image.

In the Waveform monitor, the dots spread out as contrast is increased, moving upward or downward.

Contrast at 0   Contrast at 100

Any dots that started above 50 percent start to work their way up the scale, and any dots below 50 percent head toward the bottom. In other words, light grays get lighter and dark grays get darker as you increase contrast.

The Blacks, Mids, and Whites

It's often nice to have more control over the contrast than you can get by applying a global Brightness/Contrast filter. For instance, you may want to control the shadows without affecting highlights. In the image on the opposite page, for example, the shadows are too light, causing a milky effect, so you might want to selectively darken just the shadows.

Shadows

Final Cut Pro's color correction filters let you isolate different shades of the image separately from one another.

The controls for these filters allow you to target the image's contrast in three unique areas: blacks, midtones, and whites.

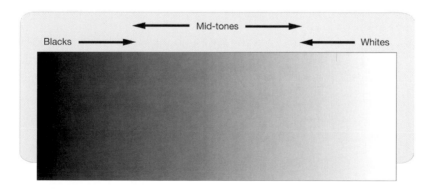

Any control that targets the blacks will affect only the shadows of the image, from full black up into the mid-gray tones.

Any control that targets the whites will affect only the highlights, from the mid-gray tones up to white.

Any control that targets the mids affects the midrange of the image, which constitutes the largest percentage of the viewing area. Controls for mids extend their impact into the blacks and whites, but the effect tapers off. This range of the grayscale, the middle grays, is also often referred to as *gamma* in some colorists' circles.

3-Way Color Corrector

There are two main color correction filters that operate by isolating the three separate areas of grayscale: the Color Corrector 3-way filter and the Color Corrector filter. We'll explore the 3-way filter now.

Among its many virtues, the Color Corrector 3-way filter is more likely to play in real time to an external monitor, depending on the configuration of your computer. Remember that the ability to see color correction on a broadcast monitor is of critical importance when preparing a program that will be distributed in NTSC or PAL video format.

Before using the 3-way color corrector, it will be enlightening to first try the effect with the Brightness/Contrast filter.

1   From the Timeline, open clip **3A_3** into the Viewer and go to the Filters tab. The Brightness/Contrast filter should still be applied to this clip.

2   Reset the Contrast and Brightness sliders to 0.

3   Use the Brightness slider to darken the clip. Try to make the scene look less washed out. Notice that as you darken the clip, the bright parts of the frame also darken.

Darkening the whole clip doesn't resolve its washed-out look. You need to alter the balance between the highlights and shadows. This means isolating the shadows, which we'll do now using the 3-way color corrector.

4   Remove the Brightness/Contrast filter from clip **3A_3**.

5   With the clip selected in the Timeline, in the Filters tab, choose Effects > Video Filters > Color Correction > Color Corrector 3-way.

Normally, you would expect to find all the controls for making adjustments in the Filters tab. Notice, however, that there is a button in the tab labeled Visual.

There are actually two places to make adjustments with the color correction filters: either here, or in a more visually user-friendly display. Click the Visual button to go to the more visual Color Corrector 3-way tab.

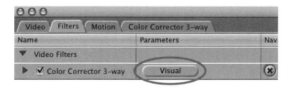

NOTE ▶ In the Visual Color Corrector 3-way tab, you can click Numeric to go back to the Filters tab.

The Color Corrector 3-way Visual tab has all the controls you need to adjust this image. Are you already curious about the color wheels themselves? Don't worry, we'll get to them. For now, we are going to focus on the slider controls under the three wheels.

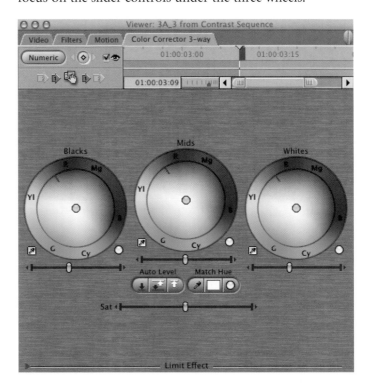

These sliders independently adjust the luminance or brightness of the black levels, the mids, and the white levels. When a slider is dragged to the left, it will decrease brightness values for that range; when it's dragged to the right, it will increase brightness in that range.

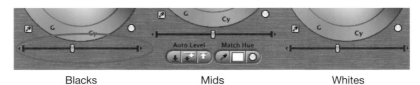

Blacks   Mids   Whites

6   Drag the Blacks slider to the left a bit to decrease luminance in the shadows of the image.

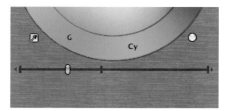

7   Observe the changes in the image in the Canvas and in the Waveform monitor as you drag.

> **NOTE ▶** A color correction filter like Color Corrector 3-way cannot be removed from the clip directly from the Color Corrector 3-way tab. Instead, you would click the Filters tab and remove the filter there, as you would remove other video filters. For this lesson, leave the filter on the clip.

Grading the Contrast

Now we'll see how fiddling with the contrast in the three regions can enhance an image in a real-world scenario. We'll also focus on how to approach the scene.

You'll continue to use the 3-way color corrector in these next steps.

Optimizing Contrast for Video

As you just saw, setting a nice black level in the image can go a long way toward enhancing the detail of the image. Setting a proper black level also helps to define one end of the video signal, which is generally the first step of the color correction process. You have to determine which parts of the image are set to absolute black (0 percent) and which are set to absolute white (100 percent). Your video should have deep, rich blacks, and your whites should be clean and bright.

In this example, the waveform shows a rich mix of full black and white levels.

Such a balance helps ensure that the image is viewed as correctly as possible. Consumer television sets are often designed to compensate for images that don't have an even balance between black and white. Having a good black and a good white can give the television a clear reference for display levels. After all the work you put into making sure that the image looks great, you want to see that it's interpreted correctly by the video equipment.

Let's set the blacks first.

1   Shift-click the reset button next to any color wheel to reset the **3A_3** clip's filters back to their defaults.

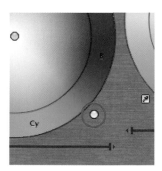

Begin the grading process by setting the bottom of the luminance scale for the blacks. What you need to decide is: What should be black? This means you want to determine what part of the image is mapped to 0 percent. In this case, your goal is to create rich, deep shadows to enhance the detail throughout the image.

2   Move the Blacks slider until the dots at the bottom of the scale in the Waveform monitor start to hit 0 percent (black).

As you continue to drag the slider toward the left, the dots begin to bunch up at the Black line. As dots hit the bottom, they bunch up on top of one another. This technique of bunching up at the bottom end of the scale is called *crushing the blacks*. In the Canvas, notice that the darkest part of the woman's hair becomes black.

Pixels will *crush* at 0 when darkening the black levels—there is no way to create "blacker than black." This is a very good thing when readying the video for broadcast, as the different systems like NTSC have regulations about black levels being lower than a certain amount. When working in Final Cut Pro, the values are simply digital percentages, so you don't have to worry about blacks being unsafe, as there is a limit to the bottom end of the scale. This is also good news when working with both digital and analog video in Final Cut Pro, as they both have the same standards when they are digital. It is only when dubbing tapes from digital to analog that you have to be concerned—and then it is simply a matter of setting up the deck properly, not working with the blacks inside Final Cut Pro. If that all sounds confusing, it can be summed up simply: When color correcting, regardless of the system and format, aim for Black (0 percent) on the scale in the Final Cut Pro video scopes.

Now let's set the whites.

When setting whites for NTSC, there should be no video levels above 100 percent. Additionally, any values at full white (100 percent) may not be desirable, as well; it all depends on the content. In the next set of steps, you will set the brightest portions of the scene to 100 percent. The sky is completely without detail and would look natural at 100 percent, so we'll start there.

3 Click the Whites slider and drag to the right until the top dots in the Waveform monitor reach White (100 percent).

TIP There are two good ways to use the mouse to make incremental adjustments with any effects slider: Click one of the little arrows at either end of the slider to nudge it in one-degree increments or, if you have a mouse with a standard scroll button, point the cursor at a slider and scroll upward to slide left or scroll downward to slide right. This is actually more accurate than dragging on the slider itself.

This step accomplishes two things: The levels of the video are set within NTSC standards, and the brightness of the sky is enhanced, making it pop out more.

Setting the Mood with the Mids

Once the range of the scene is established by setting the black and white levels, it's time to set the overall mood of the video. This is done by adjusting the image's Mids slider. For example, is it a bright day, or dark and gloomy? Is it early morning, or midday? These are questions you answer with the Mids slider. The mids not only help set the feeling of time of day, they also can change a scene from high-key to low-key or anywhere in-between.

The midtones in the image are the viewer's main focus. This is the area of the frame with the most detail, and is generally where faces are exposed. Setting the mids is a subjective task and is up to individual interpretation. If you can, consult with the cinematographer and director to get an idea of their intentions.

In this case, the scene is a sunny day, but the face isn't directly lit by the sun. You will keep the face a little dark, but not too much. It should be easy to read.

1   Drag the Mids slider slightly to the left. (Or, you can click the arrow on the left of the slider to nudge it in small increments.)

   After you adjust the mids down, you will find that the level of the whites have been pushed down a bit from 100 percent.

2   Go back and use the Whites slider to boost the whites back up to 100 percent for the sky.

   NOTE ▸ Each slider has some impact on the surrounding areas of luminance, so after you adjust one slider you may need to go back and forth between other sliders to get the right balance.

   At this point, this image's contrast has been enhanced to create a nice balance between elements in the frame. The scene's color balance could still be enhanced, but that will wait until the next lesson. For now, it's time to judge the quality of this enhancement.

3   Uncheck the Enable box to temporarily disable the filter so that you
can compare the filter settings.

Filter enabled   Filter disabled

Quite a change, isn't it? Your eyes may have been getting accustomed
to the new contrast settings. This is a good comparative tool, and you
can use it to see just how far you have traveled away from the initial
look of the video.

4   Check the Enable box on and off.

Do you like the new contrast, or would you prefer something between
the current color correction and the original state of the image? This
is a judgment call, and it's yours to make.

Additionally, look at the Waveform monitor for a before and after
view of the grading. Notice how the luminance of the original image
is clumped together between about 20 percent and 90 percent. In the
final image, if your corrections were similar to those described in the
previous instructions, you should notice that the adjustments have
stretched the contrast of the image. Now the image has a nice rich
contrast, with a good proportion of whites, blacks, and midtones.

Before   After

5 Move to the next clip in the Timeline, clip **1A_3**, apply the Color Corrector 3-way filter, and rebalance the contrast of this clip. Start by setting the blacks and whites, then use the mids to set the feel of the scene.

Find the balance that works for you.

6 Move to the next clip in the Timeline to see how your choices vary from a finished example. Remember, tone is subjective. There are no right or wrong answers here, as long as the video stays between 0 percent and 100 percent.

Finished example

Using High-Contrast Effects

So far, you've been adjusting the contrast to create a natural look. However, you might also want to deliberately create a high-contrast image, which can be used for a number of creative purposes: enhancing the separation of different elements of the frame, hiding a flaw in the exposure, or simply creating an interesting look. High-contrast looks, like any other visual trend in advertising and feature films, tend to cycle in and out of fashion.

Creating the High-Contrast Look

In this exercise, we will treat the image we've been working with as high contrast. Then we will explore the Broadcast Safe filter.

1   Move the Timeline playhead back to clip **3A_3**. This is the medium shot of the woman holding the golf ball.

2   Open this clip in the Viewer and go to the Color Corrector tab.

In order to create high contrast, you need to push more pixels up toward white (as seen in the Waveform monitor), and more pixels down toward black.

3   Move the Blacks slider to the left.

As you drag, more and more of the bottom end of the scale is crushed.

4   Drag the Whites slider right to send more and more pixels up the scale, toward white.

White values, instead of bunching up as the black values do, continue upward into the Superwhite range. As you already know, this is not good for broadcast. We will rectify this next by applying the Broadcast Safe filter.

Applying the Broadcast Safe Filter

The Broadcast Safe filter limits luminance and saturation levels. In this case, it is the perfect complement while you extend the contrast of the clip.

1 Add the Broadcast Safe filter to clip **3A_3** (Effects > Video Filters > Color Correction > Broadcast Safe) and click the Filters tab. Notice that the Broadcast Safe filter's default mode is Conservative. This setting is generally fine for most situations.

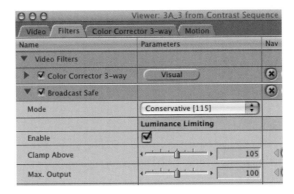

In the Waveform monitor, you should see that the white values have been clamped down to 100 percent.

The Broadcast Safe filter has clamped the top part of the scale from the Superwhite section down to 100 percent and lower.

2 Click the Color Corrector tab.

3   Drag the Whites slider to the right so that you can see how the
Broadcast Safe filter has put a limit on whites.

As you drag to the right, values climb to 100 percent and bunch up. The
Broadcast Safe filter is clamping any Superwhite values. This filter is
good to use whenever you want to make a range of light values brighter
but don't want to worry about going into unsafe luminance ranges.

4   Click the Filters tab.

5   Click the Mode pop-up menu in the Broadcast Safe filter to see the
choices available.

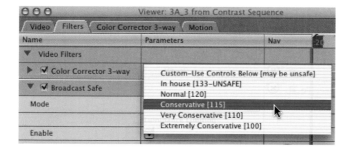

As a rule of thumb, you can use the default choice of Conservative,
as this limits values to 100 percent. The other choices, including the
Custom option, let you customize the top end of the luminance scale
with more precision. When in Custom mode, these controls are all
manual. In choices other than Custom, the sliders have no effect.

If you choose Custom, the following dialog box appears:

	Luminance Limiting		
Enable	☑		
Clamp Above	◄——⌂——►	105	◄◉►
Max. Output	◄——⌂——►	100	◄◉►
Start (Threshold)	◄——⌂——►	95	◄◉►
	Saturation Limiting		
Enable	☑		

Clamp Above sets the top percentage of luminance. Anything above this point is limited to the value in this field. Start (Threshold) is a percentage level above which light values are shifted. All values between Start (Threshold) and Clamp Above are shifted up or down together, with the Max. Output as the limit.

How High-Contrast Effects Work

What is the result of all this pushing and pulling of the contrast? The texture of the new image is certainly stylized, but how?

The image's gradations in the upper and lower end of the luminance range are removed. Where there used to be dark grays, all that is left is black. Where there used to be light grays, there is now white. A large proportion of the image now falls into one of these two extremes. Previous detail in these regions is now gone.

This focuses more attention on the remaining detail, the middle portion of the image, the middle grays. Adding contrast also makes the whites and the blacks *pop*, or draw attention to themselves.

High contrast can also bring out certain elements that you may wish to keep concealed. For instance, increased contrast can make the image appear more grainy, by highlighting its grain (film) or noise (video). If you want to amplify this texture deliberately, increasing the contrast is one way to do so.

What You've Learned

- The Brightness/Contrast filter can enhance or diminish the overall contrast of an image; the 3-way color corrector lets you selectively alter the contrast of the image's blacks, whites, or midtones.

- Crushing occurs when many pixels in the image bunch up at 0 percent luminance (the blacks).

- Tweak the midtones to set the mood of scene.

- A deliberate high-contrast look can hide a flaw and make whites and blacks pop, but it may look unrealistic or add an unwanted grainy appearance.

- Use the Broadcast Safe filter to clamp Superwhite values.

12

Color Balancing

So far, the focus has been on luminance and contrast. What about color? After grading the contrast, the next step in the primary color correction process is to work on the color balance of the image.

Establishing the look of your film is a subjective undertaking. Yes, you have to ensure that the video is broadcast legal, but beyond that, color correction is a creative endeavor. You may want to use color to enhance or alter the mood of a scene, or you may want to simply use color controls to make the scene look as natural as possible. In either case, you will need to understand how to affect color and what controls to use.

This lesson will focus on everything (of consequence) related to color. You will learn how to read the color balance of an image and use color correction to alter the colors of a scene. Additionally, you will explore the use of color as a way to imply different moods and ideas. First we will focus on identifying and creating a neutral color balance in video images so that the image closely represents the colors you would expect to see in real life. With a neutral balance, grass should look green, the sky should be blue, and most importantly, skin tones should look realistic.

Compensating for Lighting

Have you ever shopped for clothing only to get home and discover that the color of what you bought seems somehow different than it was in the store? If the lights in the store are fluorescent, and at home you are under incandescent light, then the clothing was viewed under two different kinds of light sources. Each light source has its own color temperature, which is a unique shift in color. The shift is so subtle from one location to the other, the light doesn't appear to have a noticeable color in either situation. You might even say the light seems relatively *white*, or without color. But even if you aren't aware of that color, it has an impact on the objects under that light. In this hypothetical situation, the lighting in the store affected your perception of the color of the clothing.

This phenomenon is similar in the photographed image. The lighting of the scene affects the color balance of the image, and therefore the depiction of colors in the film or video. If there is too much of any color in the light (in other words, if the light isn't *white*), then grass isn't the right green, and people don't look quite the way they should. There are many possible lighting conditions in which to photograph, and unless the image is balanced for that particular lighting scenario, the colors will seem off, unnatural. All the colors of the scene would have a color cast, or tint.

Identifying Color Casts

Colorists need to be able to see nuances in color and color casts in a video image, and must know how to alter the colors if necessary to create a natural appearance for the scene. And although every colorist may have his or her own subjective viewpoints on the use of color, finding a natural balance is often the first step to creating the final look of the video.

> **NOTE ▶** This lesson assumes that you are working on a calibrated external NTSC monitor. A computer monitor displays video images differently than an NTSC monitor or TV does; only an external NTSC monitor or TV provides a true representation of the final broadcast image. You may complete this exercise using only a computer monitor, but beware that it is not accurate for finishing purposes, and your images when broadcast may appear differently than how they are described here.

1   Open the file Lesson_12 > **12_Project_Start.fcp**.

The sequence **Color Balancing1** should be open and in front in the Timeline. If not, click the Color Balancing1 tab to load it into the Timeline.

2   Choose Window > Arrange > Color Correction.

This opens the Tool Bench window next to the Canvas with the Video Scopes tab forward.

3   In the Video Scopes tab, use the Layout pull-down menu to display the Vectorscope.

4   Move the playhead to the gap before the first clip in the Timeline, if it is not already there.

5   With the Timeline active, press the down arrow to move to the first clip in the Timeline, **6F_2**.

An image of a golfer appears in the Canvas.

Does the color of the scene look natural, or does it appear off? Look around the frame at the walls, the ceiling, and the man's face.

Your first impression is very valuable. Once you study an image for a period of time, you become less sensitive to any color cast in the image and are less likely to identify it.

Notice that the image has a slightly blue, or cold, quality to it.

6 Press the down arrow to move to the next clip in the Timeline.

It is the same clip with one major exception: a different color balance. This clip has a more neutral color balance than the previous clip did.

7 Compare these two clips with one another by going back and forth between the two in the Timeline.

TIP ▶ Press Ctrl-up arrow to temporarily visit the previous edit point. Press Ctrl-down arrow to temporarily visit the next edit point. When you release the keys, you return to the original playhead position.

Notice the differences between the ceiling, the man's face, his shirt, and the walls. The first clip in the Timeline has a bluish color cast, and the clip to its right is more neutral and natural. In particular, the shirt is a clean red, the ceiling is white, the face is warm, and the walls are a light green.

8   Make another comparison between these two clips, this time watching the Vectorscope as you go back and forth between the two clips.

Notice the differences in the Vectorscope. In the bluish clip, the main clump of values (traces) leans between blue and cyan, with the exception of the shirt, which is the clump in the red area.

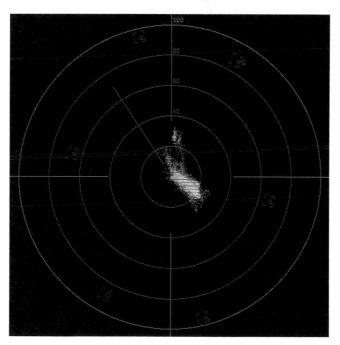

In the neutral clip, the majority of values cluster around the center of the Vectorscope.

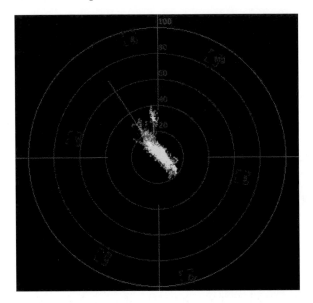

9   Use the same comparative techniques to check the different balances between the next two clips in the Timeline, starting with clip **201_6**.

The first clip has a slightly greenish color cast, and the clip after it (to the right) has a neutral color balance. Again, as with the previous two clips, study the different elements of the frame. Look at the walls, the face, and even the color of the brown bag that the man is holding. Look at the Vectorscope to see the overall difference in the layout of traces from one shot to the next.

Understanding the Color Wheel

Before we go in and actually remove the unwanted cast from our sample clip, let's take a few minutes to get a better understanding of the color wheel. As mentioned in Lesson 10, the Vectorscope could be described as a type of color wheel. In its various forms, the color wheel is an effective way to show different combinations of color, and it is used by many of Final Cut Pro's color correction tools and features, including the Vectorscope and both of the main color correction filters. Once you understand how the color wheel represents color and color controls, you can better predict the outcome of color correction actions.

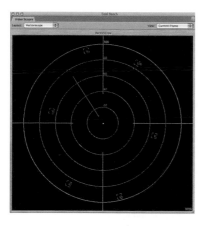 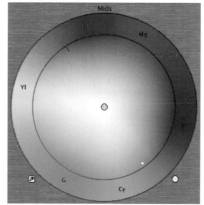

Primary and Secondary Colors in the Color Wheel

There are three main colors on a color wheel: red, green, and blue. Mixing varying amounts of these three colors results in the widest possible array of color combinations. Mixing equal amounts of all three results in white, or a lack of color. It's because of this that red, green, and blue phosphors are used to create the images on a television screen. Similarly, red, green, and blue substrates are used in film photography to create the color combinations when exposed to light.

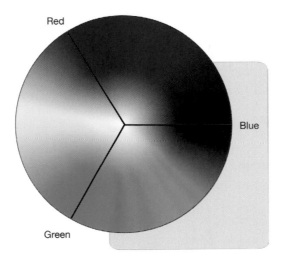

An equal mixture of any two primaries added together creates the secondary colors on the color wheel. These colors are cyan, magenta, and yellow. For example, yellow (a secondary) is a combination of green and red (both primaries).

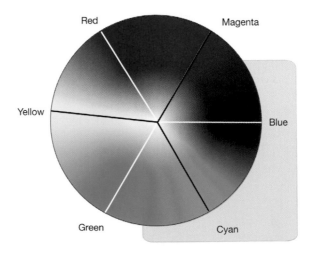

Notice that each secondary color falls directly opposite a primary color. A combination of any two opposite colors on the wheel creates white, or in color correction terms, a lack of hue, a neutral shade. These two opposite colors are *complementary*. One example of two complementary colors is yellow and blue.

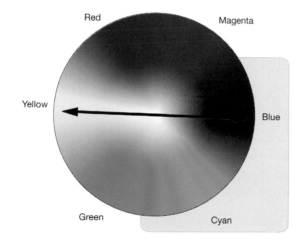

Understanding primary and secondary color relationships will help you color balance images in this lesson.

Saturation and Brightness in the Color Wheel

Mixing colors, however, involves more than adding two hues in the color wheel. Colors also have varying degrees of saturation and brightness.

The final result of color corrections in a video image is affected by all three of these components. This concept can be explored very easily using OS X's Color Picker.

1   Open a Color Matte into the Viewer. This is in the Effects tab in Video Generators > Matte > Color.

2   Go to the Controls tab to change the color of the matte.

3 Click the color picker icon (color box).

This will open the Color Picker window; you should see a color wheel. If not, click the little color wheel icon in the upper-left corner of the window.

4 Drag the bottom-right corner of the window to expand it, giving you a clear view of the color wheel.

In the center of the color wheel is a little white box. This box indicates the chosen color—in this case, gray. Notice that the color bar at the top of the window is gray.

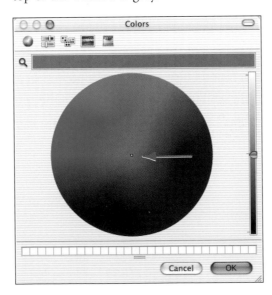

5   Click somewhere near an outside edge of the color wheel to select a color. The chosen color appears at the top of the window.

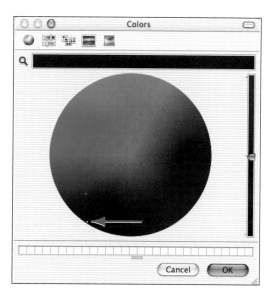

6   Click and drag around the edge of the wheel.

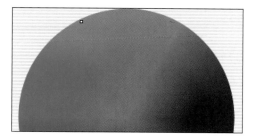

Notice the color change in the top of the window. The various colors you see are different hues.

7   Following a straight line, click and drag from the center of the wheel outward to the blue edge. As you move from the center toward the edge, you should see different saturation levels increase for that color, from no saturation at the center to full saturation at the edge. This demonstrates that a color has many possible saturation levels. Leave the icon at the outside edge of the wheel, at blue.

8 Use the vertical slider at the right of the Color Picker window to adjust brightness.

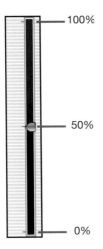

100%

50%

0%

Notice that the slider is at the midway point by default. Click and drag upward to the top of the scale, and watch the impact on the blue shade as you drag. There is now a whole new set of shades possible for blue, from the center out to the edge, depending on the brightness level.

9   Watch the rest of the color wheel as you adjust the slider. Notice the variations of colors available around the wheel.

Lower levels of brightness   Higher levels of brightness

Now you can see how color is a mixture of hue, saturation, and brightness.

10   Once you have experimented with the brightness slider, click OK in the window to close the Color Picker.

Basic Color Balancing Controls

Now let's use NTSC color bars to begin working with color balancing controls. Color bars are a good precursor to working on a video scene, as they demonstrate how a wide mix of colors can be altered with balance controls.

1   Make sure the Vectorscope display is still open.

2   Move to the last clip in the Color Balancing1 sequence, **Bars and Tone**.

3   Choose Effects > Video Filters > Color Correction > Color Corrector 3-way to apply a 3-way color correction filter to this clip.

4   Open this clip into the Viewer and go to the Color Corrector 3-way tab.

You have already explored the luminance controls in this filter; now it's time to explore the color controls.

There are three color balance wheels here. These balance wheels let you change the mix of colors in the scene. There are color balance controls for the blacks, mids, and whites. This means that color can be altered in these unique regions of the video image. When to use which wheel will be explored later in this lesson.

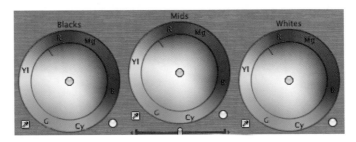

Right now we're going to explore how a color balance wheel shifts the colors of the scene.

These color wheels mimic the color targets in the Vectorscope.

In the center of each balance wheel is a small, round, light gray indicator. This is the default position for each wheel.

5   To change the mix of colors with the test clip of color bars, click the balance indicator for mids and drag it toward yellow (to the left).

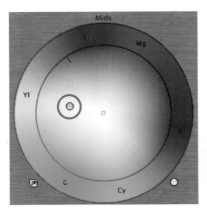 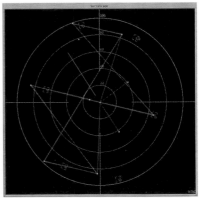

TIP ▶ At first you may not notice any movement while dragging on a balance indicator. By default, the balance controls in the color correction filters move in very small increments. Cmd-drag to make adjustments in larger increments.

As you drag, watch the Vectorscope. Notice that most of the color traces shift to the left.

Release when the balance indicator is approximately midway between the center and the symbol for yellow.

6 Look at the Canvas to see the color shift on the different bars of color.

In the Vectorscope, most of the traces have shifted to the left. In the visual display of the color bars, you should also see that the colors are a little warmer, more yellow. This is most obvious in the cyan, magenta, and green bars. The cyan bar, for instance, is now much closer to green.

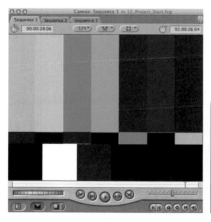
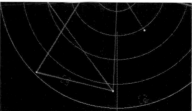

NOTE ▶ To reset any balance wheel to its default, click the white reset button at the bottom right of the wheel. To reset the entire filter, Shift-click any of the three white reset buttons. This will reset all three balance wheels, all luminance sliders, and the saturation slider.

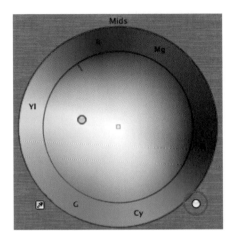

Now you can see how the balancing controls shift the balance of colors in the color wheel and redistribute their display in the Vectorscope. You add more of the color in one direction or the other, but you do not replace colors with completely different hues. For example, notice that adding yellow (dragging toward yellow) has not made the magenta into yellow, but instead has created a blend of yellow and magenta, resulting in a hue closer to red.

To remove a color cast in a video image, you would add color in the opposite direction of the color shift on the balance wheel. This helps shift the colors of the scene closer to the center of the wheel, where they're more neutral.

For instance, to remove or lessen a color tint of red, you would drag a balance indicator toward cyan.

Color Balancing a Scene

Now that you have explored the color wheel and the basic concepts behind color balancing, it's time to apply this understanding to balancing a video image. You can think of color balancing in this example as "relighting" the photographed scene to create a natural look and remove unwanted color casts.

1   Open the **Color Balancing2** sequence by clicking on the Color Balancing2 tab in the Timeline to bring the sequence to the front.

2   Move the playhead to the first clip in the Timeline, **201_6**.

Before color correcting this clip, you need to isolate the color shift. The color in the scene has a slight cast, but it would be difficult to find it without a little help from something objective in the frame.

3   Select the clip in the Timeline and set the Canvas to View > Image+Wireframe.

4   Select the Crop tool.

5   Crop the right side of the image (drag inward from the right side of image) so that only the wall and doorway next to the man are visible.

This wall should be light gray. If the image had a neutral color balance, there would not be any noticeable color in this wall.

6   Study the image in the Vectorscope. If there were any gravitation away from the center of the scope, it would indicate a color cast in the clip.

Notice that in this case, the Vectorscope reads this wall as a bit toward green and cyan, so let's remove this cast.

7 Ctrl-click in the center of the Vectorscope window and choose Magnify
from the contextual menu.

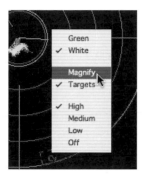

This enlarges the display of the center of the Vectorscope to allow for
a more discerning view of traces near the center.

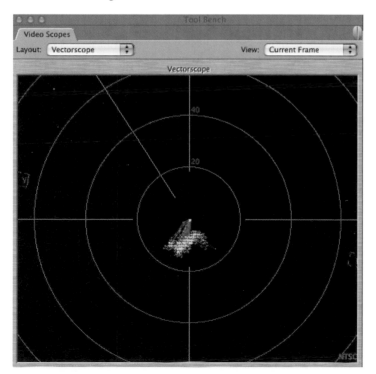

8 Add the Color Corrector 3-way filter to this clip.

9 Drag the balance indicator for mids upward a little bit to compensate for the cast.

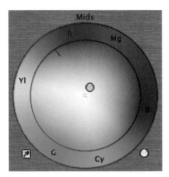

Release when the traces in the Vectorscope are hovering around the center of the Vectorscope. The wall now has no noticeable hue. It is gray, as it is in real life.

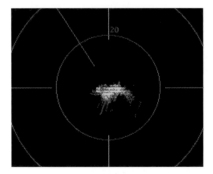

10 Uncrop the image to see how this color correction has affected the entire image.

You should now see that removing this little bit of green/cyan in the image has had a positive effect on the rest of the image by creating natural-looking colors—including the skin tones in the face. In this case, making the wall less tinted was a choice that helped the face become more natural looking as well.

11 On the Color Corrector 3-way tab, check the Enable box to turn off
the filter.

As discussed earlier, the longer you study an image, the less sensitive
you are to subtle shifts in color. One of the quickest ways to get a fresh
look at the color corrected scene is to turn off the color correction
temporarily.

12 Turn the filter off and on a couple of times to study the effect and
make any final adjustments you deem necessary.

Rendering Faces Naturally

When trying to create a natural color balance, the human face can be a
good reference point. Not only is the face usually the primary focus of
a scene, but there is also a simple, objective guide in Final Cut Pro's
Vectorscope that can help determine whether faces have a natural hue:
the flesh tone line.

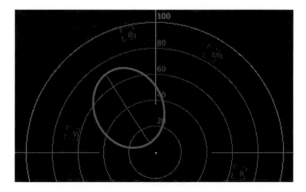

There are a multitude of skin tones in this world, with varying levels of saturation and luminance. Regardless of ethnicity, however, all faces have a similar hue, which is what this line denotes. As a result, it makes a good reference point.

1   Make sure the Vectorscope is still open, using Tools > Video Scopes.

2   Ctrl-click in the Vectorscope display and uncheck Magnify in the contextual menu.

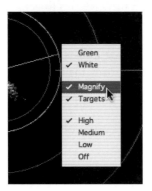

3   In the Color Balancing2 Timeline, move to clip **2B_4**, the second clip from the left, and select it.

The skin tone on this clip is a little unnatural. Let's isolate the face to read it in the Vectorscope.

4   Select the Crop tool.

5   Crop the image down until only the face is left onscreen.

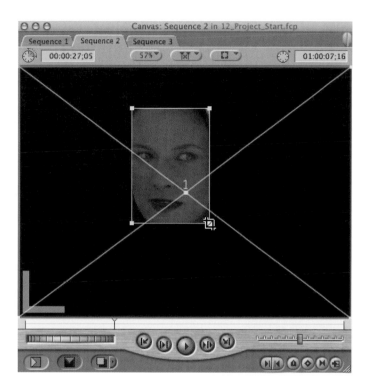

Notice that once the clip is cropped, the only values left in the Vectorscope fall about 45 degrees away from the flesh tone line. The face is closer to magenta than it is to the yellow/red of the flesh tone line.

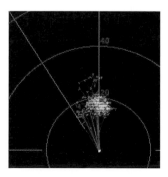

6 Add the Color Corrector 3-way filter to this clip, open it into the Viewer, and go to the Color Corrector tab.

Skin color will look more natural and realistic when the clump of traces that represent the face move to the same angle as the flesh tone line.

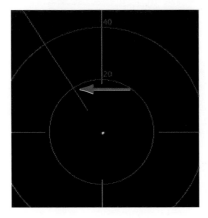

Equally important is aiming for a similar amount of saturation—in this case approximately 20 percent.

7 Use the Mids balance control to add a little bit of yellow (drag left) until the traces are hovering around the flesh tone line, at about the same saturation percentage (around 20 percent). The flesh tone line is your guide to creating a neutral balance.

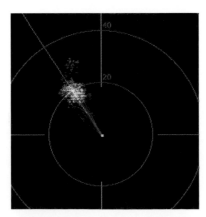

8   Uncrop the clip so you can now see the whole image.

Although you were focusing on the face in the previous steps, you were still affecting all the colors in the image. As everything in this scene was shot under the same light, the correction will have the same positive effect on the rest of the frame. The entire image, not just the face, appears more natural than it did before the correction.

9   Check the Enable box to turn the filter off and on.

The Vectorscope is a helpful tool for objective color analysis, but turning the filter on and off triggers a visual response that is purely subjective. Both techniques are valuable, and it is up to you, the colorist, to determine the extent of the color balancing that's appropriate for each situation and scene.

Auto Balance Eyedroppers

In addition to using the Vectorscope as a guide during the grading process, you also can access controls that automatically rebalance an image so that it appears more natural.

1   Move to the next clip in the Timeline, **1A_4**.

> This clip does not have a neutral balance, but it does have elements that Final Cut Pro can use to neutralize the scene. Notice the door in the background: This appears to be white, but there is such a strong tint to the clip that that the door appears bluish.
>
> If we make the assumption that this door should be white, we can use a function that rebalances the scene automatically.

2   Apply the Color Corrector 3-way filter to this clip, open it into the Viewer, and go to the Color Corrector tab.

3   Locate the Eyedropper button beneath the Whites balance wheel.

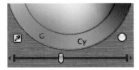

> This button is used to sample a color in the Canvas that should be white.

4   Click this button to activate the eyedropper.

5   Move the cursor to the Canvas. It becomes an eyedropper icon over the image.

6   Click a spot on the door in the image.

A new color balance to the scene is triggered by clicking on the part of the door that you want to be white.

The Whites eyedropper samples the pixels in an object in the frame that should be white and then rebalances the colors of the image to make the object white. Notice that the indicator for the Whites balance wheel has shifted up and to the left, between yellow and red.

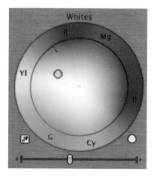

NOTE ▶ When sampling white, avoid picking something that has no detail at all, something too high on the luminance scale. When you sampled from the door, you selected values that are only about 70 percent on average, when reading a Waveform monitor.

Sampling from the Mids

When working with contrast, all three luminance sliders may need to be adjusted to enhance the contrast. With color, only one color balance wheel needed to be adjusted to balance the image. Why? Because the Whites balance wheel affects the top 75 percent of the image. Everything from dark gray shades of color up to white is affected; as a result, in the last example, the image was balanced by adjusting that one wheel.

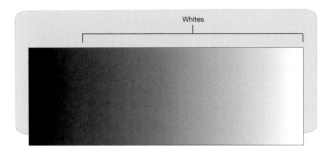

You probably noticed, however, that there are three eyedroppers, one each for white, mids, and blacks. This means that you can sample different elements in the frame to create a more natural color balance.

In general, you should begin to color balance a scene to make it natural and realistic by working in the whites or the mids. Then, depending on the scene, additional adjustments may or may not be necessary.

If there is nothing white in the frame, sample something that should be gray using the Mids eyedropper. The mids typically make up a large percentage of an image, and a balance wheel for the mids affects 25 percent to 75 percent of the luminance.

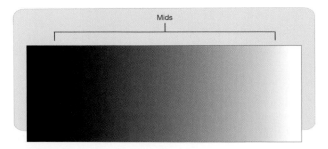

If the entire image is lit with the same color (temperature) lighting, as is often the case, you may get away with balancing in just the mids. The advantage of doing the primary color balancing with the mids is that you can avoid overly tinting the bright whites or deep blacks. This is a real gray area (yes, that's a pun), and it is of course highly dependent on the composition of the image. Every image is different and requires a unique approach.

> **NOTE ▶** When dealing with strong, saturated colors, the Whites wheel has the strongest influence on yellow, cyan, and green. The Blacks wheel has the strongest influence on red, blue, and magenta.

So let's use the Mids eyedropper to color balance the scene.

1   Shift-click the reset button under any of the three color wheels to reset the entire filter back to its default settings. This restores us to the uncorrected image. Now, instead of balancing with the whites, you will balance the same image with the mids.

2   Click the eyedropper under the Mids color wheel.

3   Move the cursor to the Canvas and click with the eyedropper on a part of the phone, which is supposed to be gray.

The image should balance when you click. If the result appears similar to those of the last exercise, then you sampled correctly. Notice that the indicator for the Mids wheel is up and to the left, between yellow and red. The original bluish-cyan cast is now gone. The door is white, the face is natural and the phone on the table is gray.

Using Color to Create a Stylized Look

So far, we have color balanced images merely to achieve a neutral, natural look. But if the world were always portrayed so neutrally, so antiseptically, it would become monotonous and boring.

By altering color and its intensity, veering away from this neutral approach, you can alter the mood of the scene and the viewer's perceptions. Indeed, color is a powerful tool. It can be used to suggest different moods and feelings, portray the time of day, and give texture to the photographed environment. Color can elicit subtle or dramatic emotional responses. A general knowledge of color and its effects can be a great aid in the color correction process.

People build relationships with color from an early age. Parents and teachers often say things like, "It's green, like grass," or, "A red light means stop." These associations become ingrained, and you as a colorist can use color to try to trigger feelings, moods, and memories in your viewers, as well as to make other nonverbal associations. A sophisticated use of color makes a scene dreary and bleak, warm and inviting, or frightening and cold.

In the remainder of this lesson, we will use color to achieve a more stylized and sophisticated look for a scene.

Creating Color Tints

The cinematographer may have implemented a color cast while filming through a use of color in lighting and/or colored filters on the lens. The color cast, or tint, may also be created after shooting, through color correction.

In this exercise, you will use color balancing controls to create or enhance a color tint.

1 Open the **Color Balancing3** sequence (or click the Color Balancing3 Timeline tab to bring sequence to the front, if already open).

2 Move to the first clip in the Timeline, **2B neutral**.

3 Add the Color Corrector 3-way filter to this clip.

4   Open this clip into the Viewer and go to the Color Corrector 3-way tab.

This clip has a neutral color balance. We will now make it look like late afternoon by warming the highlights of the image, which are the areas most directly affected by the setting sunlight.

5   Drag the luminance slider for Whites to the left.

This can help to emulate the perception that sunlight is less intense at this time of day.

6   Add a warm color by dragging the Whites balance indicator somewhat toward yellow and red, as indicated in the illustration.

Notice that the highlights in the hair are more yellow, as is the glow around the little bit of sky. The face appears warmer, but not as warm as the hair. Yet the shadows, the darkest part of the image, remain neutral. If the time of day were a little later, you might add a little blue in the shadows, as the darkening sky would have a colder color than the direct sunlight.

Using the Whites indicator to warm up the color balance was appropriate in this situation.

The scene is still realistic, but is now more suggestive of late afternoon sunlight.

7   Move to the next clip in the Timeline, **6D neutral**.

8   Add the Color Corrector 3-way filter to this clip.

9   Open the clip into the Viewer and go to the Color Corrector 3-way tab.

10 Use the Mids color wheel to experiment with a more extreme color balance. Drag toward the flesh tone line to add warm light.

You might be wondering why we're using the Mids balance. This is only one option. Using the mids to create a tint will tend to add this color to everything in the frame except the darkest shadows and brightest highlights. This means that the tint is seen mostly in the face, the lighter part of the shirt, and the walls. This is a good option when you want the whites and blacks to be clean, without any tint. If you wanted the highlights to have color, then you could use the Whites slider instead to add the tint.

11 Turn the filter off and on to compare the tinted look with the original.

12 Drag between green and cyan. This will create a somewhat surreal tint that could be used to suggest fluorescent lighting or a spooky mood. This cast is currently popular in many TV commercials.

13 Cmd-drag the Mids balance indicator in a small circle around the center of the wheel.

As you drag, watch the resulting image in the Canvas. Although not accurate for choosing final color, this technique can help you to pick a hue for a look, or try to match a hue from another clip (something you will do in another lesson).

14 Release when you see a hue that looks interesting.

15 Click and drag along an imaginary line from the center of the Mids balance wheel outward toward the edge, staying within the same hue (angle).

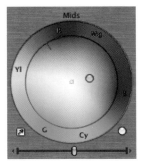

This allows you to fine-tune the color tint, as you pick less or more saturation of the color.

16 Turn the filter off and on for comparison.

Viewing the uncorrected clip and then the corrected clip back-to-back can help you decide if the effect is too heavy. Turning the effect on and off jars you back to seeing the real strength of the color tint. Basically, the more saturated the tint, the less realistic it appears.

NOTE ▶ Keep an eye on the Vectorscope to ensure that you stay within legal levels. Don't let color go outward past any target.

Tinting Black-and-White Images

In addition to adding a color cast over a color image, you also have the option of processing the shot as black and white first, and then putting a color tint over that. This look is similar to that of applying a color tint to a black-and-white photograph. If this is the goal, then you can treat the video clip with the same kind of options as the photograph. In this case, you will create a sepia tone.

When adding the tint, you can choose whether the color affects the blacks, or the blacks stay neutral. You have this same choice with respect to the whites and highlights. In the following exercise, you will create the color tint with only the Mids and Whites balance wheels. This will keep the color tint out of the blacks. For television images, clean blacks have a tendency to look less noisy (grainy) than blacks that have color.

You'll use two filters. The first filter will make the video appear black and white (grayscale, technically). The second filter will create the color tint.

1 Move to the third clip in the Timeline, **TV_wide**.

2 Add the Color Corrector 3-way filter to this clip.

3 Open this clip into the Viewer and go to the Color Corrector 3-way tab.

4 Drag the saturation slider all the way to the left.

  The clip now has no apparent color.

5 Add another Color Corrector 3-way filter to this clip.

  When a second color corrector filter is added to a clip, it appears in the Filters tab and as another Color Corrector tab, in this case labeled Color Corrector 3-way - 2.

6 Click the Filters tab to see the two filters.

The first color correction filter that you applied is on top, and the second filter is on the bottom. Clicking the Visual button for either of them will take you to the color controls for that filter.

7   Click the Color Corrector 3-way - 2 tab.

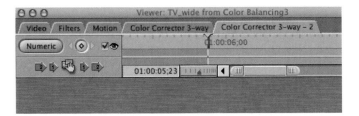

At this point, you may be wondering why you added one filter, removed saturation, and then added another filter. Why not just add the color tint in the first filter? The final effect is a result of the order of effects as they are applied to a clip. Adjusting the order of clips adjusts the final result. In this case, you applied a filter to desaturate the clip, and then applied another color correction filter to which you will add the tint.

8   Drag the Mids balance indicator outward from the center toward yellow and red, as shown in the following illustration.

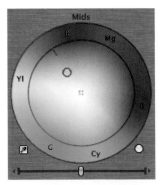

Notice the dramatic effect of this sepia color over black and white. This look may be desirable when you don't have to represent colors naturally.

9 Experiment with different angles by dragging the Mids balance indicator in a small circle around the center of the wheel.

> **NOTE ▶** You can also adjust the saturation slider on the first filter somewhere between full color and no color to experiment with tints that have varying amounts of the original color. This expands your color palette to create many more possible and interesting variations.

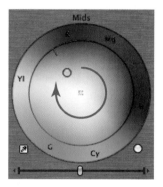

As you drag, watch the resulting image in the Canvas. Checking out these sample colors will give you an idea of the palette available to you when creating a tint effect.

What You've Learned

- Use cropping, the Vectorscope display, and its flesh tone line to achieve a realistic color balance with human subjects.

- Most realistic color balancing can be done by using the whites and/or midtones, which comprise the majority of pixels in a frame.

- Use the balance wheels in the Color Corrector 3-way filter to change the mix of colors.

- Desaturate an image to make it look black and white, and then apply a 3-way color correction filter and adjust the Mids to create a sepia-toned image.

13

Lesson Files   Lessons > Lesson_13 > 13_Project_Start.fcp

Media   Media > Lesson_10-14_Media

Time   This lesson takes approximately 90 minutes to complete.

Goals   Use comparison to aid in color matching

Color correct a scene from beginning to end

Learn a workflow for color matching

Use Frame Viewer, Copy Filter controls, and Playhead Sync
during color correction

Color Correcting for Scene Continuity

So far, you have worked sequentially on evaluating images, modifying contrast, and color balancing. In this lesson, you bring it all together and color correct a scene from beginning to end.

You will create a look for an image, based on techniques that you have already explored. To create a sense of consistency and harmony throughout the images, you will use some familiar techniques and some new ones to match the look throughout all the clips in the scene.

The Importance of Visual Harmony

When a scene is supposed to portray a continuous event, the shots that make up that scene should work toward one goal: making you believe that everything is happening at one point in time. Creating continuity between more than one shot means that the action matches as you cut from one shot to another in a way that makes the audience believe it is one continuous action. The audience should believe in these moments, although they are artificial in nature. We often judge a film's success by its ability to suspend the audience's disbelief, or to engage the audience in the story even though it's a series of contrived images strung together.

The ability to suspend your audience's disbelief may be affected by subtle changes in the look, or color balance, of consecutive images. A discontinuity in the look of consecutive images during a film can be jarring or feel disjointed, and can take the viewer out of the moment just like mismatched action between shots can.

Creating continuity or harmony between images keeps the audience's attention where you want it to be: on the story. Continuity can be created by correcting color from scene to scene to match shots to one another. When images are color corrected to match, the multiple angles of a scene appear as though they happened at one point in time.

Configuring Resolution

This lesson uses a window arrangement in Final Cut Pro that is available only when your computer monitor is set to a minimum resolution of 1280 dots per inch. So let's start out by locating and possibly adjusting your display settings.

1   Quit Final Cut Pro if it is currently running.

2   Go to the Apple menu and choose System Preferences.

3 In the System Preferences window, click on the Displays icon.

4 Set a horizontal resolution of 1280 or higher. The horizontal resolution is the first number (the number on the left) when reading from the available resolutions.

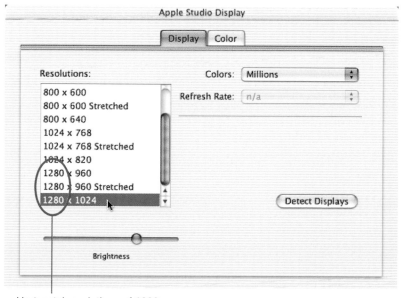

Horizontal resolutions of 1280

NOTE ▶ If you are using a PowerBook or other small screen, you may not be able to set your resolution this high. You can still complete the exercise, but the steps will vary slightly as your window arrangement will be different.

5   Press Cmd-Q to quit System Preferences.

Making Visual Comparisons

To determine if there is any discordance between shots, you need to first compare them, and then you can color correct images to match one another.

1   Open Lesson_13 > **13_Project_Start.fcp**.

The **Intro Sequence** should be open and in front in the Timeline. There are three clips in this sequence. The first two clips, **9A_final** and **3A_final**, have been color corrected. The third clip, **2B_5**, has not.

2   Move the playhead to the head of the sequence, at clip **9A_final**, if it is not already there.

3   Play back the sequence.

The second and third clips have a substantial visual discontinuity between them. There is an overall difference in contrast and colors. The wide shot has deeper blacks, and the colors are warmer and more vibrant than the close-up.

Side-by-Side Comparisons with the Frame Viewer

As we've discussed in previous lessons, human eyes become less sensitive to shifts in color over time, so you can use the video scopes for a more analytical study of the colors in the scene. A third technique is to make a side-by-side visual comparison, which is highly effective at determining differences in color and contrast. To get the most from a side-by-side comparison, we will use the Frame Viewer.

1 Press Home to move the Timeline playhead to the beginning of the sequence.

2 Choose Window > Arrange > Multiple Edits.

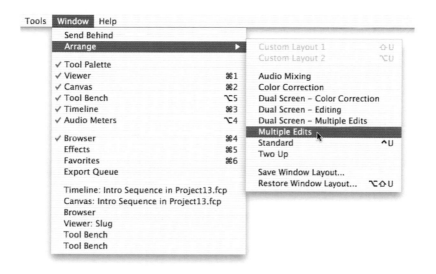

This option rearranges the windows on the screen, opening up two new Tool Bench windows in addition to the main interface windows. Two Frame Viewer tabs (each in a Tool Bench window) open on either side of the Canvas.

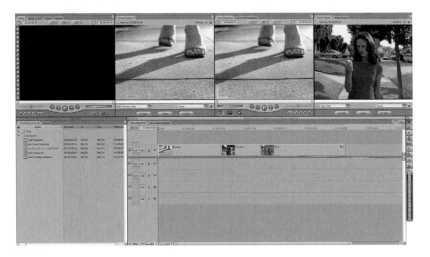

NOTE ▶ The Multiple Edits option appears in the menu only when you have a minimum horizontal resolution of 1280. If you are not using a resolution of 1280 or higher, and do not have a Multiple Edits option, choose Window > Arrange > Color Correction. A Frame Viewer tab will open as a tab behind the Video Scopes tab. Click the tab to bring it to the front whenever the instructions direct you to use a Frame Viewer window. You may also open a Frame Viewer window by choosing Tools > Frame Viewer.

The Frame Viewer helps you compare the shot you are working on with a previously color corrected clip. Let's start out by becoming more familiar with the different options available in a Frame Viewer window. If you chose the Multiple Edits layout, a Frame Viewer window will appear between the Viewer and the Canvas.

3   Choose Previous Edit from the pop-up menu at the bottom left of the Frame Viewer, if it is not already chosen.

When Previous Edit is chosen, the window is set to display the last frame of the previous clip in the Timeline (the first clip to the left of the playhead).

4   Choose None from the pop-up menu in the bottom right of the Frame Viewer, if it is not already chosen.

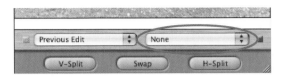

5   Scrub the playhead forward into the second clip and then into the third clip.

As you navigate from clip to clip, the Frame Viewer to the left of the Canvas updates to display the clip to the left of the current clip under the playhead. When color correcting, if you work from left to right through the Timeline, the left Frame Viewer shows the clip that has just been color corrected. If the two clips are supposed to cut together, like two shots of a scene, this gives you a way to see both clips at the same time so that they can be matched to one another.

NOTE ▶ A Frame Viewer's contents update only when playback is paused.

At the bottom of the Frame Viewer window are three buttons that act as a shortcut to opening up the split-screen features of this window.

6   Move the playhead to beginning of **2B_5**.

7   Click the V-Split button in this Frame Viewer window.

3A_final is on the left and **2B_5** on is the right.

Notice that the pop-up menus at the bottom of the window now read Previous Edit and Current Frame. That is the default combination of displayed frames.

8   Click the H-split button to display **3A_final** on top and **2B_5** on the bottom.

9   Click the Swap button.

As the name of the button implies, this switches the arrangement of the two images.

10 Click the V-Split button to return the window to a vertical split screen.

11 Click the Swap button again to reset the split screen to its default state, with Previous Edit on the left and Current Frame on the right.

When you click V-Split, notice that the two pop-up displays change to reflect the switch.

NOTE ▶ If the last step left the two images reversed in position (**3A_final** on the right), click the V-Split button again until **3A_final** is on the left.

To take maximum advantage of comparing different images with one another, you can fully alter the split screen to customize it as you wish.

12 Move your cursor over the center of the split screen, where the two images meet.

The cursor changes to the Resize pointer when it is directly over the line separating the two images.

13 Click and drag left and right (using the Resize pointer).

This action rolls the line of the split screen left or right to compare different parts of the two images.

14 Click the V-Split button to reset the split-screen border to the center of the screen, with the default view of the previous clip (with the green squares) on the left and the current frame (with the blue squares) on the right.

15 Hover the cursor over the left side of the split screen (which shows the frame from the previous edit, with green squares).

The cursor becomes a hand icon.

NOTE ▶ If the cursor does not display a hand icon while over the left side of the screen, you may have clicked one of the split-screen buttons one too many times. Move the cursor over the right side of the screen, with the green squares, to get the hand icon.

16 While the cursor displays the hand, click and drag to the left or right.

The image slides in the same direction across the Frame Viewer, revealing different parts of the two images.

17 Click the V-Split button to reset the split screen to its default state (**3A_final** on the left side of split screen).

18 Click and drag any of the four green corner points of the left side of the split screen. You are able to move any of the corner points up or down, left or right.

Frame Viewer Color Coding

A Frame Viewer is flexible enough to compare other images aside from Previous Edit and Current Frame. In order to take the most advantage of this window, let's take a moment to identify its components. Basically, everything in the Frame Viewer is color-coded green or blue. Each pop-up menu has an associated green or blue square that corresponds to the dots bordering the two images.

▶ Saving Customized Tool Bench Windows

When you have two computer monitors or a large single monitor like a Cinema Display, you may want to keep additional video scopes and/or Frame Viewers open onscreen, or set the Frame Viewer to a vertical split screen. Saving a custom window arrangement saves more than just the position of windows; it also saves several Tool Bench parameters:

- Number of Tool Bench windows open.

- Specific combination of Video Scopes and Frame Viewer tabs.

- In the Video Scopes tab, a custom window arrangement will save the layout, frame, and contextual options like the brightness of the overlays and whether targets are displayed. For instance, you could save the following to be restored: Vectorscope window, magnified, targets off, viewing the Previous Edit.

- In the Frame Viewer, the green- and blue-labeled pop-up choices are saved, as well as the split-screen border. This saves all the custom options of the Frame Viewer.

To open additional Video Scopes or Frame Viewer windows, choose Tools > Video Scopes or Frame Viewer. The additional window will open as a tab on an open Tool Bench window. To break Tool Bench tabs into separate windows, click and drag the tab itself, and let go when it is away from the original window.

To save a customized window layout (that incorporates all Tool Bench parameters), choose Window > Arrange > Save Window Layout and give the saved file a name that reflects its purpose. In the future, you can always restore this saved custom layout by choosing Window > Arrange > Restore Layout.

To take a customized window layout with you to another computer, you'll find the file you saved located in the Finder at Volume > Users > User (logged in user) > Library > Preferences > Final Cut Pro User Data > Window Layouts.

Several choices from these pop-up menus are available to aid you during color correction and other effects work.

1   Click the green-labeled pop-up menu to view the video display options for the green-labeled side of the split screen.

   Each of these choices is useful in a different situation. For now, you will continue to use Previous Edit. (If the option says anything other than Previous Edit, reset it.)

2   Click on the blue-labeled pop-up menu and choose None from the choices. This resets the window to displaying only a single image.

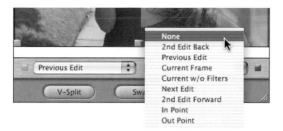

Choosing anything other than None returns the window to a split screen. The options in this menu are the same as in the green-labeled pop-up menu, with the exception of an additional choice here for None. During the following exercise, switch back to a split screen whenever it may be of help.

Color Correcting Across Scenes

Having compared the images, we're now ready to match the color balance across two scenes We'll correct clip **2B_5**, a close-up, and match it to the wide shot, 3A_final, which is already finished. We'll use the Frame Viewer and the video scopes to help us make decisions.

Setting up the Multiple Edits Window Layout

In addition to the Frame Viewer in the Tool Bench on the left, between the Viewer and the Canvas, there is also a Frame Viewer tab in the Tool Bench to right of the Canvas. In the Tool Bench window to the right of the Canvas, there are two tabs: one for a Frame Viewer and another for Video Scopes.

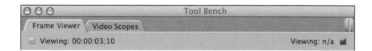

NOTE ▶ If your screen does not have the resolution for Multiple Edits, then skip to the next section, "Setting up the Color Correction Window Layout."

During this exercise, you will use one Frame Viewer window (to the left of the Canvas) and one Video Scopes window (to the right of the Canvas), which will give you a mix of subjective and objective information.

1   Click on the Video Scopes tab in the Tool Bench to the right to bring it to the front.

2   In the Video Scopes window, choose Waveform from the Layout pop-up menu, and be sure the View pop-up menu is set to Current Frame.

Setting up the Color Correction Window Layout

NOTE ▶ If you are using the Multiple Edits layout, skip to the next section, "Matching Contrast Range."

1   In the Tool Bench window to the right of the Canvas, click the Video Scopes tab to bring it to the front.

2   In the Video Scopes window, go to the Layout pop-up menu and choose Waveform.

3   Switch back and forth between the Video Scopes and Frame Viewer tabs as needed during the next exercise.

Matching Contrast Range

As the medium shot and close-up are similar angles of the scene, achieving a similar distribution of luminance values in the waveforms of those two images would be a good place to start with the color correction.

One of the main differences between these two clips is in the black and white levels. The medium shot has values that extend from 0 percent to 100 percent. The close-up, on the other hand, has a narrower range of values, mostly between 10 percent and 90 percent.

1   Move the Timeline playhead to the first frame of clip **2B_5** (if it's not already there) and select it.

2   Choose Effects > Video Filters > Color Correction > Color Corrector 3 Way to apply the Color Corrector 3-way filter to the clip **2B_5**.

3   Choose Effects > Video Filters > Color Correction > Broadcast Safe to apply the Broadcast Safe filter to this clip.

    The Broadcast Safe filter allows you to push the white levels of the clip upward and still remain within broadcast standards by clamping white levels at 100 percent.

4   Open the now-broadcast-safe clip into the Viewer and click on the Color Corrector tab.

5   Drag the Blacks luminance slider to the left until the blacks in the scene start to crush at 0 percent, similar to the blacks in **3A_final**.

3A_final

2B_5, after setting black levels

6   Drag the Whites luminance slider to the right until the waveforms representing the sky in the left part of the frame begin to clamp at 100 percent.

Now the overall range of the contrast is similar between the two shots.

Setting the Midtones

One more aspect of the contrast still needs to be set: the mids level. This is something that isn't easily discernable looking at the Waveform monitor, and it may be easier to use a visual comparison instead. You will set an approximate mids level, which can be fine-tuned later, after color balancing this clip.

1   Use the Frame Viewer and the Canvas to make a comparison between the medium shot and the close-up, paying particular attention to the face in each shot. Look for any apparent change in luminance.

The more experience you have with this type of comparison, the easier it will be to see the differences between the two clips. In this case, the close-up is a little brighter in the mids range than the wide shot is.

2   In the Color Corrector tab, adjust the Mids luminance slider to better match the two clips.

As there is just a subtle difference between the two shots and only a small adjustment is necessary, click the arrow to the left of the slider four times or so, to create somewhat similar levels between the two clips.

3 In the Frame Viewer, click the H-Split button to see if the contrast adjustments hold up to a closer side-by-side scrutiny.

Balancing the Color

You may have already noticed the differences in overall color between the two clips, but it's hard to tell how to change the close-up to match the wide shot without help. You will use Vectorscope readings of both clips, a little experimentation, and the Frame Viewer in this exercise as a guide to color balancing **2B_5**.

1 In the Video Scopes window, set the Layout to Vectorscope, and View to Current Frame.

2 Move the playhead back to the clip **3A_final** (press the up arrow).

Take note of the image in the Vectorscope.

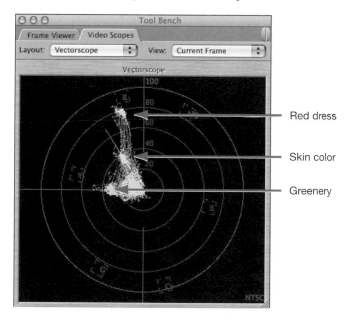

Although these two clips are not identical and should not have identical Vectorscope readings, there are some overall differences that can help guide you on how to color balance the close-up.

The majority of traces in the Vectorscope for the medium shot extend outward toward the flesh tone line. Another clump of values, which indicate the greenery in the scene, extend toward yellow (leaning a little toward green). There is also a clump of values close to the red target, representing the red dress the woman is wearing.

3   Move the Timeline playhead forward to the close-up (press the down arrow), and notice the Vectorscope readings.

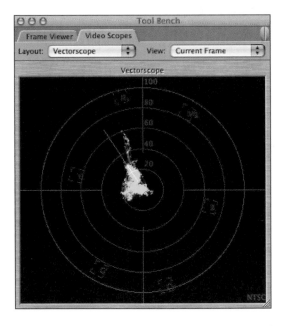

The close-up also has three general clumps of traces, but they all are somewhat closer to the center of the Vectorscope. In general, this clip needs to have color added in the direction between yellow and the flesh tone line, as well as a little boost in the saturation to better match the wide shot.

4   In the Tool Bench window between the Viewer and Canvas, click the Frame Viewer tab to bring it to the front.

5   In the Frame Viewer, click the V-Split button twice.

You should now see the close-up on the left screen and the wide shot on the right, with the woman's face in both views.

6   In the Viewer, Cmd-drag the Mids balance indicator in a small circle around the center of the wheel.

As you drag, watch the two images in the Frame Viewer. Trying out different hues can help you see what color is closest to matching the two images. Although this does not necessarily show you how much color to add in the balance wheel, it gives you an idea of which direction (angle, hue) to move in the wheel.

In this case, adding color between yellow and the flesh tone line gets you closest to matching the wide shot. This experimentation confirms the information you gained in the Vectorscope.

7   Set the Mids balance indicator between yellow and the flesh tone line. Not much color is needed here; set it just a touch away from the center of the wheel.

At this point, the color balance between the two shots should be fairly similar. There does still appear to be an overall lack of saturation, which will be addressed in the next step.

8   Drag the saturation slider slightly to the right to intensify the colors in the scene.

Now the clips are closely color matched.

9   Use the Play Around button in the Canvas to play back from the previous final images and then into the newly color corrected close-up. Render if needed before playing it back.

This is the final test to see if the images flow well one after the other, as they will eventually be seen by the audience.

10 After playback, determine whether any additional correction is needed in contrast and/or color balance, and make any adjustments. Use the Frame Viewer and the video scopes to aid you.

> **TIP** If the comparison frame of the clip you want to see is not available when using a Frame Viewer to compare clips, choose In Point from the green-labeled pop-up menu and set an In for the Timeline over the frame that is good for comparison. This is handy when you are set to Previous Edit, for example, and the last frame of the clip is one in which the actor has already left the frame. If you set an In point in the Timeline on a frame when the actor is in the shot, you can use this frame when you're comparing it with the next clip in the Timeline.

11 Play back the entire clip (**2B_5**) to be sure that the color correction holds up well throughout the shot.

> **NOTE** ▶ For additional practice in color matching, open the **More Practice Sequence** in the Browser and practice with that series of clips.

Executing a Complete Color Correction Workflow

In addition to using the Frame Viewer and video scopes to compare and match shots, you can employ other techniques to simplify the color correction process. These include automating the opening of clips in the Viewer with Playhead Sync and using Copy Filter controls to copy color correction settings.

In this exercise, we will use a broad complement of techniques, old and new, to color correct a full scene. Used together, these techniques can be highly effective aids in matching shots and minimizing steps in the process. As time is always precious in post-production, having an efficient color correction workflow can allow you more time to be creative.

Starting the Scene

1   Click the Ice Cream Sequence tab in the Timeline to bring it to
the front.

2   Switch to the Multiple Edits window layout if it is not currently chosen (or the Color Correction layout if Multiple Edits is not available
on your system).

3   Play back the sequence to get familiar with the content and to see how
the clips need to be color corrected.

4   Press Cmd-A to select all the clips in the Timeline.

5   Choose Effects > Video Filters > Color Correction > Color Corrector 3
Way to apply the 3-way color corrector to all the clips in the Timeline.

Although you will work on one clip at a time, applying the filter to the
whole scene will save steps later in the process, as you will come to see
in this lesson.

6   Deselect the clips in the Timeline by clicking anywhere in a blank space.

Setting Playhead Sync to Open

In preparing to color correct a group of clips, you can use the Playhead
Sync button in the Viewer or Canvas to automate the process of opening
clips into the Viewer. Then you can scrub through the Timeline, observe
an image in the Canvas, and instantaneously be able to make color correction adjustments on the Color Corrector tab in the Viewer. Not only does
this save a couple of steps, but it also helps to ensure that you are working

on the correct clip in the Viewer. You can simply dive right in and make the appropriate color correction adjustment.

1   Double-click the first clip in the Timeline to open it into the Viewer. This clears out the clip from the previous Timeline from the Viewer.

2   Click the Video tab in the Viewer to confirm that you have opened the correct clip. You should see the same frame in the Viewer and Canvas.

3   Move the Timeline playhead forward into the second clip.

Now the Canvas displays one image and the Viewer displays another. In the next step, we'll lock these two playheads to one another so that the clip in the Viewer is always the same as the one in the Canvas.

4   In the Viewer, set the Playhead Sync pop-up menu to Open. The Playhead Sync button is located at the top, between the Zoom and View pop-up menus.

TIP The Playhead Sync option can also be chosen from the Canvas's Playhead Sync pop-up menu.

5   To see how this Playhead Sync option works, click and drag the Timeline playhead from left to right through the Timeline.

As you scrub from clip to clip, the Viewer window automatically displays the same image that the Canvas does. The clip under the Timeline playhead is opened into the Viewer automatically.

6   With the Timeline window active, press Home to return to the beginning of the sequence.

7 Click on the Color Corrector 3-way tab in the Viewer.

8 In the Timeline, scrub the playhead slowly throughout the sequence.

As you drag, observe the name of the clip in the title bar of the Viewer.

The Viewer is opening up clips in the Timeline to the same tab, in this case the Color Corrector 3-way tab. Since color correction filters are already on each clip, you can start making adjustments as soon as you move the playhead in the sequence over any shot in the scene.

In other words, what you see in the Canvas can be immediately color corrected in the Viewer. You don't have to worry whether you have opened the right clip. Whenever the Playhead Sync option is set to Open, you are always looking at the same clip in the Viewer and the Canvas, as long as there is only one track of video clips. When you have more than one video track, Option-click on the Autoselect icon to select only the track you want to color correct.

NOTE ► As it is possible to accidentally turn off Playhead Sync, routinely check that the icon in the Playhead Sync pop-up is set to Open.

Playhead Sync: Open   Playhead Sync: Off

Also note that Final Cut Pro always opens the clip on the highest track that has autoselect turned on.

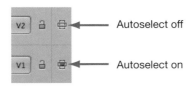

Autoselect off

Autoselect on

Choosing the Base Shot

When approaching a scene, first determine what shot should be used to create and fine-tune the look. Often, the first shot in the scene may be an appropriate starting point, especially if it is a wide shot. In general, a wide shot is a good place to begin, as it sets the visual foundation for any shots that are closer up.

If the first shot of the scene is a close-up, then you may want to develop the look of the scene on another shot. Communicate with the director and cinematographer to see if they have an opinion about which shot most represents the intended look of the scene.

In this exercise, we will use the first shot, a wide-angle shot, as the basis of our color corrections. Clips color corrected after this clip will be matched to this look.

Developing the Initial "Look"

Creating the look of a scene is a creative and subjective undertaking. As a guideline, make adjustments based on your own taste, and have fun with it. In this exercise, we've only provided suggested changes. Feel free to veer off at any time and create your own look.

> **TIP** To see a complete, color corrected sequence, open **Ice Cream Sequence/finished** from the Browser.

The only rule is to keep your adjustments within broadcast standards. This is a good habit to get into right away. If you want to create a high-contrast look, then add a Broadcast Safe filter to the clip in addition to the 3-way color corrector. That way you can push up the whites of the image without creating any illegal values. The examples given do not require the use of the Broadcast Safe filter.

1   Press Home to move the Timeline playhead back to the beginning of the sequence.

2   In the Video Scopes window, switch to the Waveform monitor to prepare to manipulate the contrast.

> **TIP** During this exercise, switch to the Waveform monitor when working on luminance and to the Vectorscope when working on color balance.

3   In the Color Corrector tab in the Viewer, use the Blacks luminance slider to set the black level for the first clip, **301_1**.

For example, drag the slider slightly to the left to bring down the overall fill level, making the shadows deeper and more reminiscent of nighttime.

4   Use the Whites luminance slider to set the white level.

For example, drag the Whites slider to the left somewhat to minimize the glare and make it easier to read detail in other parts of the frame.

5   Use the Mids slider to set the midrange of the shot, the mood.

For example, drag the Mids slider slightly to the left to enhance the nighttime lighting. Dragging too far left will eliminate too much detail and make the actors' expressions less readable.

6   Set the color balance for the shot, using any combination of the three balance wheels as needed, although only a mids adjustment is really necessary.

For example, the magenta cast in the image can be removed by adding a little green with the Mids balance wheel. This will result in a warm, incandescent feel.

Checking Your Work

Take a moment to test out the new color correction. See how it holds up with a fresh eye, and view a side-by-side comparison with the original clip.

1   Check the Enable box for the color correction filter to disable it; then turn the filter back on.

Turning the filter off and on should help you determine whether the color correction is enough or too much.

2   Play back the entire clip to see how the color correction holds up over the duration of the clip.

3   Make any further adjustments to the shot as needed on the Color Corrector tab.

Applying Copy Filter Settings

Before making manual adjustments on any two clips, you may be able to start by copying color correction settings from similar clips that have already been color corrected. Each Color Corrector 3-way filter has buttons that let you copy settings from one clip to another clip in the Timeline. This can give you a good starting point for adjusting a new image, and it may be the only adjustment needed.

Clicking on a button to the left of the Drag Filter icon (the little hand) will copy the settings from a color corrector filter on a clip to the left of the current clip.

These settings are then pasted into the current clip's color corrector filter.

Clicking on a button to the right of the Drag Filter icon will copy the settings of the current clip and paste them into the same filter on one of the next clips to the right in the Timeline.

If there is already a filter on the clip to the right, then only the settings of the filter are applied to that clip. If there is no filter, then the whole filter and its settings are applied to the clip.

In either case, the color correction created on one clip may be used as a starting point on another clip in the sequence.

1   Move the Timeline playhead to the second clip, **302_1**.

This clip is another wide angle of the scene, with coverage similar to that of the previous clip. As it appears to have been shot under lighting and exposure similar to the first clip's, copying the color correction from the first clip may be the next step.

At worst, the copied filter settings may be a good starting point. At best, this may be all that is needed to match the two shots.

2   In the Color Corrector tab in the Viewer, click the 1 button to the left of the Drag Filter icon.

This copies the filter settings from the first clip back (to the left) in the Timeline. In this case, it has gone a long way to matching the two shots.

3   Make any other necessary adjustments to match the two clips with color balance or contrast controls.

NOTE ▶ Copy Filter controls are also available to other filters applied to a clip, and are available to copy all filters to or from a Timeline clip, regardless of whether they are color correction filters. To copy all filters from one clip to another, choose Modify > Copy Filters and select an option from the available choices in the sub-menu. These controls are especially helpful when you want to copy more than one filter at a time. To copy filters beyond the two-clip range, you could always copy the clip with the filters and use Paste Attributes to apply them to one or more clips.

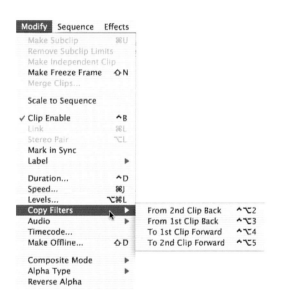

Grading the Rest of the Scene

Now that you have established a look for the first establishing shots, you can color correct any similar shots that come later in the scene to match these established shots.

The next few shots take place in another room, the kitchen. Although it is another location, you may still be concerned with matching the overall look and feel of the clip. In other words, if the living room scene was graded as high contrast, for example, you might want to grade the kitchen as high contrast as well.

As a reminder, the following tools are at your disposal:

- The Vectorscope, to evaluate color

- The Waveform monitor, to evaluate contrast

- Cropping, to identify color casts

- The Frame Viewer, to compare images or display a before-and-after of the color correction

- Copy Filter buttons

- The Enable check box, which lets you evaluate color corrections by turning filters off and on

- Rendered full-resolution real-time playback, to evaluate final color correction (this is the last thing you'll do)

Keep in mind that you generally want to:

- Maintain consistency in shots that take place in the same location.

- Maintain overall consistency in the project by remaining aware of other parts of the program.

Use the following steps as a guide for color-matching the next shots in the Timeline.

1   Move forward in the Timeline to the next clip, **201_6**.

    The man enters the kitchen in this shot.

2   Color correct this clip, including contrast and color balance.

As mentioned, it's up to you as to what look you may want to create. As this is a new room, the balance on color does not necessarily have to match that of the living room.

For example, drag the Mids and Whites sliders slightly to the left to lessen the intensity of the background and deepen the shadows for a richer contrast. Then drag the color balance indicator slightly outward from the center, between red and magenta, to remove the greenish cast and simulate cooler lighting in the kitchen than in the living room.

3   Move on to the next clip in the Timeline, **203_1**.

4   Color correct this close-up of the ice cream container being pulled out of the bag.

For example, drag the Mids luminance slider to the right slightly to open up a little more detail from the shadows.

The color balance of the previous clip is slightly different, as a casual observation of the shirt in each clip reveals. To determine just how to adjust the close-up, you can use a Frame Viewer split screen of Previous Edit and Current Frame, observing differences in the shirt, as well as the skin color, any color cast in the whites, and the overall saturation of the two clips.

To better match the balance and intensity of the wide shot, drag the Mids balance indicator outward slightly toward yellow, and drag the color saturation to the left somewhat.

5   Move on to the next clip, **201_1**.

This is a return to the wide shot similar to the second clip back in the Timeline, already color corrected.

6   Use Copy Filter controls to copy the filter settings from the second clip back to this clip, **201_1**. Do this by clicking the 2 to the left of the Drag Filter icon. This is done from the Color Corrector 3-way tab in the Viewer.

This allows you to take advantage of the color correction already done. As this clip appears to be another take of the same shot, chances are the lighting and exposure are the same, and the same color correction may do the job.

TIP ▶   Using Copy To or Copy From for the second clip back or forward is common when working on a narrative scene. If you cut back and forth between a wide shot and a close-up, then every other shot is the same and uses the same color correction. Additionally, when cutting back and forth between coverage—close-ups of two people, for instance—again every other shot is the same and may use the same correction.

7   Move on to the next clip in the Timeline, **202_1**, and color correct it.

For example, lower the contrast blacks and mids, and raise the whites. This results in a higher contrast and a larger separation between foreground and background elements. For color, drag outward from the center in the direction of the flesh tone line.

8   Move on to the next clip in the Timeline, **101_1**, and color correct it.

As this is a new angle, there is no previous color correction that is probably of much value to copy from. Notice that the background is the kitchen. The previous shot was inside the kitchen. You can use the Frame Viewer to compare this new angle with the Previous Edit.

9   Move on to the next clip, **103_1**.

This clip is similar to the first two clips in the Timeline and could benefit from the same color correction. Since the first clip in the Timeline is more than two clips back, you will use another method to copy this filter setting.

10   Select the clip **103_1** to be corrected in the Timeline by clicking on it with the Selection tool.

NOTE ▶ This clip is being highlighted so that it may easily be found again after the next two steps. For this reason, do not deselect the clip until you have completed the next three steps.

11   Press Shift-Z with the Timeline window active to resize the Timeline to fit all clips.

12   Move the playhead over the first clip in the Timeline.

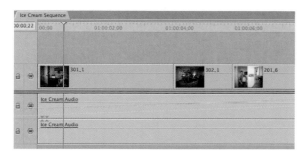

As Playhead Sync is still set to Open, the first clip in the Timeline, **301_1**, is opened up in the Viewer.

13 In the Viewer, click the Drag Filter icon and drag to the clip, **103_1**, still highlighted in the Timeline, to copy this filter from **301_1** to **103_1**.

NOTE ▶ When you drag the Drag Filter icon, make sure that you do not click and then release the mouse over the same spot in the Color Corrector tab. Doing so will copy the filter to the same clip, and it will show up as a separate Color Corrector tab. To correctly copy to another clip, click and drag, then release when the cursor is over the new clip in the Timeline.

14 Move to clip **103_1** in the Timeline.

In the Canvas, notice that this clip now has the same color correction as the first clip. In the Viewer, notice that there are now two Color Corrector tabs.

15 In the Viewer, click the Filters tab.

You should see two filters here. The one you placed originally shows up as the filter on top, and the one you just copied shows up on the bottom.

16 Click the first filter on this tab and delete it.

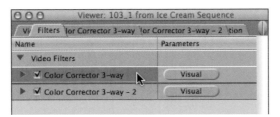

Remove this filter.

Only the second filter has the settings copied from the other clip in the Timeline.

17 Finish color correcting this scene, matching clips to ones that have already been color corrected. The remaining clips are similar to those you've already corrected, so you can use Copy and Drag Filter controls to copy the color correction for similarly shot images.

18 If RT playback cannot output to an external monitor in full quality, render the whole scene.

> **NOTE ▶** If you are not using an external monitor, you can skip this step. Anything other than seeing the color correction in its intended medium (an external monitor) should be used only as a close approximation, and will not be considered broadcast ready until judged on an external video monitor.

19 Play back the sequence, and make any final changes as needed.

20 Pat yourself on the back.

What You've Learned

- Use the Frame Viewer to make side-by-side comparisons.
- Use the color coding in the Frame Viewer to choose custom viewing options.
- Use the Multiple Edits window arrangement when color matching.
- The Copy Filter controls save time when color correcting clips similar to previously corrected clips.
- Set Playhead Sync to Open to automate the process of opening clips in the Viewer to be color corrected.

14

Lesson Files	Lessons > Lesson_14 > 14_Project_Start.fcp
Media	Media > Lesson_10-14_Media
Time	This lesson takes approximately 60 minutes to complete.
Goals	Perform secondary color correction for color enhancement on specific colors
	Become familiar with the options in the Limit Effect controls
	Create special-effects looks using secondary color correction

Lesson **14**

Secondary Color Correction

In this lesson, you will fine-tune specific colors in the frame using the Color Corrector filter and Limit Effect controls.

These controls let you isolate colors to create effects that range from subtle enhancements to surreal transformations. You can use them to create a look that rides the wave of the latest commercial trend, or experiment with variations and create the next trend yourself.

When to Use Secondary Color Correction

Final Cut Pro's Limit Effect controls let you make color enhancements that are limited to individual colors in the frame. The process of enhancing individual colors is often referred to as *secondary color correction,* which is performed after the scene has been color balanced overall.

Secondary color correction is sometimes optional, as overall adjustments in contrast and color balance may be sufficient. Often, though, secondary color correction is a vital step in the process of creating finished images. As you move through this lesson, you will learn how to make these corrections as well as discover different real-world applications for such color enhancement as making a dingy sky into a richer, deeper blue.

Before   After

First you will open a project and fine-tune color with the same controls you've used in earlier lessons. As you will see, those controls will be adequate when balancing an overall image, but not precise enough when enhancing individual colors.

In this scenario, which is a video clip of a bowl of fruit, we will intensify the color of the green apples.

1   Open Lesson_14 > **14_Project_Start.fcp**.

2   Choose Window > Arrange > Color Correction.

3   In the Video Scopes window that opens, choose Layout > Vectorscope.

4   Move to the first clip in the Timeline, **L4-fruit-1** (in the Secondary Color Sequence).

This clip is a close-up of a bowl of fruit.

Often in commercials, a product shot like this may need to have one of the colors in the frame enhanced.

5   Choose Effects > Video Filters > Color Correction > Color Corrector 3-way to add the Color Corrector 3-way filter to this clip.

6   Open the clip into the Viewer and go to the Color Corrector 3-way tab.

7   On the Mids balance wheel, drag between yellow and green about halfway outward from the center of the wheel. This intensifies the color of the green apples.

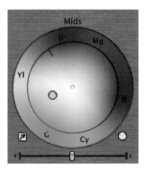

In the Canvas, notice that the apples have a richer color but that the effect on the rest of the scene is undesirable.

Now let's try another method to modify the color of the apples.

8   Click the Mids reset button to return the Mids color wheel to its default position.

9   Drag the saturation slider to the right to try to intensify the green.

Again, this correction has a positive effect on the green apples but an undesirable effect on the rest of the fruit in the scene. In fact, as soon as you start to add saturation, you can see in the Vectorscope that the reds in the frame attain illegal values.

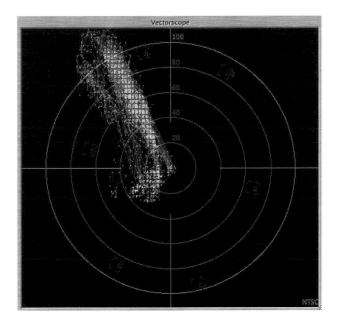

Color balancing the entire scene doesn't work in this situation, when you want to enhance only one color. In the rest of this lesson, you will work on color correcting individual colors, such as the green apples, without negatively affecting other colors in the scene.

10 Switch to the Filters tab, click the name of the Color Corrector 3-way filter, and press Delete to remove the filter from the clip.

> **NOTE ▶** The term *secondary color correction* should not be confused with secondary colors in the color wheels. Secondary color correction refers to altering a single color or a unique range of colors, regardless of whether those colors are primary or secondary on the wheel.

Using Balance and Hue Wheels

Before moving into secondary color correction, it's important to take a closer look at the color correction filter that will be used: the Color Corrector filter. This filter, although similar in some respects to the 3-way color corrector, has some unique controls that will come in handy in this lesson.

1   Move the Timeline playhead to the second clip in the Timeline, a generator clip of **Bars and Tone**.

    You will use this test clip to demonstrate the effects of two different methods of color correction. Later in this lesson, you will use what you've learned here in some common color correcting scenarios.

2   Choose Effects > Video Filters > Color Correction > Color Corrector to apply the Color Corrector filter to this clip.

3   Open this clip into the Viewer and go to the Color Corrector tab.

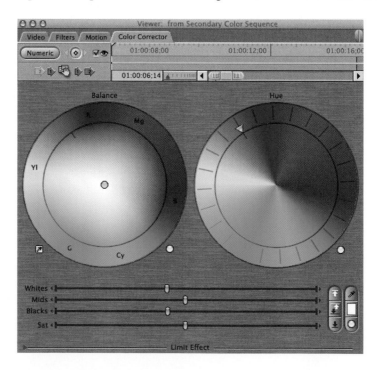

The two color wheels found in this filter, one for Hue and one for Balance, represent two distinct methods of color correction.

The Balance wheel is similar to the Color Corrector 3-way balance wheel, but simplified. When color balancing with the Color Corrector filter, colors are affected throughout the entire range of luminance.

Remember, altering color in a Balance wheel shifts the color toward that side of the color wheel.

4   Click and drag on the balance indicator toward the yellow side of the wheel and then toward the blue side of the wheel. As you drag, alternate between looking in the Canvas and the Vectorscope, and study the blue bar in the image.

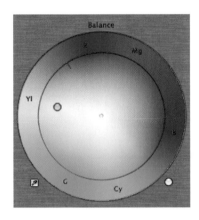 

Notice that the blue intensifies when you drag toward the blue side of the wheel. Adding yellow on the wheel lowers the blue bar's saturation. With an extreme addition of yellow, the bar basically becomes black, a complete lack of saturation or hue.

5   Click the reset button under the Balance wheel to reset it to the center.

You can alter a limited range of hues with color balancing. The Hue wheel, on the other hand, lets you alter a wider range of hues. Instead of color mixing, using the Hue wheel is more like color mapping. It's like rotating or dialing in hue values around the color wheel. The tick marks along the perimeter of the wheel act as guides to allow you to accurately stop the wheel where you wish to reassign the color values.

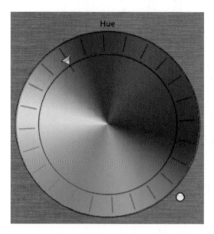

6   Click and drag the hue indicator clockwise or counterclockwise around the outer rim of the Hue wheel.

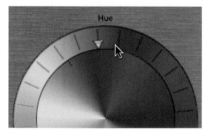

As you rotate the wheel, alternate between looking at the Vectorscope and the Canvas.

Notice that instead of shifting the colors toward one side of the wheel or the other like the Balance wheel, this method rotates the colors in a circular fashion around the color wheel (Vectorscope) to alter them.

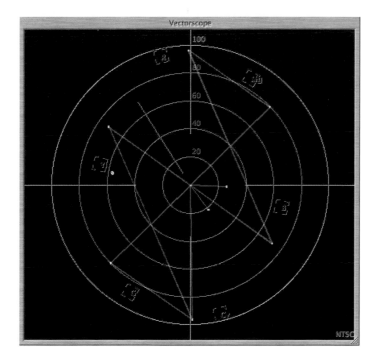

7 Reset the Hue wheel to its default with the reset button.

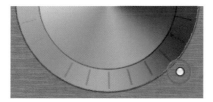

8 Drag around the Hue wheel again, this time watching the blue bar in the Canvas.

Using the Hue wheel is a great method for manipulating color when you need a vastly different color from the original color. Going counterclockwise around the wheel, you can change a blue bar into magenta, then red, through yellow and green, and finally back to blue in a full 360 degrees around the wheel.

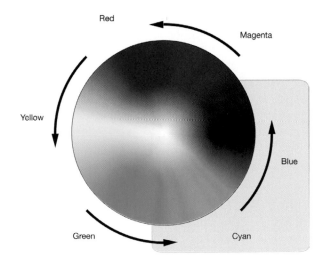

Sometimes, one color correction method is more appropriate than another. Other times, you may find that a combination of both is the right choice.

Using Limit Effect Controls

Let's use the Color Corrector filter in a new way: to alter only one of the colors in the frame. To do this, the color has to first be defined. In principle, this is similar to keying. The color to be altered is selected with an eyedropper, and then the selection, or matte, is fine-tuned with additional controls. Keying makes the selected color transparent, whereas secondary color correction replaces the selected color with a newly chosen color. In other words, to limit the effect of the color correction to only one color, you use Final Cut Pro's Limit Effect controls.

We'll do that now to intensify the green in the apples from our previous exercise without affecting other colors in the frame.

Making the Initial Color Selection

First we need to select the green that we'll intensify.

1 Move to the first clip in the Timeline, **L4-fruit-1-final**. Choose Effects > Video Filters > Color Correction > Color Corrector 3-way to add a filter to this clip.

2 Open this clip into the Viewer and go to the Color Corrector tab.

3 Shift-click either of the color wheel reset buttons, just like with the Color Corrector 3-way filter, to make sure the filter is reset.

4 Toggle open the Limit Effect controls by clicking the disclosure triangle at the bottom left of the Color Corrector tab.

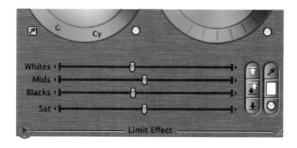

The Limit Effect controls are used to modify the behavior of this filter to isolate and manipulate specific colors. Controls that are below the Limit Effect line are used to choose the target color, while the controls above the Limit Effect line are used to alter the target color.

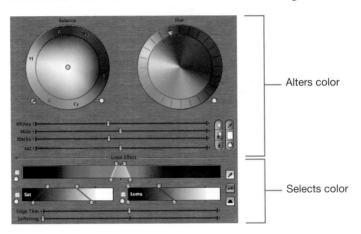

Alters color

Selects color

TIP On smaller computer monitors, opening the Limit Effect controls makes the color wheels fairly small. To compensate, drag the lower-right corner of the Viewer window to enlarge it and to automatically scale up the color wheels and other controls. Using larger controls increases the spacing in the different controls, thereby letting you make smaller and more subtle adjustments in any of the controls. Using a relatively large Viewer window is helpful for any situation in which you want subtle control in a color correction filter.

To activate the Limit Effect controls of the filter, you must make an initial color selection. Start by selecting a spot on one of the green apples.

5   Press Cmd-+ to zoom in on one of the apples in the Canvas.

Zoom until the Canvas looks similar to the next illustration.

You may have to use the scroll bars in the Viewer to center on the apples after zooming in.

6   In the Viewer, click to select the Limit Effect eyedropper.

NOTE ▶ Be careful to select the Limit Effect eyedropper, not the Hue Match eyedropper directly above it.

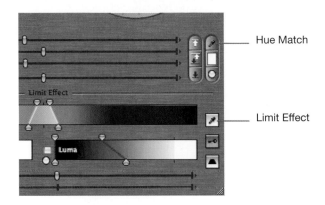

7   Move your cursor to the Canvas.

It becomes the eyedropper icon.

8   Click somewhere on the green apple to define the initial color range of the apples.

You may notice that nothing visually appears to have happened after you clicked on the apple with the eyedropper. Actually, a lot has just happened. Looking in the Limit Effect controls of the clip shows that each of the three controls now has a check mark.

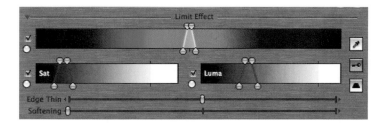

Once any of these three controls is checked, a Limit Effect function for the filter is active. This means that any of the color controls above the Limit Effect line will affect only the selected portion of the frame, instead of everything in the frame.

TIP If at any time you want the Limit Effect controls disabled, Shift-click any of the three Limit Effect reset buttons. To quickly reset Limit Effect and the top part of the filter at the same time, click the Filters tab and then click the red X reset button for the filter.

Refining the Color Selection

So far, all we've done is define a matte. We don't know if the selection is complete or partial, or whether it needs to be fine-tuned. There are a couple of ways that you can get a view of the selection: by using a matte-like view of the image or by applying a temporary color effect to reveal the scope of the selection.

Let's do the latter—desaturate the selection so that we can see its scope—and then we'll add to it until the entire desired range, from the lightest and least saturated areas of the apple to the darkest shadows, is completely selected. Then, a final color effect can be fine-tuned.

1   Click the saturation slider and drag all the way to the left.

Since the Limit Effect section is activated, this desaturation affects only the selected part of the apple, removing any color from it. You should notice that only a small part of the apple is black and white (grayscale). This part of the apple is the only selected color so far.

Although the final effect will not be a desaturated look, this effect does serve to show you how much of the apple is selected and how much is not. At this point, not much of the apple is selected.

Next, we'll use the eyedropper to increase the selection.

2 Shift-click with the Limit Effect eyedropper in another spot on the apple in the Canvas. Repeat until all areas of the apple are selected, as indicated by the grayscale areas.

Shift-clicking allows you to add to your selection. Notice that each time you Shift-click, more of the apple becomes grayscale. If you don't hold down Shift before clicking in the Canvas, you replace any previous selection with the new one. You can tell when you're adding to the selection because a + appears next to the eyedropper in the Canvas.

TIP ▶ Instead of Shift-clicking to add to a selection, it is sometime quicker and more dynamic to Shift-drag: Select the eyedropper, press Shift, then click and drag in the area as many times as you need to until you've selected all of it—in this case, until all of the green apples appear grayscale in the Canvas.

3 When your selection is complete, choose Zoom > Fit to Window in the Canvas or press Shift-Z with the Canvas window active.

Toggling Through Views with the Key Button

Our selection is final, but Final Cut Pro's Limit Effect controls offer one more tool to help you assess the scope of a selection: the key button. Let's explore it quickly so you can see how it works. Then we'll finish off our color correction.

1 Locate the key button in the Limit Effect controls.

By default, the key is red with a gray background. This represents the Final view, in which the Canvas shows the video image with the final color effect.

2 Click the button once.

The key becomes black on a white background. This is Matte view.

In the Canvas, you should now see only a black-and-white image. This view represents the selected and nonselected pixels of the image. Any pixels that are displayed as white represent a selected part of the image. Any pixels that are black are not selected by the filter.

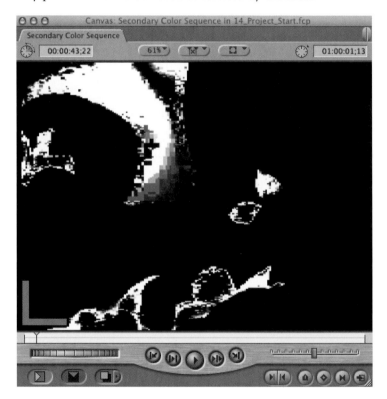

In this case, you may notice that too much of the image is selected—that the other greenery in the frame is also selected, not just the green of the apples. In this case, the extra greenery selected will help enhance the look. In other cases, you may not want anything else in the frame selected. This Matte view is very helpful in seeing something that you may not have noticed otherwise.

This view is critical to evaluating your selection, but it is not used all the time. Click back to this view whenever you need this information during the lesson.

NOTE ▶ Your Matte view may vary from the screen shot in this book. It depends on the precision of your selection.

3   Click the key once again.

The key changes to red with a blue background, which indicates Source view.

In the Canvas, you should now see the original video image. This view shows the image without any of the color effects from this filter. In other words, this is the "before" image. In this case, the apples appear in color again.

4   Click the key again to return to Final view.

This is the view you started out with. Anything you do to the video image with this filter is seen when using Final view.

It is easy to confuse Source and Final views. If you click only once on the key after viewing the Matte, then you are looking at the image without any effects. Whenever you are using the color correction filter and you don't see the result of any action, make sure the filter is turned on with the Enable check box. Then make sure the key is red on the gray background, showing the Final view.

Creating the Final Color Effect

Now that the selection is complete, we can finally intensify the green of the apples.

1   Reset the saturation slider to its default (normal color).

2 Click and drag the indicator in the Balance wheel outward between green and yellow, about halfway between the center and the outside of the wheel.

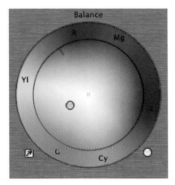

This time, color balancing only the selected color allows you to heighten the intensity of the green apples (and other greenery) without affecting the strawberries or other fruit.

3 Drag the saturation slider to the right a little.

Notice that the Vectorscope shows that only the traces that represent the green apples are getting more saturated.

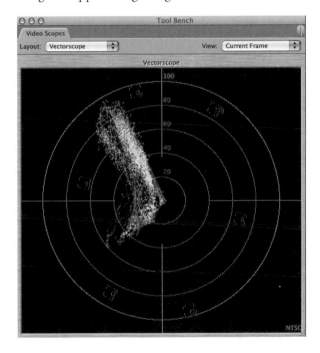

The reds of the other fruit are left alone. This is an important control, as the reds in this clip are already extremely saturated and shouldn't be extended outward any further.

4 Turn the filter off and on using the Enable check box to test out the new color correction and see how it compares with the original image.

Success! All that work has paid off. This subtle enhancement has resulted in a more vibrant image.

5   To see a finished version of this shot, open **Finished Examples Sequence** from the Browser.

Creating a New Color with Limit Effect Controls

The subtle enhancement you just applied to the apples is only one possible use of Final Cut Pro's Limit Effect controls. You can also use the controls to create more dramatic color changes. Instead of creating a more saturated green, for instance, you could turn the apples cyan or purple.

When the aim is to change the color to a vastly different hue, there are some things to remember. Namely, your selection needs to be precise, just like with keying. Any imperfections in your selection become apparent in the final image. To that end, we'll now learn how to change a color altogether using Limit Effect controls, and how to fine-tune selections even more to make the new color look as clean as possible.

Choosing a New Hue

Use the Hue wheel to make a large shift in hue, and look for any problems that may be created as a result.

1   Switch back to **Secondary Color Sequence** if you switched to another sequence, open clip **L4-fruit-1-final** into the Viewer, and go to the Color Corrector tab.

2   If you turned off the filter in the final part of the last exercise, turn it back on now.

3   Click and drag clockwise on the Hue wheel to change the color of the apples. Start out by rotating the Hue wheel in small increments. Closely watch the apples as you do this. Continue to rotate the Hue

wheel until you have changed the hue to a purple (the indicator will be 180 degrees from the default).

The Hue wheel is a good choice when you want an end color vastly different from the original.

Notice that the edges between the apples and other fruit are pronounced. A little bit of the apple's original color remains, producing a fringe around the edges of the selection.

Unless you like these imperfections, you will want to get a more precise selection so that all of the originally green pixels turn purple.

4   Click the Hue wheel and continue clockwise until the apples are blue-green (cyan) and the indicator is close to its original angle.

When the apples become this new color, notice that the edges aren't quite as noticeable as before. This color is close to the original green. As a result, the edges don't look quite as bad. The edges will still need some fine-tuning, but not as much as when they were purple.

5   Rotate the Hue wheel again to return the apples to purple.

If an extreme color change like this is desired, then the edges will definitely need to be improved to remove this color fringe.

NOTE ▶ You are working here with film images that have been transferred to DV format. When keying or using secondary color correction, the choice of video format is critical to achieving good results. The higher the resolution of the video format, the better the edges will look. Working with a video format like Digital Betacam or a high-definition format with an uncompressed codec will produce results superior to those when working in the limited color space of the DV format. To put it simply, the better the video format, the better the edges.

Removing Color Fringes

To get rid of the unsightly color fringe, one thing you can do is use the Edge Thin and Softening sliders at the bottom of the Limit Effect controls.

These sliders affect the edge of the selection of the purple apples, where purple (new color) and green (old color) meet. Uncorrected, these edges may look bad when paused, but what's worse, when you play back this heavily modified color, the edges may appear to dance, as pixels along the edge flicker between colors. Hiding or softening the color contrast at the edge may lessen or completely remove this unwanted effect.

1 Drag the Edge Thin slider all the way to the left.

Notice that the edges become sharper, and you more easily see the green/purple contrast.

2 Drag the Edge Thin slider all the way to the right.

The edge becomes bluish (results on your selection may vary). As you can see, neither extreme is the correct choice. But why?

The Edge Thin slider expands or contracts the edge, similar to choking a matte. At the same time, it is enhancing the edge with the opposite of the current edge color. When applied subtly, this may be a quick fix when the selection is slightly too narrow or too wide overall, or has a slight color fringe.

When using this control in other situations, try dragging a little left of center and then right of center to see the edge shift. You can then narrow in on the appropriate adjustment from there.

3   Move the slider back to the center.

In this situation, the default centered position is fine.

4   Drag the Softening slider all the way to the right.

Looking at where the apple meets the strawberry, you can see the results of extreme Softness setting.

Adding softening blurs the edge of the matte (your color selection). As this is the location of a noticeable color contrast, this can help to hide the edge, make it less noticeable. But the trick is: A little goes a long way.

5 Drag Softening back near the left, just a little bit away from its default.

Another way to create cleaner edges is to simply fine-tune the selection so that it is more precise. Oftentimes, you may find that a precise selection combined with a little edge softening is a good combination: To finesse the selection further, Shift-click or Shift-drag with the Limit Effect eyedropper in the Canvas. You can also alter the selection directly in the Viewer, which we'll try next.

Controlling Selections with Limit Effect Ranges

The selections you make with the Limit Effect eyedropper are plugged into three bars in the Limit Effect section of the filter: chroma (hue), saturation, and luminance.

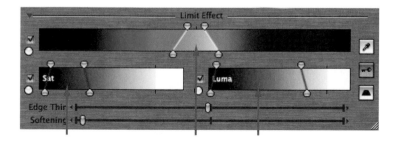

Every time you Shift-click with the eyedropper, any or all of these three ranges is modified. Once you get the selection fairly close with the eyedropper, you can go back and make any adjustments directly into this part of the filter.

The areas of the chroma, saturation, and luminance spectra within the white handles indicate the range of the color selection.

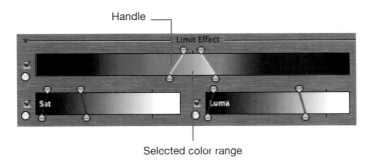

Modifying the top handles affects the width of the selection. The top handles are like a broad stroke, creating an overall selection.

Modifying the bottom handles, on the other hand, has a more refined impact on the image. The bottom handles define the *tolerance* of the top handles, or how strictly the control will select the range. In a way it is a softer approach to selection, as it helps to bridge the transition from one shade to another.

Instead of over-selecting with the top handles, use the top handles to make the broad selection and the bottom handles to fine-tune it.

The handles for Chroma, specifically, affect the hue selection. Drag the Chroma handles to select a wider or narrower range of colors. For instance, dragging the top handles of the Chroma range outward selects more greens and yellows.

Drag the Saturation handles to include or exclude color that is saturated more or less than the original selection.

Drag the Luma handles to include or exclude darker or brighter shades of the originally selected color.

Enough theory. Let's use these controls to further fine-tune our apple selection. You may find that a little experimentation and intelligent guess-work is the best way to approach these Limit Effect controls.

During the next steps, switch between Final view and Matte view as you finesse the selection. As a reminder, Matte view is a great aid to quickly spot whether the selection is over- or under-reaching other parts of the frame.

1   Drag the bottom Chroma range handles slightly outward. If the selection is extremely close, adjusting the bottom handles may be all that is needed.

> **TIP** To move handles in small increments, Cmd-drag.

2   If that doesn't improve the selection, try dragging the bottom Sat and Luma range handles.

Again, use subtle adjustments.

3   If needed, use the top handles in the three ranges to expand the selection.

Use the image in the Canvas as a guide to determining what range may still need to be selected.

For example, if the darkest shadows on the apple still appear green, then expanding the handles into the darker regions of Sat and Luma will help select that portion of the apples.

4　Adjust the three ranges, using top and bottom handles as needed, until the apples are completely selected.

5　Play back the image at full quality. Depending on your computer setup, you may need to render first. When you play back (not just study a paused video clip), you will notice imperfections in the color selection that can cause the pixels to appear to dance on the screen.

6　After playback, determine whether there are any problems that need to be addressed, and make necessary adjustments.

NOTE ▶ You can always add filters as needed. For example, you can use one color correction filter to work as a secondary control for one color in the frame, and then add another filter to work as a secondary for another color in the frame. Each filter will have its own tab in the Viewer, and if Limit Effect is enabled in both, then they each work on only one portion of the frame.

| Video | Color Corrector | Filters | Motion | Color Corrector – 2 |

Real-World Secondary Color Correction

In the real world, there's not much call for purple apples. Now let's see how to use secondary color correction and Limit Effect controls in some real-world scenarios, starting with brightening up a muted fabric color and making the color of a sky more vibrant.

Fixing the Color of a Shirt

In this exercise, we will enhance the color of a man's shirt, which is dim in the original clip.

1   Move Timeline playhead to the head of the third clip in the Timeline, **201_6 neutral**.

   In this clip, a man walks into the kitchen and over to the counter.

2   Apply the Color Corrector filter to this clip.

3   Zoom in on the Canvas to get a close-up view of the shirt.

4   Open the clip into the Viewer and go to the Color Corrector tab.

5   Toggle open the Limit Effect controls by clicking the disclosure triangle at the bottom of the filter.

6 Click to select the Limit Effect eyedropper.

7 Move the cursor to the Canvas and click a spot in the blue shirt.

NOTE ▶ The first time you click with the eyedropper, you should not yet be holding the Shift key. The initial selection will not set correctly if the Shift key is pressed.

8 Drag the saturation slider all the way to the left to desaturate the selection.

Just as in our previous exercise, this is a temporary effect so that you can better see the selection as you work on it.

9 Shift-click and/or Shift-drag to add to the selection, including as much of the shirt as possible.

10 When you are finished making the selection, zoom out in the Canvas to Fit to Window.

11 Set the saturation slider slightly to the right of center.

12 In the Balance wheel, drag the indicator between blue and cyan, about halfway from the center of the wheel to the perimeter.

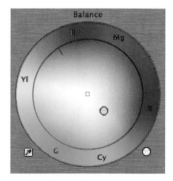

13 Turn the filter off and on with the Enable check box.

This subtle correction is enough to make the shirt pop out a little more, without looking unnatural.

14 With the filter turned on, scrub through the clip.

When the man walks in the door, the shirt moves through different lighting. The selection may be fine at the beginning of the shot, but not at other points. If it is not fine throughout the shot, your job isn't quite finished.

15 Expand the selection as needed so that the shirt is fully selected throughout the duration of the clip. Shift-click or adjust the handles in any of the ranges as needed.

16 Switch between Final and Matte view as needed.

As a reminder, Matte view is a great aid to quickly spot whether the selection is over- or under-reaching other parts of the frame.

17 Render if needed and play back the clip at full quality.

18 Move the playhead back to the first frame of this clip in the Timeline.

19 Rotate the Hue wheel counterclockwise until the shirt is purple (between magenta and blue) to test out a larger color shift.

20 Increase saturation by dragging the saturation slider about halfway to the right.

21 Scrub through the clip to see if the selection holds up throughout.

This larger color shift now shows any imperfections in the selection. There is a greater chance that as the man walks, different parts of the shirt will show up as blue instead of purple.

22 Attempt to fine-tune the selection and the edges to make the new color appear more realistic throughout the duration of the clip.

This will be challenging. The shirt has many shades as it travels through the light.

23 When finished, compare the correction against the original clip.

24 To see a finished example of this clip, open **Finished Examples Sequence**.

Brightening the Sky

On the day of any given shoot, the sky isn't always the color that the film-makers might desire. Enhancing the sky in post-production is a common adjustment. Just like the previous exercise, when the adjustments are subtle, the clip doesn't need a lot of fine-tuning.

1 Move on to the next clip in the Timeline, **L4-clouds-1**.

2 Using the Color Corrector filter and Limit Effect controls, enhance the color of the sky. Be sure to keep the correction subtle for best results, using the Balance wheel and a little softening.

3   Move through the clip looking for problems in the selection as the clouds roll by, and make any adjustments as necessary.

4   Check the correction against the original clip.

5   Play back at full quality as a final check.

Creating a Look Using Selective Color Controls

Selective color control can also be used to create a whole range of nonnatural effects, limited only by your imagination and the video format with which you are working. Some examples are a surreal mood and a one-color "splash" look. As discovered earlier in this lesson, when making broad strokes with color, you need to be able to isolate color with precision.

> **NOTE** ▶ If you can plan for your video's look before production, try to choose colors that are unique from other colors in the frame, rich in saturation, and evenly lit. This makes them easier to select in post-production. This is just as crucial as the use of green screens or blue screens when color keying.

Making a Color Surreal

Let's use bold strokes with secondary color correction controls to veer away from the natural.

1   Move forward in the Timeline to the clip **woman in red**.

2   Apply the Color Corrector filter to this clip.

3   Apply Limit Effect controls to select all the greenery in the frame.

4   Fine-tune the selection as needed.

5   Rotate the Hue wheel clockwise until the greenery becomes an unnatural shade, such as in the following example. The specific color you pick is up to you.

Assuming you have fine-tuned the selection, the color effect is a success. The original greenery was a unique color in the frame and did not exist anywhere but in the grass and the tree leaves. As there is no green in the woman or her wardrobe, it is fairly easy to color in only the greenery, and the resulting video takes on a painterly effect.

6   As always, before you are finished, test the success of the effect with full-quality playback.

Making One Color "Splash"

Now we'll turn the scene black-and-white except for the woman's red dress. This effect was popularized in *Schindler's List* and *Pleasantville*. More recently, this effect has been used (and sometimes overused) in commercials and music videos.

NOTE ▶ This kind of look is possible only with a high-quality video format, just like with keying. See Lesson 9 for more information. In this example, you will get an idea of the effect—but because you are working with this shot in a DV color space, the result is not as good as when you are working with a higher resolution video format.

1   Reset the filter for **woman in red** by clicking the Filters tab and clicking the red X reset button.

   TIP ▶ This is the quickest way to reset all sliders, color wheels, and buttons, as it only requires one click.

2   Click the Color Corrector tab.

3   Select the red dress with the Limit Effect eyedropper.

4   Set an initial color effect by dragging the saturation slider all the way to the left.

5   To invert the color correction and affect everything in the frame *except* the dress, click the Invert button at the bottom of the Limit Effect controls.

 ——— Invert

Now the image is black and white except for a portion of the dress.

6 Drag the top and bottom handles in Chroma, Sat, or Luma outward as necessary.

As you widen the selection, more of the dress becomes red.

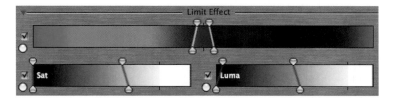

NOTE ► Remember, you can get close, but for the purposes of this exercise, don't worry if the selection is not perfect. If you accidentally select the woman's lips as well, don't worry about it.

7 Toggle between Matte and Final views while you work on the selection.

8 Add a little softening. In this case, it will definitely help smooth out the edge.

Using Matting or Cropping

In **woman in red**, the woman's lips may unintentionally get selected when you select the dress. To avoid this, isolate the area to be affected by cropping or matting the clip and superimposing it over another clip. The premise is similar to keying but different in technique. One clip will have the Limit Effect control, the other clip will not.

1 Duplicate **woman in red** in the Timeline by selecting it and Shift-Option-dragging upward to V2.

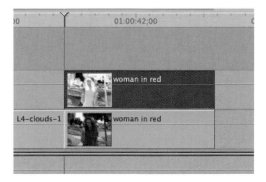

2   Open the clip from V2 into the Viewer and go to the Color
    Corrector tab.

3   Reset the entire filter by clicking the Filters tab and clicking the
    red X reset button.

4   Click the Color Corrector tab.

5   Set the saturation slider all the way to the left to make the entire
    clip black and white.

6   Turn off Visibility for V1.

7   Select View > Image+Wireframe in the Canvas and select the clip
    on V2.

8 Use the Crop tool in the Canvas to crop the bottom edge of this clip up to the woman's neck.

9 Turn Visibility back on for V1.

You now see a combination of two clips. The top part of the image is the clip on V2, and the bottom part of the image is the clip on V1.

Now you have successfully made the woman's dress stand out in red while the rest of the image is black and white.

V2 clip

V1 clip

What You've Learned

- The Limit Effect controls allow you to change one color in a scene without affecting other areas of the frame, which is a form of secondary color correction.

- The Color Corrector filter and its Hue wheel can be used to manipulate a color.

- The Saturation, Luminance, and Chroma controls can be used to fine-tune a selected area.

- Edge Thin and Softening help minimize unwanted color fringe around a selected area.

- Using duplicate clips stacked on top of each other and a matte or cropping lets you isolate one of two areas of similar color for secondary color correction.

Working with Audio

Mary Plummer has been editing film and video professionally for 15 years using on-line, off-line, linear, and non-linear systems. An Apple Certified Trainer in Final Cut Pro, she has edited music videos, documentaries, educational videos, pilots, trailers, and independent feature films. Mary's original music has been used in film and video projects from coast to coast. In 1998 she started her own BMI music publishing company. Mary's instrument of choice is a baby grand piano, an heirloom from her great-grandmother who played the piano for silent movies.

Martin Sitter is a veteran audio producer, multimedia artist, and author specializing in track-based video and audio applications. After producing electronic music albums (house/tech house) for record labels including Peng Records UK and Phatt Phunk Records LA, Martin went on to embrace interactive video design. Based in Vancouver, Martin is the author of *LiveStage Professional 3 for Macintosh and Windows: Visual QuickStart Guide*, *DVD Studio Pro 2 for Macintosh: Visual QuickPro Guide*, and *Apple Pro Training Series: Logic 6*. When not writing or producing DVD-Video, Martin teaches DVD Studio Pro and Logic Platinum as an Apple Certified Trainer.

15

Lesson Files

Lessons > Lesson_15> Daydream in A.loop

Lessons > Lesson_15> 15-2 Starting.loop

Lessons > Lesson_15> 15-4 Starting.loop

Lessons > Lesson_15> 15-2 Finished.loop

Lessons > Lesson_15 > 15-4 Finished.loop

Lessons > Lesson_15 > 15-3 Bonus.loop

Media

Media > Lesson_15_Media

Time

This lesson takes approximately 90 minutes to complete.

Goals

Create music and sound effects with the Soundtrack program

Learn the basic elements of audio and music

Split and join tracks

Sync sound clips with video in the Timeline

Work with effects and envelopes

Save a project with collected media files

Working with Soundtrack

Music has always been a fundamental component of the motion picture process. Even silent movies relied on live music to help evoke the emotion and mood of a story. Whether it is used as the foundation of a fast-paced action promo, or a single note for the drama of a scene, editors rely on music to support and enhance their projects. In the past, finding the right music meant wading through hours' worth of music libraries, or hiring a composer. Both choices can be costly and involve royalty issues.

The Soundtrack program that comes bundled with Final Cut Pro 4 offers an alternative to finding music. Now editors can score projects themselves in a Timeline-based music arrangement program. Soundtrack allows you to customize music and bring it directly into your Final Cut Pro sequences.

Most editors are not musicians, let alone composers. Fortunately, Soundtrack requires no musical background because it uses thousands of high-quality music loops as building blocks. The only instruments you need are your keyboard and mouse to create your own royalty-free music.

We will be working with several different Soundtrack projects in this Lesson. Before you start, drag the entire Lesson_15 and Lesson_15_Media folders from your DVD to your computer hard drive.

Understanding Soundtrack Basics

This lesson will focus on the Soundtrack interface, letting you understand the basic anatomy of a song, as well as use advanced techniques to edit, mix, and distribute your music. In the next lesson, you will use Soundtrack to compose music for a Final Cut Pro sequence.

Soundtrack uses loops of prerecorded music as building blocks for a song. A loop is basically a piece of music, usually created by one instrument, that can be repeated over and over seamlessly. Soundtrack also contains one-shots, which are single-event sounds like the ringing of a bell, and sound effects like a gunshot or door slam.

You arrange loops and one-shots that sound good together in a Timeline to build a score, just as Final Cut Pro uses a series of clips in a Timeline to create a scene.

Don't worry if you are tone-deaf or rhythmically challenged, because the Soundtrack Media Manager helps you select loops that go well together based on key and tempo.

Analyzing a Soundtrack Project

Let's take a look at a finished song to get a feel for some of the editing techniques we'll be exploring in this lesson.

Since we are looking at an existing project, we'll start with the Project workspace.

1   Open **Daydream in A** from the Lesson_15 folder. This will launch the Soundtrack program and open the finished song.

When you first launch the project, you might have to reconnect the media. To do so, simply navigate to your Lesson_15_Media folder and select the media file that the dialog box is asking for. Make sure to check "Use selected path to reconnect other missing files" before you reconnect the first file. All other media files should reconnect after that.

2 Press Cmd-1 to separate the window layout. Press Cmd-3 to hide the Media Manager window. We will use it later in this lesson.

3 Click the Zoom button in the upper left of the project workspace window to make the window fill your screen.

TIP It's a good idea to maximize the size of your workspace within your screen, especially when you are mixing and don't need the Media Manager window.

4 Click the Audio tab, located in the upper left of the workspace window.

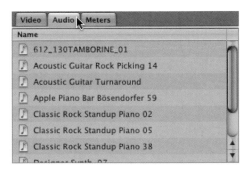

This window displays all music files used in the current Timeline. This song has nine separate instrument tracks and uses ten different loops. The guitar track contains two different loops.

> **TIP** ▶ You can drag files directly from the Audio Files window into your Timeline. This is a great technique when you want to use a loop more than once in a song.

5   Press Home to move the playhead to the beginning of the score. Now play the song using the transport controls located in the upper middle of the workspace window. You can also press the spacebar to start and stop, just as you can in Final Cut Pro.

You should hear all of the tracks except for the **Rain Stick Percussion 02** track located near the bottom. That track has been temporarily muted.

6   Click the Mute button in the **Rain Stick Percussion 02** track to turn that track on.

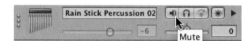

This track is optional, and may or may not make it to the final mix.

7   Click the Meters tab. This will show you the music levels for your project and indicate any peaks or clipping.

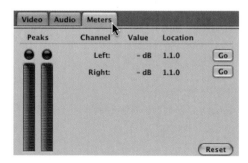

NOTE ▶ Soundtrack projects do not require video. If you are working on a project without video, you may wish to keep the Meters
window active in the Viewer to keep an eye on your audio levels as
you work.

8   Click the Stop button or press the spacebar to stop.

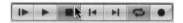

9   Press the up arrow key several times to zoom in to the playhead in the
tracks, then scroll through the Timeline to examine the song more
closely.

You can also adjust track height and zoom using the Track Height and
Zoom controls at the bottom of the Timeline.

Some of the loops have round edges, and some have straight edges.
The round edges indicate that the beginning and end of the loop play
exactly as recorded or created. The straight edges indicate that a split
or cut was placed in the loop to achieve a desired result. We'll work
more with editing loops later in this lesson.

10 Type *1600* into the project timecode window located at the top of
your workspace, then press Return. The playhead should jump to the
measure that starts at 16 seconds in the Timeline.

Music timecode is similar to video timecode, except it uses hours,
minutes, seconds, and hundredths of seconds instead of frames.

11 Ctrl-click the first **Classic Rock Standup Piano 02** loop on Track 2.

A contextual menu appears that gives you editing options for that clip.

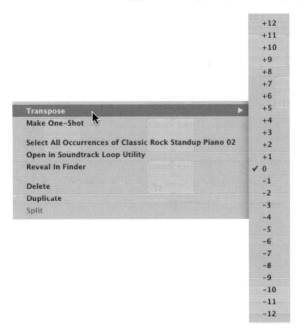

12 Choose Transpose.

A pop-up list of numbers appears from +12 to –12. This allows you to change the key of a loop. The loop is currently set to 0, which is equal to the key of the current project. To see the original key of a loop, you will need to look at it in the search window.

NOTE ▶ We will discuss musical keys later in this section.

13 Choose +2 to change the key of that loop by two semitones.

A small +2 appears in the lower left of the loop to show how much it has been transposed. The key of this loop will now be two semitones higher and may or may not fit with the song.

TIP ▶ Generally if you change loops by +/–2 it will sound pretty good. If you are composing a more upbeat song, +/–3 usually works because it corresponds with the major chords.

14 Ctrl-click again and choose Transpose > 0 to set the clip back to the original key for this song.

Each number changes the key of the song by +/–1. The maximum you can change a loop's key is +/–12, which is a full octave higher or lower.

Notice that the **Classic Rock Standup Piano 05** loop on Track 4 has been transposed to –12, which lowered the loop by one full octave while maintaining the key.

TIP ▶ Duplicating a loop and transposing it by one octave (+/–12) is a good way to add depth and range to a melody or song. The duplicate clip can be placed on any track, as long as it is in the same position as the original clip to maintain sync.

15 As with Final Cut Pro, you can press Shift-Z to make the entire Timeline fit in the workspace window.

All of the music loops will be visible in the Timeline. You may need to move the horizontal scroll bar at the bottom of the window all the way to the left to see the entire song.

16 Select View > Layouts > Single Window, or press Cmd-2, to reveal the Media Manager window.

This layout setting will create one large window for both the Media Manager and the workspace. If you prefer to keep the windows separate, select View > Layouts > Separate Windows, or press Cmd-1.

17 Repeat the last step for all five different views in the View > Layouts menu. These are the most common layouts for Soundtrack.

Press Cmd-2 to return to Single Window view.

NOTE ▶ There are additional layout choices that are not in the layout menu. To examine these choices, press Cmd-6 through Cmd-9.

Now that you have looked at a finished song, let's back up and learn about the basic elements of music.

Basic Elements of Audio and Music

Sound is created by vibrations that travel through the air in waves. Our ears translate these vibrations into specific, identifiable sounds based on the fundamental elements that make up the sound wave.

Understanding Sound Waves

A sound wave repeats as it radiates over time and distance from the original source. The basic wave has two main elements: the *amplitude*, or height of the wave from the high to low peaks, and the *frequency*, or time between two peaks.

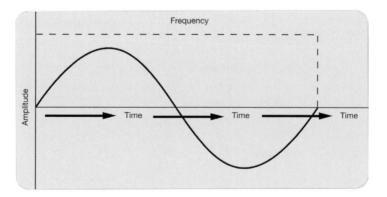

A frequency repeats in cycles per second, called hertz (Hz). An average person's ears are capable of hearing roughly between 20 hertz and 20 kilohertz (kHz). We recognize low frequency as a low sound, such as the rumble of a car engine or the musical tones of a tuba, and high frequency as a higher sound, such as a bird chirp or the musical tones of a flute.

A sound's volume is measured in decibels (dB) and is determined by the height, or amplitude, of the sound wave. We can hear an approximate range of 0 to 130 dB. The smaller the amplitude, the lower the decibels and perceived volume; the larger the amplitude, the higher the decibels and perceived volume.

The visual curve of a sustained note by an individual instrument is called its *envelope*.

The shape of the envelope varies depending on the instrument and how it is played. Imagine hearing the sound of a cymbal crash. Now imagine seeing the sound from the instant it starts until it is no longer perceived. The crash's envelope would start large and loud and slowly taper off over time until it vanished altogether.

Sustained envelope   Percussive envelope

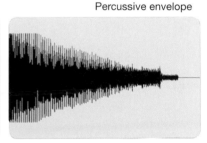

The envelope of a violin or cello would be quite different depending on how it is played. If the strings are plucked, the envelope will reveal short, quick (staccato) bursts of sound. If the cello strings are slowly played with the bow, the envelope may start small and slowly grow in intensity as it is played.

The envelope—the calling card of each instrument—allows our ears to recognize and distinguish different instruments.

You can see the envelope of a loop or one-shot by looking at the waveform located in the Additional Info section at the bottom of the Media Manager window, or in the music tracks on the Timeline.

Understanding Music

Writing music is like writing a story. A thousand miscellaneous words strung together on a piece of paper are nothing more than letters on a page. Similarly, a thousand musical notes played in random order will sound more like acoustic graffiti than music.

Soundtrack has taken a lot of the guesswork out of arranging music because all of the loops sound good individually. Soundtrack will automatically change the key and tempo of any loop to match the current project.

Now that you know a little more about the anatomy of a sound wave, let's look at the essential elements of a song.

Musical Sounds

Musical sounds are unique because each note has a specific frequency or pitch that can easily be duplicated, measured, and repeated.

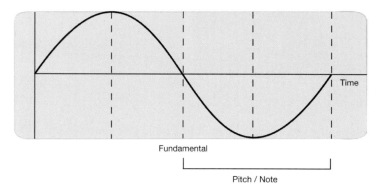

The dramatic, easy-to-recognize frequency that we hear as a note is the fundamental part of musical sound. We can hear and identify a note, such as C, whether it is played on a piano, violin, or guitar, because we recognize the fundamental sound or note. What identifies the sound of a note from one instrument to the other are the subtle elements of the sound, often called *timbre*. Timbre can be further divided into the concepts of overtones and harmonics, and help us distinguish the voices of different instruments.

Effects and EQ play on the harmonics and overtones of a sound but don't actually change the fundamental note or frequencies.

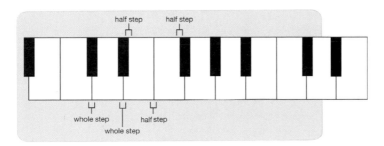

In Western music, there are seven different notes: A through G. Each note has a different sound, or pitch, and can be performed individually by many different instruments. Remember "Do-Re-Mi," the famous song from *The Sound of Music*? Each of the "do, re, mi, fa, sol, la, ti, do" sounds represents one of the notes, a step at a time, until the scale repeats an octave higher.

From any key on a keyboard, there are a total of 11 black and white keys to the right or left before the same note repeats at the 12th key, an octave higher or lower. That is why you transpose a clip by +/−12 to change it by one octave.

The black keys represent half steps between the white keys. These create the sharp and flat variations of the notes A through G. Two white keys next to each other with no black key between are also half steps.

Melody

The melody of a song is the part that stays with you long after the music stops playing. If you think of the theme to your favorite movie, the part you remember or hum to yourself is the melody.

Many of the loops in Soundtrack contain a melody or melodic parts and can be combined with other loops to create a different melody.

1   Click the Horn/Wind button in the Search tab of the Media Manager.

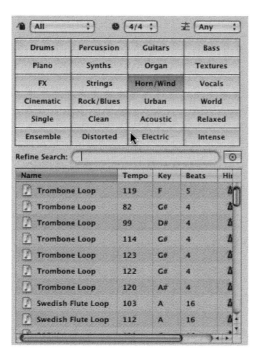

The button will darken to indicate that it has been selected. If you do not see buttons in your search window, change the search view selection to View as Buttons in the upper left corner of the Media Manager.

2   Type *Orchestra* in the Refine Search window and press Return.

Most of the orchestral sounds are a good example of melody.

3   Click the first sound to select it. Press the down arrow key to scroll down through the selections and listen to the samples.

4   Scroll down and select **Orchestral Brass and Woodwind 16.aiff**.

> **TIP**   Click and drag the right edge of the Name column in the search results window to extend your view of the names. Many of the loops have the same name except for a number at the end. The numbers, which distinguish the pieces, may not be visible without extending the Name column.

5   Listen to the **Orchestral Brass and Woodwind 16.aiff** loop.

6   Click the Stop button at the bottom of the Media Manager window.

The melody of a song is easily recognizable and remembered, like the plot of a great story.

Rhythm and Tempo

Rhythm is the heartbeat of the song and sustains a sense of timing and mood for a piece of music. Editors use the rhythm of a song to set the pace for a scene.

1   Play the song **Daydream in A** in the Timeline. Listen to the rhythm of the song as it plays.

The rhythm is subtle and relaxed in the first few measures. The song's mood is slow, quiet, thoughtful, and lonely.

Notice how the feel and mood of the song change when you hear the guitar, and again with the added percussion. The tempo of the song has not changed, but it feels more alive.

The percussion takes over toward the middle of the song, and the rhythm becomes more dominant in the mix. Instead of just feeling the timing of the song, you hear it. Now, the entire mood of the song has changed.

2   Press the spacebar to stop the song.

You can feel rhythm changes in a song as they happen. Slow and moody, or fast and frenetic, rhythm drives the mood of a song, theme, or underlying score. Rhythm is active and catchy. Without warning, you move your body to the beat.

There can be several layers of rhythm at the same time in a piece of music.

3   Type *4800* in the timecode window and press Return.

4   Press the spacebar to play the song starting at 48 seconds.

This section of the song has four different rhythm parts: classical piano, guitar, shaker, and tambourine.

NOTE ▸ There is a fifth rhythm part visible, the rain stick loop, which is muted at this point in the score.

Rhythm is often created with drums and percussion, but it can also be created by other instruments, like a piano or guitar.

5   Click the Solo buttons on the different rhythm tracks to hear them individually.

6   Press the spacebar to stop the song.

The dominating rhythm layer occurs in regular intervals called measures. Measures are made up of individual beats. The first beat of a measure is called the downbeat.

The Soundtrack interface has a beat ruler and a beat display to show the measures and beats for the current Timeline.

Time signatures represent the relationship between beats and measures, and are displayed as fractions. The upper value indicates the number of beats per measure, while the lower value reveals the duration of the beat.

Think of a waltz—1-2-3, 1-2-3. The time signature would be 3/4, or three beats per measure.

Most rock songs, on the other hand, have a fast, steady beat and follow four beats per measure.

The default meter for new projects in Soundtrack is 4/4, or four beats per measure, with each beat represented by a quarter note. You can change this by clicking the time signature window before you start composing. Keep in mind that this is just a method of counting bars and beats per measure and has no effect on the actual music that you create in the Timeline.

NOTE ▶ The time signature of a loop is set when it is first created. You will hear the difference between 3/4 and 4/4 time only in original loops that were recorded in these different time signatures.

You can also change the tempo of a song in the Timeline.

Tempo is the rate at which the beats occur in a piece of music, and is measured in beats per minute (bpm). Music with a slower tempo feels more relaxed, while music with a faster tempo tends to have a more energetic, upbeat feeling.

7   Type *200* in the BPM (beats per minute) text box in the upper-right corner of the workspace.

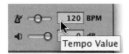

Play the song. It sounds more upbeat and lively—a bit too lively, when the percussion kicks in.

8   Type *60* in the BPM text box. Play the song again. This time it feels almost comatose.

These are extreme examples of tempo change, but it is important to understand how much tempo can change the feel of a song.

9   Type *120* in the BPM text box to go back to the original settings.

Instrumentation

If melody is the plot/story of a song, and rhythm sets the mood/feel, then instrumentation represents the characters. A typical story has main characters, supporting characters, and even bit parts and background players. The same is true for music. There are the main parts that are usually carried by one or two lead instruments, then the supporting instruments that round out the musical cast.

The choice of instruments you cast, and the parts they play, will help determine the overall sound and expression of a piece of music. Combining and creating the different instrumental parts of a song is called *arranging* a piece of music.

Soundtrack is a musical arrangement program that makes it simple to place musical elements into a Timeline. You then manipulate those elements to create a song.

> **TIP** ▶ The wrong instrumental parts can be as destructive to a song as bad acting or characters can be to a film, so choose wisely.

Key

Each loop was recorded in a specific key (except for some sound effects and percussion). Loops will sound best if used in their original key; however, the key can be changed by several semitones without stretching or distorting it too much. You can search for loops recorded in the same key, or change the key for your score in the key display window.

1   Click the Key pull-down menu at the top of your Timeline window.

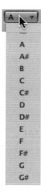

2   Change the key of the song to A# (A-sharp) and listen to the change as you play through the Timeline.

3   Change the key to C. Listen to the change.

4   Change the key back to A, the original key for the song.

The default key for a project is A, but it can be changed in the project preferences.

Soundtrack will automatically change the key of a loop to match the current project when you place it in the Timeline.

Setting Soundtrack Preferences

Soundtrack preferences can affect the way the application works and looks. Let's go through the settings before working with the application.

1   Choose Soundtrack > Preferences to open the Preferences window.

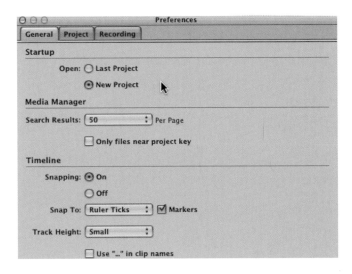

There are three tabs: General, Project, and Recording.

General Preferences

▶   The Startup section lets you chose whether Soundtrack will open a new project or your last project when the program is launched. The default is set to New Project.

▶   The Media Manager section determines how many sample selections you can view per page. If you check the "Only files near project key" box, Media Manager will display only those files that match your project's key.

▶   The Timeline section allows you to predetermine your Timeline display settings for new projects. You can turn snapping on and off, as well as specify items the playhead will snap to. You can also change the default track height.

Project Preferences

These preferences are pretty self-explanatory. You can set the length, tempo, key, and default time signature of a project.

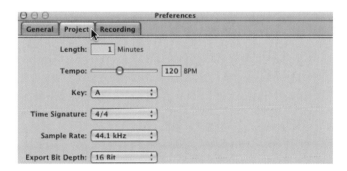

You can also specify sample rate and bit depth. If you will be exporting your Soundtrack project for CD recording or for playing strictly as a music file, leave the sample rate set to 44.1 kHz. If you will be using your music in Final Cut Pro or as a Soundtrack composition to accompany video, change the sample rate to 48 kHz. You can also export at the highest rate, 96 kHz, for projects requiring that quality.

The bit depth can be set to either 16 bits, which is CD quality, or 24 bits, which may be required for high-end video projects.

NOTE ▶   24-bit AIFF audio files can be imported into Final Cut Pro projects and exported as one or more files at 24 bits. FCP is also 24-bit playback compliant, and a project's mix can be exported as 24-bit AIFF files. These 24-bit features are new in Final Cut Pro 4.

Recording Preferences

Recording preferences allow you to select devices used for input and to monitor your session. Fade-in/Fade-out applies a fade of specific length to each take when you record audio.

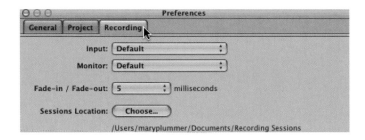

NOTE ▶ You will learn more about recording with Soundtrack in the next lesson.

Finally, the Sessions Location button lets you choose where recording sessions are saved. You can change the default location by clicking the Choose button and navigating to a new location, just as you would with any other application.

Adding Effects and Splitting a Track

You don't have to be a musician to use Soundtrack. In fact, having skills as an editor can be just as valuable. In the next series of exercises, we will work on a score for several scenes from the feature film *Chocolate Curse*, and in the process learn many of the advanced music editing techniques available in the Soundtrack program.

1 Close the current project (File > Close) and open **15-2 Finished** from the **Lesson_15** folder. Reconnect media if necessary. (See "Analyzing a Soundtrack Project," Step 1, for instructions.)

This Soundtrack project includes a video clip and dialogue track exported from Final Cut Pro. There are also five music tracks.

2   Press Home to bring your playhead to the beginning of the Timeline.

3   Play the finished sequence to see and hear the final score.

4   Close this project without saving and then open **15-2 Starting** from the **Lesson_15** folder.

5   Press Ctrl-2 to change your layout to Single Window view.

This layout works well for scoring because it allows easy access to both the Media Manager window and the project workspace.

The first step when starting to score a scene is to contemplate the feel of the scene and understand what type of musical sound the director wants. In this case we use a classic orchestral feel for the music, to play on the mood and movement of the actors.

TIP ▶ Matching the underlying music to a character's movement is an effective way to enhance the action as well as to play on emotion. In this case, the girls are going through typical teenage angst, and the music accents their overreaction in a whimsical way.

6   Press the spacebar to play the sequence in the Timeline.

Think about the beginning, middle, and end of the scene. The music should reflect the tonal changes.

The score is already in place, but there is a significant moment that has been overlooked.

7   Press the right or left arrow key on your keyboard to move the playhead to 27;29 in the Timeline, or type *2729* in the timecode window and press Return.

8   Press the spacebar to play the scene from that point.

In this scene, one girl has an idea and the other loves the idea. As the music interprets the mood, we will add an instrument to accentuate the characters' actions. A visual interpretation of this moment might be a lightbulb turning on above the character. The musical equivalent to the lightbulb can be anything from a rim shot to a whistle. In this case we'll use a wind chime to maintain the orchestral genre of this scene.

9   Select View as Columns in the Search window.

You will see two columns, Keywords and Matches. Use these columns to refine the search.

10 Select Chime in the Keywords list.

NOTE ▶ The number in parentheses next to the descriptor words in the Matches column refers to the number of matches.

11 Select **Synthetic Designer FX08.aiff** from the search results in the Name column to audition it.

This chime is better suited for a horror film score.

12 Press the Down arrow to select the second chime choice, **Synthetic Designer FX 09.aiff**. Listen carefully. It takes a while for the sound to play.

This chime loop works for our scene, but it will need to be edited.

There are two Orchestral Brass tracks, one above the other, in the Timeline.

13 Drag and drop the **Synthetic Designer FX 09 loop** into the Timeline and release it beneath the lower Orchestral Brass track. Click the center of the loop and drag left to place the beginning of the loop (the left edge) at the start of your score.

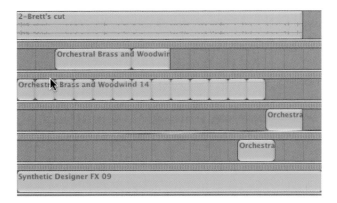

14 Click the largest track height button so you can see the new track clearly.

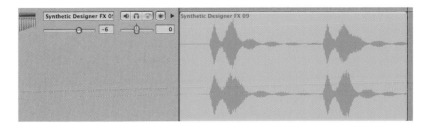

15 Click the new **Synthetic Designer FX 09** clip in the Timeline to select it.

The clip will turn slightly darker in color to indicate it is selected.

16 Use the left arrow key to maneuver the playhead to the measure just before the first chime sound starts. Use the visual waveforms as a guide.

Your playhead should be at 8;00 in the timecode window.

Unlike with clips in Final Cut Pro, you cannot click and drag the front edge of a loop to trim it. If you click and drag the head of a loop, it always keeps the beginning of the loop intact. To discard the first part of a loop, you must split (cut) the clip.

Our goal now is to split the track before and after the chime sounds, then discard the excess from the Timeline.

17 Select Edit > Split to cut the track, or press the S key.

NOTE ▶ Make sure the Chime loop is selected (it will be slightly darker in color than the other loops). If no loops are selected, Soundtrack will beep to let you know it cannot perform the edit until you select a track.

18 Click the first piece of **Synthetic Designer FX 09**, just before the splice you've made, to select that section.

The selected section turns a darker green.

19 Press Delete to remove the section from the Timeline.

20 Select the remaining portion of **Synthetic Designer FX 09** and press the right arrow to move the playhead to the end of the first chime sound before it repeats. Use the waveforms as a visual guide. Your playhead should be at 12;00 in the timecode window.

21 Press S to split the track.

22 Click to select the part of the track after the new edit, then press Delete.

There should be only one chime sound in the Timeline.

Now you are ready to move the edited loop to the appropriate place in the scene. If placed correctly, this wind chime loop will not only accent the first character's idea, but also the second character's smile.

You have been navigating in the Timeline using timecode. Try using the beat measure window to move the playhead.

23 Watch the Time in Beats window, just to the left of the timecode window, and move the playhead to 15.1.000 in the Timeline. This refers to the first beat of the 15th measure in the Timeline.

24 Click and drag the edited clip so it starts at the playhead position.

> **NOTE** ▶ Using the playhead to mark a position in the Timeline is useful only if the playhead stays in that position. When dragging a clip to the playhead, be sure to click and *hold* the mouse button as you move the clip. If you release the mouse button or click without holding, the playhead will be repositioned.

Play the clip to see how it fits with the video.

Sometimes the best placement for a clip is slightly offbeat. This technique is most commonly used when syncing a sound effect to picture. To move a clip offbeat, you will need to nudge it in one direction or the other.

25 Click the clip to select it, then press and hold the Option key and tap the left or right arrow keys to nudge the clip one beat at a time. Press Shift-Option while you tap the arrows to move one measure at a time.

Continue to nudge the clip until you are happy with the timing. Consider the action of the girls in the scene.

> **NOTE** ▶ Nudging moves a loop off the beat. If you nudge a rhythm track offbeat, it will sound out of sync with the other tracks.

26 Save and close the project.

Creating Stingers and Stabs

Sometimes scoring a scene means creating short musical cues rather than a full song. These short musical cues are often referred to as *stingers* and *stabs*.

Imagine a suspense thriller in which our brave hero arrives home perfectly happy, content with life, perhaps chatting on his cell phone. All is well in his world until he notices that the front door is ajar … cue the stinger!

Up to this point in the scene, there was no music, just ambient noise and sound effects. A suspenseful string sound slowly rises in volume and intensity as our character continues into the house. If you've ever been stung by a bee, you know that it generally takes you by surprise. One minute all is well, the next minute you feel something on your arm, and then, before you can do anything about it, you feel that swell of pain that lingers—and changes your emotional state. The musical stinger works in a similar way, because it creeps up on you and then out of nowhere *stings* you with music to toy with your emotions and build suspense, tension, or drama—instantly.

Stingers fade away, just as the pain of a bee sting fades, yet at any moment, when you least expect it, you can be stung again and the whole process repeats itself.

Our hypothetical scene continues: Everything seems fine inside the house. The musical stinger fades away as the hero relaxes. He casually opens the refrigerator when his eyes catch a glimpse of something … cue the stab! A quick, sharp sound, or stab of music, rattles our nerves, and stops every heart in the theater. Whether the payoff of the scene is a dismembered limb or the cliché of a cat leaping out of the fridge, the stab achieved its goal.

Stabs and stingers work well alone, with sound effects, or weaved into a musical score. In the next exercise, we will use stabs and stingers to accentuate an action scene.

1   Open **15-4 Finished** from the **Lesson_15** folder.

TIP ▶ If you are scoring an action scene, it is a good idea to start with the stabs and stingers, then add the rest of the instrumental tracks.

2   Play the scene and listen to the stabs used in the first half of the scene to accent the action. The second half starts with a stinger that stands out from the rest of the music.

   NOTE ▶ The Stabs are created by The Tad Sound. The stinger is **Designer Synth 07**.

3   Close the current project and open **15-4 Starting** from the **Lesson_15** folder.

4   Play the scene and listen to it without the stabs and stinger.

   The action feels less dramatic in the first half, and the musical suspense is lacking in the second half.

   Stabs can be made from many different instruments. In this scene, however, the action calls for something intense, accompanied by a good drumbeat.

5   Select the Search tab in the Media Manager window, then choose Search as Buttons.

NOTE ▶ If your window layout does not show the Media Manager, press Cmd-2 to change your window layout. This will bring up the Media Manager so you can search for the loop you want to use for your stabs.

6 Click the Drums button, then Cmd-click the Intense button at the lower right.

Both buttons will be highlighted, and the search will be narrowed to intense-sounding drums. As you can see, Soundtrack allows you to combine multiple parameters to help narrow the search.

Listen to the different files shown in the search results window. Use the up and down arrows on your keyboard to scroll through the selections. The forward arrow in the Media Manager will list additional selections that match your search criteria.

NOTE ▶ You can change the number of selections per page that come up in your search results by going to Soundtrack's General Preferences.

If you know the name of the specific sound you are looking for, just type the name in the Refine Search window. Results depend upon your currently active search parameters. For example, you won't be able to find a drum loop if you are currently searching through piano loops. Be sure to click the Drums button before you type the name of a specific drum loop into the Refine Search window.

7 Type *Tad* in the Refine Search window, and press Return.

The Tad Sound.aiff will show in the search results.

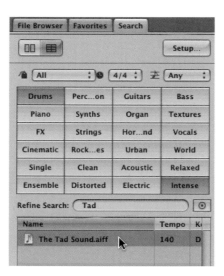

Next, you need to create a track for the stabs. Place the stabs track near the other percussion loops in the Timeline so you can adjust them for timing and alignment.

TIP ▶ It's a good idea to keep like sounds together in neighboring tracks. This will make it easier to mix, as well as to see your score graphically.

8 Ctrl-click the track selection area of the track header of the **Bass Terror Tablas** track. The track selection area is represented by three vertical white dots.

9 Choose Add Track Above from the pull-down menu. A new, untitled track appears in the Timeline.

10 Click and drag **The Tad Sound.aiff** from the search results window to the beginning of the new, empty track.

The entire loop takes two measures to play.

Notice the loop is curved on both ends, which indicates it is a complete loop.

11 Press Home to move your playhead to the beginning of the Timeline.

12 Click the Solo button on **The Tad Sound** track to isolate it from the other tracks.

The Solo button turns gray when it is activated, and all of the other tracks darken to indicate that they have been temporarily muted.

13 Press the spacebar to play the track.

The sound seems to cut off abruptly. This loop was made of two variations that can be combined or played separately. We'll use them both in this scene to create the stabs.

14 Click the Solo button again on **The Tad Sound** track to turn on the other tracks.

Now that we have a stab sound, we need to put it to work by placing it in the correct position on the track. To ease placement of the stab, turn off snapping in the Timeline.

Soundtrack's snapping feature works very much like the snapping in Final Cut Pro. Snapping affects both the playhead and the individual loops. With snapping on, the playhead and loops will snap to measures, beats, or markers.

15 Click the Snapping button at the bottom of the Timeline to turn off snapping, or press G.

The Snapping button will lighten to indicate it has been turned off. With snapping turned off, you will be able to move your playhead to any position on the Timeline.

16 Click the Solo button on the video clip track (**Action-Brett's cut**) to turn off all of the music tracks.

17 Play the beginning of the scene and find the moment of action where the ogre jumps out from behind the tree (2;22 in the timecode window).

If you want to move the playhead one frame at a time left or right, press Cmd and tap the left or right arrow keys.

You may need to press the up arrow to zoom into the track and find the exact position. You can also type *222* into the timecode window and press Return.

> **TIP** ▶ Before you zoom into or out of the Timeline, move your playhead to the point in the Timeline that you wish to view. The up and down arrows will zoom around the playhead position, while the playhead remains visible in the Timeline window.

Aligning Audio Clips to Timecode Using Markers

Soundtrack offers three types of markers: beat, time, and scoring markers. We will work more with markers in the next lesson; for now, we'll just learn their definitions and how to align clips to them.

Beat markers indicate a specific beat in the Timeline, while time markers mark a specific timecode point. Scoring markers can be created in Final Cut Pro and are used to mark a visual cue in the video portion of the scene.

Beat markers are purple, time markers are green, and scoring markers are orange.

Let's set a time marker at the playhead position in the Timeline.

1 Press M to set a time marker at the playhead position, or Ctrl-click the top of the playhead to open a contextual menu and select Add a Time Marker.

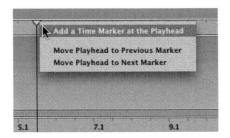

2 Click the Solo button in the video track again to unmute the other audio tracks.

Once you've set the time marker, you are ready to move your stab to that location. You will want turn snapping back on for this maneuver.

3 Press G to turn on snapping. Click the center of **The Tad Sound** to select it, then drag it forward on the Timeline and snap it to the time marker.

NOTE ▸ Selecting and moving clips in Soundtrack works the same as selecting and moving video clips in Final Cut Pro: Click inside the loop to move it on the Timeline. If you grab the end of a loop, you will stretch it in length.

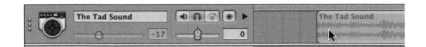

For more detailed control of the snapping feature, choose View >
Snap To and select the snapping feature you wish to use.

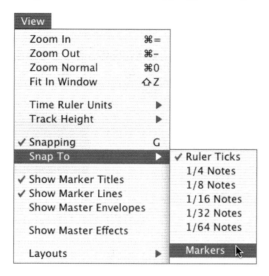

Refining the Timing and Adding More Stabs

Now we need to edit the stab to fit the scene and create additional stabs.

1 Click the Solo button on **The Tad Sound** track and press the up arrow
several times to zoom into the track.

> **TIP**▶ You will want to have a clear view of your loop before you
> start editing.

2 Click **The Tad Sound** clip in the Timeline to select it. Move your playhead to the blank space in **The Tad Sound** before it starts the second
part of the loop.

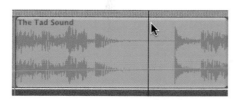

You may want to turn off snapping to do this. Listen to the loop and stop the playhead after the first part of the sound, or look at the waveform and find the straight line between the first and second parts of the loop.

3 Make sure the clip is selected and press the S key to split the music clip at the playhead position.

You will see a line through the clip where you split the track. We can now move the second half to the next stab location.

4 Type *415* in the timecode window and press Return.

The playhead will move to the new location. This is where we will place another stab.

5 Select and drag the second half of **The Tad Sound** clip to the playhead position in the Timeline.

You may wish to turn snapping on before you move the clip.

The second stab is in the correct position, but it cuts off abruptly. We will need to extend the clip.

6 Press G to turn off snapping (if it is on).

7 Click and drag the right edge of the clip to extend it until you see the straight horizontal line in the waveform indicating the end of that sound.

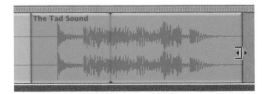

There are still two more places in the Timeline that need stabs. To create them, we will simply copy the stab we just made and paste it where we need it.

8   Click the second stab clip in the Timeline to select it.

9   Choose Edit > Copy or press Cmd-C to copy the sound clip.

10   Type *900* in the timecode window and press Return.

The playhead will move to the new location in the Timeline.

11   Choose Edit > Paste or press Cmd-V.

The clip should appear in the Timeline at the 9;00 timecode position. The playhead will automatically snap to the end of the clip you just pasted in the Timeline.

12   Press Cmd-V to paste the clip again.

You will now have two identical clips aligned next to each other in the Timeline.

Transposing Loops

Congratulations. You have created four stabs in the Timeline. However, they are all in the same key and sound very repetitious. Let's transpose two of them for variety.

As we discussed earlier in this lesson, you can change the note or pitch of a particular loop by using Soundtrack's transpose feature.

Transposing changes the key of a note. Transposing by positive numbers makes the key higher; transposing by negative numbers makes the key lower. If you transpose a clip by +/–12 semitones, you change it by an entire octave.

Our goal now is to transpose the second and fourth stabs to give them a different sound or personality.

1   Ctrl-click the second stab in the Timeline.

2 Choose Transpose > –3.

A small –3 appears in the lower-left corner of the clip to indicate it has been transposed (the sound has been shifted lower) by 3 semitones.

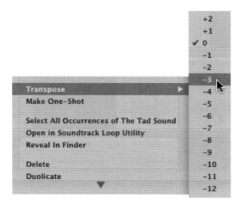

3 Repeat Steps 1 and 2 on the fourth stab to lower the sound by 3 semitones.

Listen to the transposed stabs. The variation adds an ominous feel to the scene.

Now that we have all tracks in place for the first half of the scene, let's briefly turn our attention to the stinger in the second half.

4 Click the Solo button to unsolo **The Tad Sound** track and activate all the other tracks. Listen to the second half of the scene.

The **Designer Synth 07** track should still be muted in the Timeline.

5 Click the Mute button on the **Designer Synth 07** track to turn it on. Listen to the second half of the scene again.

Notice how the slow, building string sound adds tension and suspense to the scene. This is a stinger.

Later in this lesson we will adjust the stinger's fade so it starts *after* the ax hits, as if the ax were responsible for the stinger.

As you can see, stabs and stingers add emotion and excitement to a scene and are easy to create.

All tracks for our score are now accurately placed in the Timeline, but before we work on the effects and levels, let's quickly learn how to join tracks.

Joining Tracks

You have already split a loop track using the S key. You can also remove a split or rejoin two elements from the same original loop.

1   Cmd-click the two adjacent **Bodhran Loop 35** clips on the fourth track from the top, or click in an empty part of the track near the clips and drag your pointer over the clips to select them both.

You can join the two sections into one clip since they are next to each other and are transposed the same amount (–2).

2   Press J or select Edit > Join to join the two separate clips into one clip.

You now see one long clip instead of two separate clips.

Working with Audio Effects

Editing music in Soundtrack is similar to editing video in Final Cut Pro. First you edit all of the clips into the Timeline, then you can add effects and adjust levels.

> **TIP** ▶ When you are scoring music, it's a good idea to start by putting the music tracks in the right order. When the song is finished, you can add effects and EQ. Adding effects while building the song slows the process because you won't know how the effects will sound within the mix until all tracks have been added. In other words, bake the cake first, then ice it.

You don't need to know a lot about effects to be able to use them effectively in Soundtrack. Effects are used to change or modify the sound of a clip in the same way filters are used to modify video clips in Final Cut Pro.

Audio effects can alter the sound and characteristics of the audio signal. These changes can be subtle or dramatic depending on how you set the effects parameters.

> **NOTE** ▶ For more detailed information on audio effects, read Chapter 9 of the Soundtrack manual.

In this exercise, we will add an effect to the **Basement Hit** clip to make it sound surreal and match the change in the music.

1 Type *1300* in the timecode window and press Return.

   The playhead will be at the point in the Timeline right before the ogre smashes the ax into a stump.

2 Press the spacebar to play the clip and watch the video in the Viewer.

   You should see the ax hit the stump and hear the **Basement Hit FX sound** on the eighth track.

   If you play the last half of the Timeline, you will hear the music change from classical, orchestral action music to contemporary, synthesizer-driven music.

TIP ► If the video doesn't play in the Viewer, click the Meters or Audio tab, then click back to the Video tab to refresh the window.

Our goal now is to add a delay effect to the Basement Hit FX to set the tone for the music change from classical to contemporary.

3 Click the Solo button for the **Basement Hit FX** track in the Timeline.

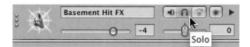

All of the other tracks should be darkened.

You can access the Effects window by clicking the Show Effects button in the track header. The Show Effects button is the farthest button to the right of the track header and looks like an asterisk.

4 Click the Show Effects button on the **Basement Hit FX** track.

The Effects window should appear in front of the Timeline. You can also access the Effects window at any time by pressing Cmd-E.

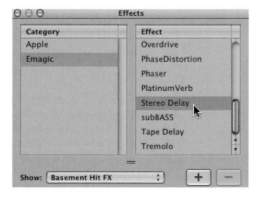

Soundtrack comes with two categories of effects: Apple and Emagic. You can also import effects from other programs such as Acid. The left side of the window shows the effects category; the right side lists the individual effects.

5   Click the Emagic category to select it.

Emagic is highlighted to indicate that it has been selected.

6   Click Stereo Delay to select it.

Stereo Delay is highlighted in blue to show that it has been selected.

The Show pull-down menu indicates which track the effect will be added to. It should say **Basement Hit FX**.

7   Click the + (plus) button to add Stereo Delay to the **Basement Hit FX** track.

Stereo Delay will appear in the Name column in the Effects list. There is a check box to the left of the effect name that you can use to enable or disable an effect. By default, when the box is checked, the effect is on.

Listen to **Basement Hit** in the Timeline with the new effect.

Once you have added an effect, you can adjust its parameters by clicking the disclosure triangle next to the effect's enable box.

Some effects have an advanced graphical interface window that reveals a visual representation of the effect's parameters.

Before digital recording, music studios required stand-alone effects boxes and rack-mounted equipment to create effects. The advanced windows are designed with buttons, knobs, and sliders that work like the analog equipment they represent.

8 Click the Advanced button to open the control panel for the Stereo
Delay effect.

9 Adjust some of the parameters and listen in the Timeline to hear the
difference in the sound. To make it easier to test the different parameters, you can create a playback loop.

Creating a Playback Loop Area

You can set a playback area, instead of resetting your playhead every time
you want to hear a portion of the Timeline. We will create a playback area
around the clip.

1 Make sure the Looping button is active (highlighted) in the transport
controls bar.

2 Click and drag the mouse to the right in the beat ruler above the **Basement Hit FX** clip to create a playback region. The beat ruler is located just below the video track at the top of the Timeline.

In and Out points appear in the playback area. These In and Out points represent the playback area that will loop.

You can click and drag the In and Out points to move them.

NOTE ▶ To "slip" the playback area to a different part of the Timeline, click inside the playback area and drag left or right to a new location. This works like the Slip tool in Final Cut Pro and maintains the duration between the In and Out points. Turning off snapping eases the placement of the loop area.

3 Press the spacebar to start the playback loop. Be sure the playhead is parked inside the marked area in the beat ruler.

Click the Effects window to resume the parameter adjustment.

Looping the playback area makes it easier to hear the effect changes you are manipulating.

4 Close the Stereo Delay interface window, and then click the reset button at the bottom of the effects panel.

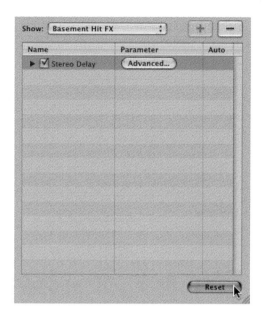

The effect will revert to the default settings. We will use the default settings for this project.

5   Close the Effects window and click the Solo button on the **Basement Hit** track to turn the other tracks back on.

6   When you are finished using loop playback, click in the beat ruler outside of the playback region.

The In and Out points disappear.

You can also turn off looping by clicking the looping button.

TIP ▶ The best way to learn how different effects sound is to apply them and practice making parameter adjustments.

7   Listen to the delayed **Basement Hit** track mixed with the other tracks.

Bypassing Track Effects

Once you've applied effects to a track, you may wish to turn the effects on or off without opening the Effects window. The Bypass Effect button is located to the left of the Effects window button on each track, and allows you to toggle the effects on and off. This is useful when you are mixing and want to hear certain tracks with or without effects in the mix.

1   Play the **Basement Hit** clip in the track with the effect.

2   Click the Bypass Effects button to turn off the effect.

The button turns darker gray when it is activated. Any effects associated with that track will be temporarily turned off while the Bypass Effects button is active.

3   Play the clip again in the Timeline to hear it without the effect.

Click the Bypass Effects button again to enable the effects on the track.

Using Envelopes to Edit Audio

Now that the tracks are in place and you've added the necessary effects, it's time to adjust the levels.

In the audio recording world, an envelope is the volume curve of a sound that can be represented on a graph. In the Soundtrack program, *envelopes* are interface elements that can be used to dynamically adjust and automate volume, panning, tempo, and effects parameters.

Each instrument track has individual volume and panning controls located in the track header. You can use these controls to adjust the levels for an entire track.

1 Locate the third track from the top, **Bodhran Loop 08**, and unsolo any soloed tracks.

The volume for that track is set to –6. This level is relatively high in the mix considering that the loudest level possible is +6 and the lowest is –96.

You can lower the volume level for that track by clicking the volume slider and dragging to the left, or typing a new volume level in the text box to the right of the slider.

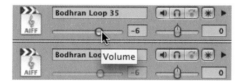

2 Click the volume slider and drag to the left until the level is –13, or type –13 in the volume text box.

The volume for the entire track is now set to –13 decibels.

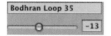

Now let's look at the panning controls for **Bodhram Loop 35** on Track 3.

The panning range in Soundtrack is –100 to +100. These numbers represent the stereo field from the extreme left (–100) to the extreme right (+100). The center of the stereo field is 0.

At the moment, all of the tracks are panned to 0, or center. This means you will hear them equally out of both the left and right speakers, and they will sound as though they are in the center of the room.

When you listen to live music, the location of the instruments affects where and how you hear the sound. All instruments in an orchestra are not in a clump at the center of the stage, for example. They are spread out from the left to the right, and our ears hear them accordingly.

When mixing the audio tracks for a film, part of the goal is to give the different elements a realistic feel, and location, in the mix. For example, if a police car zooms by traveling left to right, the audio should also sound as though it is traveling from the left to the right speaker.

An important element in scoring music is achieving a full stereo field, instead of center-panning every sound equally.

3   Click the Solo button for the **Bass Terror Tablas** track. Play that part of the track and listen to the sound.

The track is panned center (0) so you will hear it equally out of both speakers, and you will see identical levels in the audio meter for the left and right side.

4   Click and drag the panning slider all the way to the left (−100). Listen to the clip.

You should hear the sound out of only the left speaker, and only the left side of the Audio meter should display audio levels.

5   Click and drag the panning slider all the way to the right (+100). Listen to the clip.

Now, you hear the sound out of only the right side, and the audio meter displays levels on only the right side.

6   Click in the panning level window on the **Bass Terror Tablas** track and type *0* to reset the track. Click the Solo button again to turn on the rest of the tracks.

7 Change the Panning level of the **Bodhram Loop 35** on Track 3 to –50, that of the **Bodhram Loop 35** on Track 4 to –50, and that of **The Tad Sound** track to 50.

These tracks will now sound off-center: two more to the left, and the other more to the right.

Using Envelope Points to Fine-tune Levels

Envelope points can be used to dynamically change the parameters of a track over time.

Envelope points function like Final Cut Pro keyframes and allow you to fine-tune track levels. This process is called *automation* and can be applied to individual tracks or across the entire mix.

Track envelopes are horizontal lines located beneath each individual track, and they can be accessed by clicking the disclosure triangle on the left side of the track header.

In this exercise, we will fade the volume up on the stinger so that it begins after, not before, the ogre slams down the ax.

1 Click the disclosure triangle to the left of the **Designer Synth 07** track, which is the sixth track from the top. Unmute and unsolo all tracks if necessary.

A purple envelope track appears with volume and pan lines.

2 Type *1216* in the timecode window and press Return to move the playhead to the beginning of the **Designer Synth 07** clip.

3 Turn off snapping. Double-click the thin horizontal Volume envelope line at the playhead position to set an envelope point.

An envelope point appears in the Volume envelope.

TIP ▶ If you turn off snapping before setting envelope points, the points will always go exactly where you click. If snapping is on, the envelope point may snap to the nearest ruler tick in your Timeline.

4 Type *1600* in the timecode box and press Return.

5 Double-click the Volume envelope line at the new playhead position to set another envelope point.

6 Click the first envelope point and drag it down as low as possible (–96).

The Volume envelope is now bent at an angle.

Every envelope has an envelope point, or keyframe, at the beginning of the track. The first envelope point for this track is still set at its original volume level.

7 Ctrl-click the envelope point at the start of the track.

A contextual menu appears. Choose Set Value to Next Point.

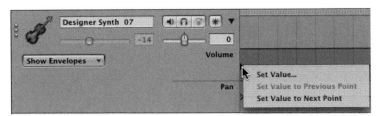

The Value of the envelope point will match the value of the next point in the Timeline.

You could also choose Set Value, which allows you to type the value for the point.

The volume for the track will now be silent until the track starts to fade in at the second keyframe.

NOTE ▶ If you add another audio clip to the silent portion of the track, you will need to raise the volume to hear the new clip.

You can move or nudge an envelope point up, down, right, or left. Click the envelope point to select it and then press one of the following:

▶ Shift-Option-right or left arrow to move an envelope point to the previous or next gridline. This distance varies depending on how much you are zoomed into or out of the Timeline.

▶ Option-right or left arrow to nudge the envelope point by one pixel.

▶ Option-up or down arrow to move the envelope point up or down by one pixel.

▶ Shift-Option-up or down arrow to move the envelope point up or down by five pixels.

NOTE ▶ You can also use these same commands to move audio clips left and right within the tracks.

We want to adjust the position of the second envelope point in **Designer Synth 07** to align it exactly with the end of the **Basement Hit**, so we'll use the **Basement Hit** clip in the track below as a visual guide to align the envelope point to the end of the clip.

8   Click the second envelope point (located at 12;16 in the timecode window) to select it.

9   Press Shift-Option-right arrow once to move the envelope point one measure to the right.

10 Press Option and tap the right arrow several times to nudge the point until it is just to the right of the **Basement Hit** clip. Listen to the timing of the stinger as it fades in.

11 Click the disclosure triangle on the **Designer Synth 07** track to hide the envelopes.

Once you set envelope points in a track, you will no longer be able to use the corresponding controls in the track header. In this case, the volume control slider is grayed out in the **Designer Synth 07** track because the envelope points override the master volume for that track.

Tips for Working with Envelope Points

The process of selecting and deselecting envelope points is similar to that of selecting and deselecting clips in the Timeline in Final Cut Pro.

- Delete an envelope point by clicking on the point to select it, then pressing the Delete key.

- Select multiple envelope points by Cmd-clicking each point you wish to select.

- To select a large group, or range, of envelope points at one time, click in the envelope area near a point and drag across all of the points to select them.

- Select a contiguous group of envelope points by clicking the first point, then Shift-clicking the last point you wish to include.

- To deselect an envelope point within a range of selected points, Cmd-click it.

- To remove envelope points from a clip so that you can adjust the static volume control slider, select and delete all of the keyframes on the track except the first one, located at the very beginning of the track.

Automating Effects Parameters

You can automate effects parameters in the Timeline using the effects envelopes. The effects envelopes are located below the Volume and Pan envelopes on tracks that have applied effects.

1   Click the disclosure triangle on the **Basement Hit** track.

Notice the Stereo Delay BPM envelope.

2   Click the Effects Window button (asterisk) on the **Basement Hit** track.

3   Click the disclosure triangle located on the left of the Stereo Delay effect in the Effects window.

The different numerical parameters for that effect appear in the Effects window. Each parameter has a check box on the far right in the Auto column.

4   Click any of the parameter check boxes in the Auto column to create a corresponding effects envelope.

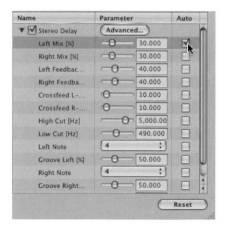

You will see a new envelope for each parameter that you check. Each of these can be automated with envelope points.

Click the disclosure triangle to hide the envelopes for the **Basement Hit** track, and close the Effects window.

Using Master Envelopes

So far, we have been working with envelopes for individual tracks. There are also master envelopes that represent the levels for the overall project.

The master envelopes are located at the bottom of the Timeline below the last track.

1   Choose one of the following methods to reveal the master envelopes:

▶   Ctrl-click in the gray space below the last track, then select Show Master Envelopes.

▶   Choose View > Show Master Envelopes.

▶   Click the Master Envelope button on the bottom left of the Timeline window.

A Master Envelope will appear at the bottom of the workspace. Scroll down if necessary.

You can use master envelopes to automate volume, tempo, and key settings for an entire project.

2   Choose Show Envelopes > Tempo from the pop-up at the head of the Master Envelope track.

The Tempo envelope disappears from the master envelopes.

3   Choose Show Envelopes > Show All Envelopes, or select Tempo to bring back that envelope.

4   Click the Master Envelope button to hide the master envelopes.

Saving Soundtrack Projects

Just as you manage media in Final Cut Pro, you can manage and copy
media you wish to save with your Soundtrack project files. In this next
exercise, we will practice different methods of exporting and distributing
Soundtrack files.

When you save a project, consider whether you need to include the associated loops along with the project file. If you are working with a Soundtrack
project on a single computer that already contains all of your loop files
(Soundtrack comes with over 4,000 loops), then you can save only the
project file, as it will continue to reference the master loops on that
computer.

You can save a project *and* all of the associated media files in the same
folder. This is a convenient way to move the entire project to another
computer, or archive the media along with the project. The Soundtrack
projects included with this book were saved as collected files, along with
all of the associated media.

We will now save the project, including the collected media files, onto your
hard drive.

1 Choose File > Save As.

2 In the dialog box that appears, name the project *Lesson 15-4 test*.

3 Navigate to a part of your hard drive where you can save the folder.

4 Click the Create New Folder Button and name the folder *Lesson 15-4
Collected*.

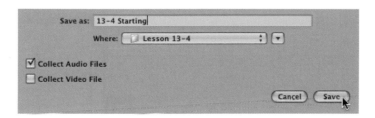

NOTE ▶ It's a good idea to create a folder when you are saving media files with your project. Otherwise, the media files will be dropped wherever your project is saved and may clutter up your desktop or document folder.

At the bottom of the Save As window are three choices of files to include with your project: Collect Audio Files, Collect Video File, Hide Extension.

5   Check Collect Audio Files.

All of the associated audio files will now be included in your project folder.

Video files are usually large, and you may or may not want to include them with your project. If you are simply archiving or mixing your Soundtrack project, you may not need the video.

Leave the Collect Video File box unchecked for this exercise.

6   Check the Hide Extension box.

This will hide the .loop extension in the name of your project. In order for OS X to recognize the Soundtrack project file, the .loop extension will be saved regardless. With this option, the extension is hidden in the filename.

7   Click Save.

8   Quit Soundtrack and look for the folder on your hard drive containing the collected files.

9   When you find the folder, double-click to open it, and inspect the collected files inside.

10   Double-click the **Lesson 15-4 test** file.

Soundtrack launches and opens your archived project, with all of the associated files linked and ready to play.

You can use this technique to save and archive any of your Soundtrack projects.

NOTE ▶ You can practice Soundtrack scoring techniques on a new scene from the movie The Chocolate Curse using the file 15-3 Bonus in the Lesson_15 folder. Listen to the score and then try adding stabs, stingers, effects, and additional loops to enhance the scene.

What You've Learned

- To discard part of an audio loop, position the playhead and split it by pressing the S key.

- Transposing allows you to change the key of a loop.

- Sound effects such as stabs and stingers can be added to enhance the dramatic effect of a visual scene.

- Snapping and markers allow you to position and sync audio with video.

- Envelopes are used to adjust and automate volume, panning, tempo, and effects parameters.

16

Lesson Files
Lessons > Lesson_16 > 16-Promo Score Starting

Lessons > Lesson_16 > Recording Bonus Project

Media
Media > Lesson_16_Media

Time
This lesson takes approximately 120 minutes to complete.

Goals
Create a temporary rhythm track using Soundtrack

Export a rhythm track to Final Cut Pro, add scoring markers, and import it back into Soundtrack

Perform advanced mixing and effects

Understand Soundtrack's various exporting commands

Create a favorites library

Record audio in Soundtrack

Using Soundtrack with Final Cut Pro

Which comes first, the picture or the music? Editors face this dilemma every time they cut a project that is driven by music.

Composers prefer to use the final cut of a piece when creating a musical score. Editors prefer to have the music before they edit the picture, so they can build the project around the timing of the music.

With the Soundtrack program, both editors and composers can be satisfied. Final Cut Pro and Soundtrack work together, making it easy to send a project between programs at different stages of the scoring and editing process.

Compose a Score from Prerecorded Loops

In this exercise, you will be both editor and composer as we score a 60-second promo from prerecorded loops.

We will follow a real-world workflow, creating a "temp score" in Soundtrack, then opening the temp score in Final Cut Pro, editing the picture, and adding scoring markers. Finally, we will bring the edited promo back into Soundtrack and complete the score. To do that, we will use advanced music editing and mixing techniques, and then learn different ways to export and distribute Soundtrack projects.

Prepare the Project

Before you begin this lesson, make sure you have copied the entire Lesson_16 and Lesson_16_Media folders from the courseware DVD to your computer.

1 Double-click the Soundtrack icon to launch the program.

   An empty, untitled project opens.

   NOTE ▶ If your preferences are set to open the last project, then close the current project and open a new one.

2 Choose File > Save As and name the project *Lesson 16 Promo Temp Score.*

3 Save the project to the Lesson_16 folder on your hard drive.

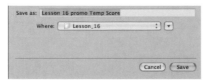

4 Press Cmd-4 to create a window layout that puts the Media Manager on the far left and hides the track header columns for maximum Timeline workspace.

   This window layout works well for building tracks and dragging clips from the search window to the Timeline.

We need to set the duration of our project. In our 60-second promo, the music will run for 58 seconds. Project duration can be set in minutes from the Soundtrack Preferences window, but since the Preferences window requires a minimum project length of one minute, we will change the project duration manually.

5 Type *5800* into the timecode window at the top of the Timeline and press Return.

The playhead will go to the 58 seconds point in the Timeline.

A red project duration marker is located to the right of the playhead one minute into the Timeline.

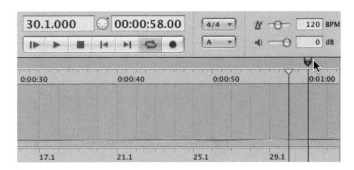

6 Ctrl-click at the top of the duration marker and select Set Song Duration from the contextual menu that appears.

7 Type *5800* in the duration window, then click OK.

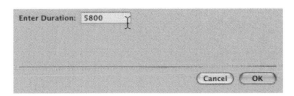

The red duration marker has moved to 58 seconds in the Timeline.

> **TIP** ▶ You can also set the project duration by clicking and dragging the duration marker to a new location in the Timeline.

8 Press the Home key to move the playhead to the beginning of the Timeline.

9 Press the down arrow key several times until you see the red duration marker on the far right.

You will be able to see the entire Timeline from start to finish, before all of the clips are in place.

> **NOTE** ▶ The up arrow will zoom out of the Timeline; the down arrow will zoom into the Timeline.

Start with a Temp Score

A *temp* score is a piece of music used temporarily in place of the final piece. Typically, editors use songs from a music library as the temp score. The disadvantage of using a temp score is that the editor must cut the picture to music that will eventually change, which inevitably changes the feel and timing of the edit.

In Soundtrack, we will create a temp score using the actual rhythm tracks of the final piece of music.

We will audition (listen to) different Soundtrack loops to find the right rhythm foundation for this project. It helps to know what feel the director or client wants for the promo. In this exercise, a promo for the Santa Clara Custom Bicycle Company, the music and the promo should be as fun, cool, and exciting as riding one of the fictional company's off-road bikes.

1 Click the Search tab at the top of the Media Manager window.

2 Click the Drums button to limit your search to drums.

There are more than 900 drum choices, which could take a while to listen to, so let's narrow the search.

3 Cmd-click the Urban button to add that parameter to your search.

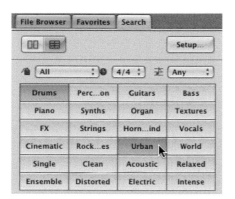

Now, both the Drums and Urban buttons should be selected.

4 Click to select the first choice on the list, **Drummers of Motown 07.aiff**.

This is a good, catchy beat that will give a strong, rhythmic foundation to the first part of the promo.

TIP ▶ Click and drag the right edge of the Name column header to the right to extend it and see the entire name of the sample, including the number. This is helpful when there are several choices with the same name.

5 Look at the bottom of the window to see more information about the clip.

You will see some information at the bottom when the clip is playing. To see all of the additional information on a clip, you need to toggle open the disclosure triangle.

Notice that the **Drummers of Motown 07.aiff** loop is eight beats in length.

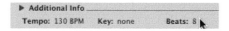

The time signature for the project is 4/4, or four beats per measure. The loop we have selected will take up two measures in the Timeline.

NOTE ▶ As you audition loops, you will hear them in the project key (the default key is A) and project tempo (the default tempo is 120 beats per minute). If you change the project key or tempo, the loops you audition will also change to match the project. You can try different project keys and tempos before you add clips to the Timeline.

6   Click and drag the **Drummers of Motown 07.aiff** loop from the Media Manager and drop it on the first track of the Timeline.

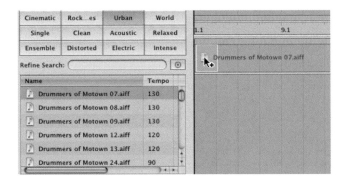

The loop will appear in the top track.

7   Click the right edge of the **Drummers of Motown 07.aiff** clip in the Timeline and stretch it until it repeats six times.

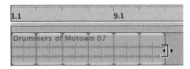

There will be six segments of the loop, and it will end at 2400 in the Timeline.

You now have a tempo for the first 24 seconds of the promo temp score.

Create a Turnaround with Percussion

If the same drumbeat repeats over and over, it becomes nothing more than a monotonous metronome that keeps tempo. It is important to mix it up a bit and periodically change the tempo of the percussion or drum track. This type of change is called a *turnaround* because it turns to a different tempo or percussion combination, then turns the track back around to the original beat or leads the song in a new direction.

Let's create a turnaround that will result in an entirely different tempo or percussion track, thus acting as a catalyst for change in the song itself.

Keep in mind that the more you know about the project you are scoring, the better. In this case, the promo we are prescoring starts with a series of magazine covers and clippings, then suddenly kicks into footage of the mountain bikes in action.

As a composer/editor, your job is to support and enhance the feel of the project with the music. Therefore, this temp track will start the Motown rhythm to support the first part of the promo, then turn around about halfway through to a completely different sound to enhance the action onscreen. In essence, the rhythm will go "off-road" just like the action in the promo.

1   Select and listen to the **Drummers of Motown 09** track in the search window.

It sounds very much like the first track, but if you look at the additional information you see that it is 16 beats, which is twice as long as the first loop we selected. The tracks' similarity will make them fit well together, and their differences will make it feel more like a live drummer is picking up the groove. Plus there is a solid kick at the end of the **Drummers of Motown 09** loop that we can use as part of our turnaround.

2   Click and drag the **Drummers of Motown 09** clip to the second track in the Timeline and place it so that it overlaps the last segment of the first **Drummers of Motown 07** clip.

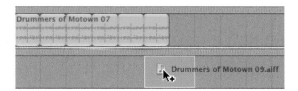

TIP ▶ Make sure snapping is turned on (press the G key) before you drag and drop any new clips to the Timeline to ensure that the rhythm and the timing of the tracks are in sync.

3   Listen to the tracks together.

We have set up our turnaround, so now it's time to add a new drum sound as the payoff.

4   Click the Drums button in the search window to search all of the drum loops.

5   Type *club* in the Refine Search window, then press Return.

Drums	Perc...on	Guitars	Bass
Piano	Synths	Organ	Textures
FX	Strings	Horn...ind	Vocals
Cinematic	Rock...es	Urban	World
Single	Clean	Acoustic	Relaxed
Ensemble	Distorted	Electric	Intense

Refine Search:	club	⊙

6   Select **Electronic Club Beat 036.aiff**, drag it to the third track, and line it up with the end of the clip on the second track.

7   Drag the right edge of the clip in the **Electronic Club Beat 036.aiff** Timeline until the loop repeats three times.

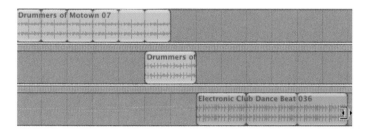

Finish Off the Temp Track

Now we need a really strong finale—something unique, fun, and full of energy to sum up the entire promo.

1   Click the Intense button in the search window.

2   Type *backward* in the Refine Search window and press Return.

   Backward and Down.aiff appears in the search results window.

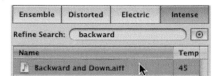

3   Click and drag **Backward and Down.aiff** to the fourth track and place it just to the left of the red duration marker in the Timeline.

The temp track is almost finished. We have built a beginning, middle, and end. Now we need something to fill the gap near the end. The music should climax with a big finish. Since we are working with drums and a rhythm track, a drumroll will be the perfect choice.

4   Select the Drums button in the search window.

5   Type *roll* in the Refine Search window, then press Return.

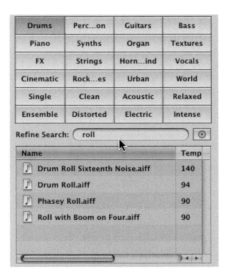

You will see four drumroll choices.

6   Audition each drumroll to see which one fits best with the rest of the rhythm track.

7   Type *3600* in the timecode window and press Return.

8 Press the spacebar to play the second half of the Timeline.

9 As the playhead nears the gap in the tracks, click the first drumroll selection in the search results window to hear it with the rest of the tracks.

10 Repeat the last step with each of the different drumrolls and listen to how each one sounds with the tracks.

The **Phasey Roll.aiff** loop has the right combination of energy and club sound that fits with the mood and energy of the piece.

11 Click and drag **Phasey Roll.aiff** to the fifth track and align it with the end of the **Electronic Club Beat 36.aiff** clip.

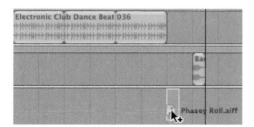

12 Click the right edge of the **Phasey Roll.aiff** clip in the Timeline and drag until it repeats one time.

The **Phasey Roll.aiff** fills the gap between the **Electronic Club Beat 36.aiff** and the **Backward and Down.aiff** finale.

The **Phasey Roll.aiff** also works as a turnaround for the Electronic Club Beat and leads us to the big finale. In fact, **Phasey Roll.aiff** works so well as a turnaround at the end of the temp track, we will also use it to enhance the first turnaround.

13 Select the **Phasey Roll.aiff** clip in the Timeline and press Cmd-C to copy it.

14 Click the fifth track in the Timeline (the **Phasey Roll** track) to make sure that it is selected.

15 Type *2400* in the timecode window and press Return.

The playhead is now at 24 seconds in the Timeline.

16 Press Cmd-V to paste a copy of the **Phasey Roll.aiff**.

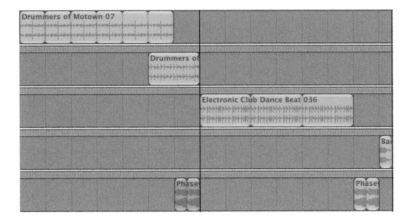

17 Listen to the finished temp score. Does it inspire you and provide rhythmic structure for the edit? If so, then you have accomplished your job as a composer.

Export the Soundtrack for Final Cut Pro

Now that the temp track is complete, you need to export a mix of the tracks for the editor to use in cutting the promo.

Later in this lesson, we will explore the ways that Soundtrack allows us to export or distribute tracks, with a focus on exporting a mix of the rhythm tracks. Mixing down the five rhythm tracks to a stereo pair allows us to easily import the temp score into Final Cut Pro.

The first part of exporting is to set user preferences for the exported mix.

1   Choose Soundtrack > Preferences.

2   Click the Project tab in the Preferences window.

3   Click the Sample Rate menu and choose 48.00 kHz.

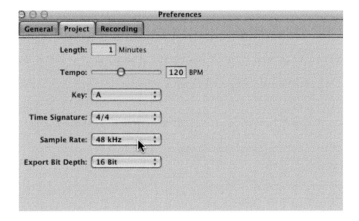

The standard audio rate for DV NTSC Final Cut Pro projects is 48.00 kHz.

NOTE ▶ If you are using a system without hardware to support 48 kHz audio, you will receive the following warning "The output device cannot support the sample rate of this project. The output will play at a rate of 44.1 kHz. Exports to disk, however, will be saved at the project sample rate."

This means that you will hear your project in Soundtrack at 44.1 kHz, but when you export it to disk for use in Final Cut Pro, it will export at the project sample rate (48 kHz). You can also change the project audio rate using the Project > Sample Rate pull-down menu.

4   Close the Preferences window.

5   Choose File > Export Mix.

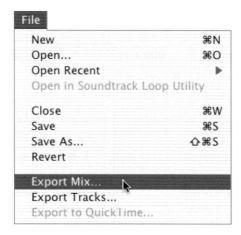

A dialog box opens to designate the name and location of the file you wish to export.

6   Type *Temp-Score* as the title of the track.

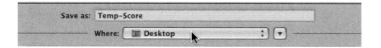

7   Select where you would like to save the document.

TIP ▸ It is a good idea to save the temp score file to the Desktop so you can easily drag and drop the file into your Final Cut Pro Browser.

8   Save your Soundtrack project and hide Soundtrack. We will come back to it later.

Import the Soundtrack into Final Cut Pro

You can import Soundtrack music files into Final Cut Pro the same way you import any other audio file. First, we will open the Final Cut Pro project we want to import the Soundtrack music into.

1   Launch Final Cut Pro and open **60 Second Promo.fcp** from the Lesson_16 folder.

NOTE ▶ If you need to reconnect media when opening, you should find all files within the Lesson_16_Media folder.

2   The **Bike Promo Starting** sequence should be open in the Timeline and empty. If not, open that sequence now.

3   Ctrl-click the Music from Soundtrack bin.

4   Choose Import File from the contextual menu.

5   Choose the **Temp-Score.aif** file on your Desktop.

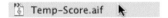

Temp-Score.aif appears in the Music from Soundtrack bin.

6   Double-click the **Temp-Score.aif** clip to open it in the Viewer.

7   Click the Timeline window, then press the Home key to move the playhead to the beginning of the sequence.

Make sure audio tracks 1 and 2 are patched as the destination tracks.

8 Click the Overwrite button to place the music onto audio tracks 1 and 2 of the **Bike Promo Starting** sequence.

9 Press Shift-Z to make the sequence fit the window.

Put on Your Video Editor's Cap

Now that the temp track is in the Timeline, picture editing can begin. For the purposes of this exercise, we will skip the editing process and bring in a finished picture edit as a nested sequence.

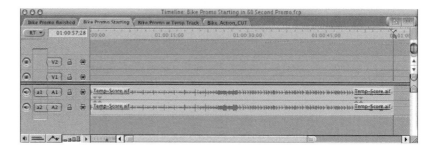

1 Click the A1 and A2 audio patches to disconnect them.

> **TIP** ▶ Nested sequences always include two tracks of audio, even when the audio tracks in the nest are empty. It is a good idea to disconnect audio patches before bringing in a nested sequence so that the nest's audio tracks do not interfere with the current Timeline tracks.

2 Double-click the sequence **Bike_Action_CUT** in the Browser to open it in the Timeline window.

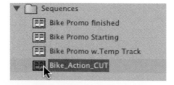

Bike_Action_CUT will serve as the picture cut for this exercise.

3 Ctrl-click the Bike_Action_CUT tab in the Timeline window and choose Close Tab.

The **Bike Promo Starting** sequence should be open in the Timeline window.

4 Press and hold the Cmd key.

5 Click and drag the **Bike_Action_CUT** sequence from the Browser to video track 1 in the Timeline. Do not release the mouse yet.

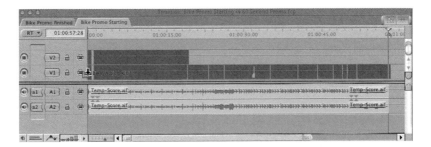

6 Make sure the arrow is pointing down for an Overwrite edit.

7 Align the nest with the beginning of Track 1, then release the mouse and the Cmd key. This reveals the nested sequence as individual clips in the Timeline, a new feature in Final Cut Pro 4.

NOTE ▶ Since we are working with music, picture timing is very important. Be sure that both the music and video clips start at the very beginning of the Timeline.

8 Watch the promo cut with the temp track. You might need to render parts or all of the sequence to watch it easily.

Note how the editor used the temp track's pacing as a foundation for the edit.

9 Listen to the first rhythm turnaround in the Timeline (01:00:20:00–01:00:29:00), and hear how it drives the changes in the picture edit, as well as the feel of the overall piece.

Setting Scoring Markers in Final Cut Pro

The promo is really starting to come together. Now that the editor is finished with the picture cut, it's time to make notes so the composer can complete the score. To do this, use scoring markers.

You set scoring markers in Final Cut Pro the same way you set any other marker. The difference is that they will be visible in Soundtrack so the composer can use them as a guide. Scoring markers can be set only from within Final Cut Pro. You cannot erase these markers in Soundtrack. This ensures that the composer will see your notes. If you are the composer as well as the editor, you can mark significant points in the cut for scoring in the Soundtrack project Timeline.

1 Play the end of the sequence.

The last shot of the paint gun would work really well with the end of the score, but the timing is off.

2 Move the playhead to 01:00:57;11, and press the M key to set a marker.

3 Press M again to open the marker window.

4 Type *fix timing – last shot* into the Name text box.

5   Click the Add Scoring Marker button.

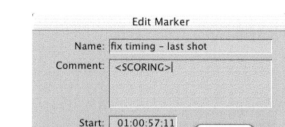

<SCORING> appears in the marker Comment field. Your scoring marker information will be included with the video clip when it is exported to Soundtrack.

You will be able to see the scoring markers in the Final Cut Pro Canvas if the playhead is stopped over the marker in the Final Cut Pro Timeline when Overlays are enabled in the Canvas.

6   Click OK to close the window and accept the changes.

7   Add the following additional scoring markers to the Timeline:

Timecode	Marker name
01:00:24;14	Santa Clara title flash
01:00:35;26	Action/mood change

01:00:39;11	Harder terrain action
01:00:43;07	Mood change effect
01:00:47;13	Airborne action
01:00:51;24	Finale title change

Completing the Round Trip

Now that the promo has been edited, it's time to export the finished video from Final Cut Pro to Soundtrack in order to complete the score. The process of exporting a project from Soundtrack to Final Cut Pro and then back to Soundtrack again is referred to as a *round trip*.

Export the Video

First we will export the finished promo video, along with the scoring markers, so that it can be imported into Soundtrack.

Before we start, make sure you have all of the markers set in the Timeline. If you did not finish setting the markers in the previous exercise, you may choose to open the completed **Bike Promo w.Temp Track** sequence in the Timeline for use in this exercise.

1   Mark In and Out points at the beginning and end of the sequence.

2   Ctrl-click the **Bike Promo Starting** sequence in the Browser.

> **NOTE ▶** If you are using the **Bike Promo w.Temp Track** sequence in the Timeline, Ctrl-click that sequence instead.

3   Choose Export > For Soundtrack.

The Soundtrack Export window appears. The check box inside the window asks whether you wish to include the Temp-Score audio track with the exported video.

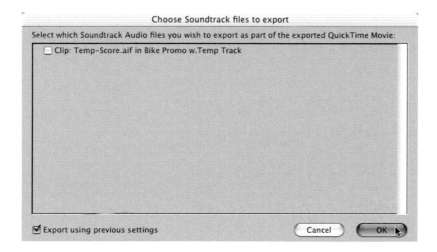

Since we already have the temp score in Soundtrack and there have been no changes to the music, we do not need to include the temp score with the export. Leave the box unchecked.

When exporting scenes with dialogue, like the scenes used in the previous lesson, you should check the box to include the base audio track as a guide for scoring music.

4   Click OK.

A Save window appears.

5   Type *Bike Promo edit* in the Save As field.

6   Select the Desktop as the destination for the file.

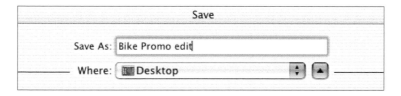

In the lower portion of the window are pull-down menus labeled Setting, Include, and Markers.

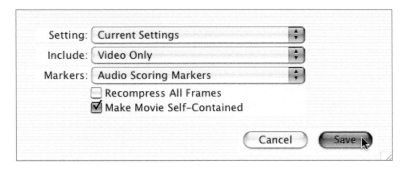

7   Choose Include > Video Only.

8   Make sure Markers > Audio Scoring Markers is selected.

9   Check the Make Movie Self-Contained box to make the video file independent of the master media clips.

   NOTE ▶ If you will be doing all of the work for Final Cut Pro and Soundtrack on the same computer, you can uncheck Make Movie Self-Contained and reference the original source media with your exported file.

10 Click Save to export the movie.

   If you haven't rendered the sequence, Final Cut Pro will now render the necessary effects and transitions before exporting the file. When the process is finished, you will find a Final Cut Pro movie of your sequence on the Desktop.

11 Now you should save your Final Cut Pro project as well, and can also quit Final Cut Pro if you'd like, as we are done with Final Cut Pro for this lesson.

Import the Final Cut Pro Project into Soundtrack

Fasten your seat belts and return your seats to an upright position—our round trip is nearly ready to land. As the flight descends, we will import the file we just created in Final Cut Pro into the Soundtrack project.

1 If you closed Soundtrack, reopen the program, then open the project titled **Lesson 16 Promo Temp Score**.

2 Press Cmd-2 to change the window layout to include the track header column and the Viewer for video, audio, and meters.

You can use the File Browser in the Media Manager to navigate to a file, then drag it into the Timeline. But we are going to drag and drop it from the Desktop directly into the Timeline.

3 Move the Workspace window to reveal the Desktop and the **Bike Promo edit** file.

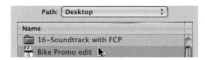

4 Click and drag the **Bike Promo edit** clip from the Desktop to the empty video track at the top of the window, and then drop the clip onto the empty track.

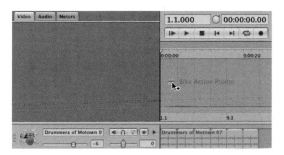

NOTE ▶ The video clip will automatically start at the beginning of the Timeline.

An image appears in the window to the left of the video track.

5   Choose File > Save As. Name the file *Lesson 16 promo score unmixed* and save it to the Lesson_16 folder on your hard drive.

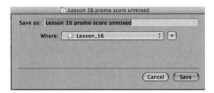

6   Press Cmd-3 to change the window layout to exclude the search window.

NOTE ▶ This window layout (Cmd-3) is excellent for mixing because it gives you a large workspace for your tracks and hides the search window, which you generally don't need when you get to the mixing phase of your project.

Congratulations! Your round-trip project has landed with ease, and now you are ready to finish scoring the promo.

Let's start by taking a look at some of the changes that occurred to our Timeline in Final Cut Pro.

Reading Final Cut Pro's Scoring Markers in Soundtrack

If you look at the Timeline you will notice a series of orange scoring markers. These are the markers that you created in Final Cut Pro. They have several properties that make them different from other markers in Soundtrack:

- Scoring markers created in Final Cut Pro cannot be deleted in Soundtrack. This is to ensure that the composer receives the notes (markers).

- A new thumbnail image appears in the video track at each scoring marker point.

- A scoring marker name appears at the top of the Timeline after each scoring marker.

To read the marker names, zoom into the track using the up arrow.

You can navigate between markers by using Shift-M to move forward in the Timeline and Option-M to move backward.

Syncing the Timing

Let's look at the last scoring marker in the Timeline and make the appropriate changes to the score. The last scoring marker is labeled *fix timing–last shot*.

1   Place the playhead near the end of the sequence and press the up arrow several times to zoom in on the last part of the Timeline.

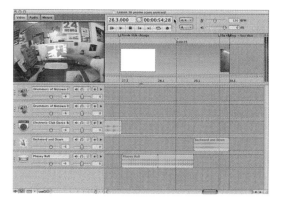

You should be able to read the last two scoring markers and clearly see the last two clips in the Timeline.

2   Type *5428* in the timecode window and press Return.

The playhead moves to the new location, and you should see the image of a desk and computer screen in the Viewer.

3   Press the spacebar to watch the end of the promo.

Notice that the **Backward and Down** sound effect works well with the paint gun, but it starts too late and ends too early.

> **TIP** ▶ When you play the end of a sequence, the playhead automatically resets to the beginning of the Timeline. Press the End key to move the playhead to the end of the Timeline.

4   Click the center of the **Backward and Down** clip to select it in the Timeline.

5   Press the Cmd key and tap the left arrow or right arrow to move the playhead back and forth a frame at a time. Watch the Viewer and move the playhead left until the man moves the paint gun toward camera—right before it's aimed directly at the lens (56;28).

> **NOTE** ▶ Syncing music clips to picture is a subjective process. You may decide to move the clip slightly to the right or left depending on what works best for you.

This is where the **Backward and Down** clip should start.

6   Press Shift-Option and tap the right arrow to move the **Backward and Down** clip toward the playhead position. When you get closer, release the Shift key and hold only Option while tapping the arrow to move the clip toward the playhead position (56;28).

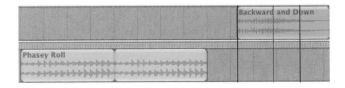

The **Backward and Down** clip is now in the perfect position, but we need to fix the pause between the **Phasey Roll** and the **Backward and Down** clips.

7   Click and drag the right edge of the **Phasey Roll** clip to extend it one more full segment to the right.

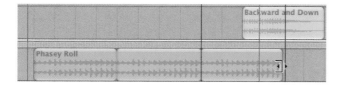

The ending is almost finished; we just need to fix the song duration. At the moment our duration marker is still at 58 seconds and doesn't include the entire **Backward and Down** clip.

8   Click and drag the Red Duration marker to the end of the **Backward and Down** clip.

The duration now extends farther than the video clip. This will keep all of the sound in the export files and add a nice, snappy ending to the entire promo.

Finalize the Score

Now it's time to finish the score. You have the picture edit to use as a visual guide, and the temp track to use as a blueprint for the music.

Our goal is to find music loops for the score, add them to the Timeline, mix the project, and, finally, distribute or output the finished piece.

We'll start with finding music loops to use for the score.

Finding and Sorting Loops

Creating and editing a song is very much like editing a project in Final Cut Pro. As an editor, you want to get all of the clips together in the Browser *before* you start editing them. The same logic applies to scoring music. First, we will audition a variety of music loops and choose the ones we want for the score. Then, we will start the scoring process.

Soundtrack allows you to sort music loops by creating favorites. In this exercise, you will create numerous favorites that can be added to the score.

The more you know about a project, the easier it is to find appropriate loops. At this point, you no longer need to guess but can actually watch the promo to get a feel for its energy and genre. This is essential when selecting favorite loops to use in the score.

1   Press Cmd-1 to change the window layout.

    The Media Manager appears as a separate window on the left side of the screen.

    TIP ▶ The Cmd-1 layout is an easy way to search for loops and gather favorites.

2   Grab the right edge of the Name column in the Media Manager window and drag it to the right, just to the edge of the window. Be careful not to drag it too far to the right.

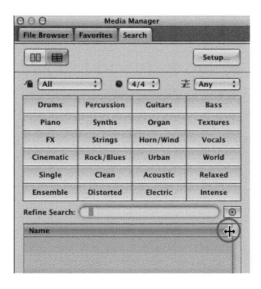

Now you will see only one column as you search for loops. This will make it easier to search and identify loops by name. The other data about the clips will be available in the additional information area located at the bottom of the search window.

Though we will be searching by name, you can also search by any of the categories in the other columns.

Auditioning loops for a song is like auditioning actors for a role. It's a good idea to work with one instrument or group of instruments at a time for easier comparison and selection. We will start with guitars.

3 Click the Guitars button in the search window, then Cmd-click Electric.

Drums	Percussion	Guitars	Bass
Piano	Synths	Organ	Textures
FX	Strings	Horn/Wind	Vocals
Cinematic	Rock/Blues	Urban	World
Single	Clean	Acoustic	Relaxed
Ensemble	Distorted	Electric	Intense

You will see more than 260 choices (if you installed all of the Apple Loops that come with the Soundtrack Program).

There are many ways to refine the search parameters. In this case, we'll go for a particular, prerecorded effect—delay.

4 Type *delay* in the Refine Search window and press Return.

The list narrows to nine choices, which should all be similar in sound and should work well together in the Timeline.

5 Press the spacebar to start the rhythm track in the Timeline.

6 Select the first choice in the search results to listen to the track.

7 Press the down arrow to hear the next selection.

You can also press the up arrow to return to the previous selection.

8 Repeat step 7 until you have listened to all of the choices.

9 Press the spacebar when you have finished listening to all of the choices.

The track will stop playing in the Timeline. You are ready to select your favorites.

10 Select **Delayed Guitar String 01.aiff** in the search results.

11 Click the Add Favorite button located at the bottom right of the search window.

12 Click the Favorites tab at the top of the Media Manager window.

You will see the **Delayed Guitar String 01.aiff** loop. Later in this lesson, you will be able to drag this clip directly from the Favorites window to the Timeline.

13 Click the Search tab to return to the search window.

14 Select **Delayed Guitar String 02.aiff** in the search results window, then click the Add Favorite button.

15 Repeat Steps 13 and 14 with **Delayed Guitar String 06.aiff**.

You should now have three delayed guitar string sounds in your favorites.

Let's move on to additional guitar sounds.

16 Type *Rock* into the Refine Search window and press Return.

17 Scroll down through the choices and select **Modern Rock Dirty Guitar 03.**

18 Add this loop to your favorites.

The **Modern Rock Dirty Guitar 03** loop has a fun, action feel that is different from the other guitar sounds and will work well with the bike promo.

This method of searching and selecting individual favorites is a great way to collect music loops before arranging the actual song.

You can also select an entire folder of loops to add to your favorites. Later in this lesson, you will learn how to build a favorites library. At this time, we will focus on adding a folder of Apple Loops to the favorites.

19 Click the File Browser tab at the top of the Media Manager window.

20 Navigate to the Lesson_16_Media folder.

21 Select the Bike Promo Favorites folder.

22 Click the Add Favorite button.

23 Click the Favorites tab.

You will see the Bike Promo Favorites folder with the other favorites.

24 Double-click the Bike Promo Favorites folder to open it in the Favorites window.

We will use these loops to finish the score.

Building the Score

In Lesson 14, you learned how stabs and stingers can heighten dramatic tension at certain moments in a clip. We want the music in our promo to have the same impact. We'll start by finding the visuals that we want to emphasize with rhythm, then layer the other instruments on top to build up the song.

We'll start with the titles near the beginning of the promo.

1   Press Cmd-4 to change the window layout.

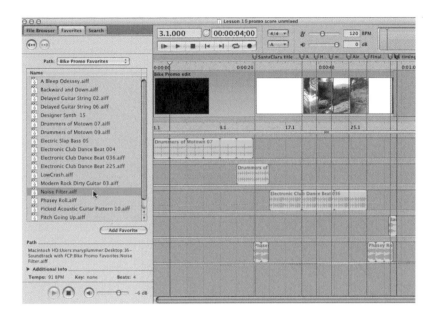

2 Press Shift-Z to make the entire Timeline visible in the workspace window.

3 Select **Noise Filter.aiff** from your imported Bike Promo favorites.

4 Listen to the loop. It has a techno-windy feel to it.

5 Click and drag the **Noise Filter.aiff** clip to the Timeline and release it at the beginning of the track below the **Phasey Roll** track.

6 Click the right edge of the **Noise Filter** clip in the Timeline and stretch it to two segments in length.

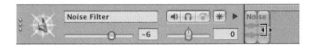

7 Type 19:08 in the timecode field to move the playhead toward the white flash frame at the start of the title.

8 Turn off snapping by pressing G or choosing View > Snapping.

9 Click the center of the **Noise Filter** clip and move it so it starts just after the playhead position (19:08).

Typically, you would place all of the clips in the Timeline before adjusting individual levels. In this case, we want to make the **Noise Filter** clip subtle in the mix, so we will go ahead and adjust it now to see how it works as we build the song.

10 Press Cmd-2 to show the track headers. Click the disclosure triangle on the **Noise Filter** track to show the envelopes for that track.

11 Press the up arrow several times to zoom into the track and focus on the **Noise filter** clip and envelopes.

12 Double-click directly on the Volume envelope line in the center of the clip, between the two segments.

An envelope point appears on the volume line.

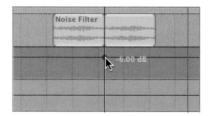

13 Add two more envelope points at the beginning and end of the clip.

14 Click the first envelope point to select it, then press Option-down arrow to lower the point to around –18.

NOTE ► The further you zoom into a track, the more control you will have on the levels when you drag an envelope point to change the value.

15 Ctrl-click the third envelope point and choose Set Value from the contextual menu.

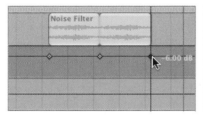

16 Type *–18* for the value.

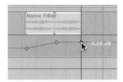

17 Repeat steps 15 and 16 for the first envelope point.

18 Play and listen to the sound of this clip mixed with the other tracks.

Now, we want to repeat the same audio clip and envelope points when the second video title begins in the Timeline.

Copying and pasting works, but copying a clip with its associated envelope points requires using a timeslice.

Working with Timeslices

A timeslice in Soundtrack is exactly what it sounds like—a slice of time. It can include one track, multiple tracks, or all tracks. Timeslices are used primarily for cutting, copying, and pasting portions of a Timeline.

There are several differences between using timeslices and using the basic cut, copy, and paste commands. First, the basic editing commands work only with individual clips, and they always include the entire clip that is selected. A timeslice allows you to start at any point in the Timeline and capture as many tracks as you want within that point in the Timeline. Timeslices also include the envelope points and settings.

Let's copy and paste the **Noise Filter** clip using a timeslice.

1   Click the down arrow several times to zoom out of the Timeline.

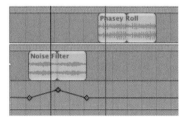

You should be able to see the entire **Noise Filter** clip, as well as the first **Phasey Roll** clip in the Timeline.

At the top of each track is a thin horizontal bar consisting of small, vertical lines. This is called the selection bar, and it is used to create timeslices.

2   Click and hold in the selection bar above the first envelope point on the **Noise Filter** track. Do not release the mouse. This is where the timeslice will begin.

3   Drag the mouse to the right across the selection bar. Stop and release just past the third envelope point.

The selection bar turns blue, along with everything in the track within that timeslice.

4   Press Cmd-C to copy the timeslice.

5   Type *2325* in the timecode window and press Return to move the playhead to just before the **Phasey Roll** clip.

6   Press Cmd-V to paste the timeslice.

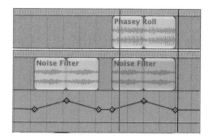

You will now see a copy of the **Noise Filter** clip with its envelope points in the Timeline just below the **Phasey Roll** clip.

7   Click the disclosure triangle to close the envelopes for the Noise Filter clip.

Advanced Editing and Mixing

Let's take a look at the finished score so we can see the results of the advanced mixing techniques we're about to learn.

1   Close the **Lesson 16 Promo Score Unmixed** project.

2   Open the **16-Bike Promo mix finished** project from the Lesson_16 folder. Use the suggestions in the note above if you have trouble reconnecting the media.

3   Press Cmd-5 to change the layout to view the Timeline only.

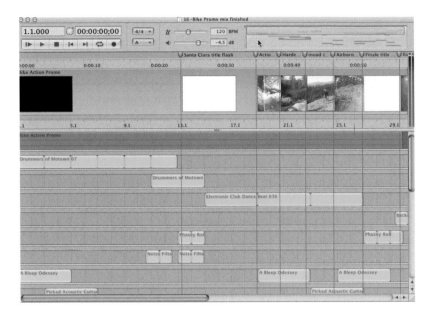

TIP ▶ This window layout (Cmd-5) is great for looking at your entire Timeline, consolidating tracks for mixing, and changing the placement of clips by using other clips as a reference.

4   Press the Home key, then press Shift-Z to fit the entire length of the Timeline in the window.

You can use Global view to see the overall map of your Timeline. The blue window at the top of Global view shows the current window. You can move that view to see other parts of the Timeline.

5   Move your cursor into the Global View window and stop over the shaded blue area.

Your cursor becomes a hand icon to move the view.

6   Click and drag the blue viewing area to the bottom of the Global View window to see the lowest tracks in your Timeline.

The tracks in the Timeline will change to the lowest tracks selected in the Global view area.

The Global view is very useful when working on long projects with many tracks.

7   Use the Global View window to move back to the top tracks in your Timeline.

8   Press Cmd-3 to change the window layout to reveal only the Viewer, track headers, and Timeline.

9   Watch the entire promo with the finished score.

Notice the instrumental changes that occur at the scoring markers, accentuating the changes in action onscreen.

Repairing Audio Clipping

In the last lesson, we learned how to adjust panning, volume, and effects for individual tracks.

Now, we'll focus on techniques for adjusting the mix levels of the entire project.

The volume and panning levels in each track have been set individually, but we still need to adjust levels for the entire project as a whole. At least one track is too loud in the mix and will distort if not adjusted.

One of the first things you need to look for after setting the individual track levels is *clipping*. Clipping occurs when volume level exceeds the maximum limit that can be reproduced, causing the digital signal to distort. In Soundtrack, clipping occurs when audio meters rise above 0 dB.

Remember, the maximum audio level for a track is +6 and the lowest is –96. Levels are relative for each sound and do not correspond with the levels on the meters.

To accurately evaluate the sound levels, you need to work with the Meters tab in the Viewer.

1   Click the Meters tab in the Viewer.

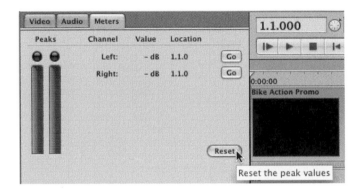

2   Click the Reset button at the bottom right of the Meters window.

The numbers in the window all reset to a 0 value.

When you play your project from the Timeline, the Meters tab will display the audio levels. The loudest levels are reproduced in the audio metering windows and displayed in decibels for the left and right channels. The location of the loudest level is marked to make it easy to find and fix any problems that arise.

If any audio is clipping, the round, red indicators above the level meters will light up and stay lit to let you know that clipping occurred.

3   Press the Home key, then press the spacebar to listen to the tracks.

4   Watch the meters carefully as the tracks play. Press the spacebar to stop if you see the red clipping indicators.

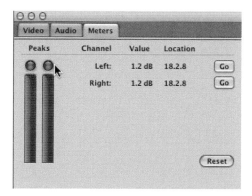

The two red clipping indicators should be lit up on top of both meters around the 34:36 mark in the Timeline. Now that you've detected clipping, you need to find the errant track and fix it.

Soundtrack offers a simple solution to the problem of finding clipped tracks—the Go button. Clicking Go will take the playhead to the exact point of clipping in the Timeline so you can easily find and fix the problem.

5   Click the Go button next to the left channel.

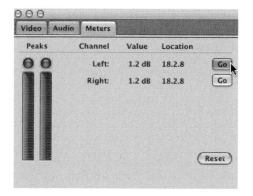

The playhead moves to 34:26 in the Timeline (18.2.799 time in beats). Notice under the Value column that the highest level in this clip is 1.2 dB. The Wood Block track seems to be the cause.

6   Scroll down to the Wood Block track, and click the disclosure triangle to see the envelopes for that track. You can make the tracks larger if you wish.

7   Select and lower the first volume envelope point to –9.

8   Lower the third envelope point to –9.

9   Lower the center envelope point to –6.

The Clipping indicators will stay red until you reset them. Notice that the meters to the far right of the video track also show red clipping indicators.

10 Click the Reset button in the Meters window to reset the meters.

11 Watch the Wood Block section of the Timeline.

There should not be any other clipping in the tracks now.

You can use this method to fix clipping throughout a project and to find the highest levels.

Equalizing the Mix

The score is finished, but let's equalize the entire project before we export it.

1 Press Cmd-E to open the Effects window.

2 Choose Show > Master Effects.

3 Select the Emagic Category, then Fat EQ for the effect.

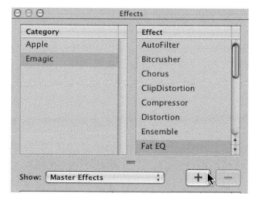

Now, click the Add Effect button (+). The Fat EQ effect appears in the Name column.

4 Click the Advanced button to open the effect's advanced options.

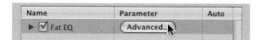

5   Adjust the EQ parameters to your individual taste. Be aware that the EQ may raise the overall volume levels.

If the EQ caused clipping in the tracks, you can lower the entire master volume to compensate.

6   Close the Fat EQ effect's advanced settings window, then close the Effects window.

7   Click the Master Envelope button at the bottom left of the Timeline to show the master envelopes.

8   Click the Envelope point at the beginning of the master volume envelope and lower it to −10.

You can use this same technique to add different types of effects to the entire project.

9   Save the project as *Bike Promo Tempo Test*.

Experimenting with Tempo Changes

Tempo changes can be gradual for a subtle effect, or sudden for a more dramatic effect. Let's experiment with tempo changes to see the different effects they have on a project.

> **NOTE** ▶ You can also change tempo by moving a scoring marker to the playhead.

1   Type *1908* in the timecode window and press Return to position the playhead at the beginning of the first title.

2   Option-click the Santa Clara title scoring marker and drag it to the playhead position.

3   Look at the master tempo envelope at the bottom of the Timeline.

Two keyframes have been set automatically to reflect the change in tempo.

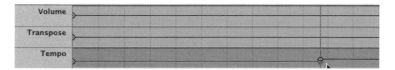

Moving a scoring marker to the playhead keeps all of the tracks in sync and in relative positions to one another. The tempo preceding the marker will change to adjust the timing accordingly.

Everything beyond the scoring marker remains at the original tempo.

TIP ▶ This method is very useful for syncing an effect to picture after all of the tracks have been scored.

Scoring markers are a powerful feature in Soundtrack. Keep in mind that they change only your master project tempo, not the timing of your video.

The video track appears to change in length as you change the tempo, but this is only for visual reference. The Soundtrack program shows tempo changes in the project as master envelope points. It does *not* make audio loops longer or shorter visually in the Timeline to illustrate tempo changes.

Now let's create a gradual change in tempo using envelope points.

4 Undo your tempo drag by pressing Cmd-Z. Move the playhead back to 19:08.

5 Double-click the tempo envelope at the playhead position to set an envelope point.

6 Move the playhead to the Santa Clara title flash scoring marker.

7 Set another tempo envelope point.

8 Set a third tempo envelope point at 29:25.

All three tempo envelope points should be at the original value of 120 bpm.

9 Change the value of the middle tempo envelope point to 90.

Play that section in the Timeline and listen to the changes.

Notice that everything gradually slows down, then speeds up again.

10 Move the playhead to 23;27 in the Timeline. Drag the second envelope point to the playhead.

11 Click and drag the third point directly over the second.

Both points will be at 23;27. The lower point should have a value of 90.

12 Ctrl-click the point on top and set the value to 120.

13 Listen to this section in the Timeline.

You will hear the tempo gradually slow down, then suddenly jump back to normal speed.

This is a more dramatic effect and can be used to enhance a dramatic change in the song.

14 Save the project.

Exporting Projects

Earlier in this lesson we exported a mixed track out of Soundtrack so it could be opened in Final Cut Pro. There are actually three export commands in Soundtrack.

The first is File > Export Mix. This mixes all of your tracks down to two tracks that can be burned to CD or imported into another program such as Final Cut Pro. This is the method we used to export the temp track to Final Cut Pro.

> **NOTE ▶** Be sure to set the audio rate in the project preferences before exporting your projects: 44.1 kHz for CD music; 48 kHz for most Final Cut Pro projects, including DV format.

The second is File > Export Tracks. This keeps all of your tracks separate, but they maintain their reference to one another, as well as their levels and position. Export Tracks is useful if you are using Soundtrack for sound effects and background sound that you want to maintain as separate audio tracks in Final Cut Pro.

When you use Export Tracks and bring the separate tracks into Final Cut Pro, they appear as separate audio tracks in the Timeline. Be sure to create a folder for exported (separate) tracks so they stay together when imported into Final Cut Pro.

Soundtrack's third export command is File > Export to QuickTime. This combines the video track and a mix of the audio tracks into a QuickTime file that can be imported as a clip into a program such as Final Cut Pro, compressed for a DVD, or streamed on the Web.

Exporting to QuickTime is a terrific feature if you are completely finished with the project in Soundtrack and there is no additional work to be done on the picture or sound. It exports a finished product.

Building a Favorites Library

Soundtrack comes with over 4,000 loops, which would take more than a bit of time and gray matter to memorize. That's why it's a good idea to build a library of your favorite sounds.

You can pick a category, such as drums, and slowly listen to each and every loop. When you come across a sound that inspires you, add it to your Favorites list. Eventually, you will have quite a few favorites and may want to remove some.

A more organized approach is to create Timelines of favorites that can be saved in folders with the collected files.

1   Choose File > New.

2   Press Cmd-4 to set the window layout.

3   Click the Search tab.

4   Click the Guitars button.

5   Listen to the Guitar loops. If you find a loop that you like, drag it to a track in the Timeline.

6   Select at least 10 guitar loops and add them to the Timeline on separate tracks.

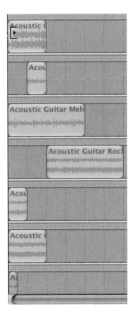

Once you have placed the selections into the Timeline, you're ready to collect them all into a folder.

7   Choose File > Save As.

8 Name the file *Guitar Favorites*.

9 Create a new folder and call it *My Favorite Guitars*.

You may need to click the disclosure triangle to expand the window and create a new folder.

10 Select the Guitar Favorites folder.

11 Check the Collect Audio Files box at the bottom of the Save window.

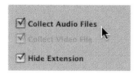

12 Click Save.

All of the files from the Timeline will be saved in the Guitar Favorites folder.

13 Click the File Browser tab.

14 Navigate to your Guitar Favorites folder and click the Add Favorites button.

15 Click the Favorites tab.

Your Guitar Favorites bin is ready to work with.

Recording Audio in Soundtrack

Although Soundtrack is a music arrangement program used primarily to build music using prerecorded loops, you can also record audio directly into the Timeline to create your own loops or one-shots.

There are two methods for recording into Soundtrack: single take and multiple takes. Both methods create stereo AIFF files that can be used as is or tagged using the companion application Soundtrack Loop Utility (found in your Utilities folder inside your Applications folder) to optimize their flexibility for stretching and search parameters.

In this exercise, we will record tracks into the Timeline, choose takes, create a loop from our best take, and process it through the Soundtrack Loop Utility to add metadata.

Preparing to Record

Before you record, set up and test the recording equipment you plan to use. Then make sure you have enough space on your hard drive: a 1-minute 44.1 kHz stereo audio file requires about 10 MB of disk space. Then get ready to roll in Soundtrack.

1   Make sure Soundtrack is open and all projects are closed.

2   Open the **Recording Bonus Project** from the Lesson_16 folder.

The **Recording Bonus Project** opens in your Timeline.

3   Reconnect media if necessary.

4   Press Cmd-3 to change the window layout.

You will now have one large window with the track headers column and Timeline.

5   Press Shift-Z to see the entire Timeline in the window.

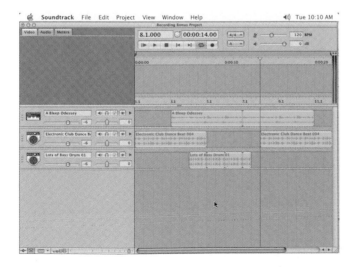

Now check Soundtrack's recording preferences.

6 Choose Soundtrack > Preferences and then click on the Recording tab.

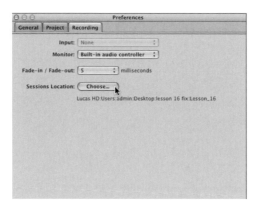

7 Set the Input and Monitor devices to fit whichever devices you are using for your setting. If the Input pop-up is grayed out, your Mac probably has no built-in audio input jacks. You can read through this section, but won't be able to record anything without connecting a USB adapter or PCI sound card.

If you are using the built-in computer microphone and speakers, change both to the built-in audio controllers.

8 Set the Fade-in/Fade-out to 5 milliseconds (the default setting).

9 Choose the hard drive location where you would like the recorded files for the sessions to be located.

Select the Lesson_16 folder to save your recordings.

10 Close the Preferences window.

Single-Take Recording

Single-take recording is designed for recording a single take into the Timeline at the current playhead position.

1 Play the Timeline and listen to the short rhythm track.

The drums stop at 13.00 in the Timeline, leaving a gap or break in the percussion before it picks up again.

Sometimes gaps are used for dramatic effect in the rhythm track, and can be very effective after—or as part of—a turnaround. This example uses a "call and answer" technique The **Lots of Bass Drum 01** starts a four-beat measure (the call), and the **A Bleep Odessey** sequencer sound finishes the four-beat rhythm (the answer).

You will record a finger snap to place in the gap to set up the return of the **Electronic Club Dance Beat 004** clip.

2   Type *1300* in the timecode window and press Return.

The playhead moves to the beginning of the gap.

3   Click the Record button in the transport controls located at the top of the workspace window.

NOTE ▸ The Record button will be grayed out if you were unable to set an input source in the Recording preferences.

The Single Take Recording window appears. The name of the current project is the default session name.

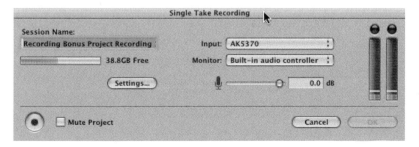

4   Type *SNAP* in the Session Name field.

5   Snap your fingers near your microphone to test the audio recording levels.

Watch the audio meter on the right side of the recording window, and make sure your levels aren't clipping (in the red).

6   Adjust the recording input slider to set the recording level.

7   Check the Mute Project box if you are monitoring through speakers so the playback will not contaminate your recording with feedback.

If you are using headphones, you can leave the Mute Project box unchecked.

8   Click the red Record button at the bottom left of the window to begin recording.

9   Snap your fingers once.

The snap was recorded but does not show up in the Timeline—yet.

10   Click the Stop button to stop the recording.

11 Click the OK button at the lower right of the Recording window to save the recording.

A new track appears in the Timeline, titled **SNAP**.

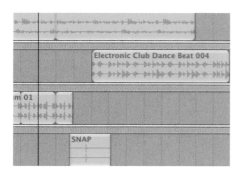

NOTE ▶ The **SNAP** clip has straight lines at each end, which indicates that it is a one-shot recording.

12 Select the **SNAP** clip in the Timeline. Look at the waveform in the clip for the actual snap.

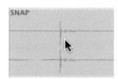

Next, you will move the clip so that the timing of the snap is a half beat before the **Electronic Club Dance Beat 004** clip.

13 Press Option and tap the left and right arrows to nudge the **SNAP** clip into position.

Count the beats of the gap while listening to it. One, two, three, four, and **Electronic Club Dance Beat 004** picks up the tempo: one-two-three-four.

The **Lots of Bass Drum 01** is the one-two, the **A Bleep Odessey** is the three-four. Your **SNAP** clip is the "and" right before the **Electronic Club Danced Beat 004** starts.

This is a tricky maneuver, so it might take a few attempts to get it right. You should feel when it is in the right position. If necessary, open the **Bonus Recording Proj. Finished** project file to hear the snap in the correct position.

> **TIP** ▶ To train your ear for rhythm and tempo, practice counting the beats leading up to the gap. Start at the beginning of the song and count the beats or tap your foot to the beat as it plays. You should feel/hear four distinct beats per measure: one-two-three-four. That is the 4/4 time signature, or four beats per measure. These distinct beats are called the *downbeats*. Try again. This time, count one-two-three-four-and, one-two-three-four-and. You should feel the "and" even if a beat isn't there.

Multi-Take Recording

Multi-take recording offers several advantages over single-take recording. As the name suggests, you can record multiple takes at a time, then choose and save only the takes that you want to keep. Multi-take recording gives you the option of making your new AIFF files into loops or one-shots.

Let's try recording a series of snaps using the multi-take recording method.

1 Move your playhead to the 13.00 position on the Timeline.

2 Make sure the Looping button is active in the transport controls.

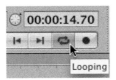

> **NOTE** ▶ If looping is inactive, the playback region will still set a region with In and Out points, but they will not loop the playback of that region after you finish recording.

3   Click and drag the mouse to the right in the beat ruler at the playhead
position to create a playback region. The beat ruler is located just
below the video track at the top of the Timeline.

In and out points appear in the playback area. These In and Out points
represent the area that will be recorded.

Extend your recording area by at least a measure on either side to allow
room at the head and tail of your recording.

You can always cut (slice) the excess heads and tails from your clips
once they are in the Timeline.

4   Click and drag In and Out points to extend the playback area or
recording duration.

Set the In point to 7.1.00 in the beat ruler and the Out point to 8.3.00.

5   Click the Record button in the transport controls at the top of the
window.

The Multiple Take Recording dialog box appears.

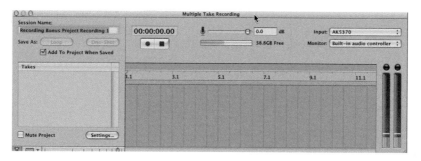

This window is similar to the single-take recording window.

Look at the Takes list box on the left side of the window. Each time the recording time lapses, a new take will start. As a take is finished, it will appear in the Takes list box.

Notice the Save As buttons: Loop and One-Shot. They are grayed out until the takes are recorded.

Also, the box Add To Project When Saved is checked by default. Leave this checked so that your takes show up in the Timeline once selected.

6   Type *Snaps-Multi* in the Session Name field.

7   Locate the Mute Project check box at the bottom left of the window.

If you are listening with headphones, leave the Mute Project box unchecked. If you are listening through monitor speakers, check the box.

Check the recording levels before starting. They should remain at the settings from the previous single-take recording exercise.

8   Click the Record button to begin.

9 Snap your fingers once per take. Record three different takes.

Don't worry about getting the timing of your Snap perfect in each take. You can always reposition the snap after it is in the Timeline. If you were recording an instrumental part that needed to fit in with the other tracks, you would want to be more careful with the timing of the take.

10 Click the Stop button to end the recording session.

It's okay if you recorded an incomplete fourth take, as you will choose only the best takes to add to your Timeline.

All takes show up as one long clip, separated by take markers.

11 Click Take 1 in the Takes list box.

The Take 1 portion of the recorded clip appears blue, like a Timeslice.

12 Click the Play button above the takes to listen to the selected take.

13 Repeat steps 11 and 12 to listen to the other two takes.

14 Choose your favorite take.

Since we recorded a single event—a finger snap—there is a lot of empty space in the clip before and after the actual snap sound.

We can isolate the area around the snap to narrow the size of the clip. This is not necessary if you choose to keep the recording as a one-shot. However, if you want to create a loop out of the snap, make it as tight as possible.

The single take we recorded earlier is a one-shot. Let's turn this take into a loop.

First, we will clean up the usable sound to make the clip shorter.

15 Click inside the timeslice selection area to change the size of the timeslice.

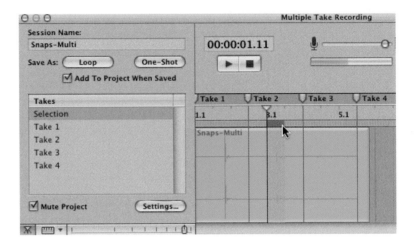

The word *Selection* appears above the first take in the Takes list box to indicate that you have chosen a selection instead of a full take.

If you try to make the selection smaller, you will be fighting the snapping function around the markers and playhead position.

16 Click the Snapping button in the lower-left corner of the Multiple Take Recording window to turn off snapping. Now try to make a smaller selection.

With snapping off, it should be easier to narrow the recording area to the section just before and after the snap.

TIP Don't make the space in front and back of the snap too tight, or it won't make a very good loop. Try to imagine, if the snap were looped, how much time you would want between snaps.

17 Click the Save As: Loop button.

A Save window appears.

If you'd like, you can click the Add to Favorites button in the lower center of the window to save the recorded loop for later use.

18 Select the Lesson_16 folder from the Where pop-up menu, then click Save.

Your new loop will be saved in the project folder.

19 Close the Multiple Take Recording window to conclude the session.

A new track is automatically added to the Timeline, and your loop will be placed in the recording area.

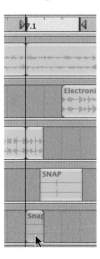

20 Select the loop and align it so that the snap is in sync with the single-take snap in the Timeline.

You can turn off snapping in the Timeline for easier positioning of the loop, or nudge it holding the left and right arrows.

21 Listen to each snap take and decide which you want to keep in the project.

22 Mute the track of the snap you do not want to use.

Congratulations! You have successfully recorded both single and multiple takes. All the snap needs now is a little reverb effect.

Adding a Reverb Effect

1   Press Cmd-3 to display the track headers.

2   Click the Show Effects button (asterisk) on your final snap track.

3   Add an Apple–Matrix Reverb effect.

4   Toggle open the Matrix Reverb parameters and choose one of the sounds, such as Plate.

Remember that music is a subjective experience, and as the composer, *you* need to appreciate the sound before others can do the same.

Tagging Loops in the Soundtrack Loop Utility

So you see, adding new files to your library of loops is easy. But finding the right file when you need it again is a different story.

One of the extraordinary things about the Soundtrack program is the extensive metadata and tags that can be added to classify, filter, and sort the loops. Metadata is simply information about the loop; adding metadata tags does not affect how the loop sounds. Apple Loops created in Soundtrack are the only loops whose format includes a comprehensive set of instrument, genre, and mood descriptors. This metadata is not available in other loop programs.

The metadata in Apple Loops together with the versatility of Soundtrack makes it easy for nonmusicians to find and work with loops that sound good together. Soundtrack even sorts major and minor keys.

Soundtrack is versatile enough to recognize loops created in other programs, such as the WAV files created in Acid. However, Apple Loops created in Soundtrack are a new format and are built with AIFF—which makes them compatible for use in Final Cut Pro.

1   Ctrl-click your Snap loop in the Timeline and choose Open in
    Soundtrack Loop Utility from the contextual menu.

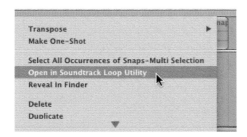

The Soundtrack Loop Utility window opens.

Now we'll set the tags so that the loop will be easy to find in the
search parameters. We'll start by giving you credit as the author of
the Snap loop.

2   Type your name into the Author field.

3   In the Search Tags area, choose Genre > Experimental.

4   In the Descriptors area, select the radio buttons that describe the loop.
The center radio button is a neutral, or off, position.

Single, Acoustic, and Clean all apply to your Snap loop.

5   Click the Assets button to open the Assets window on the right side of
the utility window, if it is not already open.

Assets list the different loops that you are going to tag. You can add
metadata to one loop at a time, or to all of the loops in the Assets
window at once.

Notice that your loop in the Assets window has a dot in the Changes
column. This indicates that you have made changes to the metadata of
the saved file.

6   Click the Save button.

The changes have been made to the data in your loop.

Notice that the Change dot is no longer present in the Assets window.

7   Close the Soundtrack Loop Utility and save your Soundtrack project.

You have created a loop that can be indexed in the Soundtrack search window and incorporated into your compositions.

> **NOTE ▶** For more information on using the Soundtrack Loop Utility, read the Soundtrack manual.

What You've Learned

- When composing audio, start with a temporary rhythm track.
- Add scoring markers to Soundtrack files in Final Cut Pro to give the composer direction for the final piece.
- Round-trip your audio loop by importing it back into Soundtrack to finalize.
- Create a favorites library to help you easily find loops.
- In addition to using prerecorded loops, you can record sounds in Soundtrack using single or multiple takes.

17

Lesson Files

Media

Time

This lesson takes approximately 60 minutes to complete.

Goals

Show and hide waveform display in the Timeline

Explore the difference between peak and average audio levels

Choose an appropriate dB level for a sequence's dialogue

Explore the Audio Mixer

Use Views to create different arrangements of audio tracks in the Audio Mixer

Record level keyframes to automate an audio track in real time, by moving faders in the Audio Mixer

Make subframe adjustments to an audio clip

Lesson 17
Audio Finishing

Have you ever heard the saying "Video is two-thirds audio?" Well, it's true. The ear is more sensitive than the eye, and viewers are much more tolerant of a dodgy video stream than they are of less-than-perfect audio. For example, if your video has too little contrast, or if the color is not quite correct, most viewers won't turn the channel. Conversely, if your video's sound constantly peaks into distortion, or if audio levels jump erratically from low to high, you're going to lose some ears and eyeballs.

Happily, there's no reason your audio should ever turn a viewer away from the video, because doing your audio right is a simple process. In this lesson, you will learn how to use a reference tone to correctly configure the level of your sequence's audio. Along the way you'll see how to set the level of audio clips, use Final Cut Pro 4's new Audio Mixer, automate audio tracks in real time, and make subframe adjustments to correctly synchronize an audio clip to a marker in the Timeline. Are you ready to face the music?

Preparing the Sequence

Movies are all about suspending your disbelief—losing yourself in the magic of the story and forgetting about reality, if only for a moment. So in the finest cinematic tradition, let's suspend our disbelief by pretending we're not video editors, and put on the hat of an audio engineer. For the rest of this lesson, you'll concentrate on sound, so set the stage by opening this lesson's start file.

1   Open the file Lessons > Lesson_17 > **17_Lesson_Start.fcp**.

2   Arrange the windows on your screen in the standard layout by pressing Ctrl-U (or choose Windows > Arrange > Standard).

Your screen should look more or less like the following figure:

3   Next, we'll turn off a setting that we'll learn about later in this lesson. Choose Final Cut Pro > User Preferences (Opt-Q), and make sure that the Record Audio Keyframes box is *not* checked.

4   Click OK.

5   Play the sequence from the beginning, and listen carefully to the audio.

Using the basic audio editing techniques you learned in *Apple Pro Training Series: Final Cut Pro 4*, some extra audio tracks have been added to the project, and the level of the clips has been adjusted to create ambient tone and background music. Listen to the whole sequence a few times until you're familiar with its content, the sounds, the places where the dialogue seems low in volume, and those where it seems high.

Displaying Waveforms in the Timeline

As you zoom or scroll around the sequence in the Timeline window, it takes a bit of time for your computer to calculate and display the waveforms for the audio clips. Although fast computers will redraw waveforms quickly, less powerful machines will slowly chug through this process, which can cause your system to seem sluggish as you zoom in, out, or even just scroll around the Timeline window. If this happens to you, speed up your workflow by turning waveform display off.

1   Choose Sequence > Settings (Cmd-0).

The Sequence Settings window opens, with the General tab showing.

2   In the Sequence Settings window, select the Timeline Options tab.

3 Click the Show Audio Waveforms check box to deselect it.

4 Click OK to close the Sequence Settings window, and look at the Timeline.

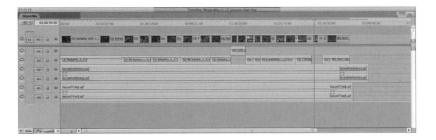

Notice that the waveforms have disappeared from your audio clips. Keep this trick in mind if your Timeline starts to feel sluggish, or if it's slow to redraw after you've zoomed in or scrolled to a different section. This chapter, however, is all about audio, and we want to see our audio clip waveforms, so let's turn Show Audio Waveforms back on using the Timeline pop-up menu.

5   In the lower-left corner of the Timeline, click and hold the pop-up menu.

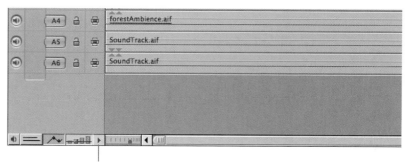

Timeline pop-up menu

The menu opens.

6   From the Timeline pop-up menu, choose Show Audio Waveforms.

The Timeline's audio clips once again display their waveforms.

Muting and Soloing Audio Tracks

The secret to good audio is getting the dialogue right. More than any other sound in your video, the dialogue is the part the viewer focuses his or her attention upon. In the following exercises, you're going to hop into the

viewer's frame of mind by focusing your attention on the sequence's dialogue alone, so let's temporarily get the audio tracks that do not contain
dialogue out of the way by disabling their sound. In Final Cut Pro 4, there
are three ways to do this:

- Disable the audio track by clicking its green Audible button (these
  buttons are often called Track Visibility controls—even on audio
  tracks—but this book refers to them as the Audible buttons). If the
  Audible button is disabled, the audio track's sound does not play.

- Mute the audio track. A muted track does not play.

- Solo the dialogue audio track. Soloing a track turns off the sound of
  all the sequence's other audio tracks (except for other soloed tracks,
  which still continue to play).

That's the theory, now let's put it into action …

1   For the next several steps, it will help to hear the sequence's audio as
you turn audio tracks on and off, so in the Timeline, move the playhead to the beginning of the sequence and press the spacebar to begin
playback.

2   On Track A5 and Track A6, click the Audible button to turn the tracks
off (disable them).

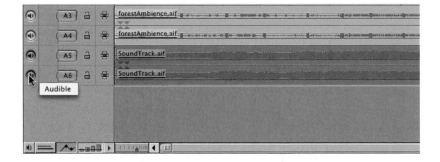

Clicking the Audible button is a good way to turn off the track's sound,
as long as you remember the following: Disabling the Audible button

not only turns the track off, but also excludes the track from the rendered or output version of your movie—this includes movies exported to QuickTime, Print to Video, Edit to Tape, and so on. A less permanent way to turn off a track's sound involves using the Mute buttons. Muted tracks are still included in the sequence's sound when you export it to a QuickTime movie or print to tape.

Before you can mute a track, you need to show the audio controls in the Timeline.

3 In the lower-left corner of the Timeline, click the Audio Controls button (or choose Sequence > Settings > Timeline Options). In the Sequence Settings dialog that comes up, click the Show Audio Controls check box to select it.

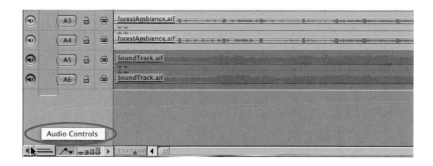

Mute and Solo buttons appear at the far left of each track.

Mute button
Solo button

Muted and Soloed audio tracks affect the sequence only while you edit it. When it comes time to output the sequence, the Mute and Solo button choices are overridden, so all muted or soloed tracks are included in your final renders. Disabling audio tracks with the Audible button has one other distinct advantage over using the Mute or Solo buttons: It removes the strain the audio track places on your computer's CPU. Muted tracks, on the other hand, still consume CPU cycles, because you can instantly turn these tracks back on by unmuting them. If your sequence drops frames as it plays, click the Audible button to disable audio tracks you don't need to hear, and save those CPU cycles for more important parts of your project (like adding more effects to the other tracks).

4   On Track A3 and Track A4, click the Mute button.

The Mute button has a black speaker on it. Clicking it turns the speaker yellow and temporarily turns off a track's sound. Consequently, Track A3 and Track A4 can no longer be heard.

5   Click the Mute buttons again to unmute Track A3 and Track A4, and then re-enable Track A5 and Track A6 by clicking their Audible buttons.

All audio tracks are now playing together.

6   On Track A1 and Track A2, click the Solo buttons.

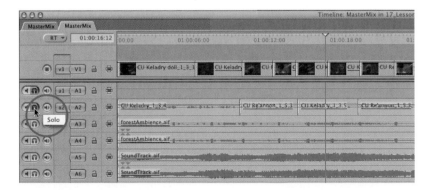

Track A1 and Track A2 are soloed. All the sequence's other tracks are automatically muted so you can't hear them. That's great, because for the next few exercises you are going to concentrate on getting your dialogue right, so it's fine to have the other audio tracks temporarily silenced. You'll turn Track A1 and Track A2 back on a little later, but for now leave them soloed and continue on to the next exercises.

Setting the Level of the Dialogue

Imagine you're in your living room channel surfing. As you switch through the programs, you pay the most attention to the dialogue, which is the main way for a program to deliver aural information to you. The music and background sounds all slip into the, err … background, and the focus of your ears' attention is the spoken words. You'll also notice that the sound of dialogue across all television channels is more or less uniform, and always reaches your ears at the same volume level. In other words, the average volume of the dialogue has purposefully been configured to be consistent across all broadcast programs. This allows a more pleasant viewing experience, because you can confidently flip between programs without having to jump for the remote control's volume buttons to raise or lower the television's sound.

To keep the level of dialogue constant, broadcast television uses an average level of dialogue that corresponds to approximately –15 dB to –12 dB on Final Cut Pro 4's digital level meter. For example, if you were to take a video sequence from Final Cut Pro, use DVD Studio Pro to turn it into a DVD-Video, and then play that DVD on your TV, dialogue that used an average level of –12 dB in Final Cut Pro would sound exactly the same level as the dialogue on a television broadcast. Consequently, if you want your sequence to play at the same volume as broadcast television programs, it's a good idea to ensure that the average level of your sequence's dialogue is between –15 dB and –12 dB as you edit in Final Cut Pro. You'll learn more about this a bit later in this lesson, when we discuss reference levels.

Peak Versus Average Level

One of the most important audio concepts to understand is the difference between peak versus average audio levels.

Peak level is represented by the spikes in the waveform. These spikes represent short bursts in volume that last only a fraction of a second. In music, the peaks usually correspond to rhythmic elements in the song, such as kick drums and cymbal crashes. In dialogue, on the other hand, peaks typically fall on the "plosive" sounds, or hard consonant sounds such as *p*s, *t*s, and *k*s. In fact, if you say the word *peak,* you can even hear how your own voice sounds louder and more pronounced during the "p" and "k" portions of the word, while it's quieter during the "ea."

A waveform's average volume level is represented by a line that distinguishes the waveform's solid body from its peaks. As you listen to an audio stream, you are much more sensitive to the stream's average level than you are to the peak level, and if the audio sounds too loud or too quiet, it's very likely the average level that you are noticing, not the peak level.

Dialogue: Common Average and Peak Levels in Final Cut Pro

Delivery Format	Average Volume	Peak Volume
Broadcast television	–12 dB	–6 dB
VHS tape	–12 dB	–3 dB
Theatrical Dolby Digital	–20 dB	–3 dB

TIP ▶ Dynamic range compression offers a way to sonically shave the peaks off a waveform while increasing the level of the wave's quieter parts. This gives you more precise control over the wave's average level. Final Cut Pro 4 comes with a great dynamic range compressor, available by choosing Effects > Audio Filters > Final Cut Pro > Compressor/Limiter.

Let's take a moment to explore peak and average levels using the project's **SoundTrack.aif** file. This file contains music, not dialogue. Nonetheless, music is very dynamic in nature, with noticeable spikes that provide a good example of the difference between peak and average audio levels.

1   In the Browser, double-click the **SoundTrack.aif** audio file.

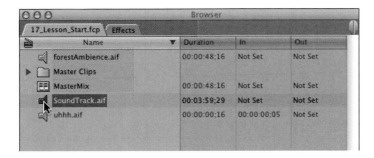

The file opens in the Viewer.

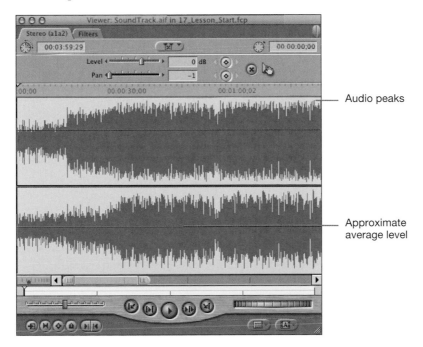

2 Press the Viewer's Play button to audition the audio file and see if you can hear the difference between the peaks and the average levels.

This Viewer is quite narrow, while the audio file itself is fairly long. To get a bit more space to display the file, let's tear the Audio tab out of the Viewer and drop it into the Timeline window.

3 In the Viewer, grab the Audio tab, called Stereo (a1a2), and tear it out of the window. Don't release the mouse button.

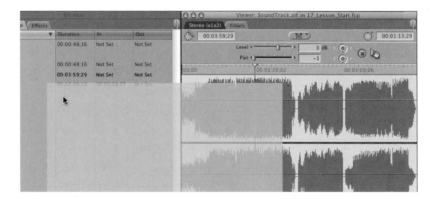

The tab tears out of the Viewer and is shadowed as you drag it across the workspace.

4 Drag the pointer over the gray area just under the Timeline's title bar.

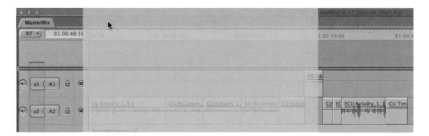

With the pointer over the gray area, the Timeline is outlined in a thick border. This border indicates that you can drop the audio tab into the Timeline window.

5   Drop the Audio tab.

The audio waveform fills the Timeline window.

Approximate average level

With the waveform spread across the Timeline window, it becomes much easier to see it in detail. Notice the peaks in the waveform, and then look closely at the more solid part of the waveform—its body. While it takes a bit of practice to identify a file's average level, you can get close by thinking of it this way: If you shaved the peaks off of the waveform, you'd be left with a flat, smooth wave. This smooth wave would come close to representing the waveform's average level. Can you see it?

Exploring Dynamic Range

Dynamic range is the difference between your audio stream's loudest and quietest portions, and it's important to take dynamic range into consideration when you determine how loud your sequence's dialogue should be. For example, film soundtracks are often mixed using a large dynamic range. They are meant to play on the big screen, with big sound systems that are very efficient and accurately reproduce a large difference between loud and quiet sounds. In a movie, you want to be able to hear the lovers whisper, and you want to be shocked by the exploding car. You want to hear the rumble of the low-rider car as it drives by, and you want the thrill of the roar as the low-rider revs its engine. You want big sound, and consequently big dynamic range is required. For this reason, movies typically mix in dialogue at between –20 dB and –31 dB. At first glance this may seem surprisingly low on the level meter, but add an explosion that peaks at –6 dB, and you've got a very dynamic—and dramatic—soundtrack.

Television, on the other hand, has different concerns. Most televisions today are not equipped with efficient speakers, and the mono 3-inch driver on the front of a typical budget television has a hard time reproducing sound, period, let alone the full dynamic range of a film score. Consequently, audio destined for TV uses a severely reduced dynamic range. The following chart lists the dynamic range required for several different types of programs:

Dynamic Range Versus Program Delivery Format

Delivery Format	Dynamic Range
Broadcast television	6 dB
Videotape	12 dB
Theatrical Dolby Digital	20 dB

Using the Audio Meter

In Final Cut Pro, –12 dB is a very significant number because it makes a good reference level to use for video destined for broadcast. When you output your sequence to analog tape formats, such as BetaSP or U-matic, you should adjust your tape recorder so that –12 dB on Final Cut Pro's level meter is 0 dB on your tape recorder's analog, or volume unit (VU) level meter. If you do so, your audio will come out perfect, guaranteed!

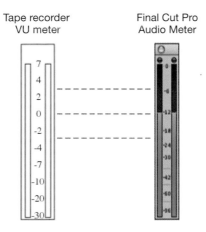

Tape recorder
VU meter

Final Cut Pro
Audio Meter

NOTE ▶ 0 dB on an analog level meter is often referred to as *unity gain*.

Digital videotape recorders such as DV, DVCAM, DVCPRO, and digital Betacam receive digital audio straight from Final Cut Pro and will record audio at the same levels as those you see on your Final Cut Pro Audio Meter.

With this in mind, let's take a moment to look at Final Cut Pro's Audio Meter.

1 In the Timeline window, click the **MasterMix** tab to bring the sequence back into view.

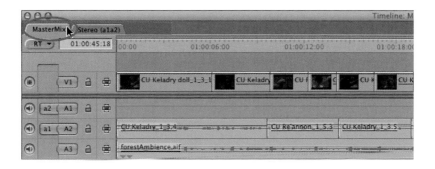

2 Play the sequence.

Right now the dialogue tracks are soloed, so all you hear is the children talking.

3 Look at Final Cut Pro's Audio Meter, and note the peak levels compared with the average levels.

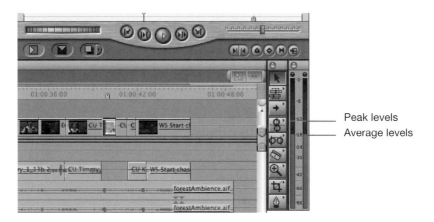

Peak levels
Average levels

As the sequence plays, the Audio Meter pulses between a high and a low value. The high value represents the sequence's peak level, and the low value generally comes close to showing the sequence's average levels level. The difference between these two levels determines the audio stream's dynamic range.

The Audio Meter helps you determine peak values by holding a yellow line temporarily in position at audio peaks (this is called a *peak and hold* display). The average volume level, on the other hand, takes a bit of practice to work out. As you watch the Audio Meter pulse between its high and low levels, notice that some green is almost always displayed in the Audio Meter, and the volume level very rarely drops to silence. Pay careful attention to the lowest level of the green in the display.

For all intents and purposes, this is the average level of the audio stream. In this example, the average level of the dialogue is approximately –18 dB.

4   Press the spacebar to stop playback, and look at the Audio Meter.

Even though the sequence stops playing, the Audio Meter continues to show the level of the frame the playhead is currently parked on.

Choosing a Reference Level

So, we've examined a lot of the theory involved in audio—now let's start mixing! The first step to creating a great mix is calibrating your speakers using a reference tone. A *reference tone* is a steady 1 kHz sine wave that sounds like a long, sustained note. It's important because this reference tone helps you set a comfortable monitoring level and provides a volume refcrence to use as you set the levels of your sequence's dialogue.

If you've ever surfed around late-night television, you've seen the color bars and test tone that comes onscreen when a channel goes off air. This test tone is usually a 1 kHz sine wave that plays at 0 dB on the analog VU meter. In fact, this test tone is exactly the same as the one you'll use to calibrate your speakers before working on your sequence's audio, and it's available from the Viewer's Generators pop-up menu.

The reference level is used for two purposes. First, if you are outputting your sequence to tape in preparation for broadcast, you should always include a minute of test tone and bars at the beginning of the sequence. This test tone plays at the same average level as the dialogue in your sequence, and it allows the broadcaster to calibrate its equipment to play your audio at the correct level. The test tone also provides a steady signal you can use to calibrate your audio signals to an appropriate listening level, and that's the purpose we'll put it to in the next few steps.

For this example, let's assume you want your video to play at the same level as standard broadcast television. To achieve this, we'll use a reference level of –12 dB and then calibrate our speakers to an appropriate listening level for mixing.

1   Double-click any video clip in the sequence. This will get a Video tab back into the Viewer. Click the Viewer's Video tab, and in the lower-right corner of the Viewer, click and hold the Generators pop-up menu.

Generators pop-up menu

The Generators pop-up menu opens.

2   Choose Bars and Tone (NTSC).

The Bars and Tone Generator appears in the Viewer.

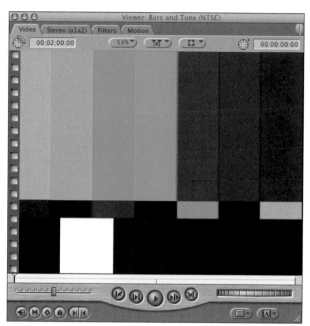

3   Press the Viewer's Play button.

The 1 kHz test tone plays. Notice that Final Cut Pro's Audio Meter holds steady at –12 dB as the test tone plays.

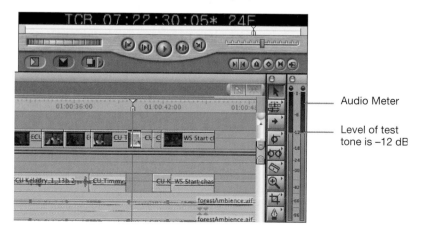

Audio Meter

Level of test
tone is –12 dB

At –12 dB, this test tone plays at exactly the same level as the test tone you hear on those late-night, off-air channels.

If you intend to mix your sequence with more dynamic range than is required for television, you will need to lower the level of the test tone. In a later step, you will still mix in the dialogue at approximately the same volume level as this lower test tone, which in turn gives you more *headroom*, or more level gain above the dialogue level to mix in effects such as those explosions and revving car engines we referred to earlier. In this situation, you will need to lower the level of the test tone from its default –12 dB, as demonstrated in the following steps:

4   Click the Viewer's Stereo(a1a2) tab to display the test tone.

Toward the top of the Stereo tab, you'll see Level and Pan sliders. If you look closely, you'll notice the Level slider is set at –12 dB. This, of course, is exactly the same value displayed on Final Cut Pro's Audio Meter.

5   Move the Level slider down to –20, and check out Final Cut Pro's Audio Meter. (If the test tone is not playing, press the Play button to start playback once again.)

The Audio Meter now displays a level of –20 dB.

6   Set the Level slider back to –12 to ensure that the test tone plays at –12 dB.

Finish preparing to mix by setting your speakers to a comfortable listening level.

7   Play the test tone, and adjust your speakers so the tone sounds neither too loud nor too quiet.

NOTE ▶ Adjusting speaker volume is not the same thing as adjusting the Viewer's Level slider. You can adjust the speaker volume by increasing or decreasing the output volume of your computer using the speaker keys at the top of the keyboard's keypad. (For a PowerBook, the speaker keys are on the F4 and F5 keys.)

The test tone should be loud enough so you can hear it clearly, but not so loud that it tires your ears. As you mix your audio in Final Cut Pro, don't change the volume of your speakers. Maintaining a consistent playback level lets you get used to the volume you're working at, which in turn gives you a good feel for how the your audio sounds and helps you avoid having audio in one part of your video that's louder or quieter than in another part. When it comes to volume, consistency is the key!

Adjusting the Dialogue Level

Now that you've decided upon a reference level and have properly configured your speakers, it's time to attack the sequence's audio. The first step in this process is setting the level of the sequence's dialogue in the following fashion: Set the dialogue so its average level is approximately the same as the level of your reference tone.

In other words, if your reference tone is at –12 dB, this is approximately the level you should use as the average level for the dialogue. If you decide to you want more dynamic range in your audio streams, then a reference level of –20 dB might be more appropriate, and in this case you'll mix your dialogue at an average level level of –20 dB. After that, you need simply mix the rest of the sequence's audio relative to the dialogue. The long and short of this process comes down to ensuring your dialogue is at the same level as the reference tone, because you'll use this reference tone to calibrate the audio inputs on your analog video recorder to 0 dB. If you take care to set your dialogue to the same level as the reference tone, all of your sequence's other sounds fall naturally into place! For the purpose of this lesson, we'll use a reference tone of −12 dB.

> **NOTE ▶** You also must pay attention to your sequence's peak level. For broadcast, audio that uses a reference level of −12 dB should never peak above −6 dB on Final Cut Pro's Audio Meter. For tape formats such as VHS, −3 dB is an appropriate peak level for sequences that use a reference tone of −12 dB.

1   Play the sequence again and determine the average level of the dialogue.

Right now the average level of the dialogue is approximately −18 dB. Furthermore, this level is consistent across the entire sequence. Your reference tone is at −12 dB, so you need to raise the level of each audio clip by 6 dB. You could progress clip by clip through the sequence, grab the pink level overlay line, and raise the level of each clip by hand. But that would be a slow and arduous task. Instead, use the following trick to boost the level of all the clips at once:

2   With the Selection tool, drag a selection range around all of the audio clips in Track A1 and Track A2.

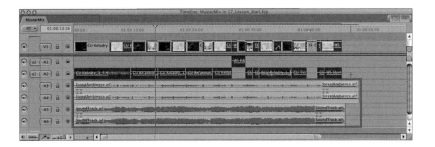

All of the clips in Track A1 and Track A2 are selected.

3   Choose Modify > Levels (Cmnd-Opt-L).

The Gain Adjust window opens.

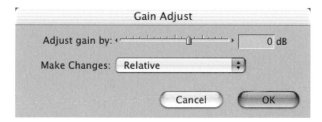

This window lets you adjust the level of several audio clips simultaneously. It's simple to use; just grab the slider and set an amount to adjust
the gain by. Positive values increase the level of the selected clips, while
negative values decrease it.

However, there is one important setting in this window, and that's Make Changes. This setting has two different values: Absolute and Relative.

▶ *Absolute.* All gain adjustments are absolute, which means each selected audio clip is moved to the exact value indicated on the Adjust Gain By slider. If the clip contains keyframes, the keyframes are erased.

▶ *Relative.* This is the default setting. All gain adjustments look at the current level of each individual clip, and then adjust the clip by the amount specified in the Adjust Gain By slider. If the clip contains keyframes, each individual keyframe is adjusted by the amount specified in the Adjust Gain By slider.

4   Leave the Make Changes setting at Relative, set the Adjust Gain By slider to 6, and click OK.

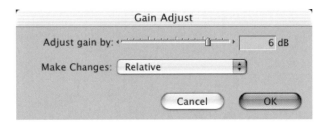

The level of each clip increases by 6 dB.

5   Play the sequence again and watch the Audio Meter.

Now the average level of the dialogue is approximately –12 dB. Perfect!

With the dialogue finally set to the correct level, it's time to adjust the level of the sequence's other audio tracks. You'll do that in the following exercises using Final Cut Pro 4's Audio Mixer.

Exploring the Audio Mixer

Final Cut Pro 4's new Audio Mixer is a great addition to this program's audio arsenal. With a fader (level slider), a Pan slider, and Mute and Solo buttons for every audio track in your project, the Audio Mixer mimics the functionality of a hardware audio mixing console.

Using the Audio Mixer

Let's open up the Audio Mixer and take a look around.

1   Choose Tools > Audio Mixer (Opt-6).

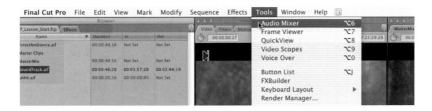

A Tool Bench window opens to show the Audio Mixer.

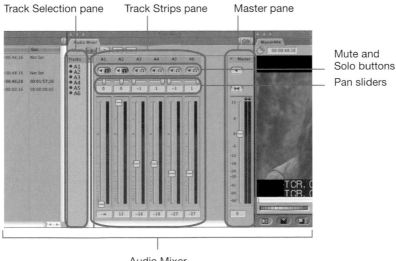

Track Selection pane   Track Strips pane   Master pane

Mute and
Solo buttons

Pan sliders

Audio Mixer

This window is dominated by a central section that contains a dedicated level fader for each track in your project. At the top of each track's fader is a Pan slider, a Mute (speaker) button, and a Solo (headphones) button. The Mute and Solo buttons in the Audio Mixer provide exactly the same function as the Mute and Solo buttons you enabled by clicking the Timeline's Show Audio Controls button. A quick glance at these buttons shows that Track A1 and Track A2 are currently soloed. This means Tracks A3 through A6 cannot be heard. It's time to create a mix, so let's unsolo A1 and A2 so all of the audio tracks play.

2 On both Track A1 and Track A2, click the Solo button to turn soloing off for those two tracks.

3   Play the sequence, and watch the track faders.

In Final Cut Pro, levels are assigned to the individual clips rather than to the track as a whole. Consequently, as the sequence plays you will often see the level faders jump up and down to reflect the level of each individual clip. Areas of the Timeline that do not have an audio clip are silent, and the track faders obligingly drop to $-\infty$ (infinity) when these blank spaces are encountered.

4   Grab A2's Pan slider and move it to the left.

A2's audio is now heard completely in the left speaker.

5   Option-click A2's Pan slider.

The Pan slider jumps back to the center. Holding Option while clicking a fader is a quick way to jump the fader back to its default setting, and it works not only on the Pan slider, but on each track's level fader as well!

TIP To gear down and make a fader's movement more precise, hold the Cmd key as you drag the fader. This works with all faders in Final Cut Pro.

6   Grab the master fader and drag it to the bottom.

The master fader controls the level of the entire mix, so lowering the master fader causes the entire mix to drop in level.

TIP If you are using a mouse with a scroll wheel, you can position the pointer over the fader and then use the scroll wheel to move faders up and down. This is often easier and more precise than dragging the faders.

The scale used for the master fader can be a bit confusing at first. By default, the master fader sits at 0, which does not indicate whether the 0 refers to unity gain or –12 dB on the digital scale. In fact, the 0 setting here indicates that no boost or attenuation has been applied to the level of the sequence as a whole. However, should you so desire you can apply up to 12 dB of boost to the entire mix, or attenuate the mix until it is silent.

7   Option-click the Master fader.

The Master fader returns to 0, and the mix is neither boosted nor attenuated.

8   In the Track Strips pane, raise or lower the faders on tracks A3 through A6 to set the level of these audio tracks.

Listen closely to the dialogue as you adjust these faders, and set the level so that the dialogue in Track A1 and Track A2 is still clearly present and easily heard above the other elements of the mix.

Congratulations! You've just created a basic mix.

Working with Views

This sequence has only six audio tracks, which is a very manageable number. Indeed, a quick glance shows that all six tracks easily fit in the Audio Mixer. But what happens if you have 20 audio tracks, or 50? Or even the maximum number of audio tracks available in Final Cut Pro, 99? In those situations, your audio mixer would be very crowded. Happily, the Audio Mixer lets you get audio tracks out of the way by hiding them, which in turn lets you focus only on the audio tracks you currently need to adjust.

Even better, Final Cut Pro 4 gives you access to four different views, or custom track configurations, in the Audio Mixer. For example, you can create one view that is only the dialogue tracks, and one that is the background sounds. When it comes time to adjust the dialogue, just enable the View that contains your dialogue tracks, and only dialogue tracks will appear in the Audio window. Let's try this feature out.

1   In the Track Selection pane on the left edge of the Audio Mixer, click Track A6.

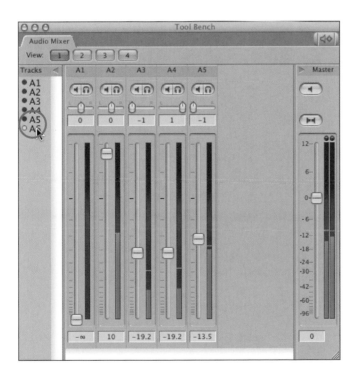

The dot beside Track A6 turns from black to an outline. Track A6 is hidden, and its track strip disappears from the Audio Mixer.

2   In the Track Selection pane, click Tracks A3, A4, and A5 to hide them.

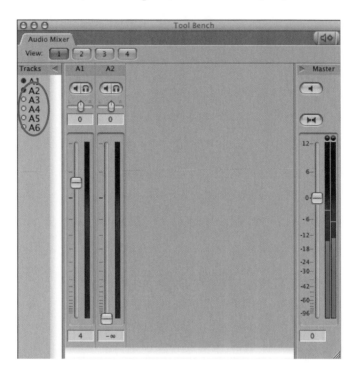

Track strips for A1 and A2 are the only ones that remain visible in the Audio Mixer. You've just created a custom view that contains only the dialogue tracks!

3   If the sequence is not playing, play it now.

Although Tracks A3 through A6 are hidden in the Audio Mixer, you can still hear them. This demonstrates an important point: Hidden audio tracks are not turned off—they continue to play.

4   In the top-left corner of the Audio Mixer, click View button 2.

All of the audio tracks are once again visible in the Audio Mixer.

5 Return to the Track Selection pane once again, but this time click Track A1 and Track A2 to hide them.

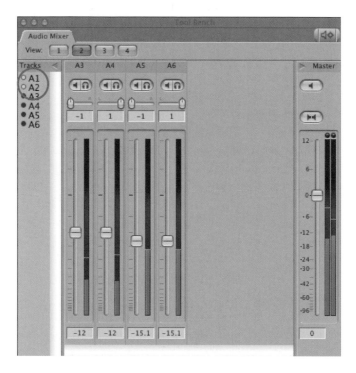

You've just created a second view that contains only the background audio tracks. Now, if you wish to adjust the dialogue, click View button 1. If you need to adjust the background audio, click View button 2.

6 Switch back and forth between View 1 and View 2 by clicking the View 1 and 2 buttons. When you're done having fun, leave View button 2 selected.

Resizing the Audio Mixer

Views go a long way to helping you deal with sequences that use many audio tracks. There will, however, be times when you need to adjust several audio tracks at the same time. In these situations, it helps to resize the Tool Bench window that holds the Audio Mixer tab, so all the tracks are visible.

Resizing the window with the Audio Mixer has another distinct advantage: If you are attempting to make very subtle level adjustments, the Audio Mixer's faders might seem a bit short, and not exact enough in their movement. You can increase the resolution of these faders by dragging the bottom of the mixer toward the bottom of your screen. This makes the Audio Mixer nice and tall, which in turn gives you precise control over your fader movements.

1 Grab the Tool Bench window by its title bar, and drag it to the left.

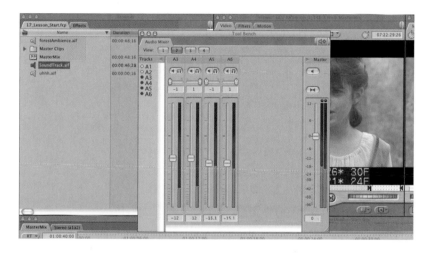

Notice that the Tool Bench is actually its own window and is not part of the Viewer. When you opened the Tool Bench, it completely covered the Viewer, but it's actually an independent window that you can open, resize, and close as needed.

2 Grab the bottom-right corner of the Tool Bench window and drag down toward the bottom of the screen.

The Tool Bench window becomes taller—and so do its faders! You now have very precise control over your fader settings.

Using the Audio Mixing Window Arrangement

Right now the Audio Mixer is obstructing a lot of your valuable screen real estate. Final Cut Pro 4 contains a new window arrangement that is tailored for audio mixing. Let's open it up and take a look.

▶   Choose Window > Arrange > Audio Mixing.

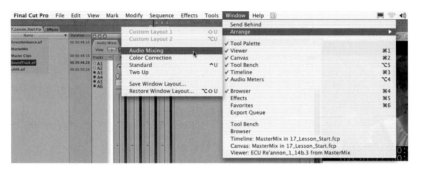

The Tool Bench window opens in the top-right corner of the screen, displaying the Audio Mixer in a tab.

Keyframing Audio

Keyframes can be used in many places in Final Cut Pro; basically any parameter that can be modified over time can be keyframed. In earlier lessons, you learned how to use overlays to adjust the opacity of video clips as the sequence plays, and keyframing audio works more or less the same way. By now you've had quite a bit of practice keyframing video clip opacity and effects, and keyframing should be old hat. The next exercise covers the addition of keyframes to an overlay by hand in order to change an audio track's level as the sequence plays. Time is money, so we'll keep this overview brief. If you are comfortable with keyframing, skip the next exercise and jump ahead to "Real-Time Keyframing."

Adding Keyframes

For audio clips, the Timeline gives you access to the Level overlay, which is used to change the levels of a clip over time. Using the mouse, you can click level keyframes directly onto the Level overlay. Let's add some keyframes now.

1   If overlays are not enabled, click the Clip Overlays button located in the lower-left corner of the Timeline window (Option-W).

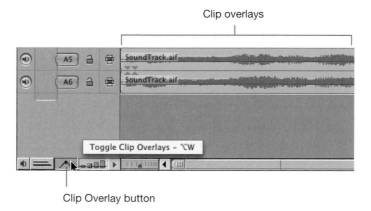

Clip overlays

Toggle Clip Overlays – ⌥W

Clip Overlay button

2   From the Tool palette, grab the Pen tool.

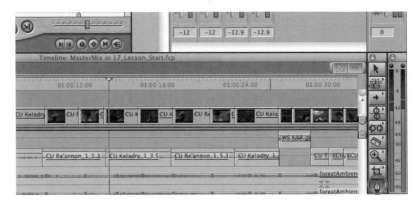

3   Focus on the **forestAmbience.aif** clip (Track A3 and Track A4), and click its overlay twice with the Pen tool to create keyframes. Don't worry about getting the keyframes' placement too exact, because you will move them in the next step.

Notice that clicking the overlay creates a keyframe on both Track A3 and Track A4. This is because these tracks are a linked stereo pair. Look closely at the figure above, and you'll notice that directly under the pointer, the clip on Track A3 has two downward-pointing green arrows. These match up with the two upward-pointing green arrows on the clip in Track A4. This is Final Cut Pro's way of graphically showing you that the audio tracks in the **forestAmbience.aif** clip on Track A3 and Track A4 are a stereo pair.

NOTE ▸ If you'd like to keyframe only one track in a stereo pair, you must unlink the stereo pair by selecting the audio clip and choosing Modify > Stereo Pair.

4 With the Pen tool, grab the first keyframe and drag it to the lower-left corner of the clip.

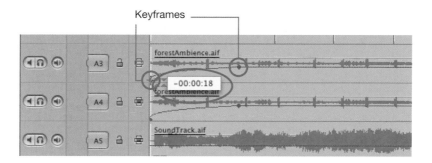

As you drag the keyframe, the pointer turns into a crosshair. By dragging the keyframe to the bottom-left corner of the clip, you've just hand-created a fade-in.

5 Move the playhead to the beginning of the sequence, and then play the sequence to hear the effect of your new fade-in.

As the sequence plays, watch the Audio Mixer and note how the level faders on Track A3 and Track A4 fade in automatically. You've just automated the tracks' levels.

Cool, but unnecessary. Track A3 and Track A4 do not need to fade in, so let's delete these keyframes.

6   Press Option and move the pointer over the first keyframe (the one at the front of the clip).

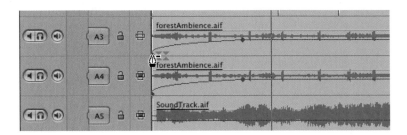

A minus sign appears to the right of the Pen tool, indicating it is in the delete mode.

7   Click the keyframe.

The keyframe is erased.

8   Option-click the second keyframe to delete it.

No keyframes are left in the **forestAmbience.aif** clip.

Real-Time Keyframing

Real-time keyframing is arguably the coolest new audio feature added to Final Cut Pro 4, because you can now record level fader, pan slider, and audio effects changes in real time simply by moving a fader or slider. This works much the same way as automation in full-featured audio editing programs like Emagic Logic, and it's a great time-saver. Real-time keyframing really shines if you need to do quick edits like ducking (temporarily lowering) background music so it doesn't drown out a section of dialogue, or for creating custom level fades. Let's try it out.

1   In the upper-right corner of the Audio Mixer, click the Record Audio Keyframes button (Shift-Cmd-K).

Record Audio Keyframes button

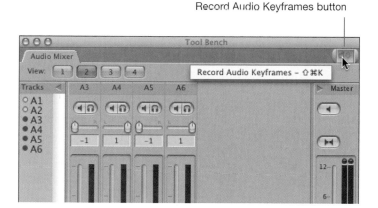

You can now record keyframes in real time, as the sequence plays.

NOTE ▶ You can also enable and disable audio keyframe recording by opening the User Preferences window (Final Cut Pro > User Preferences) and checking the Record Audio Keyframes box.

2   Let's open the User Preferences once more (choose Final Cut Pro > User Preferences or press Option-Q) and make sure that All is selected from the Record Audio Keyframes pop-up menu. Click OK.

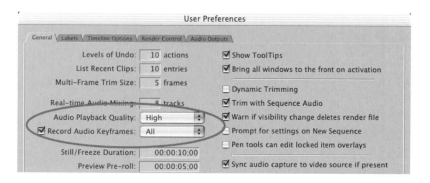

3 In the Timeline, move the playhead to the beginning of the sequence, then start playback.

4 In the Audio Mixer, grab the fader for Track A5, and move it up and down as the sequence plays.

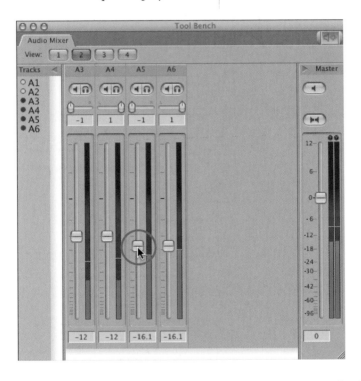

Track A5 and Track A6 are a stereo pair, so as you move the fader for Track A5, the fader for Track A6 comes along for the ride.

5 After you've made a few changes to the fade, stop playback.

In the Timeline, notice that your fader movements have been recorded as keyframes in the **SoundTrack.aif** clip overlay.

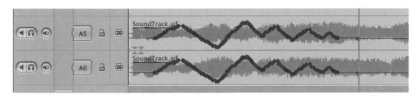

With the Record Audio Keyframes option set to All in User Preferences, Final Cut Pro records keyframes for every fader movement. Computers are getting faster all the time, but each of those little keyframes still takes up a small amount of your system's resources. To conserve CPU power for other processes, you can smooth the way Final Cut Pro records keyframes by selecting a different keyframe option from the User Preferences window.

6   Once again, choose Final Cut Pro > User Preferences.

7   Choose Record Audio Keyframes > Peaks Only. Click OK.

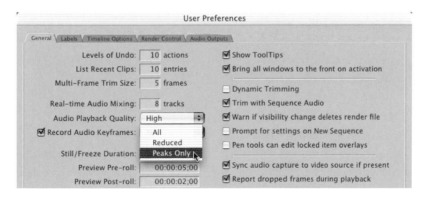

8   The playhead should now be somewhere in the middle of the sequence. Start playback from that point, to re-record the keyframes, but this time recording only the peaks.

9   In the Audio Mixer, move the fader for Track A5 up and down.

10 After a few movements, stop playback.

In the Timeline, only the peaks of your fader movements are recorded.

NOTE ▸ Peaks are represented by the points in the recording where the fader changes direction.

11 Click the Record Audio Keyframes button to disable real-time keyframing.

A word of warning: When you're done recording real-time keyframes, always disable this button! If you don't, adjustments you make to Level and Pan sliders in the Viewer and Timeline will automatically be recorded as keyframes, which may not be the exact effect you're after.

Resetting a Clip's Keyframes

If you record keyframes into a clip, either intentionally or accidentally, and then decide you don't want them, you can reset the clip and delete all keyframes by using the following technique.

1   In the Timeline, double-click the **SoundTrack.aif** audio clip in Track A5 to open it in the Viewer.

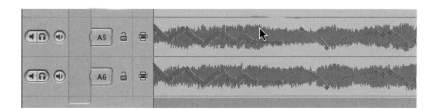

2   In the Viewer, click the Reset button.

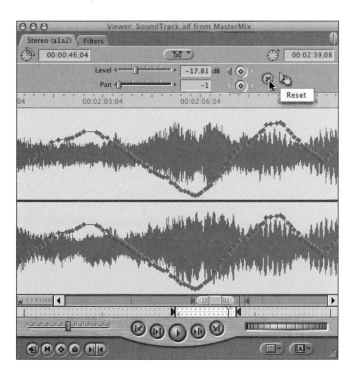

3   All of the clip's Level keyframes are deleted, and its overlay is set back
to its default value of 0 dB of boost/attenuation. However, at 0 dB this
track plays a bit too loud, so let's lower the level.

4   In the Viewer, grab the overlay and drop the level by approximately −16 dB.

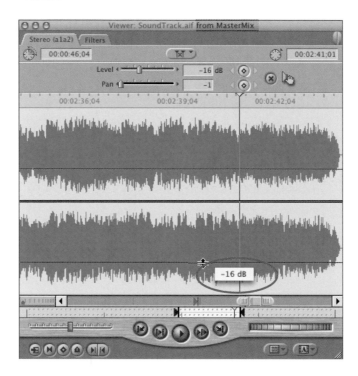

NOTE ▶ If you find it tricky to adjust the level overlay to −16 dB, Cmd-drag to gear down, and force Final Cut Pro to drag the overlay through all available dB settings. You can also enter a number directly into the Level numerical input box at the top of the Viewer.

5   Click the Timeline window to make it the active window, and play the sequence.

Give the sequence a good listen, and really concentrate on the level of the different parts that combine to make the mix. If it helps, close your eyes or turn off your computer monitor so don't have any visual distractions and can focus on the sound. If everything sounds great, then you're ready to move on. If not, head over to the Audio Mixer and make some more adjustments.

Subframe Audio Trimming

This sequence is more or less finished. However, there's one final edit to be made. If you look at the end of Track A2, you'll notice there's a hole in the dialogue.

Dialogue from A1 covers the first hole in A2

Holes in dialogue track (A2)

There's actually a hole a bit earlier, too, but the earlier hole is filled by dialogue from Track A1 so you don't notice anything missing. The second hole, however, is wide open, and as the young girl huffs, there's no audio to accompany her puffing cheeks. There's no sound! And let's face it, only the isolation tank industry is built on complete silence. You want to hear that fierce girl huff as she puffs, so let's fill this hole with the **uhhh.aif** clip located in the Browser.

1   In the Browser, double-click the audio file named **uhhh.aif**.

    The file opens in the Viewer.

2   Press the Viewer's Play button to audition the file.

    It sounds like someone saying, "Uhhh!" Okay, this is a great sound to fill the second hole in A2. Let's turn our attention back to the Timeline for a moment.

3 Make sure that overlays are on in the Canvas. If not, click the Canvas window to make it the active window, then choose View > Show Overlays.

By choosing View > Show Overlays in the Canvas, marker names (and properties) appear on top of the video in the Canvas and Viewer. For example, take a glance down the Timeline and note the marker above the second hole on Track A2.

4 Move the playhead so it's directly over the marker by pressing Shift-M (to jump to the next marker) or Option-M (to jump to the previous marker).

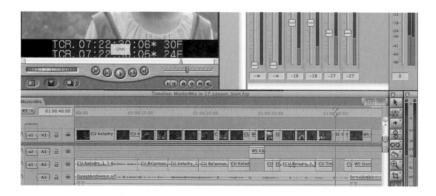

In the Canvas window, the marker's name (*Uhh*) is printed on top of the video. The audio file is named Uhh, the marker is named Uhh ....
It looks like the editor is trying to tell us something here. And indeed, the **uhhh.aif** clip should be dropped in Track A2 at the marker Uhh. But first, the **uhhh.aif** clip needs to be trimmed.

5   In the Viewer, move the playhead to the end of the silent portion at the front of the **uhhh.aif** waveform.

Notice that no matter how close you try to get, there's a little bit of space between the playhead's position and the beginning of the wave. This is quite common when you are trying to sync up short, percussive sounds such as punches, car crashes, and grunts of displeasure. Why? In video, the smallest unit of temporal measurement is the frame, which for NTSC video lasts for exactly 1/29.97 of a second and for PAL lasts 1/25 of a second. The smallest unit of temporal measurement for an audio file, on the other hand, is a sample. Assuming a sampling rate of 48 kHz, this means 48,000 samples pass per second, or roughly 1600 samples per frame. As you can see, audio's temporal resolution is much finer than video's—when it comes to sound, a lot can happen in the space of a frame.

Indeed, this **uhhh.aif** wave begins almost halfway through the frame, so to sync up the playhead to the wave, you must use the following trick:

6   Shift-drag the playhead to the beginning of the wave.

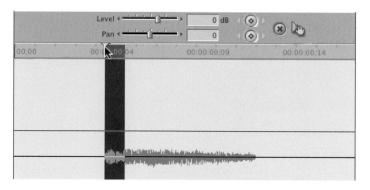
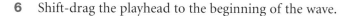

Holding Shift lets you adjust the playhead in increments of 1/100 of a frame, which in turn lets you snug the playhead right up the beginning of the wave.

7   Press I to set an In point.

8   In the Timeline, move the Source slider to Track A2.

9   In the upper-right area of the Viewer, grab the clip drag handle, drag the **uhhh.aif** clip into the Canvas window, and choose Overwrite.

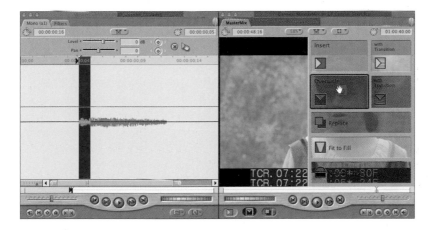

The **uhhh.aif** clip is placed into the hole (gap) in Track A2.

10 Play the sequence from just before the newly inserted audio.

An "Uhh!" sound plays in time with the girl's huff.

11 Adjust the level of the new clip until it mixes well with the other audio in the sequence.

What You've Learned

- To enable Mute and Solo buttons in the Timeline, click the Audio Controls button.
- All dialogue in a sequence should use the same average level as the reference tone used to calibrate your system, typically a 1 kHz sine wave tone.
- Broadcast video, analog videotape, and DVD video use different average and peak dialogue levels.
- The Audio Mixer provides an interface similar to a hardware mixing console, with faders and Mute and Solo buttons you can use to adjust the levels of your sequence's sound.
- To record audio keyframes in real time, enable the Record Keyframes button in the Audio Mixer.

18

Lesson Files   Lessons > Lesson_18 > 18_Lesson_Start.fcp

Lessons > Lesson_18 > 18_Lesson_Finished.fcp

Media   Media > Lesson_18_Media

Time   This lesson takes approximately 45 minutes to complete.

Goals   Configure and use multiple audio outputs

Configure Final Cut Pro to use a hardware audio interface

Create a custom audio outputs preset

Insert sync beeps to help the post-production facility line up audio tracks

Convert sync beeps into actual two-pops

Remove level, pan, and audio effects information to flatten audio clips for export

Export audio to AIFF(s) and OMF

Configuring Audio Output

When it comes to audio editing, Final Cut Pro has many great features—you'll find it offers all of the effects and mixing functions you need to create great-sounding audio mixes. If, however, you have access to a dedicated audio editing program like Logic Platinum, or if you send your audio out to a post-production facility for final mixdown and mastering, you should know a few extra things in order to export your audio out of Final Cut Pro and move it into your audio finishing application. This chapter covers all of those things, from using multiple outputs to exporting AIFF and OMF (Open Media Framework) files.

Working with Multiple Outputs

In previous versions of Final Cut Pro, all audio tracks were mixed to a single pair of stereo outputs. That was sufficient for most editing purposes, but if you intended to output your sequence to a multichannel recording device such as a Digibeta deck, some extra work was required. With the release of Final Cut Pro 4, you now have access to 24 separate audio output channels. The advantages of this feature are many and varied. For example, you can now output dialogue to the first and second audio tracks on a Digibeta deck, and music/effects to the third and fourth tracks. Or if you are archiving a complex score created in Final Cut Pro, you can now link three ADATs together to record that complex score over all 24 channels available to Final Cut Pro 4.

The true power of this feature shines clearly for users working in the various surround-sound formats that are the new hot-ticket item in video (particularly for DVD-Video). Although Final Cut Pro 4 does not currently allow surround mixing directly in the program, you can nonetheless import surround audio stems (finished surround-sound files) mixed in a program such as Logic, then hear these stems in all their larger-than-life, surround-sound glory as you edit the sequence's video.

MORE INFO ▶ *To mix in surround sound, you need a few extra tools. For starters, you must have a sound card with multiple audio outputs, such as the Emagic EMI 2|6 (two inputs and six outputs), and a separate speaker for each channel in the surround mix. For example, if you are mixing 5.1 surround, you need six speakers (one full-range speaker for each of the five main channels, plus a sixth speaker that is a subwoofer used to output the ".1," or low-frequency effects channel). But that's not all; you also need an audio editing program capable of surround mixing. Logic Platinum 6 is the most cost-effective program for surround mixing currently on the market. The Apple Pro Training Series includes a great book on using Logic Platinum, with a whole lesson devoted to mixing 5.1 surround. To learn more, check out* Apple Pro Training Series: Logic 6.

Logic Platinum's Pan
window lets you place
sounds anywhere in the
Surround spectrum.

Choosing Your Audio Interface

In order to fully use multiple outputs, you *must* have an audio interface that
has more than two outputs, such as Emagic's EMI 2|6. If you don't have an
audio interface with multiple outputs, you can still follow the exercises in
this section, though you will not be able to hear tracks assigned to outputs
other than output 1 and 2. If, however, you do have an audio interface with
multiple outputs, you may find that Final Cut Pro does not automatically
recognize it. This is easy to fix using Final Cut Pro's Audio/Video Settings
window.

1   Open the file named Lesson_18 > **18_Lesson_Start.fcp**.

2   Choose Final Cut Pro > Audio/Video Settings (Option-Cmd-Q).

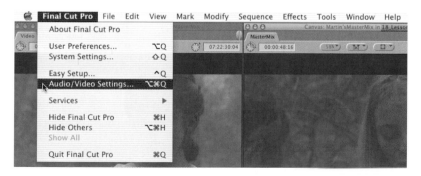

The Audio/Video Settings window opens. At the bottom of this window is a setting labeled Audio Playback. This setting tells Final Cut Pro which audio interface to send sound through.

3   Choose your audio interface from the Audio Playback menu.

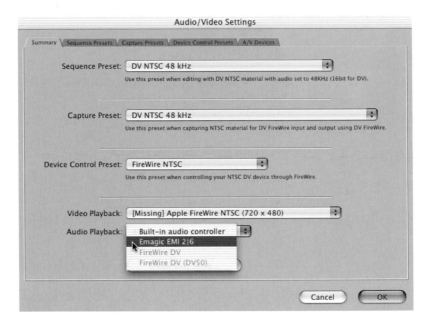

TIP If your audio interface doesn't appear in the Audio Playback menu, there are a few things you need to check. First, make sure the cable connecting the audio interface to your computer is plugged in and working, and that the audio interface itself is getting power. If that's all fine, then check to ensure you've installed the audio interface's drivers! Although OS X's Core Audio architecture is exceptionally proficient at recognizing the many different audio interfaces on the market, Core Audio can't see an audio interface if it isn't told how to find it. That is the driver's job. For more information, refer to your audio interface's manual or visit the manufacturer's Web site.

4   Click OK to close the Audio/Video Settings window.

Setting Up the Sequence

Before you can use multiple outputs, you must configure Final Cut Pro so that it knows exactly how many outputs you need. In the following example, you will configure Final Cut Pro to use 6 separate audio outputs, though you can follow these steps to configure up to 24 discrete audio outputs.

1   Click anywhere in the Timeline to make it the active window.

The audio tracks are part of the sequence we are currently working on, so to change them we need to use the Sequence Settings window.

2   Choose Sequence > Settings (Cmd-0). The Sequence Settings dialog opens with the General tab displayed.

The Sequence Settings window is used to adjust the settings of the sequence you are currently working on. All of the settings located here can also be found in Final Cut Pro's User Preferences dialog. However, the User Preferences window affects only the settings of newly created sequences, not currently open ones. To change the settings of the current sequence, you *must* use the Sequence Settings window.

3   In the Sequence Settings window, select the Audio Outputs tab.

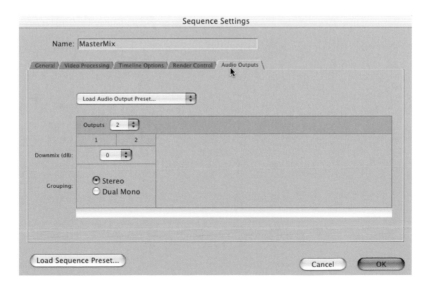

Toward the middle of the Audio Outputs tab is a setting labeled Outputs, which currently shows two audio outputs available. Let's enable six outputs. By setting up six discrete audio outputs, you can use Final Cut Pro to monitor a 5.1 surround mix Six discrete audio outputs provide one output for each channel in the surround mix.

4   From the Outputs menu, choose 6.

To the right of the two original outputs, four new ones appear.

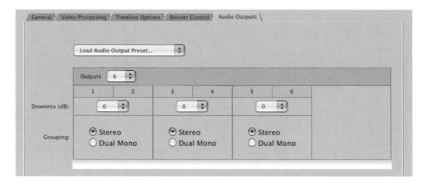

Notice the area labeled Grouping. Right now each output is grouped as one-half of a stereo pair. If you are outputting to a multichannel device such as a Digibeta deck where you want stereo dialogue in channels 1 and 2 and music/effects in channels 3 and 4, stereo grouping is a good option because it maintains the stereo shape of the file, as determined by the panning you have set. Dual Mono, on the other hand, treats each track as a mono source, and the option to pan the track from left to right is removed. This is perfect for playing surround audio files mastered in an audio program like Logic 6 Platinum, but if you still want to pan tracks in Final Cut Pro, Dual Mono is not the correct setting. To demonstrate this fact, let's assign outputs 3 and 4 as dual mono outputs.

5   In the Grouping area for outputs 3 and 4, choose Dual Mono.

NOTE ▶ In audio, an interesting phenomenon occurs when you play two tracks containing exactly the same content The overall volume of the tracks increases by 6 dB. Tracks that are close in content but not exactly the same will still cause volume spikes of 3 dB (sometimes even more). This creates problems in Final Cut Pro, because a stereo track that doesn't clip Final Cut Pro's Audio Meter can suddenly cause clipping if played in dual mono. To help you avoid this, Final Cut Pro automatically attenuates dual mono outputs by 3 dB, as you can see in the Downmix (dB) menus for outputs 3 and 4 in the preceding figure.

6   Click OK to close the Sequence Settings window. (If you get a dialog warning that your audio device doesn't support the selected number of outputs, just click OK.)

7   If the Audio Mixing windows arrangement is not open on your screen, choose Window > Arrange > Audio Mixing.

In the Audio Mixer, notice that the Master pane now has six instead of just two level meters—one for each output.

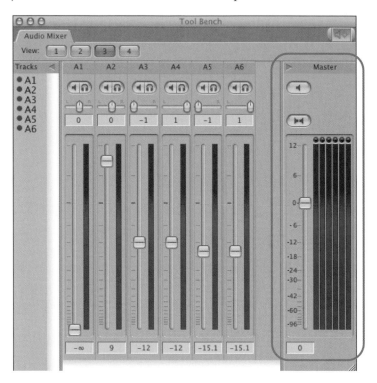

Setting a Track's Audio Output

Final Cut Pro is now configured to use six audio output channels. The next step is to tell each audio track in the Timeline which output channel to send its sound through. To do so, you'll use shortcut menus available in both the Audio Mixer and Timeline.

1 In the Audio Mixer's Track Selection pane, Ctrl-click Track A3 and choose Outputs > 3.

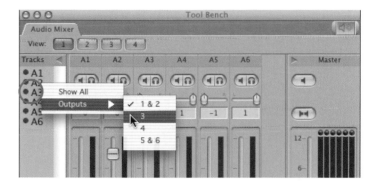

Track A3 is now assigned to audio output 3. You can also assign audio track outputs right in the Timeline window.

2   In the Timeline window, locate Track A4 and Ctrl-click close to the right edge of the track header.

A menu appears.

3   Choose Audio Outputs > 4.

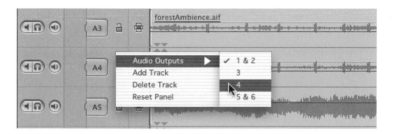

4   Using one of the techniques you've just learned, assign Track A5 and Track A6 to audio outputs 5 and 6. Because Track A5 and Track A6 are a stereo pair (as determined by the Audio Output settings we made earlier), you need to assign only one of them to outputs 5 and 6; the other one will come along for the ride automatically.

So, Tracks A1, A2, A5, and A6 are assigned to stereo outputs, and Track A3 and Track A4 are assigned to mono outputs. Look at the Audio Mixer's pan sliders—and notice that the tracks assigned to stereo outputs have a pan slider available, but the two tracks assigned to mono outputs have their pan sliders deactivated. The moral of this story is: If you need to pan a track, you must assign it to a stereo pair of outputs. (If need be, you can always open the sequence settings and change the audio outputs grouping for 3 and 4 back to a stereo pair.)

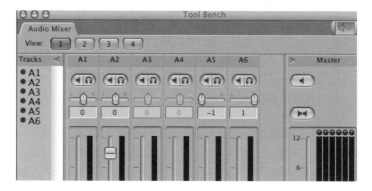

Downmixing to Stereo

If you don't have an audio interface with multiple outputs, you can still edit a sequence configured to use multiple audio outputs by using the Audio Mixer's Downmix button. Downmixing is the process of taking the audio from several outputs and mixing it together so it plays from a stereo pair of audio outputs. Let's check it out now.

1   Play the sequence from the beginning.

     Notice that all six level meters in the Audio Mixer's Master pane are active, which means audio is being sent to all six outputs.

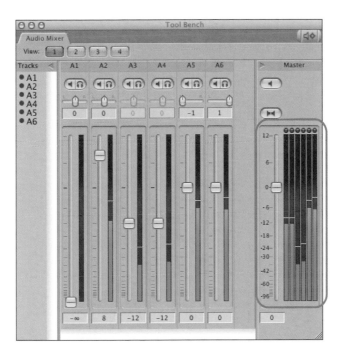

2   Above the Master pane's fader, click the Downmix button.

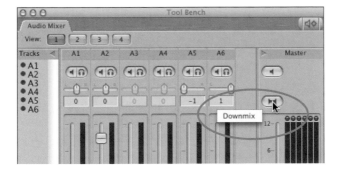

All six outputs are downmixed to outputs 1 and 2, and only the level meters for outputs 1 and 2 are now active in the Master pane.

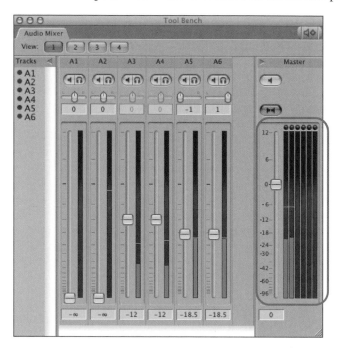

Creating an Output Preset

If you find yourself editing a lot of projects that use multiple outputs, save yourself some time by creating an output preset. For the sake of example, the following steps show you how to create a 5.1 audio output preset, though you can use the same steps to create a preset with any configuration of outputs you use often.

1   Choose Final Cut Pro > User Preferences > Audio Outputs tab.

2   Select the Default Stereo preset and click the Duplicate button.

    The Audio Output Presets Editor dialog opens.

3   Name the new preset *5.1 Surround*, type a brief description in the Description field to remind you of this setting, assign the Outputs setting to 6, and set each group of channels to Dual Mono.

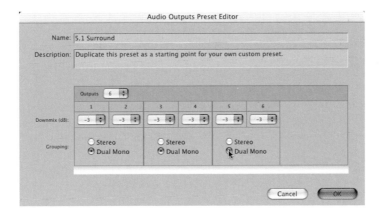

4   Click OK to close the Audio Output Presets window, and then click OK to close the User Preferences window.

5   Click the Timeline window to make it active, then choose Sequence > Settings.

The Sequence Settings window opens.

6   In the Sequence Settings window, choose the Audio Outputs tab.

7   From the Load Audio Output Presets menu, choose the new 5.1 Surround preset.

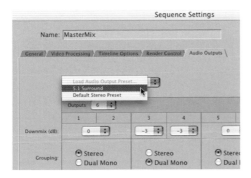

The 5.1 Surround preset is loaded and ready to go.

8   Click OK to close the Sequence Settings window.

Exporting Audio for Sweetening

Final Cut Pro 4's audio mixing capabilities are well developed, and you can confidently create full audio mixes right in the application. But just the same, if you have access to a specialized multi-track audio editor such as Logic Platinum, you may want to use the audio editing program's high-quality effects and dedicated audio features to *sweeten* the sound of your sequence.

Flattening Audio Clips

Specialized audio programs like Logic Platinum have some great digital signal processing effects designed to take audio that already sounds good and make it truly sparkle. Consequently, if you have a program like Logic, it's often best to sweeten your audio there. To prepare your sequence for export to an audio editing program, you should remove any audio filters applied in Final Cut Pro, reset the audio level of all clips to 0, and return the tracks to their default pan positions. This provides a blank canvas with all audio clips returned to their default settings, which is exactly what you want if you intend to touch up your audio outside of Final Cut Pro.

You can easily flatten your audio clips using the Remove Attributes feature:

1   Click the Timeline window to make it active, and then press Cmd-A.

All of the sequence's clips are selected.

2   Hold the Ctrl key, click any of the sequence's audio clips, and then choose Remove Attributes from the contextual menu.

The Remove Attributes dialog box opens.

NOTE ▶ You can also remove the attributes of an individual clip by selecting it, Ctrl-clicking, and choosing Remove Attributes.

3 Under the Audio Attributes section of the window, check the Levels box and also the Pan and Filter's boxes, if they are available. If the Pan and Filters choices grayed out, there is no pan data or audio filters applied to the sequence's audio clips.

4 Click OK.

All filters and level and pan information are removed from all of the sequence's selected audio clips. As a result, each clip's level overlay is returned to 0 dB (note that in the Audio Mixer, each fader has returned to the 0 dB setting) and each track's Pan slider is returned to its default setting.

Using Sync Beeps

Sync beeps are short, one-frame audio blips used for synchronizing audio tracks once they are imported into the audio editing application. If you are exporting your audio tracks for sweetening in an external audio editor such as Logic Platinum, a sync beep is an important element that you should add to every track in your project. The reason for this is simple When you bring your exported audio files into the external audio editing program, you need some way to sync up all the individual tracks—voilà, sync beep. And there are other benefits as well. For example, if you are using a noise filter such as Waves X-Noise (www.waves.com) to clean hiss or unwanted clicks and sputters out of your audio, a slight amount of delay is always added to the sweetened audio. This delay is small, but it's enough to throw a track out of sync with the other tracks in the sequence. Noise filters are often used to clean up dialogue tracks, which can quickly throw the dialogue out of sync with the actor's lips. Without a sync beep, you'll have one heck of a time trying to line these tracks back up.

A sync beep can be any short blast of sound. To keep it easy, we'll create a sync beep using the test tone from the Test Bars and Tone generator, and place it at the very beginning of each track in the sequence.

> **NOTE** ▶ It's also a good idea to add a sync beep at the very end of each audio track. Audio tracks might be in sync at the beginning but grow progressively out of sync over time, due to audio effects such as noise filters. Adding sync beeps at the end of the sequence's tracks helps you detect this problem. This exercise only covers adding sync beeps at the front of each track, though you can easily apply what you learn here to add them at the end as well.

1   In the Viewer, choose Bars and Tone (NTSC) from the Generators pop-up menu.

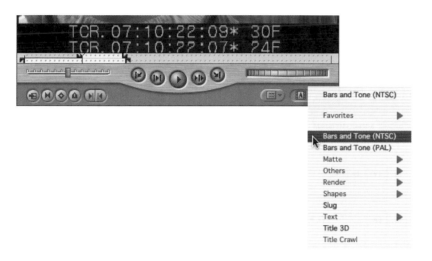

2 Press I to mark an In point in the Viewer.

Since the sync beep should be only one frame long, let's also set an Out point at the end of this same frame.

3 With the playhead still on the same frame, press the O key to mark an Out point, to mark a one-frame duration.

You are about to drop this one-frame clip at the beginning of your sequence. It's a small clip, so to see the results of this edit, let's zoom in on the beginning of the sequence.

4 In the Timeline, zoom in as close as you can on the first frame of the sequence.

5   From the Viewer, drag the one-frame color bars clip and insert it into the A1 track, at the very front of the sequence.

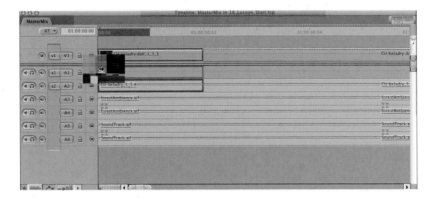

Since we had the V1 source track patched to the V1 destination track in the track controls panel, all of the tracks push right to make space for this one-frame clip. Notice that one frame of test bars has been inserted at the beginning of the V1 video track. You probably don't want this frame in your video stream, so let's get rid of it.

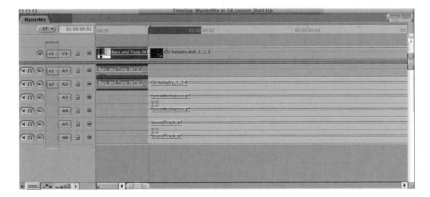

6   Option-click the test bars in the V1 track.

Holding Option temporarily disables the link between the video and audio portions of the clip, which in turn lets you select the video portion without selecting the audio portion.

7   Press Delete.

The test bars are removed from the sequence, but the test tone is left behind.

8   Select the test tone at the front of the A1 track, and press Cmd-C to copy it.

9   Drag the a1 and a2 source controls until they are lined up with the A3 and A4 destination controls.

10 Press the Home key to jump the playhead to the beginning of the sequence.

11 Press Cmd-V to paste the one-frame sync beep into Track A3 and Track A4.

12 Repeat steps 9 through 11 to paste the sync beep into Track A5 and Track A6.

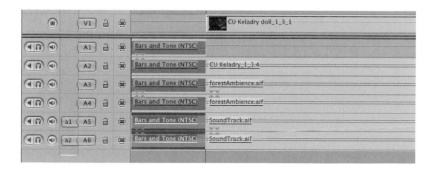

Using Two-Pops

Two-pops originated as a way for movie projectionists to ensure the movie's sound was in sync with the picture. You've probably seen this at the beginning of films where there's a visual countdown that looks like a second hand sweeping around a clock: 10, 9, 8, 7, 6, 5, 4, 3, *pop*. The "pop" is only a single frame, and it falls directly on the countdown's number 2. A two-pop!

Two-pops are still used today to synchronize audio with video. Like a sync beep, a two-pop is placed at the very beginning of the sequence, though unlike a sync beep, there's always *exactly* 2 seconds of black and silence between the two-pop and the first frame of video. In the last exercise, you added sync beeps to each audio track in the sequence, and it's very easy to convert those sync beeps to actual two-pop. Let's do that now.

1   Choose Sequence > Settings (Cmd-0). The Sequence Settings window opens.

2   In the Sequence Settings window, click the Timeline Options tab.

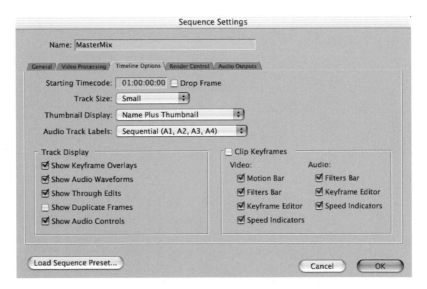

At the top of the Timeline Options tab is a setting called Starting Timecode. The Sequence currently starts at 01:00:00:00, which is exactly where we want the first frame of the video to begin. However, to create a two-pop we need to add two seconds to the beginning of the sequence. This means the sequence must be altered to start at 00:59:58:00.

3   In the Starting Timecode text box, enter *00:59:58:00*, press Return to lock in this change, and then click OK to close the Sequence Settings window.

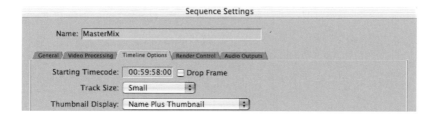

Back in the Timeline, your sequence updates to begin at 00:59:58:00.

In the next few steps, you'll move all of the sequence's audio and video clips—except for the sync beeps—forward so they begin at 01:00:00:00.

4   Click the Timeline to make it active, and then press Cmd-A to select all of the sequence's clips.

5   Hold the Cmd key and click each of the sync beeps to deselect only the sync beeps.

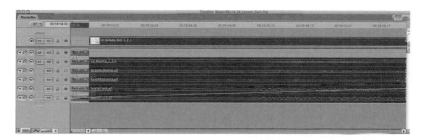

6   In the Timeline, zoom out so you can see the first three or four seconds
of the sequence.

7   Move the selected clips forward to 01:00:00:00.

This sequence is almost finished. Before moving on, let's fill the gap at
the beginning of the V1 track with a black slug.

8   Ctrl-click the gap at the front of the V1 track and choose Fill with Slug.

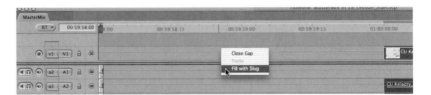

A black video slug fills the gap. Your two-pop is added, and you are
now ready to output this sequence's audio.

Exporting Audio to AIFF

Final Cut Pro's export options include an Export Audio to AIFF(s) function that creates a single AIFF file for every audio output in your project. It's important to understand that this option exports a single AIFF file for each *output channel* assigned in the sequence settings, not for each *track* in the sequence. Consequently, if you have two or more tracks assigned to the same audio output channel, these tracks will be combined into one AIFF file.

1   Choose File > Export > Audio to AIFF(s).

The Save dialog appears. Like all Save dialogs, this one lets you name your file and navigate to the folder you wish to save it in, so let's do that now.

2   Leave your AIFF file(s) as the default name, **MasterMix.aif**, and navigate to the Lesson_18 folder.

At the bottom of the Save dialog are three menus: Sample Rate, Sample
Size, and a final option called Files. The next three steps involve these
menus.

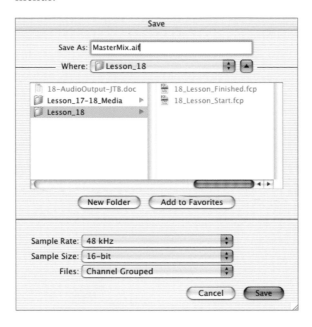

3   From the Sample Rate menu, choose 48 kHz.

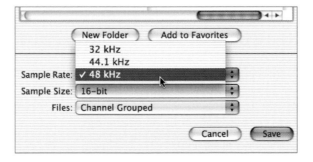

The general rule of thumb here is to choose the sampling rate that
matches the sampling rate of your sequence. Because most video projects use a sampling rate of 48 kHz, that is the default sampling rate
and the one you'll most often choose when exporting AIFFs. You also
have the option of choosing 32 kHz or 44.1 kHz.

NOTE ▶ An audio file's sampling rate determines the number of samples in a second of the file. A sample is the audio equivalent of a video frame, and it holds a discrete, single unit of the audio file's sound. When played in quick succession, these samples combine to create music in much the same way as a series of video frames combine to make a moving picture. At 48 kHz, 48,000 audio samples combine to make 1 second of music, while 44.1 kHz uses 44,100 samples per second, and so on.

4 From the Sample Size menu, choose 24-bit.

Sample size determines the file's *bit depth*, or the amount of information that is recorded to represent the sound of each individual sample. A 24-bit file stores more information per sample, which in turn preserves more of the audio file's sound. Even if the source audio files that make up your sequence are 16-bit, you should still export to AIFF using the 24-bit Sample Size option. The reason? Final Cut Pro internally processes audio using 32-bit calculations, which yields an even higher sound quality than 24-bit. Consequently, if you've raised or lowered the volume of the file, added effects, or even just panned the sound from side to side, Final Cut Pro has performed its aural manipulations at a very high sample size. To preserve as much of that quality as possible, choose 24-bit.

NOTE ▶ The Audio to AIFF(s) export option provides the only method of exporting a 24-bit audio file from Final Cut Pro. QuickTime export is limited to 16-bit.

However, you should keep a few things in mind. First, make sure your audio editing program can use 24-bit audio files (some don't). Second, think about what you intend to do with these files. For example, CD-Audio discs use only 16-bit audio files, so if you are going to record these AIFFs to an audio CD, choose the 16-bit option.

5   From the Files menu, choose Channel Grouped.

Channel Grouped tells Final Cut Pro to export one AIFF for each audio output used in your sequence. It does so in the following fashion Stereo pairs are exported as a single, interleaved stereo file, while dual mono channels are output as individual, mono AIFFs.

The Stereo Mix option takes all outputs and downmixes them into a two-channel stereo file, in the following fashion:

- All stereo-paired outputs are exported with odd-numbered outputs mixed into the left channel and even-numbered outputs mixed into the right channel.

- All dual mono outputs are mixed equally into the left and right channels, which centers their stereo image.

NOTE ▶ When you downmix, each track's volume is adjusted by the dB amount specified in the Downmix menu for its audio output. This menu is located in the Audio Outputs tab of the Sequence Settings window.

6   Click the Save button.

The Exporting Audio AIFF(s) dialog opens to let you know Final Cut Pro is exporting the files. When this window disappears, your exported AIFFs are finished and waiting in the Lesson_18 folder you selected in step 2.

Exporting Audio to OMF

Open Media Framework (OMF) files are the best choice for moving your sequences into an audio application for sweetening, because OMF files maintain the layout of clips in each track. An OMF file maintains audio clip positions in the sequence by including the source media for all clips, each clip's source media In and Out points, the clip's In point and time position in the Timeline track, and any handles (if desired). Consequently, OMF files are self-contained and can be easily transported from system to system.

> **NOTE ▶** Being self-contained, OMF files are often very large. However, there's a 2 GB limit on the size of OMF files. This equals approximately 7 hours of 48 kHz, 16-bit mono audio.

Level, panning, and audio filter information is not exported into the OMF file, so any changes you've made to clip volume or pan position will be ignored, and audio effects will be stripped from the clips when you export to OMF. In fact, only cross-fade information can be exported with the OMF file. Let's check the process out.

1   In the Timeline, click the Audible button (aka Track Visibility control) to make it green for each audio track you wish to export into the OMF file.

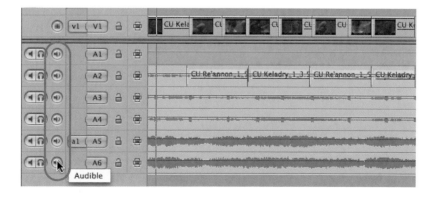

The Audible button is the only one that determines whether a track is exported to the OMF file—the Mute and Solo buttons are always over-ridden when exporting to OMF.

2   Choose File > Export > Audio to OMF. The OMF Audio Export dialog box appears.

3   From the OMF Audio Export window's Sample Rate menu, choose the desired sampling rate.

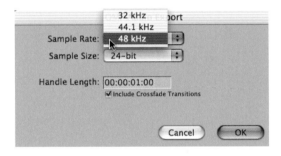

4   From the Sample Size menu, choose the desired sample size.

5   In the Handle Length setting, enter a timecode value to represent the length of the handles Final Cut Pro should apply to both ends of the exported audio clips.

Handles are extra media included before and after the active segment of the audio clip. They are used to create smooth cross fades between audio clips, and it's always a good idea to include handles of at least one second (timecode value 00:00:01:00). However, feel free to create larger or smaller handles if it suits your purposes.

6   If you've added cross fades to audio clips in the sequence, select the Include Crossfade Transitions check box.

This option creates linear cross fades only, but you can use the cross-fade function of your audio editor to turn these linear cross fades into curved fades that smoothly transition from one clip to the next. (Curved cross fades are sort of like ease-in and ease-out motion curves in animations, but for audio levels.)

If you need to, you can disable the Include Crossfade Transitions check box, and Final Cut Pro will not export your sequence's audio cross fades into the OMF file. This is useful when you are working with audio editors that do not read cross-fade information from OMF files, or if you want to create cross fades using the more advanced features of your audio editor.

NOTE ▶ Logic Platinum happily reads and displays cross-fade information from OMF files, but other audio editing programs don't.

7   Click OK.

The Save dialog box opens.

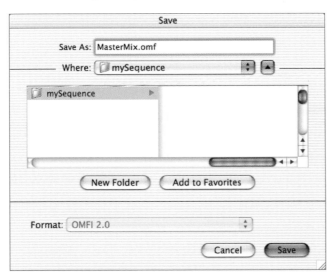

8   Name your OMF file, navigate to the Lesson_18 folder to save it, and then click Save.

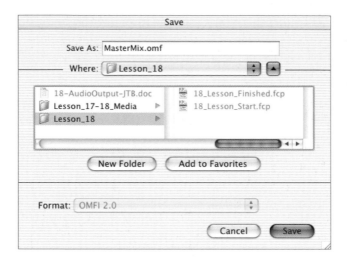

A progress dialog box opens and keeps track as Final Cut Pro exports the OMF file. When the progress dialog disappears, your OMF file is ready for import into an external audio editor such as Logic Platinum.

NOTE ▶ Nested sequences will be mixed together and exported as a single item.

What You've Learned

- To use a multichannel audio interface, set Final Cut Pro to recognize it in the Audio/Video Settings window.

- The Audio Outputs tab in the Sequence Settings window is used to configure your Final Cut Pro sequence to use multiple audio outputs.

- Flattening an audio clip removes all volume, pan, and audio effects information.

- The Export > Audio to AIFF(s) option exports a single AIFF for every audio output channel activated in your sequence settings, according to the choices defined for each sequence, in the Timeline Audio Output contextual menu.

- Final Cut Pro's Export > Audio to OMF option creates a single OMF file that contains the In and Out point, original media (with or without handles), track data, and time position of each clip in the sequence.

Titling with LiveType

Steve Martin has more than 12 years of experience as an editor, producer and trainer. He has taught workshops at NAB, Macworld, DV Expo, QuickTime Live and the American Film Institute. He is also a lead instructor for Apple's certified training program as well as president of Rippletraining.com, a site dedicated to helping people get the most from Apple's next-generation tools.

19

Lesson Files   Lessons > Lesson_19 > Lesson 19,ipr

Media   Media > Lesson_19_Media

Time   This lesson takes approximately 90 minutes to complete.

Goals   Configure the LiveType working environment

Apply and modify a background texture

Use a Webding glyph as a matte

Work with Photoshop files in LiveType

Animate glyphs

Add, modify, and apply effects to LiveFonts

Add text tracks and apply effects

Output a finished movie

Animating Type with LiveType

Welcome to the world of animated type and motion graphics. Just watch the opening of almost any television show, sit through a movie trailer, or view a commercial, and your eyes will marvel at the seemingly endless ways type can be made to fly, spin, float, and even dance across the screen. Animated type and other visual "eye candy" is the domain of motion graphics, a discipline that has come into its own in the past few years due to the proliferation of low-cost compositing and animation software and blazingly fast desktop computers.

What has changed very little however, is the often painfully slow process of bringing all of the graphic elements together, stacking them in the Timeline, then animating them through the means of keyframes and other Timeline-based conventions. Because this process can take hours—and in many cases, days—motion graphics work is frequently farmed out to design houses and other creative entities to deliver the final animation.

Enter LiveType. LiveType was created with the simple goal of giving artists, editors, and producers the ability to create incredible motion graphics in a fraction of the time it takes to create them in other applications.

At the core of LiveType is a media library that puts at your fingertips many of the necessary components to build your animations—components such as pre-rendered fonts, textures and other assorted objects. What's more, LiveType provides you with a completely different approach to animation that in many ways allows greater experimentation and creative freedom.

And with all this control, you do not want to lose sight of the fact that motion graphics, like many other commercial art forms, is a means to an end. Whether your goal is to help sell a new television show, create a DVD menu, or spice up some rather dull-looking video, LiveType will give you endless options for achieving your goals and keeping your clients happy. And maybe you might just get your weekends back.

Viewing the Finished Project

In this lesson, you will use LiveType to create an on-air promotion (or promo) for a water sports show.

1   Open the Lesson_19 folder that you copied to your hard drive, locate the movie labeled **Show Promo.mov**, and then double-click it to view the finished movie in QuickTime Player.

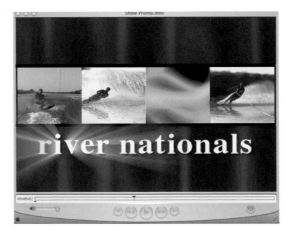

All movies that are exported from LiveType are QuickTime movies rendered with the animation codec. The animation codec is essential for two basic reasons: first, the animation codec yields extremely high image quality with little or no compression artifacts; and second, it supports alpha channels, which is the 8-bit portion of the image that defines transparency. This allows you to render out movies with or without backgrounds that can be easily and cleanly composited in applications like Final Cut Pro, Shake, or After Effects.

2   Open the LiveType project file **Lesson 19** from the Lesson_19 folder.

You may need to reconnect files to this project. You will find the two files needed in the Lesson_19_Media folder.

Double-clicking the **Lesson 19** project file opens the project file from which the promo movie was created. This is a seven-ayer composite consisting of animated text tracks, moving textures, video clips, and a Photoshop document.

3   Either click the Play button in the Canvas window or choose File > Render > Preview > Normal to render the movie to RAM, and then view the project in LiveType.

The section of the Timeline that is rendered is determined by setting In and Out point markers for the section you wish to preview. Just as you can in Final Cut Pro, you can either click-drag the markers, or you can use your I and O keys at the current playhead position to set them.

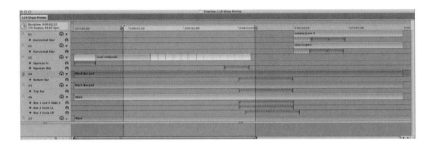

Configure the LiveType Work Environment

Start by creating a new project.

1   Choose File > New.

An untitled project tab appears next to the finished Lesson 19 tab in the Timeline. Like Final Cut Pro, LiveType allows you to work on multiple projects at once. To switch back and forth between projects, just click the tabs. For this lesson, you will want to keep the Show Promo project open to use as an occasional reference when building your animation.

NOTE ► All empty projects default with one empty text track labeled "01."

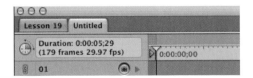

2   Save the untitled project to your Lesson_19 folder, calling it *L19 Show Promo*.

Before you begin, you will want to set up your project properties. LiveType is a resolution-independent application, which means it can output a variety of formats, from DV to HD. It is essential that you set your output resolution at the start of your project rather than in mid-production, otherwise all of your elements will have to be resized to fit the new resolution.

3 Choose Edit > Project Properties.

At the top of the window is the Presets pop-up menu. All untitled projects default to CCIR 601 NTSC output. If you are outputting your work for broadcast delivery using a third-party capture card, this is most likely the setting you will use. For this lesson, you will use the DV setting since the supplied lesson footage is in this format.

4   From the pop-up, choose NTSC DV 3:2.

Setting a Starting Timecode

LiveType sets its default starting timecode to 00:00:00:00. In many cases, you will want to change this to reflect the timecode reference of the destination application you will be compositing your animations into. For example, if you are working in Final Cut Pro, and your first frame of animation begins at, let's say, 01:02:15:12, then this is the number you would enter in this field to keep your animations in sync with your Final Cut Pro project. For now, just leave the start timecode at its default.

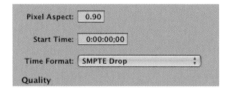

NOTE ▶ If you bring in a QuickTime movie with timecode for use as a background, the project start time will automatically inherit the starting timecode of the source movie file. This is useful because your Timeline will now reflect actual clip timecode.

Setting Render Quality

As mentioned earlier, there are two ways to preview. Therefore, LiveType gives you two separate render quality adjustments; one for Canvas previewing and another for menu previewing. There is also a third setting for choosing your final output quality. In most cases, you will want to leave this on High, which yields the maximum quality movies to disk.

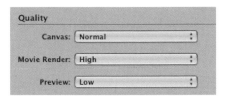

You can choose between four different render quality settings that effect both quality and render speed. The setting you choose depends largely on how long you are willing to wait while the movie compiles to RAM or disk. Generally speaking, complex projects with many layers and effects will require you to reduce the preview quality in order to speed up the production process.

Setting the Background Color

You can incorporate a background color into your projects by clicking the color box and choosing a new color from the Apple color picker. (The default is yellow.) Colored backgrounds can be useful when doing simple title treatments, like white type on black, or when you need to see greater contrast between elements that are otherwise too difficult to see over the default checkerboard background. To see the color displayed in the Canvas, you will need to increase the background's opacity.

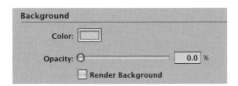

1   Click the Color box to bring up the Apple color picker. Choose a new color, then close the color box.

2   Drag the Opacity slider to 100%.

3   Click OK in the Project Properties box to accept the change.

In the Canvas window, you should now see your chosen color.

4   Choose Edit > Project Properties.

One more minor detail: Even though you have enabled a colored background, LiveType will still render out the background completely transparent unless you check the Render Background check box. As you will soon discover from the ensuing lesson, this also applies to any background elements you have in your Timeline.

5   Set the Opacity back to 0, then close the Project Properties window.

Applying and Modifying a Texture

You are now ready to begin building the show promo. A good place to start is by choosing an animated texture that will serve as the background that's in keeping with the watery theme of the show. LiveType supplies you with 174 different textures you can use as backgrounds, matte fills, and other assorted eye candy.

Adding a Liquid Texture

1   In the Media Browser, click the Textures tab.

2   From the Category pop-up, choose Liquid.

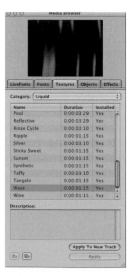

You can preview each texture in this category by clicking a name in the list. A great shortcut is to use your up and down arrow keys to move up and down through the list.

3   Scroll down until the Wave texture appears in the preview window of the Media Browser.

4   Add this texture to the Timeline by clicking the Apply to New Track button.

The texture is now added below the empty text track. Drag the thin gray track separator bar down below the wave texture, as shown.

NOTE ▸ Normally, tracks are added in a "top down" fashion, as in most compositing applications. However, because the texture is a full-screen element, LiveType placed it below the empty text track so that you don't have to reorder the layers.

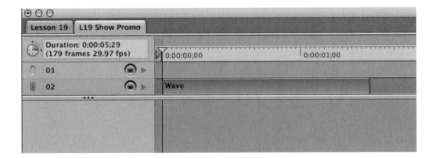

Changing the Track Duration

This promo will be tagged as part of a larger ad campaign that includes both 15-second teasers and full-blown, 60-second television spots. As such, you will be creating a promo tag that is six seconds in total duration that can be deployed at the tail of each commercial to promote the date and time of the show. Since the default length of this animated texture is only a second and a half, you will need to increase the texture's duration.

1   Click the Timing tab of the Inspector to reveal the timing properties of the selected track. Notice the current Speed defaults to 100%.

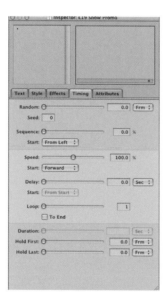

2   Click on the right edge of the track and drag to the right until the Out point of the track is just slightly past the six-second hatch mark on the time ruler.

Notice in the Inspector that the speed was auto-adjusted by the increase in duration—in this case, the clip was slowed down to roughly 25%. At this point, it would be a good idea to preview the track to see how the speed change has affected the motion of the texture.

3 Move your playhead to exactly six seconds in the Timeline, then press
O on your keyboard to mark an Out point.

4 Click the Play button in the Canvas to preview the texture between
the In and Out points. If you have a slower machine, you may want to
set your Canvas preview quality to Draft in order to speed things up.

Looping the Track

After watching the preview, you may have decided that the speed change
is now too slow for your taste, in which case you want to keep the default
speed, yet maintain the same six-second duration. The only way to accomplish this is to loop the track.

1 Make sure the track is still selected, and then enter *100* in the Speed
field in the Inspector. Then press Return on your keyboard. Notice the
clip returns to its original length.

2 In the Loop field, enter *5*, and then press Return.

3 Preview your change in the Canvas.

Changing the Track Color

As cool as this texture looks, your client thinks the blue is a bit too, well...blue. You're going to tone it down a bit.

1 Click the Attributes tab to bring up parameter adjustments for things such as Opacity, Scale, Rotation, and Color.

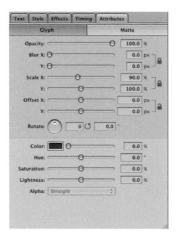

2 Drag the Hue slider to the right and to the left. Notice you get instant feedback in the Canvas window.

For this lesson, we give you the color coordinates, but feel free to use your own.

3 Enter *–3.1* for Hue. Enter *–52.5* for Saturation. Enter *–32.2* for Lightness.

TIP ▶ Use the Tab key to jump your cursor to each successive input field.

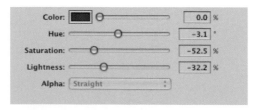

Working with Text Objects

After watching the finished piece, you may have noticed how the main visuals center around geometric shapes that animate and are filled with various clips of water skiers. These geometric shapes were created inside of LiveType using nothing more than a system font, then matting video to their alpha channels. The great thing about LiveType is that all text characters (or glyphs) on a text track are vector-based and can be independently moved, scaled, and animated without loss of resolution. Text tracks are represented in the Canvas by a blue track bar.

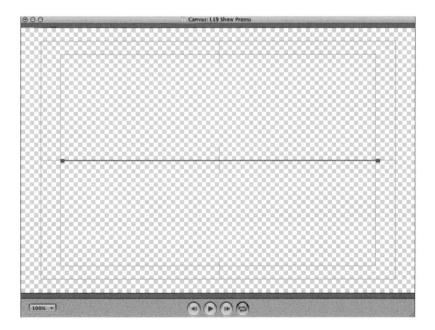

Let's see how to work with text objects in LiveType.

1   Click in the empty 01 track to make it active.

2   In the Media Browser, click the Fonts tab and scroll down the font family list in the left pane until you've located the Webdings font.

Webdings are a graphic designer's best friend. They are a library of useful little symbols and icons from airplanes to asterisks (and everything in-between) that are handy for quickly creating buttons, logos, or in our case, animated alpha mattes.

3   Make sure your playhead is parked at the beginning of the Timeline, then click Apply to add the Webdings font family to the empty text track.

NOTE ▶ You won't see the actual track in the Timeline until you enter some text in the Inspector.

Your next step is to choose a square-shaped glyph that will form the basis for the animated video squares that will contain the water skiers.

4   In the Inspector, Ctrl-click anywhere in the text input field. From the contextual menu that pops up, choose Font > Show Fonts to bring up the Fonts window.

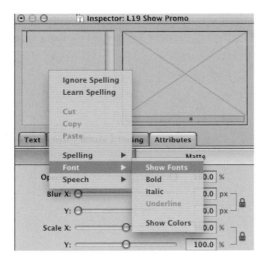

5 From the Extras pop-up menu at the bottom of the Fonts window, choose Show Characters to bring up the OS X Character Palette.

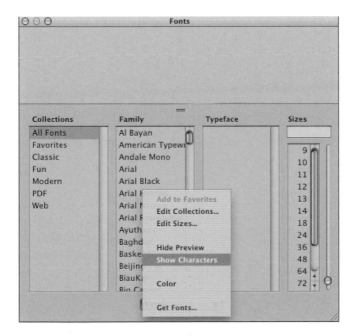

6 Choose All from the View pop-up. If your window does not look like the one shown in the following screen shot, click the triangle button in the lower-left corner. Choose Webdings from the Font pop-up in the lower-left corner of the window.

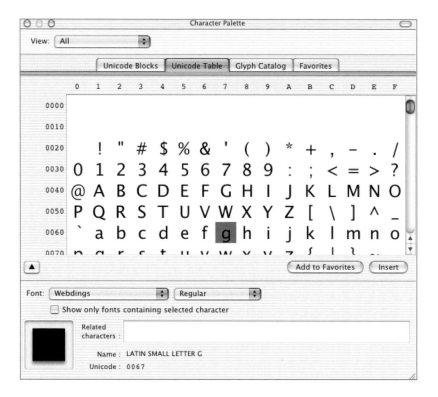

7 Click the Unicode Table tab to reveal a map of all alphanumeric keys and symbols for the Webding font family. To see which Webding glyphs map to which keys, just click a character while watching the glyph window at the lower-left corner of the window. The square glyph you are looking for is mapped to the lower-case "g." Click the Insert button on the lower left four times to add four squares to the text track.

8 Close the Character Palette window and the Fonts window.

A text track should now appear in the Timeline along with four gray squares in the Canvas window.

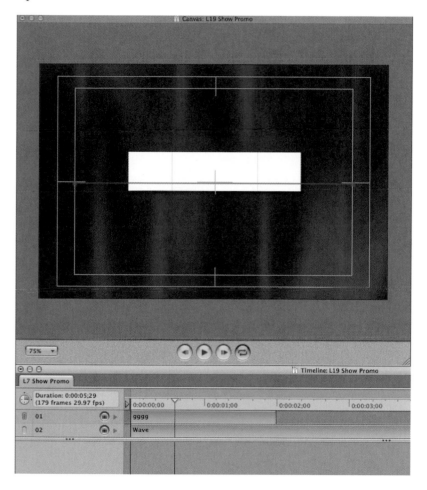

All text tracks are created with a default duration of two seconds. You can change this in the Timing tab of the Inspector.

9 Click the Timing tab in the Inspector and enter *6* seconds in the Duration field, then press Return.

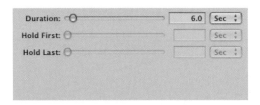

The text track is now extended to the six-second mark in the Timeline ruler area.

Next, you will adjust the tracking and size of each square in the Canvas.

10 In the Text tab of the Inspector, enter *200* in the Tracking input box, and then press Return.

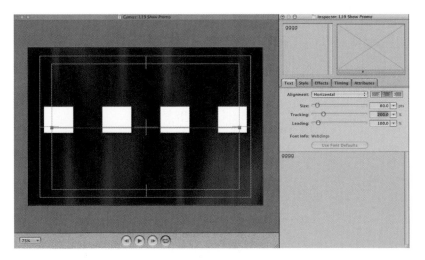

11 Click the Attributes tab and enter *200* in either the X or Y Scale property input field.

Since both X and Y values are locked, the aspect ratios of the glyphs remain locked and therefore keep the squares from becoming rectangles.

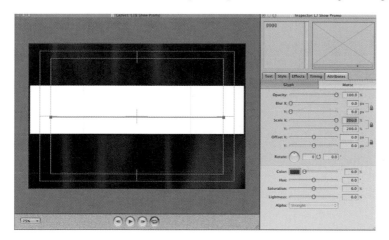

Matting Video to the Glyphs

Now that you have your glyphs placed in the Canvas, you will matte a video image into them.

1 Click the left-most glyph to select it.

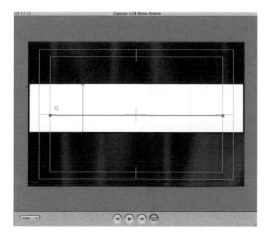

2 Click the Attributes tab (if it isn't selected already), then click the Matte subtab.

3 From the Matte To pop-up, choose Movie or Image.

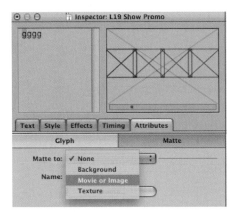

An open dialog appears that you will use to select the source for the matte.

4 Navigate to the Lesson_19_Media folder, locate the **Andrew Rips** clip and open it by double-clicking.

The video should now be filling the first box. However, it is currently scaled at 100 percent, revealing only a portion of the image.

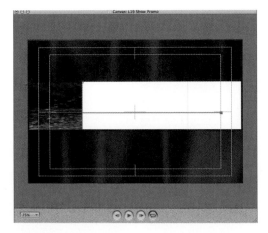

5   Still in the Inspector, drag the Scale slider on the Matte subtab to the left until the value reads zero.

At 0%, the image is scaled relative to the current size of the glyph, which after resizing, reveals most of the video image.

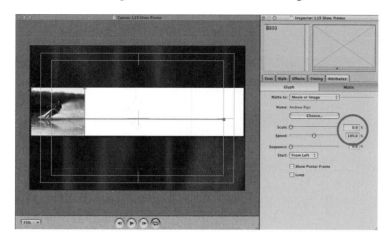

NOTE ► Using this method of matting does not allow you to reposition the video image relative to the position of the glyph. In order to do that, you will need to use the File > Place Background Movie command to add the movie to the Timeline, then choose Matte to Background from the Matte subtab. This feature is explored in much greater detail in the next chapter.

Now you will map the same video image to box 2 and box 4 (going from left to right).

6   Select box 2 and repeat steps 3 through 5.

7 Select box 4 and repeat steps 3 through 5.

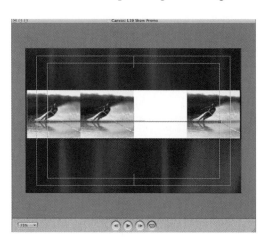

8 Choose File > Render Preview > Normal to see a low-resolution preview of your work thus far. Preview your hard work, then close the Preview window.

Changing the Video Speed

The great thing about LiveType is how quickly you can achieve different looks to your titles and animations by simply changing one or two attributes in the Inspector.

1 Click box 2 to select it, and then enter *50* in the Speed input field.

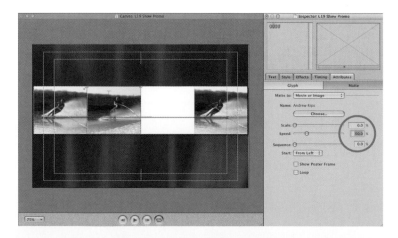

2 Click box 4 to select it, and then enter *25* in the Speed input field.

3 Render a preview to see the results.

Matting a Texture to a Glyph

You may have noticed that the third box is empty. This is because you are going to matte a texture to the remaining box for the purpose of breaking up the water ski visuals as well as providing a dynamic backdrop for the type elements that will promote the date and time of the show.

1 Click the Textures tab in the Media Browser, then choose Smoke from the Category pop-up menu.

2 Use your up and down arrow keys to locate the Waft texture.

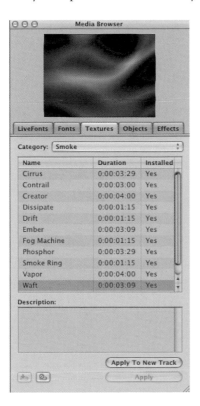

3 Click box 3 in the Canvas to select it.

4 Click the Attributes tab in the Inspector, then click the Matte subtab. (these items should still be selected from the previous steps.)

5 From the Matte to pop-up, choose Texture.

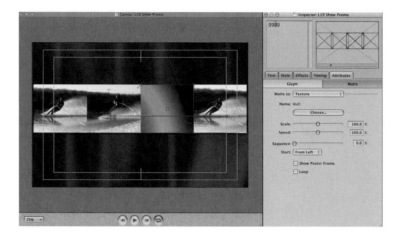

The Canvas window should now be showing the blue Waft texture matted to box 3.

Scaling and Colorizing the Texture

Although this texture looks interesting, it's not quite there yet. You are going to change its size and color.

1 Drag the Scale slider to zero to matte the glyph with the entire texture.

If you look back in the Texture tab of the Media Browser, you will notice that the Waft texture has a duration of 3:09. Because you matted this texture to a six-second text track, there are not enough frames for the texture to play the full length of the track. Therefore, you must loop the texture.

2   Click the Loop button in the Attributes tab, then preview.

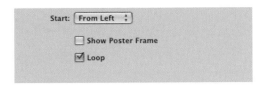

3   To change the texture's color, click the Glyph subtab and click the color box to bring up the Apple color picker. Choose a warm orange to visually offset all the blue in the background image. Then close the color picker.

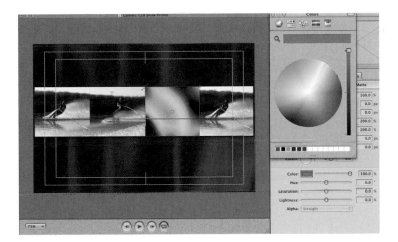

Working with a Photoshop Image

What would a still or motion graphics designer do without Photoshop? You simply cannot do without it because of the sheer amount of functionality it brings to the design process. In this promo, for example, the client decided that the images of the skiers would be greatly enhanced if they were bordered, top and bottom, by two black bars. Since there is no way to create objects of this nature directly in LiveType, the border was created in

Photoshop and saved in the Photoshop format to retain its transparent background.

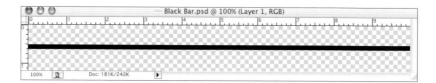

First, we place the image in LiveType.

NOTE ▶ LiveType 1.0.1 or earlier does not support Photoshop layers.

1   Make sure your playhead is at the beginning of the Timeline, then choose File > Place.

2   Navigate to your Lesson_19_Media folder, locate the **Black Bar.psd** file, and double-click it. The imported Photoshop image should now be sitting in the 01 track above the first two tracks.

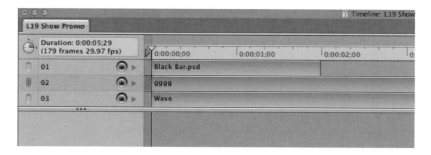

Now we change the image's duration.

3   Make sure the 01 track is selected, and then click the Timing tab of the Inspector. Enter 6 seconds into the Duration field to match the length of the 02 track below it.

You are now going to move the bar into place and then duplicate the track to create the second bar. Before proceeding, you will want to lock the 02 track to keep from accidentally moving any of the glyphs.

4   Select the 02 layer in the Timeline, then choose Layout > Lock Position to lock the four boxes into their current position in the Canvas.

5   Select the 01 track and choose layout > Lock Position to unlock the black bar.

6   Hold down the Shift key while dragging the black bar to the top edge of the skier glyphs.

> **TIP** ▶ The Shift key is a universal convention in most graphic applications for constraining the vertical position of an object while dragging. Once you get the object close to where you want it, you can hold down the Cmd key and use your arrow keys to nudge the objects one pixel at a time.

To create the lower bar, you will duplicate the track and then drag it into position.

7   Make sure the 01 track is still selected, and then choose Track > Duplicate Track.

8   Shift-drag the top bar and drag to the bottom edge of the skier glyphs.

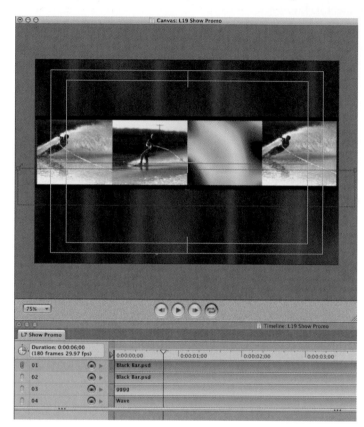

Animating Objects

At long last, it's time to animate your objects and make this promo really pop. In many motion graphic workflows, animation is generally approached after the main visual elements have been acquired or created, laid out in the Canvas, and shown to a client as a single-frame image to get their sign off that the design is still on track. The fact of the matter is, you don't want to spend a lot of time animating until you are sure your client likes your current creative direction. Of course, if you don't have any clients (yet) you can forget what I just said and start animating anytime you feel like it.

You will begin animating the glyph boxes with the matted ski clip. You might want to take another look at the finished Show Promo project to get a good idea of where you will be going. At about three seconds into the animation, all four boxes begin moving to different locations on the screen, with two of the boxes remaining onscreen, and two boxes leaving.

1   Select the 03 track and choose Layout > Lock Position to turn off locking.

A checkmark next to the menu item means locking is enabled for a particular track.

2   Drag your playhead to the three-second mark in the Timeline, then choose Track > Add New Effect.

A purple effect bar is now visible in the Timeline directly below the 03 text track.

Since we want the boxes to begin animating three seconds from the beginning of the Timeline, you will need to move the effect bar.

3   Click and drag the effect bar to the right until the left edge of the bar lines up with the playhead location.

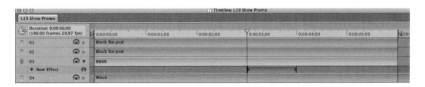

When an empty effect is initially applied, the effect is given the generic name New Effect. All effects have a default beginning and ending keyframe as represented by the left and right facing "half-diamonds." Keyframes can be selected by directly clicking them or by using the keyboard shortcuts Shift-K and Option-K.

TIP ▶ Shift-K moves the playhead forward, to the nearest keyframe to the right of the playhead, and Option-K moves the playhead backward, to the nearest keyframe to the left of the playhead. These keyboard shortcuts work only if your playhead is within the boundary of the effect, not outside of it.

In LiveType, effects are always applied to the entire text track. This means that each individual glyph that makes up a text track has the same effect applied to it initially. For example, if you animate the scale property of one glyph, all the other glyphs scale as well. To selectively choose which glyphs get effects applied to them, you will need to disable the effects for the glyphs you do not want the effect applied to. We'll do that next.

4   Click box 4 in the Canvas to select the glyph. A blue box around the glyph confirms your selection.

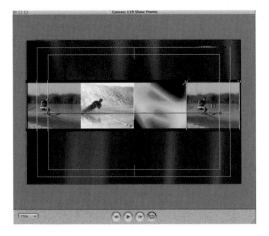

5   Click the Zoom pop-up in the lower-left corner of the Canvas and choose 50%. This will allow you to place objects outside the active image area.

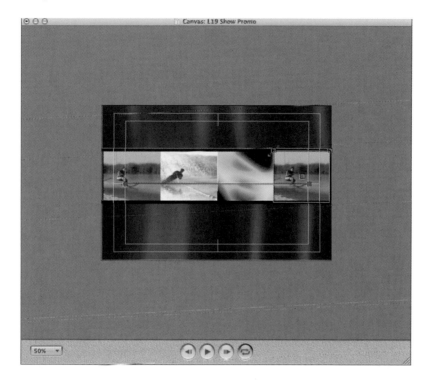

6   Make sure the effect bar is active, and then click the second keyframe half-diamond to select it. Selecting these keyframes might be a little tricky at first (be sure to click near the point of the arrow), but you'll get the hang of it.

7 In the Canvas, Shift-drag all four glyphs to the left, until the right edge of the fourth glyph is just outside of the left edge of the Canvas window.

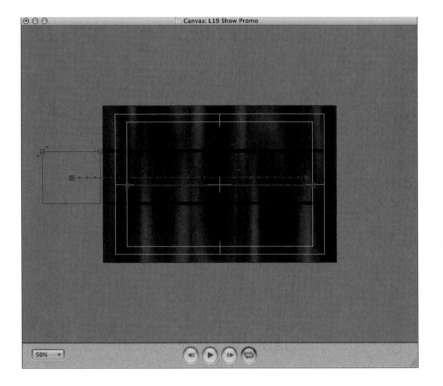

Notice that the trajectory for the glyphs is represented by a dotted line in the Canvas. If you look in the Inspector, you will also see a wireframe preview of your animation between your marked In and Out points. Notice, that the motion is applied to all four glyphs. If you want to see the animation with video, click the Play button in the Canvas.

TIP ▶ You may want to decrease your preview range so all six seconds of content does not have to be included in the render. You can set your In and Out point markers before and after the effect bar in the Timeline to render just the section you are working on.

Now you are going to selectively disable this motion effect from certain glyphs, namely, boxes 2 and 3.

8 Move your playhead to the beginning of the purple effect bar. This way, you can see all the glyphs on the screen at once, making it easier to select them.

9 Click box 2 in the Canvas to select it, and then click the Effects tab of the Inspector. If you have any trouble, check in the Inspector text box to be sure all of the text (the four letters "g") are deselected first.

10 Click the checkmark in the box to turn the effect off for this glyph.

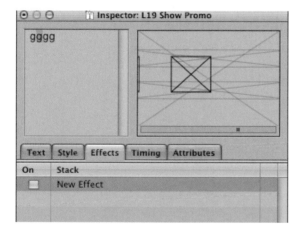

Notice the wireframe preview window in the Inspector. Now that the effect has been disabled for box 2, it just sits there motionless. If you wish, click the Play button in the Canvas to preview with video.

11 Click box 3 to select it, and then click the checkmark to turn it off the effect.

The wireframe preview updates to display the two center boxes with no motion applied to them. At this point, you are going to name your effect to more easily identify what effects are applied to your glyphs.

12 In the Inspector, double-click the name of the effect to rename it. Call this effect *Box 1 and 4 Slide L.*

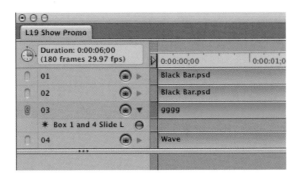

Animating the Second Glyph

To add a separate effect for box glyphs 2 and 3, you will need to create additional effect bars.

1 With the effect below track 03 still selected, choose Track > Add New Effect.

A new effect is added on the track below your first effect, at the beginning of the Timeline.

2 Drag the effect bar to the right and position it directly below the first bar in the Timeline.

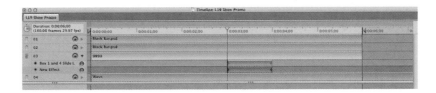

3 In the Effects tab, double-click the new effect and call it *Box 2 Scale LL*. The "LL" is shorthand for lower left.

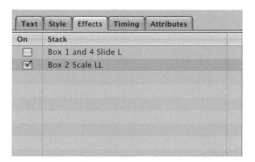

You will need to disable this effect for boxes 1, 3, and 4.

4 Click box 1 in the Canvas to select it, then turn off the effect for **Box 2 Scale LL**.

TIP ▶ A good way to quickly identify which glyph you are currently working on is to look in the text input field and notice which character is highlighted.

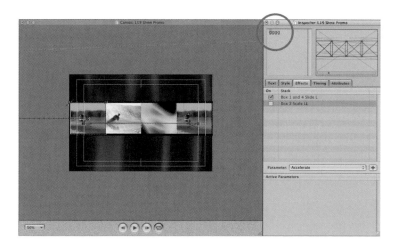

5 Click box 3 to select it and repeat step 4.

6 Click box 4 to select it and repeat step 4.

Now that you have the scale effect applied only to box 2, you are going to scale and position the box so it grows and moves to the lower-left corner of the Canvas.

7 Click the second keyframe on the **Box 2 Scale LL** effect bar to select it.

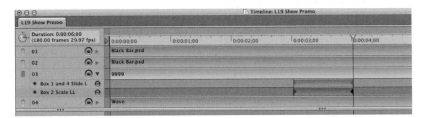

8 Click box 2 in the Canvas to select it, and then click the Attributes tab of the Inspector.

9 Enter *200* in the Scale input field and watch the wireframe preview area to see the change.

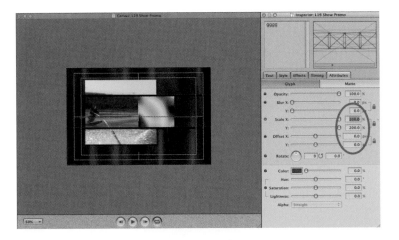

In the Canvas window, drag box 2 and position it in the lower-left corner of the frame. Again, watch the wireframe preview area to see the change or you can preview render to RAM.

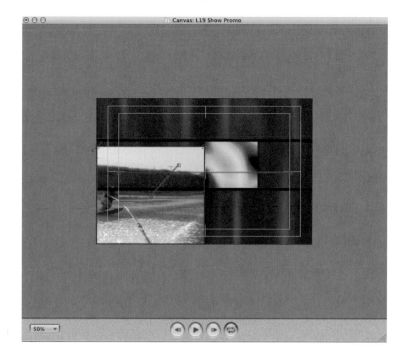

Animating the Third Glyph

The last box you will animate is box 3, the one with the Waft texture matted to it. This image will do the mirror opposite of box 2—that is, it will scale to 200 percent and land in the lower-right corner of the screen.

1   Make sure Track 03 is still selected, then add a new effect by pressing Cmd-E.

2   Drag the new effect bar to the right and position it under the first two effects.

3 Click the Effects tab in the Inspector, double-click the new effect name, and call this effect *Box 3 Scale LR*.

4 Make sure your playhead is parked just to the left of the effect bars in the Timeline. This will make it easier to select the glyphs.

5 Click the box 1 glyph to select it, and then uncheck the **Box 3 Scale LR** check box to disable it. Select the letters (g) in the Inspector text box if you have trouble selecting the individual glyphs in the Canvas.

6 Click box 2, then repeat step 5.

7 Click box 4, then repeat step 5.

8 Click the second keyframe on the **Box 3 Scale LR** effect bar to select it.

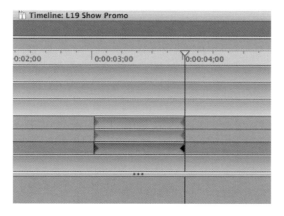

9 Click box 3 in the Canvas to select the glyph.

10 Click the Attributes tab in the Inspector.

11 Enter *200* for the Scale property and press Return.

12 In the Canvas, drag the box 3 glyph to the lower-right corner of the screen, then preview.

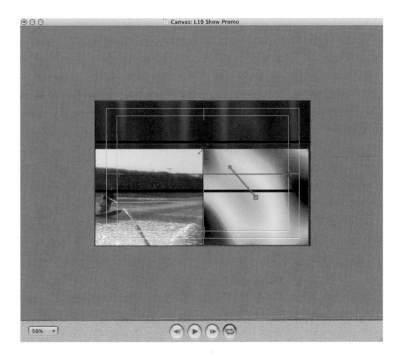

Using Ruler Guides

Ruler guides are a helpful way to make sure your objects are aligned the way you want them.

1 Set your Canvas zoom scale to 100%.

2 Choose Edit > Project Properties.

3 Check the Show Rulers check box and click OK.

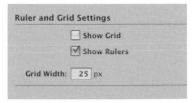

4   Drag down from the gray ruler area and position the blue horizontal ruler guide on the top edge of the box 3 glyph (the skier glyph on the left).

5   Click the box 3 glyph to select it, then carefullly Shift-drag the box until it is flush with the guide.

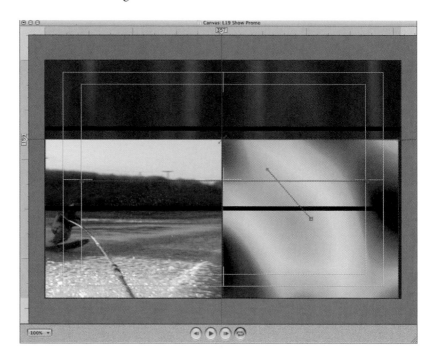

Changing the Effect Timing

In LiveType, all keyframe parameters for a given effect reside on a single effect bar. That is, there are no multi-layer keyframe stacks like you find in other programs. For example, if you click any of the keyframes you created earlier, then click the Effects tab, you will see a list of all the active parameters for that keyframe.

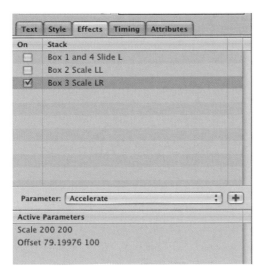

Both Scale and Position (Offset) are active for this keyframe

The beauty of this is that effects (represented by the purple bars) are treated as containers for all keyframe parameters applied to a track or object. In the example shown above, both Scale and Position are active for a single keyframe, making it easy to move the entire effect around without having to worry about moving individual keyframes for each parameter.

1   Click and drag the **Box 3 Scale LR** effect bar to the right in the Timeline to offset the timing of this object.

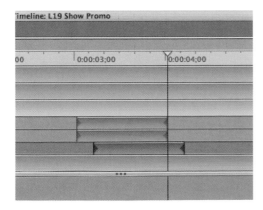

Notice how this simple time shift of the effect bar gave us a completely different motion in the preview window.

2   For fun, drag the other effect bars to new Timeline location to see how the motion is affected by the change. You can always use multiple undos to get you back where you started.

TIP▸ For more precision in your timing adjustments, you can click the Timing tab of the Inspector and enter a value in the Delay input field.

Previewing Selected Tracks

One of the most efficient ways to animate objects is to limit your previewing to the track you are working on. Because you will be repeatedly previewing your animations to judge timing and other motion properties, rendering every track could take an inordinate amount of time.

1   Select the 03 track, and then choose View > Selected Only.

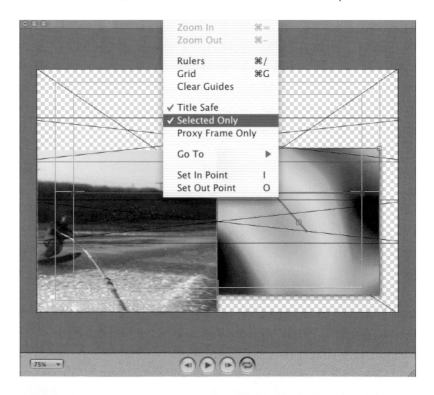

When you click the Play button on the Canvas window, only this track will be cached to RAM for playback.

2   Select 03 again, then choose View > Selected Only again to show all layers in the Canvas window.

Additionally, you can disable tracks by clicking the Enable/Disable Track button on the Timeline, and only the tracks that are enabled will be previewed. However, if you have many tracks, this may not be the best option.

Animating the Photoshop Image

Now that you have the skier boxes animated, you will focus your attention on animating the black bars you imported earlier.

1   Click the Enable/Disable Track button for Track 01 to turn off the visibility of the lower bar.

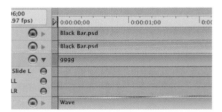

2   Click the 02 track to select it, then press Cmd-E to add an empty effect bar.

3   Enter 3 in the Delay parameter input box in the Timing tab of the Inspector, or just drag the bar to line it up with the other effect bars on Track 03.

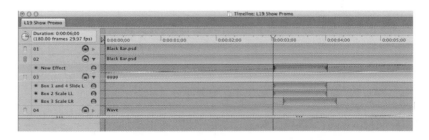

4   Click the first keyframe on the 02 track effect bar to select it.

5   Click the Effects tab in the Inspector and choose Rotate from the Parameter pop-up menu.

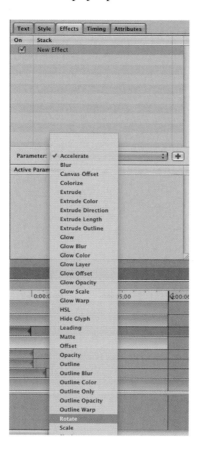

6   Click the plus button (+) to add this parameter to the Active Parameters list.

7   Press Shift-K to move the playhead to the next keyframe.

8   Double-click "Rotate 0" in the Active Parameters list to bring up the parameter input window for that keyframe. Enter *90* in the Rotate input box.

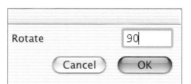

After previewing, you should now see the black bar start horizontally and end up vertically separating boxes 2 and 3.

9 Change the effect name in the Effects tab by double-clicking and entering *top bar*.

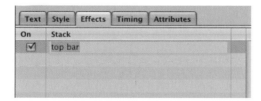

10 Click the Enable/Disable Track button for Track 02 and turn on the button for Track 01.

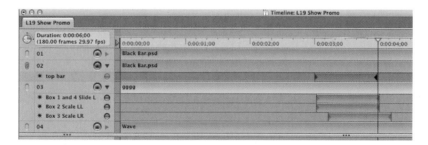

11 Click the 01 track to select it, then press Cmd-E to add an empty effect bar.

12 Enter *3* in the Delay parameter input box in the Timing tab of the Inspector.

13 Click the first keyframe to select the start of the 01 track effect bar.

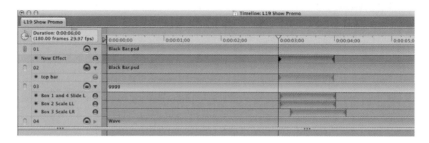

14 In the Effects tab, choose Offset from the Parameter pop-up menu, then click the plus button (+) to add this parameter to the Active Parameters box.

An *offset* in LiveType is similar to *position* in other programs. The distinction is that offset is always relative to an object's starting position of absolute zero for both the X and Y axis (not the pixel coordinates within a frame).

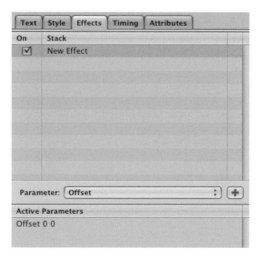

15 Press Shift-K to move your playhead to the second keyframe.

16 Double-click the word "Offset" in the Active Parameters list to bring up the Offset input box. Enter a value of *–137* for the Y offset value, then click OK. Preview your work.

Working with LiveFonts

At this point, you have worked with different type objects in LiveType but have not yet worked with any actual type. You are going to apply and modify a LiveFont for the main title of the show. LiveFonts are 32-bit pre-rendered animated typefaces you can add and customize to give your work some additional graphic "punch." The obvious pitfall, of course, is that although they have a certain "wow" factor, they can easily fall prey to overuse and abuse, if you know what I mean.

1   Move your playhead to the beginning of the Timeline, click the LiveFonts tab in the Media Browser, and scroll down to locate the Spotlight font. Click the Apply To New Track button to add this font to your Timeline. Again, you won't see anything happen until you enter some text for your LiveFont in the Inspector.

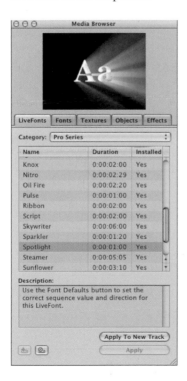

Spotlight is a volumetric lighting effect that is standard fare in many movie trailers and other action-oriented titles.

2 In the text input field, type *river nationals*.

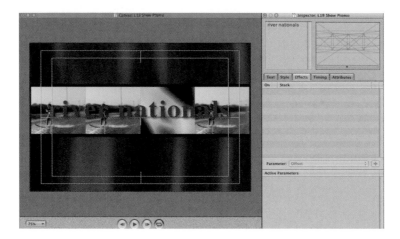

The Spotlight LiveFont appears in the Timeline with a duration of one second.

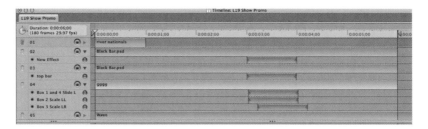

3 Set your preview range to cover from 0 to 4 seconds in the time ruler and preview your work.

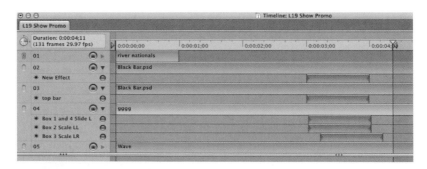

TIP ▶ Because this particular LiveFont is so processor intensive, you may want to choose View > Selected Only to reduce your screen render time to only the LiveFont track.

You will now alter the timing of the light pass across the characters by modifying the sequencing parameter.

4   With the LiveFont on Track 01 selected, click the Timing tab of the Inspector.

5   In the Sequence Input box, type *14*, then press Return and watch the result in the wireframe preview box.

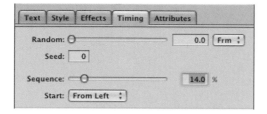

What you have just altered is the timing by which each glyph (or character) is acted upon, in sequence, by the light effect. Simply stated, a value of 0 will have all glyphs being hit by the light at the same time. A value of 14 in this case has a staggering effect that keeps each glyph from being acted upon until the previous glyph is at least 14 percent into the effect.

If you look in the Timeline, you will notice sequencing markers (one for each character) that give you a visual indication of the sequence timing you have just set. Sequence markers that are further apart indicate longer sequencing values, whereas sequence markers that are closer together indicate shorter values. Experiment with these values while watching the change in both the Timeline and the wireframe preview box.

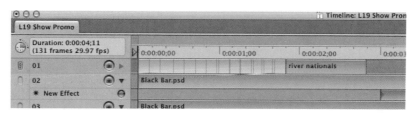

To change the direction of the light pass, you will need to change the starting side.

6   From the Start pop-up, choose From Right to reverse the direction of the light pass.

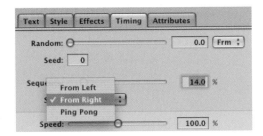

7   Preview the animation a few times. We should give the opening title a little head room before the light pass comes in. To do this, we will use a hold.

8   Drag the Hold First slider to the right or enter a value of *12* in the input box. You can enter a hold Duration in frames or seconds from the pop-up.

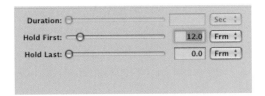

In the Timeline, the darker teal-blue section, indicating the start and native duration of the actual Spotlight effect itself, has been offset by 12 hold frames, indicated by the lighter teal-blue track sections. Also notice that hold frames have no sequencing markers.

9   Preview your work.

Applying a "Squeeze In" Effect

Your opening title is looks really good. However, you still need a way to bring the title on and off the screen. You could just create a standard fade in (and out), but this is LiveType, which puts many other creative possibilities at your fingertips.

1   Make sure the 01 track is still selected.

2   In the Media Browser, click the Effects tab.

LiveType comes with 136 preprogrammed effects you can quickly apply to your tracks. All the parameters and keyframe placements have been created for you, which leaves you with the simple task of choosing one that is appropriate for the look or feel you want to create.

3   In the Category pop-up, choose Fades.

4   Locate the Squeeze In effect and click Apply, or simply double-click the name.

The effect is added to the beginning of your Timeline with a default duration of 21 frames.

5   Preview the Squeeze In.

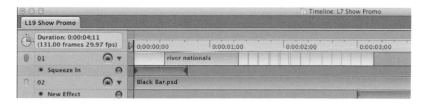

6 Make sure your playhead is sitting somewhere over the Squeeze In in the Timeline, then click the Effects tab of the Inspector. You can see that this canned effect is applying both Opacity and Tracking values over time. You can modify this effect even further by adding additional parameters from the Parameters pop-up.

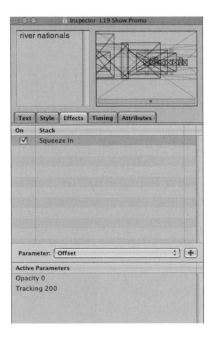

For instance, after watching the effect, you decide that you want the squeeze in effect to end before the light pass begins. This requires a change in the effect duration.

7 Click and drag the right edge of the purple effect bar until it aligns with the left edge of the LiveFont starting frame (dark blue teal area).

8 Preview again.

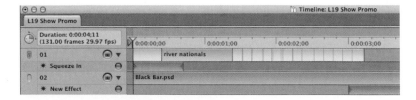

Applying a "Squeeze Out" Effect

You are now going to apply the reverse effect on the Out point of your title.

1 With Track 01 still selected, locate the Squeeze Out effect in the Media Browser, then click Apply.

The effect is intelligently added to the end of the title track.

2 Drag the left edge of the Squeeze Out effect bar to the right to shorten where the effect begins. Preview again.

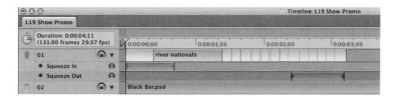

Finessing Color and Positioning

1 Click the Attributes tab, then click the color box and pick white from the Apple color picker.

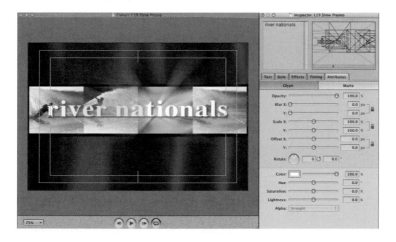

To position the title on the screen relative to the other objects, you will need to turn the other layers back on.

2   Make sure the 01 track is selected, then choose View > Selected Only.

3   Choose Edit > Project Properties and check the Show Grid box.

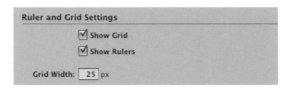

You should now see a handy grid by which you can accurately center and position your title.

4   Move the title into place under the glyphs by dragging on the blue track bar, turn off the grid, then preview if you wish.

Finishing the Promo

You are in the home stretch. By now, you should be marveling at how quickly and easily you can get professional-looking results. In this last section, you will finish the promo by creating a text track, applying an effect to it, and then duplicating the results to create text for both the upper and lower ad copy sections of the screen.

1   Set your In and Out preview markers to cover a Timeline range from zero to six seconds.

2   Move your playhead to four seconds.

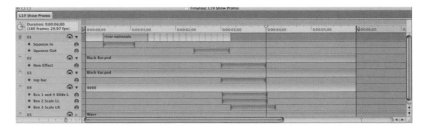

3   Click the Font tab in the Media Browser to choose Arial Black from
the font Family list.

4   Click Apply to New Track to add this font to the Timeline.

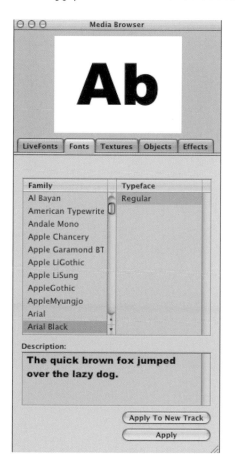

5   In the text input box of the Inspector, type *skiers*, press Return, then
type *open*.

NOTE ▶ If you are not seeing your title in the Canvas, move your playhead directly over the Ski Open text track. You also will need to drag the track up in the frame so you can see the lower line of text.

Now let's change the text formatting.

6   Click the Text tab, and set the text Size to *60* pts, the Leading to *60%*, and text justification to left.

7   In the text input window of the Inspector, highlight just the word "skiers." This will select only the characters (glyphs) on the first line on the text track in the Canvas.

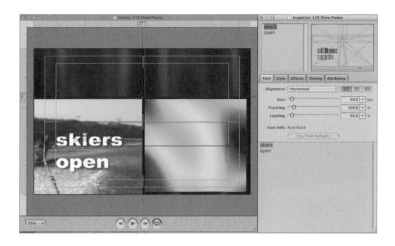

8   In the Font tab of the Media Browser, choose Arial, then double-click
     it to change the font to a narrow sans-serif.

9   Click the Attributes tab, click the Scale lock to unlock the aspect ratio of X and Y, and change the Y Scale value to 70%. (Make sure the lock icon is open before entering the Y value.)

10   In the Canvas, drag the text object to place it in the upper-left, blue quadrant.

To bring this title forcefully onscreen, you are going to apply a Horizontal Blur effect.

11 In the Effects tab, in the Media Browser, locate the Horizontal Blur. Make sure the 01 track is still selected, then double-click the blur to add the effect to the track.

Now we're ready to duplicate the track.

12 Make sure the 01 track is selected, then press Cmd-D to duplicate the track (or select Track > Duplicate Track).

13 In the Canvas, drag the newly created track to the lower-right quadrant to the screen, then replace the text in the Inspector to read *sunday* [Return] *june 4.*

14 Change the Leading to *80%.*

15 Position the text so that it is centered and within title safe. Use your grid for precise alignment.

16 Change the text color to black in the Attributes tab of the Inspector.

17 Preview the final animation and pat yourself on the back.

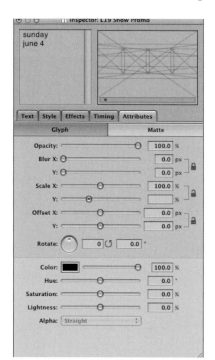

Outputting Your Movie

Congratulations, you've successfully created a fairly complex animation in the amount of time is takes to have a good cup of coffee. Your last step is to output the movie to disk.

1 Choose File > Render Movie. Be sure to save your project first.

2 Navigate to your Desktop, name your movie, then click Save.

Since you already have your render In and Out points set for six seconds, you will leave the Render Only Between In/Out Points option checked.

What You've Learned

- Fonts, textures, and effects can be easily modified in the Inspector.
- Effects can be applied to an entire text track or to individual glyphs within the track.
- Video and textures can be matted to any glyph, whether it is regular type or a symbol.
- Effects parameters are applied to a single keyframe in the Timeline effect bar, making it easy to change your animation timing.
- Photoshop images can be placed and animated in LiveType.

20

Lesson Files
Lessons > Lesson_20 > 20_Project_Start.ipr

Lessons > Lesson_20 > 20_Motion_Menu.ipr

Media
Media > Lesson_20_Media

Time
This lesson takes approximately 60 minutes to complete.

Goals
Export to and from a Final Cut Pro project

Use a background as a matte fill

Use an object as a graphic border

Combine multiple effects on one track

Customize and save effects

Use Final Cut Pro markers to align a track

Prepare content for Final Cut Pro and DVD Studio Pro.

Lesson 20

Using LiveType to Create a Motion Menu

In the last lesson, you used LiveType to create an on-air promo for a television show. In this lesson, you will use LiveType to create a motion menu to entice viewers to explore your DVD. Apart from the content itself, the menu leaves the most lasting impression on viewers because it is, in fact, the first thing they see when they pop your disk into their DVD players. Whether you're creating a Hollywood title or selling a product, your DVD will greatly benefit from a well-designed and executed motion menu.

In many ways, LiveType is a perfect DVD authoring companion because you can quickly obtain professional-looking results. And since both iDVD and DVD Studio Pro allow you to work with your own custom-designed motion menus, it makes perfect sense to use LiveType as an integral part of your DVD production pipeline.

Viewing the Finished Project

Let's view the final project so that you can see what you're about to create.

1   Open the Lesson_20_Media folder that you copied to your hard drive, and locate the Media > Lesson_20_Media > **DVD Motion Menu.mov** file. Double-click it to view the finished movie.

2   Open the LiveType Project file labeled **20_Project_Start.ipr** from the Lessons > Lesson_20 folder.

This opens the project file from which the DVD menu was created. This is an eight-layer composite consisting of an imported background movie on Track 08, animated textures and objects (Tracks 05 and 07), and Webding glyphs (Tracks 01, 02, 03, 04, and 06).

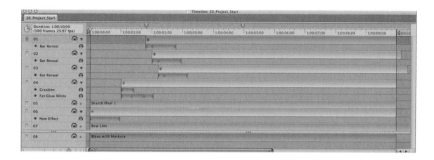

Often, it is useful when viewing someone else's completed project to disable certain tracks so you can see how the project was put together.

3   Park your playhead at 1:00:02:15. Click the Enable/Disable Track buttons for the Webding tracks (Tracks 01, 02, 03, 04, 06). Notice that a square glyph was used to create the DVD main title and chapter bars.

4   Turn the disabled tracks back on.

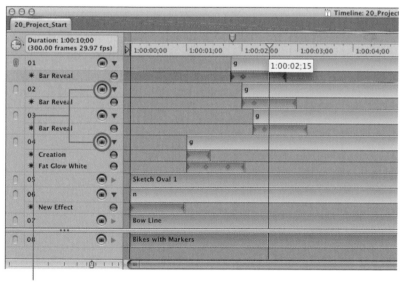

Enable/Disable Track buttons

5   Now park your playhead at 1:00:01:00. Disable Track 06. Here, a circle glyph was used as a matte for the video.

Exporting from Final Cut Pro

If you plan to use video assets in LiveType, then it's likely you will be creating your video content in Final Cut Pro and then exporting your movie to LiveType. You can set markers in the Final Cut Pro Timeline, and when they are exported, they will show up in the LiveType Timeline. This is extremely useful for syncing your animations to specific video and audio events.

1   Use the LiveType menu, or Cmd-H, to hide LiveType.

2   In the Finder, open your Lesson_20 project folder, then double-click the **Bikes.fcp** project file to launch Final Cut Pro.

A simple Timeline will open with three clips in it, with a total duration of 10 seconds.

You will use this Timeline to export your video assets for use in building your LiveType project. The Timeline you opened should have a single green marker placed at the edit point between clips 1 and 2. You are going to create a marker for the second edit point.

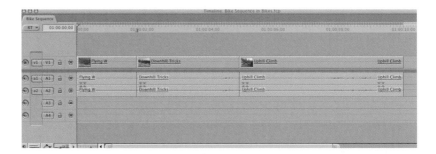

3   Move your playhead to the second edit point, making sure you have no clips selected. Press M on your keyboard twice. (The first M sets the marker, and the second M brings up the Edit Marker window.)

4   Name the marker *Uphill*, then click the Add Chapter Marker button to
set a chapter marker. Click OK to close the Edit Marker dialog.

5   With the Bike Sequence Timeline active, choose File > Export >
For LiveType.

6   In the Save window, set the Markers pop-up to Chapter Markers.
Setting chapter markers will flag QuickTime to include them in the
exported movie.

7   Make sure the Make Movie Self-Contained box is unchecked.

8   Name the movie *Bikes with Markers* and save it on your Desktop (or some other convenient location). Don't save it to the Lesson 20 Media folder.

9   Quit Final Cut Pro.

Creating the Motion Menu Background

As in the previous lesson, you will start from the ground up: building the background elements first, then compositing the various menu foreground elements such as the menu bars and main title, and finally, applying animated effects. Let's start by creating a new project and saving it to your hard drive.

1   Switch back to LiveType. If you quit the program after the previous exercise, launch it again from the Applications folder or the Dock.

2   Choose File > New.

3   Choose File > Save, and save the untitled project to your Desktop with the name *20_Motion_Menu*.

Now let's apply a texture.

4   Click the Textures tab of the Media Browser and choose Geometrics from the Category pop-up.

The Geometrics category contains colorful continuous-tone shapes that dance, wiggle, and float across the screen. They're a load of fun because they are at home in anything that requires a whimsical or playful feel—from kid's shows to extreme sports. Since your client has a thing for purple, you will use the Bow Line texture.

5   Double-click the texture name to add it to the Timeline.

You may need to zoom your Timeline out to see the entire texture.

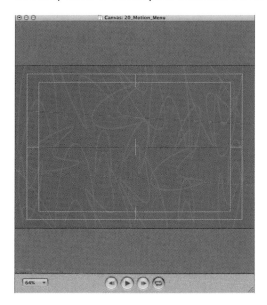

The texture is placed on Track 02 below the empty 01 text track. Drag the Background separator bar below Track 02, if necessary. The texture's default duration is 4 seconds, which will need to be increased because the movie you exported from Final Cut Pro is 10 seconds.

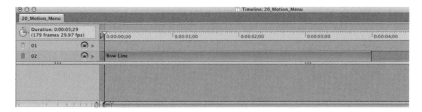

Next, you need to change the track duration.

6   Make sure the track is selected, and then click the Timing tab of the Inspector.

7   In the Loop input box, enter *3* and press Return.

Don't worry that the texture goes a bit beyond 10 seconds. You want at least 10 seconds of material to cover the video.

Matting Background Video to a Glyph

In the previous lesson, you used a square-shaped glyph from the Webding font family to create "boxes" for matting an external video clip. Other than scale, you did not have any control over the placement of the clip because it was "locked" to the matted glyph's onscreen position. Your next exercise is to import a video clip to be used as a background layer, matte it to an oval-shaped glyph, then accurately position it behind the matte to better reveal the clip's subject matter.

You will begin by creating the oval-shaped cutout for the video in the upper-right section of the screen.

1   Click the 01 text track to make it active, then click the Fonts tab of the Media Browser and locate the Webdings font family. Click Apply to add this font to the track.

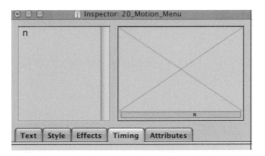

2   In the text input field of the Inspector, type a lowercase *n*. Move your
    playhead directly over the newly created text track on 01. You should
    see a white circle in the center of the Canvas.

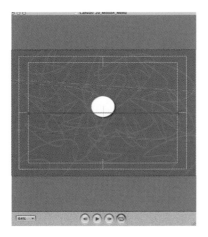

Now you will size and position it.

3   Set your Canvas view to 50%, then click the Attributes tab of the
    Inspector. Click the lock icon for Scale to unlock the X and Y Scale
    properties, and then enter *735* for the X, and *550* for Y.

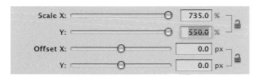

Your Canvas window should now have a nice, white egg sitting over the purple texture.

4   To position the oval in the upper-right corner of the screen, enter *162* for the X Offset, and *–92* for the Y offset.

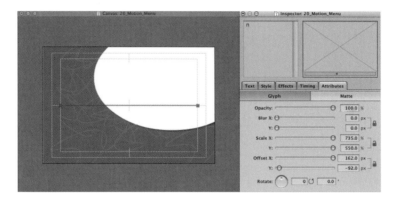

Finally, you need to set the glyph's duration.

5   Click the Timing tab of the Inspector and enter *10* in the Duration input box to extend the track to the 10-second marker in the Timeline.

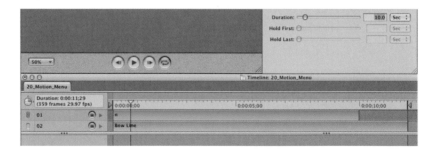

Placing and Matting a Background Movie

You are now going to bring in the movie you exported from Final Cut Pro for placement in the Timeline.

1   Choose File > Place Background Movie.

2 Navigate to the **Bikes with Markers** movie you saved out earlier to the Desktop, and then double-click it to bring it into the Timeline.

The movie should be placed on the bottom-most layer of the Timeline below a gray separator called the background bar. If it is not placed below the background bar, click and drag the background bar so that the movie is the only item below the background bar. Also notice that the markers and original timecode references were inherited from the exported Final Cut Pro Timeline.

Markers from Final Cut Pro Timeline

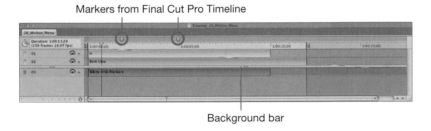

Background bar

Items such as movies, textures, and images that are placed below the background bar can have two purposes in LiveType. They can be used as an integral part of the composition and rendered into the final movie (when the Render Background box is checked in the Project Properties), or they can be used as a visual placeholder when laying out your elements and testing the timing of your animation. In this lesson, the bike movie will be included in the final render, therefore it will be an integral part of the design process.

TIP More than one track can be included as a background element, by dragging upward on the background bar.

One of the benefits of placing elements below the background bar is that they are *matte ready*. That is, any background element can be used as a matte *fill* for any foreground element (or track above the background bar).

3 Click the 01 text layer (the oval), then click the Attributes tab of the Inspector.

4   Click the Matte subtab. From the Matte To pop-up menu, choose
Background.

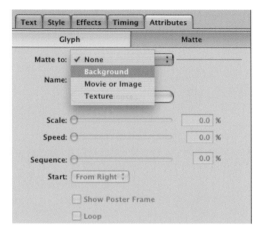

You should now see the **Bike with Markers** movie filling the oval glyph.

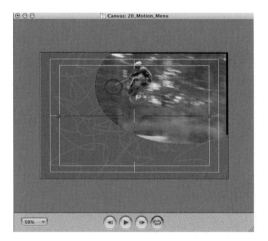

Now you'll change the offset (position) of the background movie so
that the main subject (the bikers) is nicely framed by the oval and not

cut off by the edges of the matte. First, however, you will turn off the track position lock.

5   Click the 03 track, then choose Layout > Lock Position. There should be a checkmark next to this item, indicating the track is currently locked. Release the menu to unlock Track 03 for positioning.

By default, full-screen background elements such as movie textures and imported images are placed with their onscreen positions locked. This is LiveType's way of preventing you from inadvertently moving the background when working with your foreground elements. In this case, you need to move the background in order to better place the movie behind the matte.

6   Move your playhead to Frame 21 in the Timeline. This should be a frame of a biker in midair.

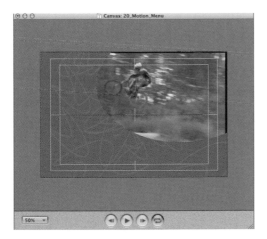

7   In the Canvas, click and drag the blue wireframe rectangle representing the background layer (Track 03) to a position where the biker can be seen centered in the matte.

NOTE ▶ If you want to match your background movie's position to mine, you can click the Attributes tab, then the Glyph subtab, and enter the same X and Y offset values (120, −4.0) shown in the following figure.

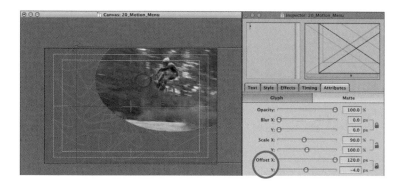

Since the biker background movie contains three different shots, spot-check your framing with the playhead at various points in the Timeline to see that nothing else of importance is cut off. Even better, render the movie to RAM to see how the effect works in real time.

8   To render a preview, first set your In and Out preview markers to cover a range of frames between 0 and 10 seconds, then choose File > Render Preview.

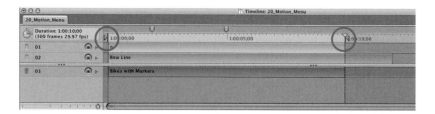

Adding a Fade-In Effect

Your next step is to add a simple effect to the matte to fade in the video.

1 Click the 01 track to select it, and then choose Track > Add New Effect.

2 Click the first keyframe triangle to select it on the effect bar.

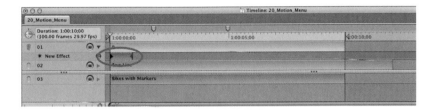

3 Click the Effects tab of the Inspector, choose Opacity from the Parameter list, and click the plus button (+) to add it to the Active Parameters list.

4 Double-click the Opacity parameter in the Active Parameters list to bring up the Opacity input window. Enter a value of *0*, and then press Return.

Because the Opacity value was initially added for both starting and ending keyframes at 100 percent, all that was necessary to create the fade was to change the starting keyframe's value to 0.

NOTE ► If you want to change the duration of the fade, just drag the right edge of the effect bar, or enter a new value in the Speed input box of the Timing tab.

Adding an Animated Border

Now that you have created a strong visual foundation for your menu, you will spice it up even further by adding an animated border to your matte. A great place to look for this element is in the Objects tab of the Media Browser. Objects in LiveType are animated elements that are designed to frame or otherwise emphasize text in your compositions.

1 Click the Objects tab of the Media Browser, and then choose Urban from the Category pop-up.

2 Use your down arrow key to locate the Sketch Oval 1 object, then click the Apply to New Track button.

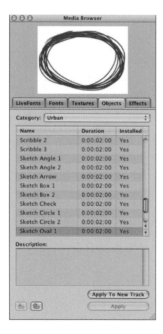

The default duration for the animated sketch is 2 seconds. Of course, you will need at least 10 seconds.

3 Click the 01 Sketch Oval 1 track to select it. From the Timing tab of the Inspector, enter *13* for the Loop value and press Return.

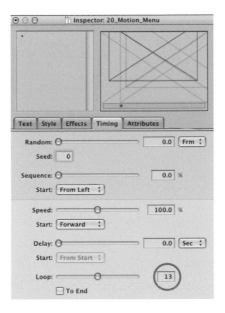

It may seem odd to enter a value of 13 to obtain a 10-second duration for a 2-second clip, but if you watch the loop play back, you will see that LiveType is calculating the duration of the loop after this initial fade up.

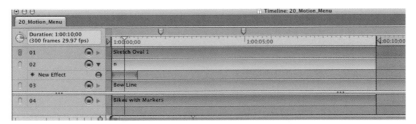

The sketch object should now be sitting roughly in the same location as the previously moved background movie. You are going to change the offset and scale so the animated sketch surrounds the matte.

4 Click the Attributes tab of the Inspector. Enter *162* for the X Offset. Leave the Y Offset at 0.

5 Click the Scale aspect ratio lock to lock it, then enter a value of *125* in either the X or Y Scale input boxes.

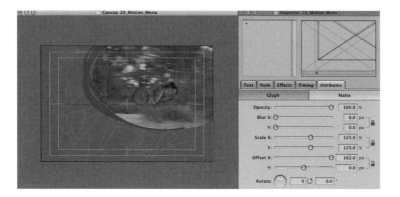

In terms of color, the object is a bit overpowering, and it clashes with the softer purple tones of the background.

6 In the Color section of the Attributes tab, drag the color slider all the way to the right, then click the blue color box to bring up the Apple color picker.

7 Choose the Crayon picker, then click the green Flora crayon and close the window.

8   Enter –*50* in the Saturation input box. This will make the green a bit
more pastel.

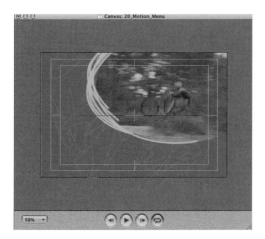

Building the Menu Bars

It's now time to build the graphical objects that will be the basis for your
DVD title and chapter headings. If you take a quick look at the finished
Lesson 19 project, you will see that these menu graphics were created with
a single glyph from none other than our favorite font family—Webdings.

Creating the Title Bar

1   Move your playhead to the first green marker in the Timeline.
This marker is where the shot changes inside the matte. You will
use this marker as the starting location for your menu graphics.

2 Choose Webdings from the Font Family list in the Media Browser, then click Apply to New Track.

3 Click the text input box of the Inspector and type a lowercase *g*, then move your playhead so it is directly over the text object. A square glyph should be centered in your Canvas window.

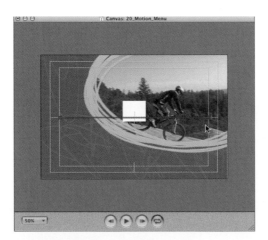

The text track should be starting at the first green marker and extending two seconds into the Timeline.

4 Drag the right edge of the 01 text track to align it with the other tracks ending at 10 seconds.

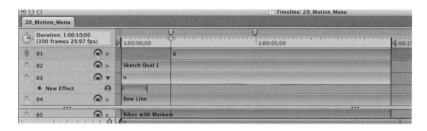

Next, you will scale, position, and add color.

5 Make sure that View > Title Safe is checked.

6 From the right corner of the glyph selection box in the Canvas, drag out a rectangle until its right and left edges line up with the inner title safe rectangle.

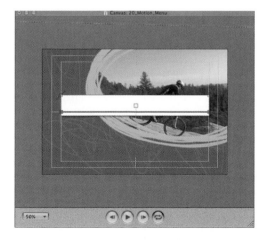

NOTE ▶ If you want your rectangle dimensions to match what's shown here, click the scale aspect lock and enter *650* for X and *100* for Y in the Attributes tab of the Inspector.

7 Shift-drag the title bar glyph upward and position it just inside the inner title safe boundary. Then Shift-drag to the left and position the bar's left edge with the screen's left edge.

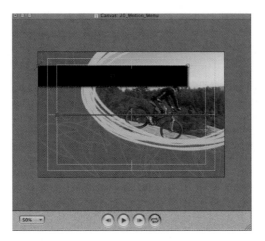

8 Click the color box, and change the color of the rectangle to black. If the crayons are still up, pick Licorice!

Creating the Chapter Bars

In order to create the chapter bars, you will duplicate this current 01 layer three times.

1 Click the 01 track to select it, and then select Track > Duplicate Track.

2 Repeat two more times to create three identical layers above the 01 title bar.

In the Canvas, all four bars are stacked on top of each other at the same screen position. You will need to reposition them.

3 In the Timeline, click the 01 track to select it. In the Canvas, Shift-drag the bar toward the bottom of the screen, making sure it is inside the title safe boundary.

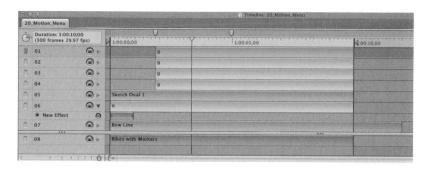

To reposition the remaining two bars, you will use the grid to help you align these objects.

4   Choose Edit > Project Properties. Click the Show Grid check box. Change the Grid Width to *50* pixels.

> **NOTE ▶** Sometimes it is helpful to display fewer grid squares rather than more, because it reduces screen clutter and in many cases makes it much easier to align large objects.

5   Zoom in your Canvas view, if necessary, and use your Cmd and up/down arrow keys to nudge the bars into alignment with the grid. Arrange the menu bars so that Track 01 is on the bottom, as shown.

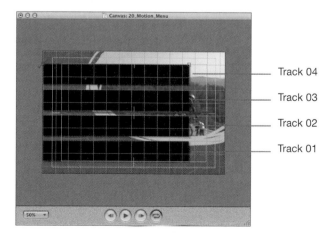

6   Turn off your grid and set your Canvas zoom to 75%.

Animating the Main Title Bar

To bring your motion menu to life, you will animate each menu bar,
staggering the entrance of each object on the screen. When working with
tracks that are all similar (or identical in this case), it is helpful to disable
the tracks you are not working with to keep your screen free from excess
clutter.

1   Click the Enable/Disable Track buttons for Tracks 01, 02, and 03.

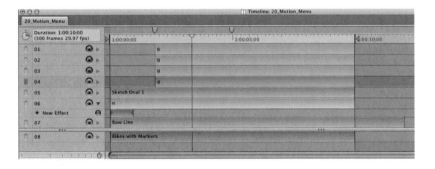

For the title bar the client wants a grand entrance—something flashy
but not cheesy. A good place to find the right effect is in the Fades
category of the Effects tab.

2   Click the Effects tab of the Media Browser, and then select Fades
from the Category pop-up. Most of the effects in thiscategory are
straight-forward fade-ins and a few fade-outs, with some blur
added.

3   Locate the Creation fade at the top of the list, then click Apply to add
it to the 04 track.

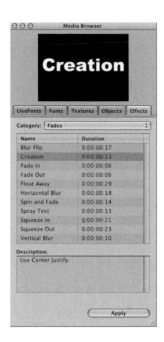

The Creation fade in is added beneath the 04 track with a default duration of 13 frames. Drag your In and Out preview markers before and after the effect and preview. If you want to change the speed of the effect, just drag the left edge of the effect to lengthen it, then preview again.

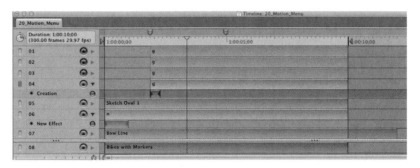

The great thing about LiveType is you can stack as many effects to a track as you want, which creates virtually limitless possibilities. This is also a good way to keep your effects from looking too canned.

4   Make sure your 04 track is still selected, then from the Effects category pop-up, choose Glows.

5   Locate Fat Glow and click Apply to add it to your track.

6   Preview your work to see how this added effect changes the animated entrance of the title bar.

Although you could go with this effect as is, you couldn't live with yourself if you didn't at least make some effort to customize it further before showing it to your client. Begin by changing the glow color from yellow to white.

7   Click the first keyframe on the Fat Glow effect bar to select it.

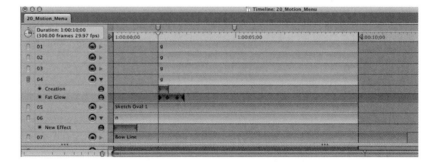

8   Click the Effects tab of the Inspector. You will see a list of all the Active Parameters for this effect listed by name as well as the current values for that parameter.

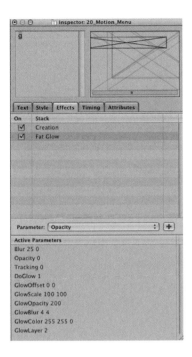

9   Double-click the GlowColor paramcter. This will bring up the parameter value input window. Notice that the current color value at this
keyframe is yellow, as indicated by the little color box.

10   Double-click the yellow square to bring up the Apple color picker,
choose the Snow (white) crayon, and click OK.

11   Click OK in the parameter value input window to accept the color
change.

12 Press Shift-K to move your playhead to the second keyframe. (You know you are parked on it when the diamond-shaped keyframe darkens in color.)

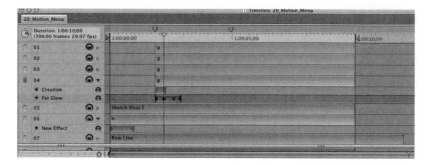

13 Repeat steps 9 through 12 for this keyframe, changing the Glow Color from yellow to white, then preview to see the change.

You should now have a glow animation that is all white. However, the glow scale is a bit too intense.

14 Click the second keyframe to select it, then double-click the GlowScale parameter in the list.

15 In the parameter value window, change the X value for Glow Scale to *100*, then click OK to accept the change.

16 Press Shift-K to move your playhead to the next (third) keyframe. Double-click the GlowScale parameter again, and change the X value to *100* like you did in the previous step. Preview the change in the Canvas window.

As you can see, it is extremely easy to change any parameter value simply by finding it in the list and double-clicking. Because all LiveType effects have their parameters listed in one location in the Effects tab, it does not take much effort to alter any effect and try different things.

Saving Effects

After getting the effect you want by customizing its parameters, you might find it valuable to save your effects for future use.

1   Make sure the Fat Glow effect you want to save is selected in the Timeline, then choose Track > Save Effect.

2   Name this effect *Fat Glow White*, then in the New category field type *My Favorite Effects* to save this effect into a new category. If you want, you can give the effect a Description. Click OK.

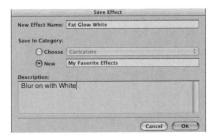

If you look in the Media Browser, you will see the new category you created with the effect you just named and saved.

NOTE ▸ Custom effects are stored in the Application Support > LiveType folder on your hard drive.

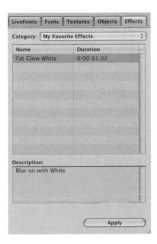

Animating the Chapter Bars

Now that you have successfully animated the title bar, it's time to turn
your attention to the chapter bars. In this section, you will animate both
the scale and acceleration properties of one bar, save the effect and apply it
to the remaining bars, and then stagger the entrance of each in the
Timeline. You will begin working on the lowest bar first.

1   Start by clicking the Enable/Disable track button for Track 04 to turn the
    track off, and then turn on the same button for Track 01, the bar at the
    bottom of the Canvas.

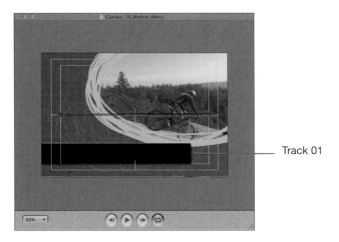

Track 01

2   Click the 01 track to select it, then press Cmd-E to add a new effect to
    the track.

3   Select the first keyframe.

4   In the Effects tab, choose Scale from the Parameter pop-up, then click
    the plus button (+) to add the effect. Do the same thing for the
    Accelerate property.

5   Double-click New Effect in the list and rename the effect *Bar Reveal*.

6   Double-click the Scale property to bring up the Parameter input win-
    dow. Enter *0* for the X scale and click OK to accept the change.

In the wireframe preview window of the Inspector, you can see a wireframe preview of the animation. You can also preview the effect if you wish.

The speed of keyframes in and out is controlled by the Accelerate property. When Accelerate is initially applied, a value of 0 is given to the effect. So that your animations change speed over the course of the animation, you will change the value of this property.

7   Click the first keyframe to select it, and then double-click the Accelerate property name in the Active Parameters list to bring up the input window.

8   Set the Accelerate value to *–100*, and click OK.

9   In the Canvas window, click the frame forward button seven times to move the playhead seven frames later in the Timeline.

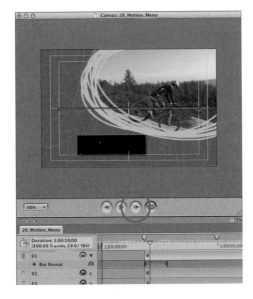

10 Double-click the Accelerate property name again and enter a value of *0* in the parameter input window, then click OK.

A keyframe is automatically added at the playhead position in the Timeline for the newly entered Accelerate value.

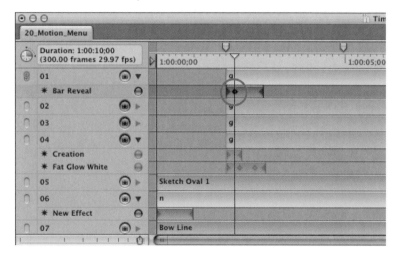

11 Press Shift-K to move your playhead to the last (third) keyframe. Double-click the Accelerate name in the Active Parameters list, and enter *100* in the resulting input window. Click OK to accept the change.

12 Preview the animation and notice the abrupt speed change between keyframes 2 and 3. Just for fun, drag the middle keyframe to a different location on the effect bar and preview again to see how the keyframe position affects how the bar is revealed.

Save and Reapply the Effect

Now you're ready to save the effect and apply it to other tracks.

1 Click the Bar Reveal effect bar to select it, then choose Track > Save Effect.

2 Click OK in the Save Effect window to save the effect into the My Favorite Effects category you created earlier.

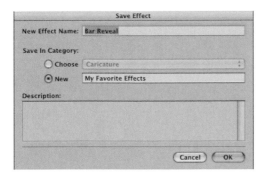

3   Enable all the remaining tracks by clicking their Enable/Disable Tracks button.

4   Click the 02 track to select it.

5   Click the Effects tab of the Media Browser and double-click the Bar Reveal effect you saved into the My Favorite Effects category (or click Apply).

The Saved effect is copied to Track 02 in the same location as the effect in Track 01.

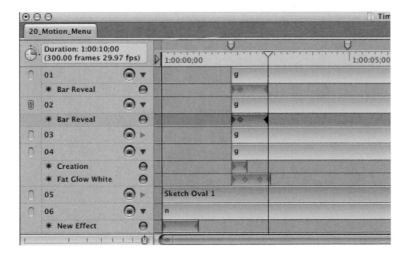

6   Click the 03 track to select it.

7   Click the Effects tab of the Media Browser and double-click the Bar Reveal effect you saved into the My Favorite Effects category (or click Apply).

Your Timeline should now have three tracks (from 01 to 03) that have identical effects at identical locations.

8   Preview the effect.

Animating the Offset of the Chapter Bars

To make the animation a bit more interesting, you are going to change the offset of the three chapter bars so they end up landing at slightly different locations in the frame.

1   Click the last keyframe on Track 01 so that it is selected.

2   Turn your grid back on in the Edit > Project Properties menu.

3   Click the bottom bar in the Canvas. You will see a blue outline around the object, indicating it is currently selected, and Track 01 will be highlighted.

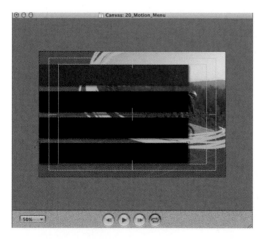

4   Shift-drag anywhere in the interior of the bottom bar (not the blue wireframe edge) until the right edge lines up with the sixth grid box

from the left. You will also see the dotted blue path trajectory indicating the motion path as you drag.

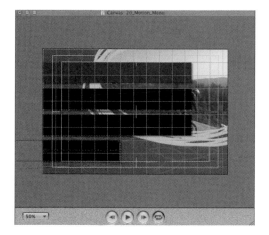

Now you're ready to animate the offset of Chapter Bar 2.

5   Click the last keyframe on the Track 02 Bar Reveal effect so it is
selected.

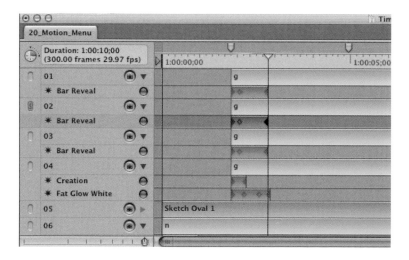

6   Click the second bar from the bottom in the Canvas. You will see a
blue outline around the object, indicating it is currently selected.

7   Shift-drag the second bar until the right edge lines up with the seventh grid box from the left.

8   Click the last keyframe on Track 03 so that it is selected.

9   Click the third bar in the Canvas (the one directly above the second bar). You will see a blue outline around the object, indicating it is currently selected.

10 Shift-drag the third bar until the right edge lines up with the eighth grid box from the left.

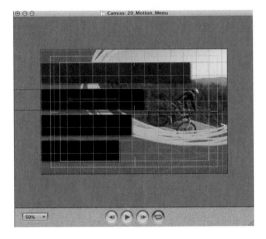

11 Preview your animations to see the effect of the offset for each chapter bar.

Apply a Delay to the Chapter Bars

For an additional touch, you'll change the delay of each bar so they appear on the screen at slightly different times. This will make the animation more rhythmic.

1   Click the 02 track, then click the Timing tab of the Inspector.

2   Enter of value of *2* in the Delay input box.

The delay change caused the 02 track to start two-tenths of a second later in the Timeline.

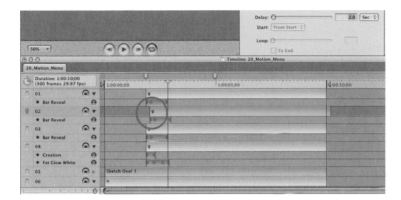

3   Click the 03 track, then enter a value of *2.2* in the Delay input box.

4   Click the 04 track then enter a value of *1* in the Delay input box.

NOTE ▶ You will need to lengthen the duration of the 04 track at the tail because it is now coming up a second short in the Timeline.

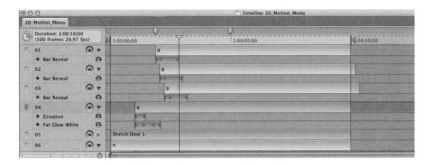

Finessing Outlines and Opacity

Let's make a few more changes. You'll make the chapter bars stand out by giving them a white border, and you'll adjust their opacity values to better reveal and enhance the background visuals.

1   Click the 01 track to select it. Click the Style tab of the Inspector, then click the Outlines subtab.

2   Click the Enable check box to turn on the outline style, then click the color box and choose Snow (white) from the color picker. Close the color picker. Enter a value of *3 pixels* in the weight input box.

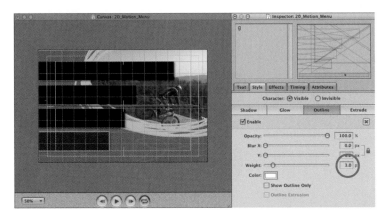

3   Click the Attributes tab and enter a value of *50* for Opacity.

4   Click to select Track 02 and repeat steps 1 and 3.

5   Click to select Track 03 and repeat steps 1 and 3.

6   Turn off the grid and preview the animation.

Preparing Content for Output

At this point, you have two options for preparing your LiveType movies for import back into Final Cut Pro. As mentioned at the start of the lesson, you can either render out a movie with the background or without the background. The default in LiveType is to render the movie without the background, which means that the matte area the movie is currently filling will be transparent when imported into Final Cut Pro. If you want to see how this will render out, click the Enable/Disable button for the 08 track.

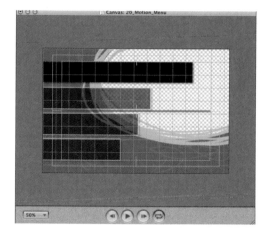

If you want the full movie rendered with the background movie, you must change this in your Project Properties window.

1   Choose Edit > Project Properties and click the Render Background check box.

2   Click OK to accept the change.

3   Drag your In and Out preview markers to mark the section of the Timeline you want to render out.

4 Choose File > Render Movie. Name the movie *DVD Menu with BG*.

5 Choose Render Only Between In/Out Points at the bottom of the Save dialog. You can also choose to render your movie without a background at the bottom of the Save dialog.

You may have noticed that this DVD menu was created without any type for the chapter bars. This is because DVD Studio Pro allows you to add type as text overlays. This means you can create and place type over any area of the background, and when the DVD is previewed and multiplexed, the viewer can see his or her selection highlighted.

What You've Learned

- Final Cut Pro can export Timeline markers that can be read in LiveType.
- Video can be placed on a background track and matted to foreground objects.
- Effects can be combined, saved, and reapplied to other tracks.
- Accelerate can be used to control effect speed between keyframes.
- Movies can be exported with or without backgrounds.

Project Management

Michael Wohl is best known as the principal designer of Final Cut Pro, a role he held for more than five years. He has also had success as a director and editor for more than 15 years. His 1993 film "Theatereality" won the coveted CINE Golden Eagle award and his latest feature film "WANT" is playing to acclaim on the international film festival circuit. He is currently in development on a new feature film and will be directing an original stageplay in early 2004 in Los Angeles.

Yan Shvalb is a creative consultant, instructor, and founder of VizualFX, a professional creative service provider and training center in New York. He collaborated with DigitalFilm Tree on the DVD training that ships with Final Cut Express and the quick-tour training movies on apple.com. He is a certified trainer in DVD Studio Pro, Shake, and Final Cut Pro. As a DVD author, Yan has created DVDs for Apple, BlueSky Studios, Central Park Media, Criterion, Fox Lorber, and BMG. He worked for Sony Music Studios as a 3D animator, compositor, and assistant editor, and was chief compressionist and DVD author at GTN, Inc. and Crush DV.

21

Lesson Files

Media

Time

Goals

Lessons > Lesson_21 > 21_Project_Start.fcp

Media > Lesson_21_Media

This lesson takes approximately 45 minutes to complete.

Master the various parameters associated with all clips

Use complex Find commands to locate specific items

Modify clip reel name and timecode

Use Auxiliary Timecode fields

Change a group of clips' reel numbers

Sync up audio and video from separate clips

Create and modify merged clips

Understand the Film Safe and Dupe Detection features

Advanced Clip Management

Good editing requires an organized workspace. Nothing is more important than managing the parameters, settings, and data associated with your clips. Even tiny errors can balloon into serious problems, including data loss, if you do not thoroughly understand how data is managed in Final Cut Pro and how to catch and correct problems.

Additionally, a solid understanding of Final Cut Pro's clip architecture can give you more flexibility in your editing decisions and improve your workflow and productivity.

Using the Browser as a Clip Database

Final Cut Pro's Browser is actually an immensely robust database containing more than 50 different parameters for each clip or sequence it contains. The first step to managing that database is to understand what those varied parameters are.

1   Open the Lessons > Lesson_21 > **21_Project_Start.fcp** file.

2   Expand the Browser window to fill your screen. Scroll through all of the columns.

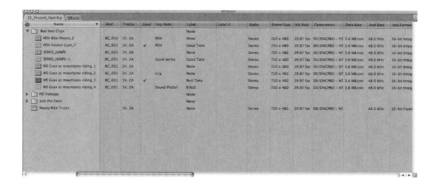

Although you can disregard many of the columns most of the time, what's important is to know where to find this information when you need it.

3   Double-click the bin called Just the Facts.

This bin has most of the columns hidden, and it has a custom-named column.

4   Ctrl-click any column header to access the contextual menu.

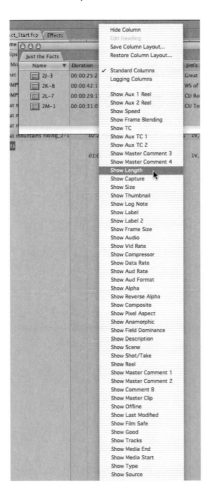

This control allows you to show and hide individual columns.

There is no right or wrong way to use the columns in the Browser. Different editing situations require different columns to be visible or hidden at any given time. If you create a set that you would like to reuse, you can save and restore the column layout.

5   From the contextual menu, choose Save Column Layout.

6   Name the layout and save it in the Column Layouts folder in the Final
Cut Pro User Data folder.

The first 10 layouts stored in this folder will appear in the contextual
menu for every Browser or bin window. Choosing it will restore that
set to the current window.

7   Close the Just the Facts bin window.

Viewing a Clip's Item Properties

Another way to view the contents of the database is to view the Item Properties for an individual clip.

1   Select the clip **SERIES_JUMPS** in the Browser and choose Edit > Item Properties.

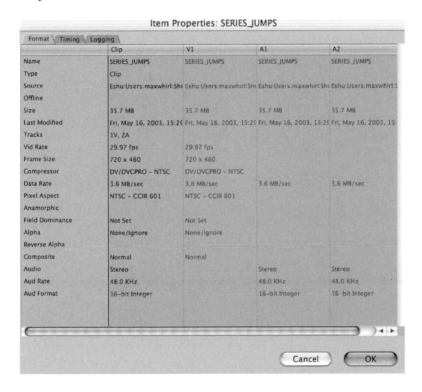

This window has three tabs that contain nearly all of the information found in the Browser columns. Because the data may be different for each of the different audio or video tracks, each track is listed as its own column. Changes you make in this window will update the Browser window and vice-versa.

2   Close the Item properties window.

Using Complex Find Operations

There are many advanced types of Find operations that can really help when working with a large, complex project.

1 Choose Edit > Find, or press Cmd-F, with the Browser active.

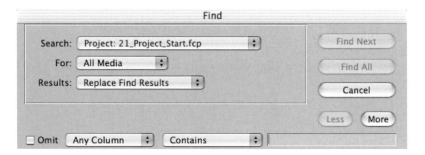

2 Set the For pop-up to Unused Media.

With this setting, you need not enter anything into the Search field. Just choose whether or not you want to search for selected sequences (or all sequences).

3   Uncheck the in selected sequences box and click Find All.

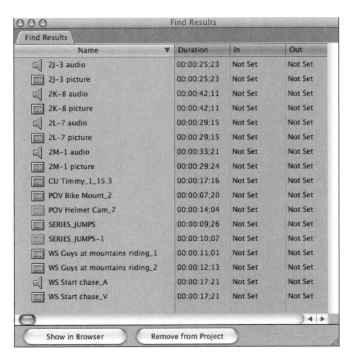

This is a useful way to assess which clips in your project are not currently used in any sequences. Alternately, you can search only for Used Media.

Once you've done a Find All and have created a Find Results bin, you can further refine your results by searching within the Find Results project.

4   Leave the Find Results bin open and press Cmd-F again.

5   Choose All Media from the For pop-up.

6 Set the Column pop-up to Media Start and set the middle column to Greater Than.

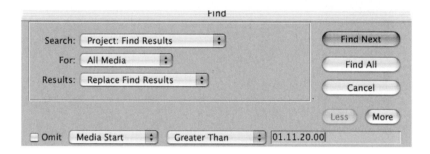

7 Enter *01:11:20:00* into the Search field and click Find All. Be sure to type all zeros and colons for best results.

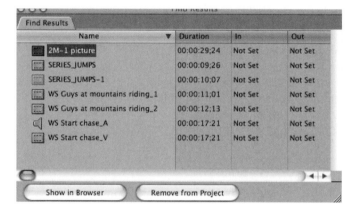

These settings will find clips with a starting timecode above hour 1. This can be very helpful if you know the rough timecode number of a shot you're looking for. You can also search on the Media End column or combine them both to find a specific timecode value.

8 Press Cmd-F again.

9 Set the first search field to Media Start, Greater Than, *02:15:00:00*.

10 Click More to add another search criteria.

11 Set the second criterion to Media End, Less Than, *02:20:00:00.*

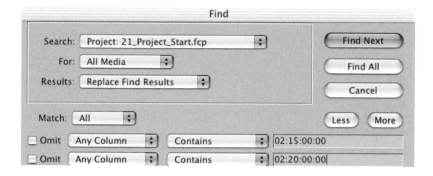

12 Click Find All.

Only one clip should remain in the Find Results bin. This is the clip that contains that precise timecode value.

You could further combine this type of search with more criteria to find clips of a certain name, from a particular reel or based on any of the comment fields you may have filled out during logging.

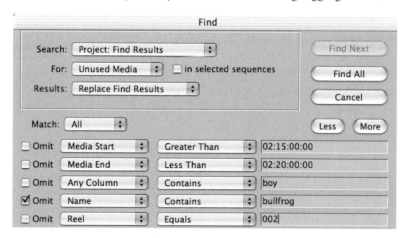

You can even omit certain criteria. The example shown in the preceding figure is searching for clips above the listed timecode, with the word "boy" in any column, but excluding clips with "bullfrog" in the name, and only from reel 002.

Working with Timecodes

One of the most important properties of any clip is its reel and timecode information. This data is the only connection between the digitized clip and the data on the tape from which it was captured. If you modify this information, Final Cut Pro might not be able to recapture the clip. Further, if you wanted to move your sequence into another application (as you might do for color correction or other special effects), you would not be able to accurately re-assemble it.

Fixing a Bad Reel Number

Still, there are occasions when you need to change this vital information. One common mistake is to neglect to change the reel number when logging multiple tapes, resulting in clips with incorrect reel numbers.

1   Close the Find Results window and double-click the bin called Bad Reel Clips to open it into its own Browser window.

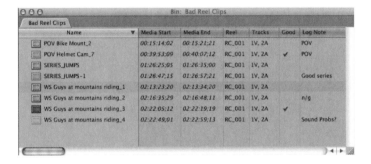

NOTE ▶ Changes made to a clip's reel number or timecode fields actually change the media file on disk. This means that every other clip that refers to the same media file will be updated to reflect the change you make. Even other applications that can read timecode will see the new information.

Often, you can identify clips with a faulty reel number based on the hours value in the timecode field. In this bin, the last four clips are marked Reel RC-001, but their timecode starts with hour 02 in the Media Start column. Although this isn't a guarantee of a reel error, it can be a good indicator, since the hour indicator is often used to differentiate sequential tapes, especially those used in field production.

2   Select one of the clips with the incorrect reel number.

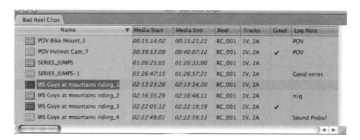

3   Type *RC_002* into the Reel column for the clip and press Return.

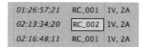

4   Click OK to accept Final Cut Pro's warning that you will be changing the file on disk.

5   Select the other three clips whose timecode starts with 02.

6   Ctrl-click the Reel column and select RC_002 from the shortcut menu.

7   Click OK in the dialog box warning you about changing the file on disk.

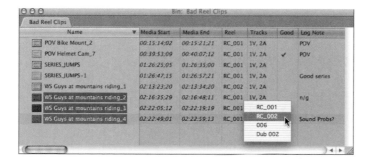

The value will be changed for all selected items.

Modifying Timecodes

Occasionally, rather than fixing the reel number, you may need to change the timecode number assigned to the clip. Although you can view the clip's current starting timecode by looking at the Media Start column, this information is not editable in the Browser.

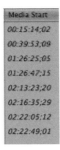

You can only modify one clip's Timecode at a time.

1   Close the Bad Reel Clips bin.

2   Open the HD Footage bin and select the clip **CU_Timmy_1_15.3**.

3   Choose Modify > Timecode.

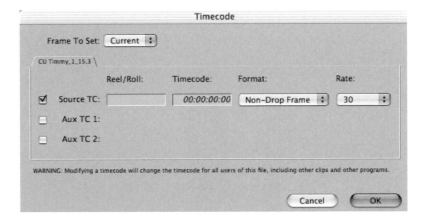

In this example, the clip was somehow erroneously reset to 00:00:00:00. To correct it, you must set the first frame of the clip to 07:24:03:10.

4 Set the Frame To Set pop-up menu at the top of the window to First.

This ensures that the number you enter in this dialog box is assigned to the first frame of the clip instead of the current playhead frame.

5 Set the Source Timecode field to *07:24:03:10*.

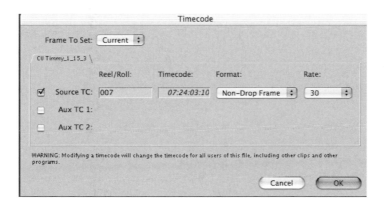

6 Set the Format to Drop Frame and leave the Rate at 30.

7 Close the dialog box by clicking OK.

Using Auxiliary Timecode Tracks

In addition to the primary timecode track, Final Cut Pro allows you to assign two auxiliary reel numbers and timecode tracks. This information is also written into the media file, so once you add such an auxiliary track, it will appear in any other clip that points to the same media file.

This feature can be used in a program such as a music video or multiple camera shoot. In the music video case, the song will have its own timecode track, separate from the video. You can keep the video's original timecode in the Source Timecode fields and use an Auxiliary Timecode field to store the version from the music. Later you can compare the timecode values to guarantee that the video is in sync with the pre-recorded song at any point in the edited sequence.

1   Arrange your windows into the Standard layout by choosing Window > Arrange > Standard.

2   Open the Just the Facts bin and open the clip **2L-7 picture** into the Viewer.

3   Park the playhead on any frame displaying the timecode slate.

This slate is displaying timecode provided by the audio playback device on set.

TIP ▶ Because the slate is providing a 30 fps timecode, and the clip you are looking at was originally shot in 24 fps film, there will be multiple frames with the same number on the slate. Be sure to step forward until you are parked on the first frame of a fresh number.

4   Choose Modify > Timecode.

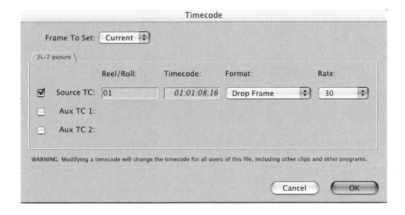

5   Check the Aux 1 check box to enable the Auxiliary timecode fields.

6   Set the Frame To Set pop-up to Current and leave the Rate set to 30.

7 Type the timecode number from the timecode slate into the Aux 1
Timecode field. Uncheck the Source TC box, since you want to modify
only the Auxillary timecode.

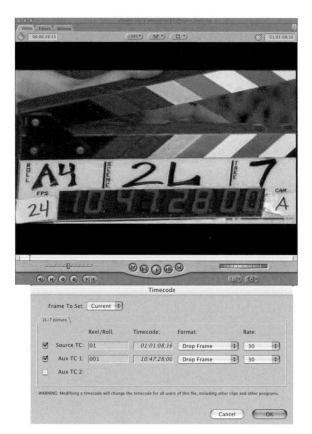

8 Close the dialog box.

Now, your clip has two timecode tracks assigned to it. You can choose
which one you want to view in the Viewer and Browser windows.

9 Access the contextual menu on the Current Timecode field in the Viewer window by Ctrl-clicking it.

10 Choose Aux 1 from the pop-up.

Now all editing of this clip (including exporting EDLs) will reference this alternate timecode value.

Recording to Dual Systems

Often, your picture and sound will be recorded on separate media. This might be because the picture was recorded on film (which can't record audio) or because production logistics required recording the audio separately from the video, usually onto a DAT recorder. This process is called dual-system recording because two decks are used (one for video and one for audio).

When your footage was recorded in this way, there is an additional step required before you can edit the footage. You must line up the audio and video elements so that lips and voices (and everything else) will play back in sync.

Syncing Clips

In most cases, dual-system media will have been shot using a slate (sometimes called a clapboard) to provide a clear frame in both picture and sound that can be easily synchronized.

1   Open the clip **2M-1 picture** from the Just the Facts bin.

2   Find the frame where the clapper on the slate closes and set an In point on that frame (at 03:05:36:11).

Although this is a timecode slate, in this case, the numbers don't correspond with the timecode in your audio clip, so you may disregard them.

3   Open the clip **2M-1 audio.**

4   Find the frame where the sound of the clapboard can be heard (at approximately 01:01:44:10).

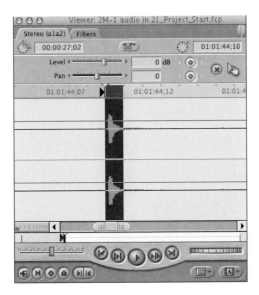

5 Set an In point at that frame.

You have now identified the same point in time on each clip.

Merging Clips
To combine these two clips into a single item for editing, use the Merge Clips command.

1 Select the two clips in the Browser window.

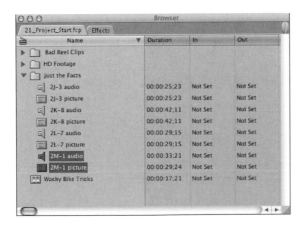

2 Choose Modify > Merge Clips.

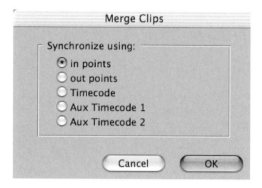

This opens the Merge Clips dialog box.

3 Set the clips to align based on the In points you just set.

4 Click OK.

A new clip is created in the Browser in the same place as the other two clips. This merged clip points to the two separate media files on disk.

You can combine up to 24 mono or 12 stereo audio tracks with a single video track in a merged clip.

5 Double-click the new clip to open it into the Viewer.

Because the audio clip starts before the video clip, there are transparent frames at the beginning and end of the clip.

From this point on, you can edit with this merged clip, and the audio and video will remain in sync.

Syncing with Timecode

In some cases, you will not have a slate to assist you in syncing your audio and video clips. You may, however, have identical timecode in the two clips. This can happen if the DAT player was slaved (synched together) to the video camera on set, or if a timecode slate was used and the numbers on the slate were identical to the ones in your audio clip.

1 Open the clip **WS Start chase_V** into the Viewer from the HD Footage bin.

This clip does not contain a slate but does have timecode numbers burned into the letterbox area below the picture. This was done when the original HD footage was dubbed to SD for editing. This is called BITC (Burned In Time Code, pronounced bit-see) or sometimes called a window dub.

Because this footage was originally shot at 24 fps, that timecode is shown on the bottom, and the 30 fps timecode that matches the audio is burned in on top. The clip's own timecode (the numbers associated with the SD tape from which it was captured) appear in the Current Timecode field at the top of the Viewer.

In this case, before you can sync the clip with the audio, you must enter the audio timecode into the Auxiliary Timecode field of the video clip.

2   Choose Modify > Timecode.

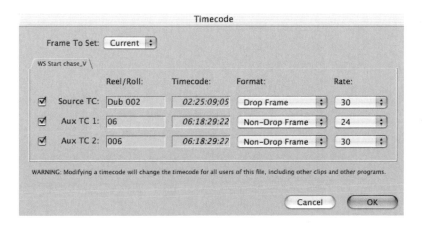

The 24 fps timecode has already been entered into the Aux 1 field.

3   Move the dialog box until you can see the timecode numbers in the Viewer.

4   Activate the Aux 2 Timecode fields by checking the box on the left, if it is not already active.

5   Set the Frame to Set to Current and type the upper timecode value from the window dub into the Aux 2 Timecode field. The Reel should be 006.

6   Set the Format to Non Drop Frame and close the dialog box.

7   In the Browser, select both **WS Start chase_V** and **WS Start chase_A**.

8   Open the contextual menu for the two clips by Ctrl-clicking one of them.

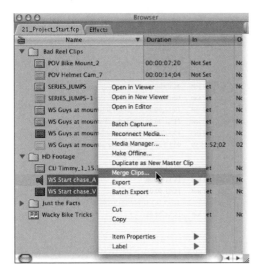

9   Choose Merge Clips.

10   Set the dialog box to Aux 2 Timecode and click OK.

NOTE ▶ Because the audio clip had no timecode in Aux 2, the merged clip synched the video based on Aux 2 and the audio based on Source.

A new merged clip is created in the Browser, linking the two media files into one item for editing. Play your new merged clip in the Viewer or Timeline to verify the audio/video sync.

Using Film-Safe Editing

The Film-Safe feature is actually used for any 24 fps material when edited in a 30 fps sequence, whether it originated on film or video. For example, footage shot on 24p HD is often dubbed to 30 fps SD NTSC tape for editing. Once you've made your editing decisions, an edit decision list is created, and the original HD footage is conformed to match the edit, creating a 24p master for broadcast, duplication, or printing to film.

Because there are duplicate frames in the NTSC version (added during the 24-fps-to-30 fps conversion process), it is possible for you to make edits on such new imaginary frames (that don't exist in the 24p original). This would cause problems when trying to conform the HD footage. However, you can prevent this by activating the Film Safe setting for your clips.

1   Select all of the clips in the bin HD Footage.

2   Scroll through the Browser columns horizontally until the Film Safe column is visible. (It's the last column.)

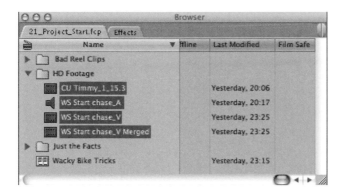

3 Ctrl-click on the Film Safe column and choose Yes from the contextual menu.

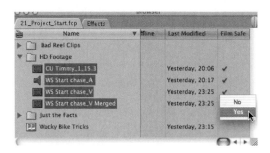

A check box will appear in all of the selected clips.

Although Final Cut Pro will let you make edits on these imaginary frames, when you perform a Media Manager trimming operation on your completed sequence, this setting will ensure that the trimmed clips will always begin and end on real frames, not imaginary ones.

Using Dupe Detection

Another feature specifically designed for clips originating in film is Dupe Detection. This allows you to identify any areas in your sequence where you may have reused the same clip more than once.

While in Final Cut Pro, you can use and reuse the same media to your heart's content. When cutting a film negative, however, there is only one copy of each frame. If you want to use a frame more than once, an additional negative must be generated.

1 Open the sequence **Wacky Bike Tricks**.

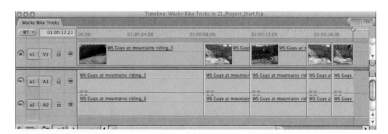

2   Open the Timeline Track Settings pop-up menu.

3   Turn on Show Duplicate Frames.

Final Cut Pro now displays the duplicated areas with a colored bar at the bottom of the clip. For each duplicated section, a new color is used. If a clip is used more than twice, the same color is applied.

If you encounter duplicate frames in a show you're cutting that will have to be conformed back to film, you have two options you can re-edit the show to avoid duplicating the frames, or you can make duplicate negatives of the scene in question.

There are a few settings for controlling the Dupe Detection feature.

4   Open the User Preferences window.

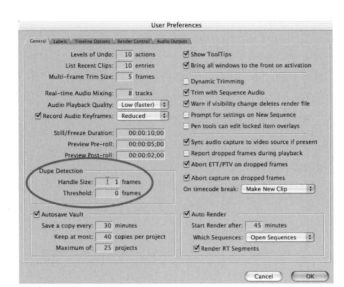

5   Set the Handle Size to *1* in the Dupe Detection area.

Because cutting film negative requires destroying at least one frame on either side of each edit, you will want to add handles to the Dupe Detection feature. This way you will be alerted if you have used a frame that would ordinarily be unavailable during negative cutting. This can occur very easily, for example, if you perform an Insert edit in the middle of another clip.

When only the handle is duplicated, a dotted indicator appears.

6   Leave the Threshold setting at 0 and close the dialog box.

What You've Learned

- Clip parameters can be modified in both the Browser and the Item Properties windows.

- Searching on selected sequences and on timecodes are ways to narrow your search parameters.

- Modifying reel and timecode information changes the media file on disk.

- When pictures and sound are recorded on separate media, their timecodes must be synched for playback and merged to be edited.

- The Film Safe setting prevents Media Manager operations from beginning or ending clips on imaginary frames of 24 fps material being edited in a 30 fps sequence.

22

Lesson Files Lessons > Lesson_22 > 22_Project_Start.fcp

Media Media > Lesson_22_Media

Time This lesson takes approximately 45 minutes to complete.

Goals Learn when and how to use the Make Offline command

Use the Reconnect Media command to resolve offline files

Use the Source column to identify a clip's media file

Consolidate media to move a project across computers

Trim a sequence to delete unneeded media

Create offline resolution clips

Replace offline resolution clips with full-resolution clips

Create an offline sequence to prepare for capturing full resolution clips

Lesson 22
Managing Media

One of the most satisfying things about working in a nonlinear editing system like Final Cut Pro is the fact that you almost never have to think about the physical realities of film and tape. Inside of Final Cut Pro, you can rename the clips, reuse them, cut them up, even combine and distort them using special effects. Because Final Cut Pro is entirely non-destructive, nothing ever happens to the weighty media files in your Capture Scratch folder. They remain intact and safely backed up on your original source tapes.

But sooner or later you're going to have to face those files, either to make room for a new show, or to move your project from one system to another, or perhaps to take advantage of the offline/online model of editing.

Understanding the Relationship between Clips and Media

Your media files are usually just QuickTime movies stored on your hard drive. There's nothing to stop you from moving them around or deleting them in the Finder, but it's not a good idea to do so. Your Final Cut Pro project relies on those media files, and if you move them around or manipulate them outside of Final Cut Pro, you may be in for a surprise. Whenever Final Cut Pro opens a project (or whenever you return to an open project in Final Cut Pro from another application), it scans your hard drive to check that all of the files referenced by the project are present and that they are the same size and shape that they were last time you opened this project. If any files are missing or have been changed, you get a warning box:

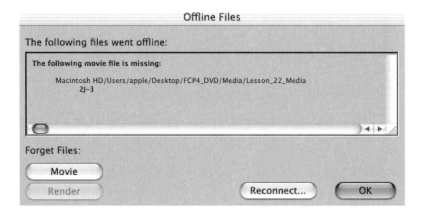

When there are clips in your project, and the media is not available, Final Cut Pro considers these files *offline*.

Making Clips Offline

There are some occasions where you will want to manually make clips offline. For example, if you had created a title in LiveType but realized you wanted to edit it, you could manually make the clip offline and then reconnect it to a new output file from LiveType.

1   Open the Lesson_22 > **22_Project_Start.fcp** project.

2   In the Browser, open the Clips bin, and select the clip **2J-3**.

3   Choose Modify > Make Offline.

You are presented with a choice to leave the media file where it was on the disk, to move it to the Trash, or to delete it outright.

NOTE ▸ Be very careful with this function! If you delete files this way, they will be gone forever. Also, if there are other affiliate clips in your project that point to the same media file, they will be made offline as well.

4   Select Leave Them on the Disk and click OK.

The offline clip should remain selected in the Browser, but it now has a red slash through it.

5 Open the sequence **Edit 1 (offlineRT)** into the Timeline.

Offline clips in a sequence will appear white in the Timeline. If you attempt to play them, you will get a warning frame in the Canvas. As you can see, when you made the clip **2J-3** offline in the Browser, it went offline in every sequence it is in as well, in the entire project.

Reconnecting Offline Files

When faced with an offline file, you can repair it at any time (providing that the corresponding media file exists on your disk) using the Reconnect Media command.

1 Select the offline clip **2J-3** in the Browser.

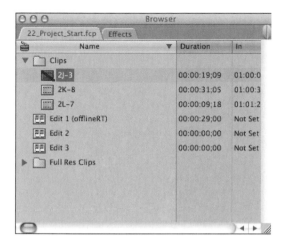

2   Choose File > Reconnect Media.

3   Check the box Select Files Manually and click OK.

4   Navigate to your Lesson_22_Media folder and find the clip **2J-3** in the
    Low Res Clips folder.

In this case, you can leave the Matched Name Only box checked, and all other media files except the one you are searching for will be grayed out, so you won't be able to select them by mistake.

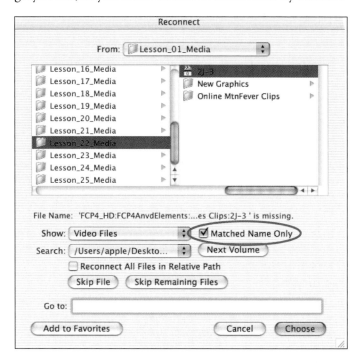

5   Select the file and click Choose.

The offline clip **2J-3** in the Browser is now reconnected to its original media file of the same name on your hard drive. The red slash is gone, and its affiliate clip in the sequence **Edit 1 (offlineRT)** is updated as well.

Deleting Media for Unused Clips

Another reason you might choose to have clips offline is to save disk space. If there are clips in your project that you are not using, you can delete the media files associated with them to make room on your disk.

1   Select the sequences **Edit 1 (offlineRT)**, **Edit 2**, and **Edit 3** in the Browser.

2   Perform a Find by pressing Cmd-F or choosing Edit > Find.

3 In the Find window, choose Unused Media and check in selected
sequences. Then click Find All.

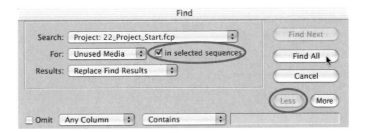

NOTE ▶ If your Find dialog has more search criteria still active from
Lesson 20 or from any previous search, click Less to disable the additional criteria and return the dialog to its default state, as shown.

4 Select all of the clips in the Find Results bin.

5 Choose Make Offline from the contextual menu or from the
Modify menu.

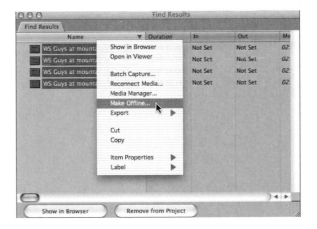

To delete the clips, you could choose either Delete from Disk or Move
to Trash. In either case, the timecode information associated with the
clips remains so you can recapture them at any time. Just don't delete
the offline clips from the Final Cut Pro project.

6 Click Cancel and close the Find Results bin.

Using the Source Column

When you encounter offline clips in your project, you may not know why those files are not available. Sometimes, an external hard drive containing the media might not have mounted. Or maybe a file or folder got renamed or moved. When moving a project from one location to another, it is fairly common to encounter some clips that have lost their links to their corresponding media files.

One trick that can help you track down the correct media for an offline clip is to check the Source column in the Browser.

▶   Ctrl-click the Browser columns and choose Show Source from the contextual menu.

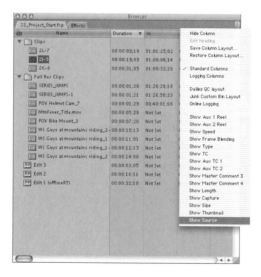

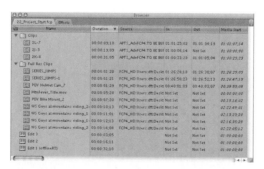

This column provides the path to the media file associated with the clip. If the clip is missing, this column provides the path to the last known location of the file. If you manually forced the clip offline, it will simply report that the clip is offline. Still, for missing clips, this might help you identify what disk is unmounted or provide other clues to the proper media file.

Using the Media Manager

The Media Manager is Final Cut Pro's versatile and comprehensive media manipulation tool.

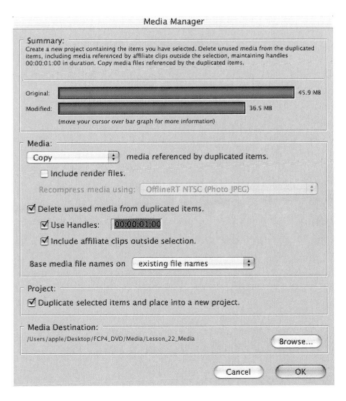

Whether you are moving your project from one computer to another, trying to eliminate clips and files you're not using, preparing a sequence for output, or even recompressing a group of files from one codec to another, the Media Manager is your one-stop shop.

Consolidating Media

When you need to move a project from one computer to another, you may not know where all of your media resides. Although most files are probably in your Capture Scratch folder, there may be a graphic or still file in another location. There may be sound effects files extracted from CD and stored in yet another location. Rather than manually scouring your disk for any related files, you can be sure not to miss anything (or grab stuff you don't need) by using the Media Manager tool.

1 Press Cmd-A to select everything in your Browser.

2 Choose File > Media Manager.

3 In the Media section, set the pop-up menu to Copy.

This will duplicate all of the media associated with the selected items (in this case, the entire project) and place them in a new location.

4 Check the box that says Include Render Files.

5 At the bottom of the window, click the Browse button under the Media Destination section and choose a location on your disk for the copied files. Create a new folder for the copied media.

In order to move your files from one computer to another, you would typically want to set this to a removable or external hard disk that you could then move to a new station.

6 Back in the Media Manager, uncheck the Delete Unused Media From Duplicated Items box in the Media section.

In this example, you want the project on the new computer to be identical to the previous one so you do not want to delete anything at all.

7 Leave the Base Media File Names On pop-up set to Existing File Names.

8 Leave the Duplicate Selected Items and place into a new project box checked.

This last setting creates a new project on your destination volume that points to the new versions of the media files. Although this step is not required (you could manually copy your existing project file in the Finder), this ensures that the new project will not have any offline files, and you won't have to reconnect media when the project gets to the new workstation.

The summary at the top of the window details your operation. The size of the bars indicates the relative amount of disk space your media is occupying. The top bar is the current state, and the bottom bar shows what will happen after you complete the Media Manager operation. Because in this example you are not deleting anything, the two bars are identical.

9 Click OK.

Immediately, you are prompted with a Save dialog box, asking you to name and save the new project file. Save it on the same disk as the new media.

10 Click Save.

The program will then perform the media management operation and open the new project in the Browser.

11 In the new project, open the sequences and clips to confirm that the new project is an identical copy of the old project. Then close the new project..

Moving Media

If you have limited disk space, or you are consolidating your media on a single disk (as you might do to prepare for backing up onto DVD), you can choose Move instead of Copy in the Media Manager.

With this setting, your original media files will be consolidated into a single location and the original files will be deleted. You will not wind up with two copies of your files.

Trimming Sequences in Media Manager
This type of trimming has nothing to do with adjusting edit points, but rather is a way to eliminate excess media after your sequence has been completed. This should usually not be done until you are completely finished making major editorial changes.

1   Select sequences **Edit 2** and **Edit 3**.

    The operation will only be applied to the media referenced in these two sequences.

2   Ctrl-click the selected items and choose Media Manager from the contextual menu.

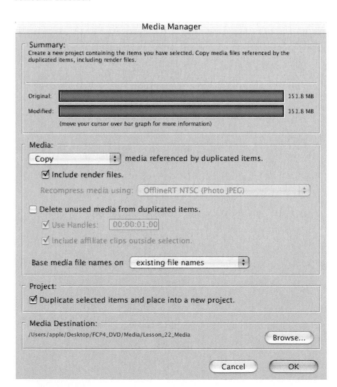

3   Set the Media pop-up to Copy.

> **NOTE ▶** Although Final Cut Pro will let you choose Move or Use Existing to modify your existing media files, doing so when trimming clips is extremely dangerous. If a power failure or crash occurred during the operation, your files could be left in an unusable state requiring you to recapture all of your media. When trimming, always create new files. Once the operation is complete, then you can delete the original media.

4   Check the box marked Delete Unused Media From Duplicated Items.

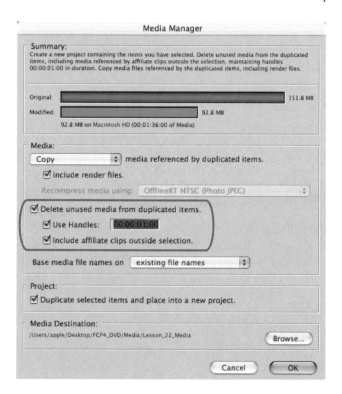

When you check this box, the summary section at the top of the window changes dramatically. Now, the modified media bar is much smaller than the original. This difference is made up of all of the media outside of the In and Out points of the clips that were used in the two sequences you selected.

5   Check the box Use Handles and set the value to one second.

Although presumably you are completely done editing, there may be an emergency or problem that might require a tiny adjustment to your edit. Adding a little bit of wiggle room is a good way to accommodate such an unforeseen issue if one should arise after this operation.

6   Uncheck the box Include Affiliate Clips Outside Selection.

If this box is checked, the Media Manager will scan the rest of your project for any other uses of the clips contained in your selected sequences. If such clips exist, and they have In or Out points set, the Media Manager will include that section in the newly created clips. This means that you will not save as much space as you would by ignoring those clips.

Because you set the whole operation to be a Copy, there is no harm in ignoring this additional media. If you had set the operation to Move or Use Existing (instead of Copy), you would be permanently deleting that media that you might be planning to use in another sequence.

7   Check the box Duplicate selected items and place into a new project.

This will create a new project containing only the selected sequences and pointing to the new, trimmed media.

8   Set your destination and click OK.

9   Name the new project file and click Save.

After the files are processed, the new project is automatically opened. If you do not plan to make any additional changes or use any of the media from the old project, you can select all the items in the old project and use the Make Offline command to delete the media files from your disk.

NOTE ▶ Do not delete these files because they will be required later in this lesson.

Working with Low- versus High-Resolution Clips

There are many times when it is impractical to make all of your editing decisions using your full-resolution media files. For example, if your original media was HD resolution captured using a PCI card, you may want to do your editing on another station that does not have that card installed.

Alternately, you may want to save disk space by working in a lower-resolution format. This allows you to store more hours of media on your disk. Also, because lower-resolution files are less taxing on a computer's CPU, you can work on a less powerful workstation and achieve more real-time effects than you could with your full-resolution media.

In this workflow, once you've made all of the editing decisions in the low-res version, you return to the full-resolution media to create the final version for output. Working in the low-resolution mode is sometimes called *offline editing*, and working with the full-resolution clips is called *online editing* (or just *onlining*).

> **NOTE ▶** Do not confuse offline and online editing with the concept of offline and online clips, as described in the section "Understanding the Relationship Between Clips and Media."

Creating Low-Resolution Clips

In order to do the offline edit, you must have a copy of your clips in a reduced-quality format. If your original format is DV, your offline format is most likely going to be Offline RT (Photo JPEG). If your original is uncompressed SD, you could still use Offline RT, but you might just reduce the resolution to DV, so you could still work with a relatively high-quality image that can be viewed in an external NTSC monitor. If your original source is HD, you could create an offline in uncompressed SD, DV, or Offline RT.

If your clips are already captured, you can convert them to your offline version using the Media Manager.

1 Select the bin Full Res Clips.

2 Choose File > Media Manager.

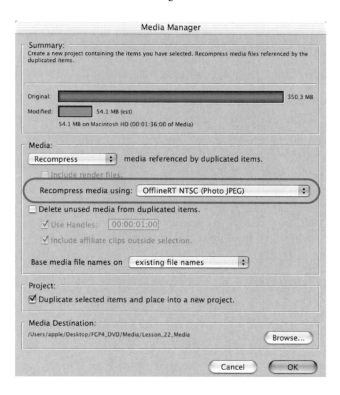

3 Set the Media pop-up to Recompress.

The Recompress Media Using pop-up menu now becomes active. From this list, you can choose the format for your offline clips.

NOTE ▶ Any sequences selected in the Media Manager operation will be altered so the sequence settings will match the format of the new clips.

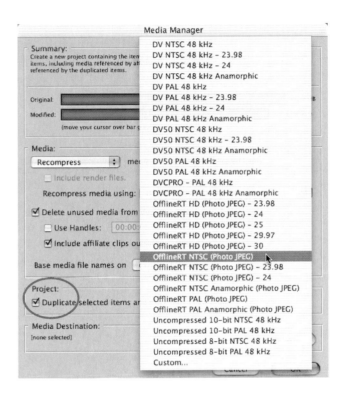

4   Select OfflineRT NTSC (Photo JPEG) from the menu.

5   Uncheck the Delete Unused Media box but be sure to leave Duplicate Selected Items checked.

6   Set your destination and click OK.

7   Name your new project and click OK.

Once the processing is complete, you are ready to edit your offline clips.

8   In your new project, create a new sequence and name it.

9   Select the new sequence in the Browser and from the Sequence menu, choose Settings.

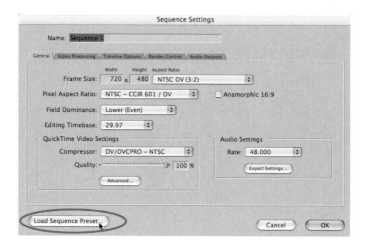

10   Click the Load Sequence Preset button in the lower-left corner.

11   From the pop-up, choose OfflineRT NTSC (Photo JPEG).

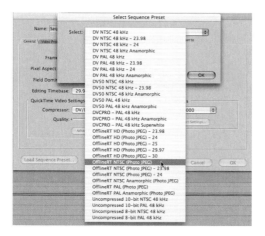

This is the same list that you were choosing from in the Media Manager dialog box. It is critical that your sequence settings match your clip settings.

12 Click OK in both the dialog boxes (first the Select Sequence Preset and then Sequence Settings).

Now your sequence is set to match your clips. You can edit your newly compressed clips into this newly created sequence. Once your editing decisions are complete, use the Media Manager to do a Trim operation as described earlier. Then, you can recapture the trimmed sequence in full resolution for your final output. So let's do that next.

Returning to Online Editing

Once you've completed your editing with the low-resolution offline clips, you're ready to return to the high-resolution clips.

If you have your original clips available on a different hard drive or a different system, you can get your project up to full resolution in a few short steps. In this case, the offline files are Offline RT, and the online clips are DV NTSC.

1 Close the offline project you created in the previous exercise and click back to the 22_Project_Start.fcp tab in the Brower, or reopen it if you've closed it.

2 Double-click **Sequence Edit 1 (offlineRT)** to open it in the Timeline.

3 Open the Sequence settings from the Sequence menu or Ctrl-click and choose Settings from the contextual menu.

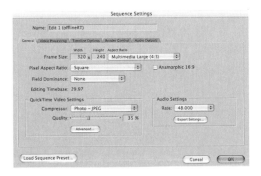

4   Click the Load Sequence Preset button in the bottom-left corner of the dialog box.

5   Choose DV NTSC 48 kHz from the pop-up and click OK, then click OK in the Sequence Settings dialog box.

Your clips in the sequence will appear to shrink, but what actually happened is that the sequence got larger. The render bar probably also changed from grey to red, or at least to green. That's because your clips no longer match your sequence settings. But this is only temporary.

6   Select the sequence icon for **Edit 1 (offlineRT)** in the Browser and choose Reconnect Media from the File menu or the contextual menu.

This will perform a reconnect operation on all of the clips in the sequence.

This time, you want to reconnect clips that are already online. The dialog box should already know this, and Online should be selected.

7 Be sure to check Select Files Manually if it is unchecked, and click OK.

A Reconnect dialog box appears asking you to choose the correct version of the clip to reconnect. Navigate to the Lesson_22_Media folder, and then to the Online MtnFever Clips folder inside, as shown.

Because you selected the Reconnect All Clips in Relative Path check box, all of the additional files in the sequence will be reconnected, and your sequence will be ready to go.

Observe that the title at the beginning has been scaled automatically to match the sequence frame size. All Final Cut Pro generators will behave in this manner.

Prep for Recapture

If you captured directly to your offline format, as described in an earlier lesson, before you can reconnect your clips, you need to recapture them at their native resolution.

To ease this process, you can use the Media Manager to create an offline sequence at the correct resolution, ready for re-capturing.

1   Select the sequence **Edit 3.**

2   Open the Media Manager.

3   Set the Media pop-up to Create offline.

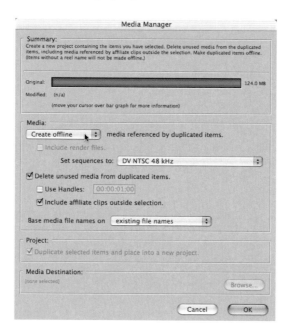

This forces you to create a duplicate project and dims the Browse button, since that applies only to situations where you are creating new media.

This setting also causes the Recompress pop-up to change function so it becomes a Set sequences to pop-up. This automatically does the work of changing your sequence settings (which you did manually in the last exercise).

4   Change the set sequences to pop-up to DV NTSC 48 kHz and click OK.

5 Name your new project file *New Project for Capture*, designate where to save it, and click OK.

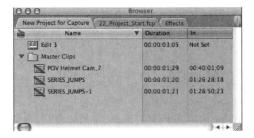

A new project opens, with one sequence and a bin of master clips. At this point, you simply select the sequence and perform a Batch Capture set to full resolution (in this case DV NTSC). Since you don't have the actual source tapes, you will not be able to do this final step now.

Once your clips have been recaptured, you are ready to fine-tune and lay your sequence to tape.

If you had any effects or elements that required rendering, you would need to re-render them in the new sequence. You should also look carefully at those sections to be sure they look correct, especially if they involved any clip motion.

What You've Learned

- When taking media files offline, choose the Leave Them On The Disk option so that you don't permanently delete your files.

- Reconnect offline clips using the Reconnect Media command.

- The Media Manager allows you to move projects to a new computer, eliminate unused clips, trim excess media from a sequence, and recompress clips into a new resolution.

- When it is impractical to make all of your editing decisions with a full-resolution file, you can perform an *offline* edit on a low-resolution copy and then reconnect the *online* (high-resolution) clip to the offline (low-resolution) sequence.

23

Lesson Files

Media

Time

This lesson takes approximately 45 minutes to complete.

Goals

Use Compressor to create MPEG-2 and MPEG-4 files

Create droplets for automatic drag-and-drop encoding

Export QuickTime reference and self-contained files

Export audio and OMF audio

Encoding and Outputting Video

In this lesson, you will learn to output your files to DVD, the Web, and third-party applications. You will use Compressor to encode MPEG-2 files for use in DVD authoring and MPEG-4 files suitable for the Web. You will export audio via OMF and export a QuickTime reference file for use in other applications.

Using Compressor

Now that you have a completed movie, you may want to output it to a medium that can be used for distribution. DVD-Video is the most popular format for distributing high-quality video. To get high-quality video onto your DVD, you will need to use sophisticated compression tools that will give you options like VBR encoding, GOP structure selection, and numerous pre-filtering options.

Compressor makes this easy and intuitive. There are numerous presets built into Compressor that will result in MPEG-2 video that is of exceptional quality, even at very low bit rates.

Exporting to MPEG-2 for DVD-Video

In this section, you'll take Compressor for a spin and encode your movie.

1   Open the **60 Second Promo.fcp** project from the Lesson_16 folder and select the **Bike Promo finished** sequence in the Browser.

2   Choose File > Export > Using Compressor.

    Compressor is launched with your sequence added to the batch.

3   In the Batch Name field, name your batch *Bike Promo*. Leaving the Batch Name untitled will make it difficult for you to track the history.

4   In the Batch window, click the Presets icon to open the Presets window.

5 Click the MPEG-2 90min Fast Encode group folder to view the summary of the presets that it contains: one for outputting the AIFF audio track and one for encoding MPEG-2 video.

6 Click the disclosure triangle for the MPEG-2 90min Fast Encode folder and view the details of the contained presets.

7 Click the disclosure triangle for the MPEG-2 90min Fast Encode preset. Inside, you'll see settings for both the video and audio encoding.

8 Click just the video setting: MPEG-2 90min Fast Encode. The Summary tab below will show you all of the details for that setting.

9 Click the Encoder, Filters, Geometry, and Actions tabs. These settings can be modified and if you change any of these settings, you will be prompted to name and save a new settings preset. Leave them at the default settings.

10 Click the Destinations button in the Presets window to open a new window with available destination templates.

Notice that in all Compressor windows, you have buttons at the top left that open or bring forward the four other main windows in the interface. There are five total windows: Batch, Presets, Destinations, History, and Preview.

Source is currently set as the default destination. The sphere at the left of the destination name indicates the default destination, which can be changed by selecting the name of an available destination and clicking the Make Default button. You can also create additional destination paths so that newly compressed files will be saved there. Destinations can be local (on your own computer), on a network server, or even on a remote Internet FTP site.

Make Default

11 Click the plus button (+) at the bottom-left corner of the Destinations window to create a new destination.

12 Choose Local and navigate to your media drive.

13 Create a new folder and name it *Encoded Media*. With the new folder selected, click Open.

14 In the Destinations window, double-click *untitled local 1* under the Name column and type *Encoded Media Folder*.

15 Highlight Encoded Media Folder and click the Make Default button.

This folder will now be the default destination for all files created by Compressor.

16 Close the Destinations window.

17 In the Batch window, select your sequence name beneath the Source Media heading.

18 From the Presets drop-down menu, choose the settings that you will use to create your MPEG-2 and AIFF files. Choose MPEG-2 90min Fast Encode, and then because your sequence contains both audio and video, choose All from the submenu.

To encode a proper MPEG-2 file, the audio must be separated and encoded into its own AIFF file. However, if your sequence contained only video, you would select MPEG-2 90min Fast Encode and choose MPEG-2 90min Fast Encode from the submenu. Alternately, if your sequence contained Audio only, you would choose DVD PCM audio from the submenu.

19 In the Batch window, select the MPEG 2 90min Fast Encode listing in the Preset column.

20 Click the Preview button at the top of the Batch window. This allows you to preview any filters you've added, as well as create frame accurate chapter markers.

Note that the name of the encoding template you are using is listed in the drop-down menu at the top-left corner of the Preview window. (If MPEG-2 90min Fast Encode is not visible in this pull-down window, use the blue pull-down arrows and select it).

21 Use the controls at the bottom of the window to navigate through your video clip.

You can set In and Out points the same way you would in FCP. In and Out points here define the boundaries for encoding, and are handy in case you want to spot check the quality of an encoding preset before committing to the whole program. Clicking the Add Marker button at the bottom-right corner of the Preview window, or pressing M on the keyboard, will add a chapter marker to the current location.

22 When parked on a marker, the Add Marker button will display a minus symbol. Click the minus marker button or press M again to delete it.

When parked on a chapter marker, you can click the Change Marker Name button to specify the name of your chapter.

23 Close the preview window and click Submit in the Batch window.

Compressor automatically quits. The Batch Monitor launches, and your files are added to its encoding queue.

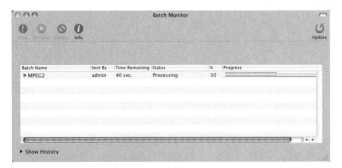

The Batch Monitor is your window to the encoding process. Progress bars indicate the status of your encode. The result of this encode should yield two files. These files will be saved in the location you selected in the Destinations window. Look for these files in the folder you created on your media drive. One of the files will be an MPEG-2 video (M2V) elementary stream suitable for DVD authoring. The second file should be an uncompressed PCM (AIFF) audio file that can be used in DVD authoring, or can be further compressed into AC3 audio using A.Pack, which is a Dolby Digital audio encoding utility that ships with DVD Studio Pro.

Exporting to MPEG-4 for the Web

Let's output the same video into a format that is suitable for the Web. In this exercise, you will encode your movie into MPEG-4 video directly to a remote server. You will modify the encoding setting to notify you that the files are available via email. You will need to be connected to the Internet for this exercise to work properly. A broadband connection is recommended for optimal performance.

1   Open Compressor again. If you have completed the first exercise, click the History button. Otherwise, follow steps 1 through 3 from the first exercise to launch Final Cut Pro and export the Bike Promo movie using Compressor. Then skip to step 5 of this exercise.

2   In the pane that opens on the right or left, click the arrow to the left of Today to view the History palette's contents for today.

    The History palette displays all submitted jobs, grouped by the date they were submitted. If you named your previous batch, you should see the name of the job and the time it was submitted.

3   Select the job and drag and drop it into the batch window.

    This is useful if you want to re-encode your job or just review the settings you used. You will use this information to reference the same source media.

4   Highlight and delete all preset entries by clicking the arrow left of the Source Media name, selecting the entries, and pressing Delete on your keyboard.

5   Choose Presets > MPEG-4 NTSC Source Material > MPEG-4 Improved NTSC Large Progressive. This will result in a high-quality MPEG-4 movie.

6 In the Batch window, click the Presets icon to open the Presets window.

7 Scroll down the list and click the MPEG-4 NTSC Source Material > MPEG-4 Improved NTSC Large Progressive.

8 At the bottom of the Presets window, select the Actions tab and check the Email Notification To box, and then enter your email address.

9 Close the Presets window and click OK when you are prompted to save the setting.

NOTE ▶ If you do not have Internet access, skip steps 10 through 12 and use the destination that you created in the previous exercise, named Encoded Media Folder.

10 Click the Destinations button to see the available destination templates.

11 Click the Create A New Destination button (the plus sign) and choose Remote from the drop-down list.

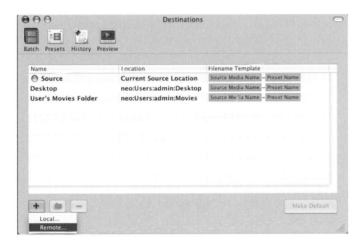

12 In the dialog box that appears, enter your FTP server information and click OK.

13 Select the new remote server destination from the Destinations window Name list.

14 Click the Batch button to launch the Batch Monitor, and then click the Submit button. Your files are added to the monitor's encoding queue.

Compressor is a powerful tool that can create high quality MPEG-2 and MPEG-4 files. Compressor is not limited only to these two formats. You can encode with any available QuickTime codec. Try experimenting with the different options that are available to you by building your own presets.

Making Droplets

You can create droplets for presets that you use frequently. Droplets are small, stand-alone applications that exist on your Desktop. Once you've created a droplet, you can drag and drop files you intend to encode directly onto it. You will create a droplet for one of your presets, and then use it to streamline the encoding process.

1 Open Compressor if it isn't already open.

2 In the Batch window, click the Presets icon to open the Presets window.

Presets

3 Choose the preset or group of presets for which you wish to create a droplet, such as MPEG 2 90min Fast Encode, and click the Save Selection As Droplet button in the upper right corner of the Presets window.

4 In the Save dialog box that appears, give the droplet a unique name, choose to save it to the Desktop (for convenience), and then choose a destination for the encoded files. (You might choose the Encoded Media folder.)

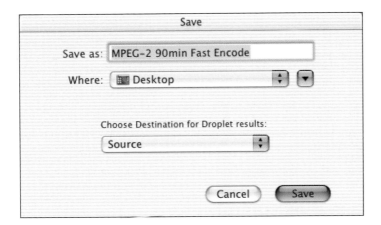

You can now drag and drop your QuickTime files directly onto the droplet to encode them. But let's automate the process one step further.

5   Navigate to the newly created droplet and double-click it.

6   Uncheck the Show At Launch box and quit the Droplet (Cmd-Q).

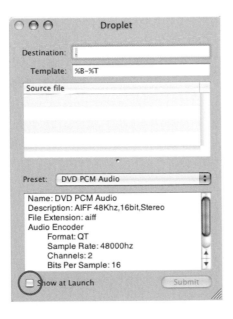

Now when you drag and drop QuickTime files onto the droplet for encoding, they will be sent directly to the Batch Monitor without any dialog boxes displaying.

NOTE ▶ QuickTime files need to have a .mov extension on the end of the filename for droplets to recognize them.

Create as many droplets as you like. They are a great way to enhance your workflow.

Exporting QuickTime Files

Exporting a QuickTime file is the most efficient way to get your video out of Final Cut Pro and into another application like Shake. A self-contained QuickTime file can be easily transported to other computers. However, you can also create a small file that contains audio media, but simply references the video media, resulting in a much smaller file. These are called *reference files*. A reference file requires that the source media be accessible to the system you are working on. In the next exercise, you will export a reference file of footage that you will key in Shake.

1 In Final Cut Pro, choose **09_Project_Start.fcp** from the Lesson_09 folder.

2 Select the **MS K STANDS_18_1B_4** clip in the Browser.

3 Choose File > Export > QuickTime Movie.

   The Save dialog box appears.

4 Type a filename and choose a destination for the exported QuickTime Movie. Leave Setting at Current Settings and leave Markers set to None.

   Notice that Include Video Only is grayed out, since this clip has only video footage. If you were exporting a clip or sequence that had both video and audio information, you could choose here whether to export either video or audio or both.

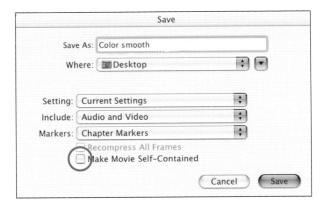

If you want to use this file independent of its media, perhaps to use it in Shake on another computer, you would check Make Movie Self-Contained. This would make the save process take longer and would result in a much larger file. For our purposes, leave it unchecked.

5   Click Save.

You can now import the reference file into Shake and use the sophisticated keyers to remove the green screen. You can also use this reference file inside Compressor, or drop it on the droplet you created earlier. The reference file you have just created is suitable for importing into any application on the same computer that accepts QuickTime files, such as LiveType, Soundtrack, iDVD, DVD Studio Pro, and QuickTime Player.

Exporting OMF Audio

You can export audio using File > Export > QuickTime Movie, but this will result in 16-bit audio files. If you wish to export 24-bit audio, you can use File > Export > Audio to AIFF(s). If you intend to work on your audio in a DAW (Digital Audio Workstation) that uses the OMF file format, you can export your audio to OMF.

1   Once again, open the **60 Second Promo.fcp** project from the Lesson_16 folder.

2   Select the **Bike Promo finished** sequence in the Browser.

3 Choose File > Export > Audio to OMF.

4 In the OMF Audio Export dialog box, choose an appropriate sample rate and size. You can also opt to add handles to your media and include cross-fade audio transitions.

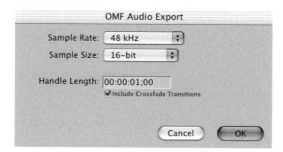

5 Click OK.

This will create a single OMF file that contains all of the audio in your Timeline plus any additional handles. The maximum file size for this export is 2 GB, so if you have a large sequence, you might have to break it up into smaller pieces before exporting. You can import the OMF file into any digital audio workstation that accepts the OMF format.

What You've Learned

- A preset in Compressor allows you to quickly and easily create MPEG-2 files for DVD authoring and MPEG-4 files for the Web.

- Compressor lets you save files on remote servers and can automatically send out an email to inform you when a batch process is completed.

- Create a droplet mini-application of your most commonly used compression presets to automate video encoding.

- To be accessible on other computers, exported QuickTime movies must be self-contained, but you can create smaller QuickTime movies for use on your own working system by exporting with audio and only a reference to the video footage.

Working with Film and 24p

Daniel Fort got his first job in the movie industry at age 16, changing the marquee at the local cinema. A Vietnam veteran who served in the Navy's elite Pacific Fleet Combat Camera Group, Dan has worked on over 20 studio and independent films such as *Desperado*, *From Dusk Till Dawn*, and *Stuart Little*. He has consulted on several features edited on Final Cut Pro, including *Full Frontal* by Steven Soderbergh, *Intolerable Cruelty* by Joel and Ethan Coen, and *Cold Mountain*, edited by Walter Murch. In 1999 he was awarded best editing for a short at the New York Film and Video Festival and in 2000 he worked on *Bojangles* for Showtime, one of the first features edited on Final Cut Pro. Dan has played a major role in the development of Apple Cinema Tools and has taught the use of Final Cut Pro with Cinema Tools at DigitalFilm Tree.

Working with Cinema Tools

Cinema Tools is a collection of special Final Cut Pro settings, prepared film leaders, a utility for converting between a 24-frame-per-second and a 30 fps edit decision list (EDL), a reverse telecine and conforming program for QuickTime movies, and a list generator. At its core, it is also a database that keeps track of all the information for even the most complex feature film.

In this special section on editing film, you will set up, edit, and complete a film or 24p project. The lesson (in PDF format) and all the project and media files you need are located in the Lessons > Lesson_24 folder and the Media > Lesson_24_Media folder.

24p Editing Basics

Ever since the talkies, film has been running through projectors at 24 frames per second. It now appears that one format is destined to become a replacement for film: 24 fps progressive high-definition video, often called 24p video. Cinema Tools, which comes bundled with Final Cut Pro 4, is used to work with film and 24p video. In this appendix, presented in PDF format on the DVD, you will get an overview of working with 24 fps material. See Lessons > x_ApdxA-Working with 24p.

Working with 16x9

Both high-definition video and theatrical motion pictures are almost always screened at a panoramic 16x9 or wider aspect ratio, which is the ratio of the picture's width to its height. Most standard-definition televisions, however, have an aspect ratio of 4x3. In this appendix, presented in PDF format on the DVD, you will learn how to work with 16x9 masters for display in 4x3. See Lessons > x_Apdx B-Working with 16x9.

Glossary

A comprehensive glossary of terms, covering both Final Cut Pro and Cinema Tools, is included in PDF format on the DVD. See Lessons > x_Glossary.

Index

education

DigitalFilm Tree's learning products are available online for purchase or download

Classes and Seminars

DigitalFilm Tree is the leading Apple authorized and Motion Picture Editors Guild authorized training center. DigitalFilm Tree has trained students with a range of backgrounds and skill levels, including schoolteachers, directors, producers, and content creators and Academy Award winning editors and filmmakers.

Color Correction for Final Cut Pro Users Guide

DigitalFilm Tree presents the definitive Color Correction for Final Cut Pro Users Guide. Printed in full color, this 270 page book is the the most advanced and comprehensive document covering 'Professional Color Correction on the desktop.'

Cinema Tools for Final Cut Pro Users Guide

DigitalFilm Tree's Cinema Tools for Final Cut Pro Users Guide is the definitive, nearly 400 page document covering the new age of film and High Definition editing.

Cinema Tools for Final Cut Pro DVD

DigitalFilm Tree's Cinema Tools for Final Cut Pro is the definitive hands-on DVD learning guide for the new age of film and High Definition editing. Developed by the industry's leading experts, Cinema Tools for Final Cut Pro provides filmmakers and editors the knowledge for using Cinema Tools and Final Cut Pro for all manner of film and HD

Color Correction for Final Cut Pro DVD

DigitalFilm Tree presents the breakthrough Color Correction for Final Cut Pro DVD learning experience. The digital video revolution has given us many innovations, including professional color and exposure correction on the desktop.

Getting the Most Out of Final Cut Express DVD

This DVD learning guide presents intermediate to advanced version of the Getting Started DVD found in every box of Final Cut Express. Getting the Most Out of Final Cut Express DVD consists of interface shots, voice over and high quality animation,

www.digitalfilmtree.com

post services   design   consulting   rentals   education

310.275.1959.t   310.275.2059.f   8969 w. sunset blvd. los angeles, ca 90069